Partners in Evaluation

Evaluating development and community programmes with participants

Dr. Marie-Thérèse Feuerstein
Ph.D, S.R.N., M.Ed., Dip.C.D

MACMILLAN

First published 1986
Reprinted 1988, 1990 (three times), 1992

Published by THE MACMILLAN PRESS LTD
London and Basingstoke
Associated companies and representatives in Accra,
Auckland, Delhi, Dublin, Gaborone, Hamburg, Harare,
Hong Kong, Kuala Lumpur, Lagos, Manzini, Melbourne,
Mexico City, Nairobi, New York, Singapore, Tokyo.

ISBN 0–333–42261–9

Printed in Hong Kong

A catalogue record for this book is available from the British Library.

Acknowledgements
The author and publishers wish to acknowledge, with thanks, the following artwork and photographic sources:
Artwork
D. Morley et al. **Practising Health for All**, OUP, 1983: p130, p131, p132 bottom
La Notica (24-10-75): p149
Tropical Child Health Unit, Institute of Child Health, University of London: p110, p132 bottom, p133 top, p144 bottom, pp156 — 8
World Health Organisation: p166 bottom
Other artwork is by illustrators and artists Joan Gammans, Jacqueline Bradshaw-Price, Sasha Kosinova, Liz Hutton and Emilio Riveiro the Third and the copyright is held by the author.
Photographs
Christian Aid/Margaret Murray: p64
World Health Organisation/J. Ling: p152
All other photographs are by the author.

The author and publishers have made every effort to trace the copyright holders, but if they have inadvertently overlooked any they will be pleased to make the necessary arrangements at the first opportunity.

Published in conjunction with Teaching Aids at Low Cost,
PO Box 49, St. Albans, Hertfordshire AL1 4AX, UK
TALC received assistance in the production of this book as a low cost edition from the Swedish International Development Authority.

Contents

Acknowledgements

This book has grown directly out of field experiences in many countries and with many groups of people. Some of these earlier groups included the dynamic peasant women of Honduras with whom I had the privilege of living and working in 1977 and 1978. Later groups have included a wide range of health and development workers, including physicians, nurses, community-based health workers, traditional birth attendants, agriculturalists, veterinarians, community development workers and school teachers in countries as varied as Laos, the Philippines and Sarawak, Malaysia. Others have used parts of the book for training purposes in Kenya and Indonesia.

This book has also drawn on evaluation experiences obtained by other people in many countries. Their labours, experience and willingness to share results and information are gratefully acknowledged and their names, where known, are mentioned in the text.

Among those who have given their encouragement and time in helping the various drafts of the book to evolve, I wish to mention particularly: Paolo Freire for early encouragement, and Mary Johnson, in Indonesia; David Werner and co-workers in Mexico and California; Maria Hamlin de Zuniga in Nicaragua; Mary Grenough in the Philippines; Professor Yusuf Kassam in Tanzania; Dr Rufino Macagba in California; Jennifer Woods of CUSO, Canada; Beryl Knotts of Oxford, UK; the staff of Oxfam, UK; Dame Nita Barrow and Dr Stuart Kingma in Geneva; Dr Susan Rifkin in Hong Kong; Dr Gunawan Nugrohu in Manila; Dr Kirsten Poulsen in Botswana; Dr Peter Oakley in Reading, UK; Dr Bob Armstrong in Manchester, UK; Dr Katherine Elliott, Dr Hermione Lovel, Dr Patrick Vaughan and Dr Gill Walt in London, UK; and Dr Axel Kroeger in West Germany.

Particular thanks are due to Professor David Morley of the Institute of Child Health in London, to Dr John Macdonald of the Department of Adult and Higher Education at Manchester University, and to Ms Jackie Menczer of the Institute of Education, University of London, all of whom read and made valuable suggestions relating to the final draft of this book. Thanks are also due to the World Health Organisation in Geneva and Manila, and to the Food and Agriculture Organisation in Rome for making it possible to use examples and illustrations from their own publications.

This book could never have been produced without the much-appreciated support and artistic talents of several artists and illustrators, particularly Joan Gammans (a freelance illustrator in the UK) and her daughter Leora; Sasha Kosinova; Jacqueline Bradshaw Price (a freelance illustrator in France); Liz Hutton (a freelance illustrator in London); and Emilio Riveiro the Third in Manila, Philippines. Their combined artistic talents made it possible to translate many of the ideas and methods in this book into visual forms that can be more easily understood and used by the reader.

The typing of the many earlier drafts was a mammoth effort on the part of my sister, Cristina Bayley, of Marilyn Spice of the University of Kent, UK, and Hazel Palmer in Geneva. The final drafts might never have emerged without the encouragement and support of Rhylva Offer of the Child-to-child Programme, assisted in part by Sarah Holder.

Sincere thanks are due particularly to Misereor of Aachen, West Germany for making possible, in 1984, production of the final drafts and completion of the artwork. Until then the book had been produced entirely on a self-financed basis.

I also wish to thank Macmillan Publishers who, through Mr Rex Parry, guided the final stages of the manuscript, despite the disappearance without trace in the post of the manuscript itself. Fortunately I had taken a copy.

Finally, I wish to thank colleagues, friends and family who have provided constant encouragement and support during the arduous stages of researching and preparing this book and who have sponsored some of the illustrations. To my husband Malcolm, daughter Rachel, son Joseph and to my mother I say: "Thank you for understanding that long periods of my time and energy have had to be devoted to producing this book in order that many may share the experiences of others as they try to find better ways of helping a whole range of people develop skills in monitoring and evaluating so that they become real partners in development programmes".

Marie-Thérèse Feuerstein,
PhD, S.R.N., M.Ed, Dip.C.D. December, 1986.

Introduction

1. WHO IS THIS BOOK FOR?

This book is for **YOU**.

It is designed to help those who want to know more about monitoring and evaluating their own work. It is based on seven years of research and experience on the part of many people across the world.

Many people are already using regular monitoring methods as a normal part of their development work. Many also use assessment and survey methods, particularly before starting a programme or expanding an existing one. On the other hand, many people may have had little training or experience in monitoring and evaluation.

What such a wide range of people have in common is their involvement in various kinds of rural and urban development programmes, such as those concerned with health, community development, adult education and agriculture.

Obviously people of many different backgrounds and levels of education are involved. These include those with little or no formal education, and, at the other end of the scale, those with advanced technical and professional training. However, they do have something in common: they are working together in the same programme, and need to monitor and evaluate their work together.

Many such people, particularly those working close to or at community level, have expressed the urgent need for a book such as this. They find that many of the available monitoring and evaluation approaches and methods are too complex, too costly or not appropriate to the real conditions under which they live and work.

2. HOW TRADITIONAL EVALUATION IDEAS AND METHODS DEVELOPED

Historically, many ideas and methods evolved in developed and often urban areas. For example, about a hundred years ago programmes aimed at helping the poor and needy found that they were required by funding agencies to explain and justify how money was being spent. These early 'evaluations' usually consisted simply of descriptions and details of services given. Later, people started to analyse the records kept by these programmes, and questionnaires were introduced to provide more information for planning and better management.

The second World War of 1939-45 saw a demand for the evaluation of training for soldiers. At this time people also started to observe and evaluate human behaviour and attitudes.

Later, mechanical instruments were introduced to collect the large (often massive) amounts of information to record programme activities and progress. These included computers, tape-recorders, cameras, and even film and television cameras.

Today there are institutions and organisations which deal specifically with evaluation. A flood of books and written material has also come into being. Many of the resulting evaluation ideas and methods have been adapted for use in developing countries. New evaluation ideas and methods have also been developed by such countries.

Many ideas and methods may be useful for evaluating some aspects of very large-scale development programmes but they still do not meet the precise needs of a wide range of development workers, including those near to community level. For example, at these levels a lot of information is often collected by people in programmes, but they may take little or no part in analysing or even using it. Also, such information may be of poor quality and not in fact very useful, although a lot of effort has been put into collecting it.

3. THE EMERGENCE OF NEW IDEAS AND METHODS

During the past seven years a range of new monitoring and evaluation approaches and methods has gradually developed. These approaches and methods are more appropriate, more easily understood and more usable by development workers themselves, including those at community level. They are not intended to replace the more traditional evaluation methods. However, they can often make those methods which are useful more appropriate and effective.

Some traditional evaluation approaches have tried to make the people suit or 'fit' the evaluation methods. The newer approaches aim to make the methods suit the people and their situation. The approaches and technology are tailored to suit the real contexts of development programmes, and the abilities and technical levels of the participants. The collective name for such approaches and methods is **participatory evaluation**.

4. WHAT HAPPENS IN PARTICIPATORY EVALUATION?

What are the objectives and different steps in the whole process? How do these steps fit together, and in what order, so that the objectives can be achieved? The flow chart below shows the steps which are necessary in participatory evaluation.

Steps in participatory evaluation

a) All those involved in a programme need to decide jointly to use a participatory approach.

b) Next, they need to decide exactly what the objectives of the evaluation are. This is often harder than they think it will be.

c) When they have reached agreement on the evaluation objectives, it is time to elect a small group of 'evaluation co-ordinators' to plan carefully and organise all the details of the evaluation.

d) Now is also the time to decide what methods will be best for attaining the evaluation objectives. The choice of method, such as analysis of programme records or use of a questionnaire, will also be influenced by the capabilities of the people involved, and by how much time and how many resources are available for evaluation.

e) As these decisions are made, the written evaluation plan is formed. This plan shows why, how, when and where the evaluation will take place, and who will be involved.

f) Next the evaluation methods must be prepared and tested (for example, a questionnaire or a weighing scale may be needed). Selected programme participants will also need basic explanation of and training in interviewing, completing written or oral questionnaires, conducting various kinds of checks or examinations, etc. All programme participants will need explanations of the objectives and general methods to be used in the evaluation. The more they understand, the more they can participate in the entire evaluation process, wherever and whenever requested by the evaluation co-ordinators.

g) Having prepared and tested the evaluation methods, the next step is to use them to collect the facts and information required for the evaluation.

h) Then the information and data are analysed by the programme participants. The major part of this work will probably be done by the evaluation co-ordinators.

i) The results of the analysis (or the evaluation findings), are then prepared in written, oral or visual form. There are different ways of reporting and presenting the evaluation findings to different groups connected with the programme. For example, a Ministry (or programme funders) will usually need a written evaluation report but community-level participants will be better able to share results if they are presented as charts or pictures, or if they are presented during discussion meetings.

j) Programme participants then need to decide exactly how the evaluation results will be used, and how such results can help to improve the performance and effectiveness of the programme.

5. FURTHER DEVELOPMENT OF SKILLS IN ANALYSIS AND ORGANISATION

Participatory evaluation means more than just a way of seeing how much has been achieved or produced at what cost and with what effect. As all these things are important, participatory evaluation naturally includes recording, counting, measuring, observing, discussing and analysing, *but it also means a lot more*. **Participatory evaluation means:**

a) Building on what people already know and do.
b) Using and developing people's abilities and skills to monitor and evaluate their own progress.
c) Helping people to see whether their activities are having an impact on programme objectives.
d) Revealing whether human and material resources are being used efficiently, effectively and at a cost which the programme can afford.
e) Enabling people to study their own methods of organisation and management.
f) Providing good information for making decisions about planning and programme direction.
g) Indicating where more detailed information is needed and how it can be obtained.
h) Enabling people to see their own programme in a wider context, such as how it relates to other development work.
i) Enabling people to analyse their individual situations and to take action to improve them.
j) Increasing the sense of collective responsibility for programme activities.

People are usually more committed to plans and activities which they themselves have had a part in making. Participatory evaluation is not just to do with the development of things. It is to do particularly with the development of people.

6. WHAT DOES THIS BOOK CONTAIN?

The first chapter looks at the main questions that always need to be asked as the first step in any participatory evaluation. Chapter two goes into the details of planning and organising evaluation, and shows how various kinds of evaluation methods or tools can be used, depending on your own evaluation objectives. There is a checklist to help you use your own resources as much as possible.

The third chapter looks more closely at how you can use existing resources, knowledge and experience in a systematic way. For example, by careful and critical study of your own work, records, programme setting, and the people involved, you can provide important data for your evaluation. You will also need to collect new and more detailed information, facts and figures.

The fourth chapter looks at different types of evaluation tools such as surveys, interviews, questionnaires, and simple measurements and tests of skills, attitudes and knowledge, that can be used for these purposes.

Chapter five examines the ways in which evaluation results can be summarised, analysed and reported. You may need to prepare a written report and to include tables, simple graphs and charts of many kinds. You may need to turn numbers into pictures to help people at community level to understand statistical evaluation results.

The last chapter looks at the importance of using evaluation results to strengthen programmes and make them more effective. For example, you may need to improve monitoring and supervision, or to collect and use better baseline information for planning and developing the programme.

Lastly, there is a short glossary of the words that are used most commonly in evaluation, and a list of useful books and information to help you improve evaluation skills in your own special area of development (whether it is health, agricultural development, education or community development).

As the entire book is designed to be useful to those who are very busy in different kinds of development programmes it has been kept short and 'to the point'. Although some of the principles and technical terms commonly used in evaluation are hard to simplify, every effort has been made to use words that are easily understood and easy to translate. This is particularly important as those who read the book may also be working directly with people at community level. Their main task is to help a range of people to participate in evaluation.

Also, to help the reader, many of the main points in the text have been set in 'boxes', and the examples of successful participatory evaluation methods that have been used in different countries have been set under the heading 'From Experience'.

Many chapters of this book have already been used to train programme participants in participatory evaluation methods in countries in South-East Asia, Africa, and South and Central America.

Some chapters have been used by people who are planning to start a development programme. For example, they have carried out baseline surveys using a participatory approach.

Participatory evaluation approaches are constantly evolving. It is hoped that practitioners will share their own evaluation experiences and results so that future editions of this book can be made even more useful.

1 Understanding evaluation

This chapter begins by looking at what the word evaluation means, why people do it, and what they expect to learn from it. A wide range of people have taken part in evaluation. However, this range has not often fully included the participants near and at community level. There are many different ways in which such groups of people can take part in evaluation.

Deciding when and where evaluation should take place, how much it will cost, and who it belongs to, are also explored in this chapter.

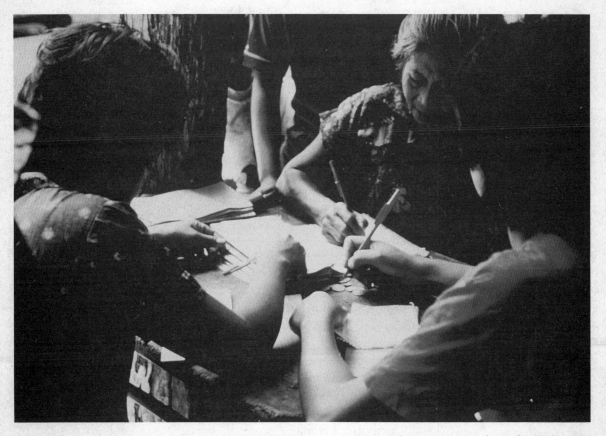

Village development workers analysing their own records in the Philippines

1.1 WHY EVALUATE?

First of all, what does the word evaluate mean? It means simply to assess the value of something. In this book, it means helping those who are involved in many different kinds of development programmes to assess the value of what they are doing. Many of them are already monitoring their own work and may have taken part in evaluating it in a systematic way.

When you ask people **why** they evaluate their work, different people give different answers. Here are some of the actual answers people have given:

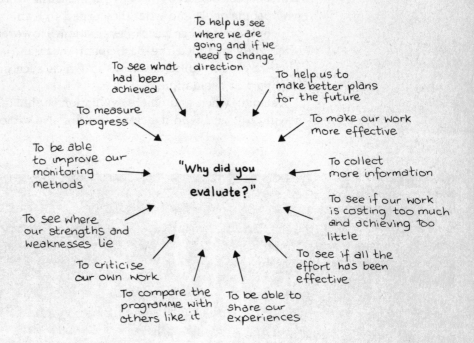

To help us see where we are going and if we need to change direction

To see what had been achieved

To help us to make better plans for the future

To measure progress

To make our work more effective

To be able to improve our monitoring methods

"Why did you evaluate?"

To collect more information

To see if our work is costing too much and achieving too little

To see where our strengths and weaknesses lie

To criticise our own work

To compare the programme with others like it

To be able to share our experiences

To see if all the effort has been effective

From the answers given by people to the question 'why did you evaluate?' **ten key reasons** emerged. These were to do with:

> **Achievement** (seeing what has been achieved)
> **Measuring progress** (in accordance with the objectives of the programme)
> **Improving monitoring** (for better management)
> **Identifying strengths and weaknesses** (to strengthen the programme)
> **Seeing if effort was effective** (what difference has the programme made?)
> **Cost benefit** (were the costs reasonable?)
> **Collecting information** (to plan and manage programme activities better)

> **Sharing experience** (to prevent others making similar mistakes,
>   or to encourage them to use similar methods)
> **Improving effectiveness** (to have more impact)
> **Allowing for better planning** (more in line with the needs of
>   people, especially at community level)

Some of these key reasons are easy to understand; some are more difficult. When you are workng with those at community level and helping them to participate in evaluation, it is necessary to use words and meanings that are even more simple and clear than those given above. One way that you can start to do this is by telling a story about other people's actual experience, such as the one below.

From experience

In one country some community development workers compared evaluation to taking a bus journey along an unknown road. While they could see through the glass windows they were happy because they could see that they were making progress. Then rain forced them to put wooden shutters over the windows and they could no longer assess their progress. They knew they were moving forward but could not tell along which road, how fast, or even whether they were nearing their destination.

Evaluation is like looking to see where and how fast you are going, and then estimating when you are likely to reach your destination.

So, from the answers that people gave it is clear that evaluation has been carried out mainly as **a way of looking at**:
programme activities, human resources, material resources, information, facts and figures;
in order to:
monitor progress and effectiveness, consider costs and efficiency, show where changes were needed, and help to plan more effectively for the future.

However, there is also another group of reasons for evaluating, and these are a little different.

Here are some of those reasons, which become clearer if we look at the answers that people have actually given.
- 'Because our funding agency asked for it.'
- 'Because the ministry asked for it.'

- 'Because our sponsors wanted to see whether they wished to go on supporting our programme.'
- 'Because the researchers wanted to try out new evaluation techniques.'
- 'Because new material was needed for publicity purposes.'

From this group of answers it is clear that evaluation has been carried out for another group of reasons. However, these reasons may not have been clear to all those who were actually involved in the evaluation.

For example, evaluations have been carried out with some programme participants believing that the results would be used to make decisions about the further funding of a programme, when in reality the decisions on further funding had already been taken by the programme funders before the evaluation began. So the evaluation results did not really make any difference to the decisions that had to be made on funding.

Evaluation has also been used in some cases as a way of justifying a weak or unsuccessful programme, or as a way of trying to cover up areas of programme failure. For example, some evaluations have looked only at those parts of a programme that were successful, not at the whole programme. If only the successful parts of a programme are being looked at, there is less chance that the weak parts will be noticed.

A few evaluations have even resulted in the destruction of programmes. This has happened, for example, where a programme had powerful individuals or powerful groups of people who did not agree with the activities or the objectives of the particular programme being carried out.

Fortunately, the vast majority of programme evaluations are not carried out for these kinds of reasons. However, they are worth remembering.

1.2 WHAT EVALUATION CAN (AND CANNOT) DO

People usually expect a lot from evaluation. Sometimes it provides clear indications of programme successes and achievements. Sometimes it provides a great deal of useful information for decision-making and planning. However, it is often the case that too much is expected of evaluation. It seems almost as if the evaluation is expected to ask every possible question and to be able to provide every possible answer.

The questions that an evaluation 'asks', and the 'answers' that it can be expected to provide, must be very carefully chosen.

Looking at success and failure

People usually expect evaluation to be able to show clearly whether success has been achieved, but it is often very hard to show clear evidence of success. In fact, it is often easier to show failure. However, failure is not popular, especially where future funding may be at stake.

One of the reasons why it is difficult to show success or failure is that success or failure can mean different things to different people. For example, what might be regarded as failure at one time can be regarded later as partly successful. Look at the following examples from the field.

From experience

In Brazil a rural development programme was set up to improve local agriculture, education and health services. It failed, largely because of the failure of a local community council.

However, a year later one of the programme organisers returned to the area for a short visit. He found that the programme had produced some results, particularly in the health field. People were using the new medicines that had been introduced for malaria, dysentery and other common diseases. Some people were still boiling and filtering their drinking water and using their latrine. Small tin racks with toothbrushes were a common feature in many homes.

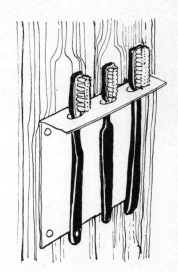

So, in the case of this Brazilian programme there were actually areas of success, despite the failure of the programme as a whole.

On the other hand it is wise to be cautious when claiming success. What can appear at first to be a success may change later into a failure. Consider, for example, two cases where latrines were built to improve community health in two South American countries.

At first the latrines in the programme area were considered a success, but as time passed the latrines were used less and less. They were never cleaned or repaired. Eventually they became health dangers, instead of health benefits.

In another programme in a very poor area, latrines were built of bricks and had locks on their doors. However, the houses did not have locks on their doors, so people used the latrines, not for sanitary purposes, but to store their valuables, such as bicycles and chickens. As far as the people were concerned the latrines were a great success – for storing valuables.

Evaluation looks at quantity and quality

Every evaluation deals to some extent with things that can be **counted** and/or **measured**. For example it may be the *number* of people involved in the programme, the *number* of products or services produced, the *amount* of material resources available or required, the *financial cost* of running a programme or the *extent* of an area cultivated.

These numbers, amounts and quantities are often described as the **quantitative** aspects of evaluation.

It is often not too difficult to determine the quantitative aspect of an evaluation. For example, a two-month vaccination programme may aim at reaching a certain number of children with a certain vaccine by a certain time. When the programme is complete it is possible to say exactly how many children were in fact reached by the programme.

However, programmes do not only consist of factors that can be counted and/or measured. They also consist of factors that are hard to count or measure, but which influence programme success or failure in important ways. These include: people's behaviour, abilities, qualities, attitudes, values, and motivations; and how people relate to one another and to the programme. These are described as the **qualitative** aspects of evaluation because they relate to the quality of what is being evaluated.

Such factors are important because they help to explain why a programme in a particular place proceeds in a particular way, and why it has particular strengths and weaknesses, problems and solutions, expected and unexpected outcomes. They also influence programme success or failure. Evaluation should look at the whole character or 'nature' of a programme.

KNOWING <u>WHY</u> A PROGRAMME SUCCEEDS
OR FAILS IS EVEN MORE IMPORTANT
THAN KNOWING IT DOES...

In answer to the question of what evaluation can do, we can see clearly that it cannot be expected to do *everything*. However, what it can often do is to:
• show the main achievement or failings;
• show where and how changes need to be made;
• show how strengths can be built upon;
• provide information and increase skills for planning and decision-making; and
• help those involved to see the wider context and implications of their own work.

1.3 WHO CAN EVALUATE?

Until fairly recently it was thought that only 'experts' could carry out evaluation. Undoubtably there are still many evaluations that are better carried out by specially-trained evaluators. These are mainly the kinds of evaluation carried out in or from laboratories, institutions, universities or hospitals.

However, what about the monitoring and evaluation of large- or small-scale community-based development programmes?

A wide range of people involved in health, agriculture, community development and adult education has been using regular monitoring methods in such programmes for a long time. These methods very often involve community-level participation of some kind or another.

However, although people at community or district level do provide or collect information and statistics relating to their own work, they usually play little or no part in analysing them. In fact, they often do not know exactly why such information is being collected or where it will go. They do not usually expect to see the results of their analysis.

Even when they do get to see the evaluation reports, they have

difficulty in understanding the specialist evaluation words and complicated ways in which the statistics and information have been presented. For community-level workers, and those who supervise them, the feeling often persists that evaluation and reports of that kind are planned and carried out for 'somebody else'. They are certainly not carried out for them.

The ways in which programme staff and community-level workers commonly monitor and evaluate their own work includes keeping records, participation in regular meetings, discussion groups, workshops to assess the progress of activities, and the writing of regular reports (weekly, monthly, quarterly and yearly).

Some programme staff, such as technical and professional workers, may have had special training or experience in evaluation. Sometimes the 'evaluator' or 'evaluators' are not part of the normal programme staff. They may work singly or as a team, and come from either within or outside the country in which the programme is being carried out. They may perhaps have been asked to carry out an evaluation themselves or they may possibly have been asked to advise others how to carry out an evaluation.

Such evaluators, who are not normal programme participants, are generally known as **external evaluators**.

External or internal evaluator: who can give the clearest picture?

An **external evaluator** is said to be a person who is able to take a fresh look at a programme because he or she is not involved personally, and so has nothing personal to gain or lose from the evaluation. For example, such an evaluator will not be influenced too much by programme staff or funders, personal friendships or dislikes. Therefore, he or she is said to be less likely to be *biased* and more able to be *objective*.

An **internal evaluator** is a person 'inside' the programme or one who knows the programme very well. He or she already knows the way in which the programme functions, and its objectives, problems, strengths and weaknesses.

However, because they know the programme it is supposed that they may find it hard to produce an evaluation report that is not biassed. For example, they may be influenced too much by their feelings, likes, dislikes, personal friendships or even their own ambitions. In other words, they may be too *subjective*, which is the opposite of being objective. Being subjective is not a bad thing in itself, but in evaluation a subjective attitude can destroy clear thinking and honest reporting.

These points will become clearer if you look at the list given overleaf.

THE ADVANTAGES AND DISADVANTAGES OF EXTERNAL AND INTERNAL EVALUATORS

External	Internal
Can take a 'fresh' look at the programme.	Knows the programme only too well.
Not personally involved, so it is easier to be objective.	Finds it hardest to be objective.
Is not a part of the normal power structure.	Is a part of the power and authority structure.
Gains nothing from the programme, but may gain prestige from the evaluation.	May be motivated by hopes of personal gain.
Trained in evaluation methods. May have experience in other evaluations. Regarded as an 'expert' by the programme.	May not be specially trained in evaluation methods. Has no more (or only a little more) training than others in the programme.
An 'outsider' who may not understand the programme or the people involved	Is familiar with and understands the programme, and can interpret personal behaviour and attitudes.
May cause anxiety as programme staff and participants are not sure of his or her motives.	Known to the programme, so poses no threat of anxiety or disruption. Final recommendations may appear less threatening.

Increasing people's confidence in their own abilities

Sometimes programme staff and participants feel that they do not have sufficient skill and ability to evaluate the work they are doing. Building on their normal monitoring and/or management methods can increase their skill, ability and confidence.

Particularly at community level people may feel that because they 'never went to school' or 'only got primary grades' or 'have difficulty with mathematics' they can play little or no part in evaluation. They may also have difficulty in expressing their opinions, particularly in public.

They may find it difficult, at first, to understand people from outside their own community. They frequently feel that they themselves are not clearly understood by such people, whether those people belong to their own country or whether they come from outside the country. These feelings arise not only because of a difference in language, culture and education; sometimes they are due to the fact that anyone who has not lived at or close to community level cannot know what it is really like.

One way of helping people at community level to see that they do have various advantages and capabilities when it comes to evaluation is to help them realise that:

- they already know a lot about the area, its characteristics, benefits, and disadvantages (for example, the type of land and its seasons).
- they know how people live; who is related to whom; who holds power and why; how people feel; what they most value; how they cope with problems; and what they hope for or fear.
- they know what people feel they can do; what they wish to avoid; what they wish to learn; and how they wish to use what they learn.
- they already know a lot about a programme (for example, its past and its present, and even its future, plans.).
  (On the other hand only programme staff may know about certain details like financing.)
- they may already be familiar with regular programme monitoring, such as collecting statistics and information, carrying out surveys, writing reports and holding meetings.

The challenge is to find the best ways in which people can be helped to make their own contribution when participating in evaluation.

1.4 PARTICIPATING IN EVALUATION

We need to look more closely at what is meant by 'participating' or taking a part in evaluation. This can take many different forms. For example, people participate in surveys by answering questions. However, they may have taken little or no part in the decision to carry out the survey or in deciding what questions to ask. What they are actually doing is *co-operating* rather than participating. Their role is mostly a passive one.

The different ways in which people do participate in evaluation can be seen more clearly from the following four examples A to D.

EXAMPLE A: The 'Studying Specimens' type of evaluation
People are only expected to play a very small part in the evaluation. When the evaluator or evaluating team have explained briefly the aims of the evaluation, people agree to be counted, examined, questioned, and so on. They are not asked, or expected, to do more. (If they did more it could be thought that they might spoil the evaluation.) The evaluation results are then removed by the evaluator(s). There is no feedback of the results to the people, and they do not expect any feedback.

EXAMPLE B: The 'Refusing to Share Results' type of evaluation

Some of the objectives of the evaluation are explained to the people. They then answer questionnaires and may even take a small part in analysing the information collected. They may also take part in other evaluation procedures.

At the end of the evaluation people receive carefully chosen feedback, but only the feedback considered suitable by the evaluator or evaluating team.

EXAMPLE C: The 'Locking up the Expertise' type of evaluation

People take part in the decision to evaluate and in selecting the aims and methods of the evaluation. They participate in carrying out the evaluation and in analysing its results. They also take part in feedback of the results to the wider community, and in putting into practice changes recommended.

However there is not a really effective monitoring system built into the programme to enable staff and participants to proceed by themselves. People are still very dependent on external help if they wish to carry out another evaluation.

EXAMPLE D: The 'Real Partnership in Development' type of evaluation

People take a part in deciding when and how to evaluate; in selecting the methods to be used; in collecting and analysing facts and information; in preparing reports; and in deciding how to use their results and put their recommendations into practice.

Where regular monitoring methods are not already being used or are inadequate, new or improved methods are built into the programme. Participants are then more able to assess regularly their own progress and to carry out periodic evaluation.

1.5 WHO IS EVALUATION FOR?

Sometimes evaluation is carried out because a ministry or national agency has asked for it, perhaps because they need more information to see whether past policies and activities have been successful.

Sometimes a funding agency asks for an evaluation for similar reasons, and because it feels a responsibility to be able to assure donors that their money has been spent usefully.

Community-level programme staff may see the main purpose of evaluation as being a practical one. They want to know what their programme has achieved, whether efforts are being effective, and whether resources are being used efficiently to achieve the objectives of the programme.

Sometimes a university is involved, and the staff and students participate in the evaluation to gain more knowledge about community-level evaluation methods. They may publish books and articles about them or use the evaluation experience for their own special studies.

When an evaluation takes place, the various people who participate in it may well have very different personal objectives or *motives* for being involved. They may also have different expectations or *hopes*. Does this matter?

Well, if we compare the progress of an evaluation to the progress of a bus, it is clear that some confusion is going to result if the people involved start off with different ideas about why they are there, what they expect and where they want to go.

Before an evaluation begins, it is essential to know what different expectations people have.

Sometimes it is difficult to find a good solution where there are many different needs and expectations. The particular situation and realities of a programme will determine what can be done about this problem. What is important is to make sure that the different needs and expectations of those at community level are not neglected. The evaluation objectives, methods, and results should also be closely related to their needs, realities, problems and expectations.

Ministries, departments, organisations, universities and agencies also have needs and expectations from evaluation. It is usually difficult for a single evaluation to provide all the information that is required at both community and other levels (which may include national and international levels).

1.6 WHEN SHOULD IT BE DONE?

Besides regular monitoring, which is (or should be) built into an on-going programme, there is a need for evaluation at regular intervals to prevent the piling up of information and also to obtain a clearer picture of programme progress and impact. For some programmes a two-to-three year gap between evaluations works well.

However, the decision about when to evaluate will depend, in each case, on many factors affecting a particular programme. For example:

Has the programme got long-term objectives?
If it has, it will be useless to try and evaluate progress too soon. Perhaps less than two years is too soon?

Has the programme got short-term objectives (like a two-month vaccination programme)?
In this case, evaluation usually takes place when the programme ends.

What kind of monitoring methods are already used?
Do records need to be gathered from places far away before the evaluation starts? Are there going to be many records to look at? Will extra time be required to do this?

Are external evaluators to be involved in the evaluation?
If so, this will affect timing. When are they able to come and how long will they take to get to the programme area? How long can they stay?

What about climate and seasons?
In the rainy season is it possible to reach isolated communities? In the dry season rivers may dry up and communities cannot be reached by boat. In a city people may find it harder to concentrate on evaluation in the hot season.

What about people's time?
During harvest time will people have time and interest to spare for evaluation? At certain times of the year people have less food and money. Is it possible to choose a time when people may be more relaxed and willing to give time and attention to evaluation?

What about the time of the programme staff?

They also have particularly busy times. Which is the best time for them?

What about ministries and outside agencies (such as departments, funding agencies and organisations)? They will also have specific ideas about timing.

1.7 WHERE SHOULD IT BE DONE, AND WHY?

An evaluation is often planned and prepared outside the area where it is to take place. For example, an external evaluator may arrive carrying a plan, and with a clear idea of which methods should be used in the evaluation. Questionnaires may already have been prepared, even though these will be tested first at community level, before they are used on a large scale.

At the end of an evaluation the information collected is often taken away to be analysed and reported, usually in the form of a written report. This is often the case where a computer is used to analyse the information.

Sometimes the evaluation results are taken away, not only out of the area, but out of the country. For example, an external evaluator may not have enough time to write up the results before leaving for home. Where this happens people who have participated in planning and carrying out the evaluation are not able to take part in one of its most important and interesting stages – that of producing its results.

By taking part in analysing and reporting the results of evaluation, participants gain a deeper understanding of programme progress, strengths and weaknesses. They can see where and why changes are needed, and can plan how to put them into practice.

The process of evaluation should be circular, like a wheel. All the parts should fit together so that the wheel can move along smoothly.

If one part of the wheel is missing, it is no longer useful. Participants need to be involved in all parts of the evaluation process. If they are left out of one part, it is like breaking the wheel.

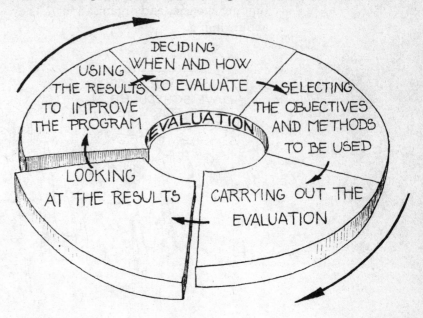

Evaluation is like a wheel turning. Don't let the wheel be broken.

Using materials and resources from 'outside'

It is likely that some of the documents and materials used in the evaluation will come from outside the evaluation area. The greater the use of outside materials and resources, the harder it will be to develop self-reliance.

1.8 HOW LONG WILL IT TAKE?

Some evaluations have taken only a few days, while others have taken many months; some have taken years. The length of time that an evaluation is likely to take will depend on many factors, some of which are listed below.

The length of time the programme has been in operation. Are there many records to look at, or only a few?
The number of people involved. Are there a hundred, many thousands or more?
Whether the programme is spread over a wide area. Are there long distances to cover between one area of the programme and another?
The number of people who can devote time to evaluation and the

amount of time they can devote. Are the evaluation activities extra to normal ones?

If programme staff only are to be involved they will know who is free to do what and how long it is likely to take.

If external evaluators are involved they may be able to stay for only a certain time and they need time to get to know the programme.

The preparation and testing of evaluation materials (like questionnaires and survey forms). This takes time.

Material resources (like paper, transport and fuel). These will be necessary and their availability influences the scope of an evaluation and the time it takes to carry it out.

The speed with which ministries, organisations and agencies need to know the evaluation results. They may be relying on the results to help them in deciding policies and plans.

Others. These depend on the particular programme.

The factor of time also relates to the next question: how much will it cost?

1.9 HOW MUCH WILL IT COST?

Some evaluations have cost many thousands of dollars, francs, pesos, marks, yen, pounds, or other currencies. Other evaluations have cost much less. In some evaluation reports the cost is not mentioned.

The cost of an evaluation will depend on many factors, some of which are listed below.

The amount of money that is available for the evaluation and its source. For example, is the programme paying, or is an agency or ministry going to pay the bill?

The objectives and scope of the evaluation. Is it to be a small-scale or large-scale evaluation and will travel be a large expense?

The material resources involved (like paper, writing materials, typing, copying, petrol, laboratory materials, correspondence, telephones, and so on).

Whether programme staff expect extra pay for the extra work involved.

Whether other people at community level who do a lot of extra work for the evaluation expect to be paid.

Whether external evaluators are involved. Will they expect travel and accommodation costs?

Others, depending on the particular programme.

Counting the entire cost of evaluation

The financial cost of an evaluation is only one of its costs. Evaluation should also be costed in terms of the amount of effort and labour put in by the people involved.

In many development programmes people often work long hours, either as voluntary workers or for minimal pay. No financial cost is usually estimated for this kind of labour.

In order to estimate correctly the costs of participatory evaluation this kind of time and effort should also be included.

```
EVALUATION  COSTS  A
     LOT  MORE  THAN
           MONEY
```

1.10 WHO DOES IT BELONG TO?

Who does an evaluation belong to? Does it belong only to those who paid its financial cost? What about those who carried it out?

Evaluation really belongs to *all* its participants, including those who paid for it (in many ways, such as with their time, effort or money) and those who carried it out.

So, the answer to this question needs to be carefully worked out before evaluation begins; afterwards is too late.

2 Planning and organising resources

The first step in planning for evaluation is to find answers to the questions asked in chapter 1. Having found these, it is then possible to move on to the next step, which is taking the decision to evaluate.

This chapter examines the need to plan carefully for evaluation, the various ways in which this can be done, some of the difficulties that may arise, and how these may be solved. The objectives of both a particular programme and its evaluation need to be clearly understood.

The chapter then looks at how you choose the evaluation methods you need, how to use existing records and written materials, and how to make the best use of the available resources.

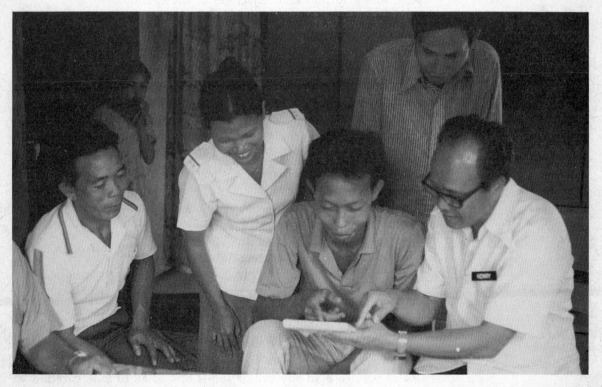

Community leaders planning with district health staff in Sarawak, Malaysia

2.1 TAKING THE DECISION TO EVALUATE

The decision to evaluate is usually a joint one made by a programme and its participants, together with a ministry, department, organisation, funding agency, etc.

The decision to evaluate, and the objectives and expectations of the evaluation, need to be clearly agreed.

> GOOD COMMUNICATION AND
> MUTUAL AGREEMENT LEAD
> TO THE BEST DECISIONS

2.2 WHY DO YOU NEED TO PLAN EVALUATION?

What does 'planning evaluation' mean? Planning is an organised method by which you can work out how you intend to reach your evaluation objectives and when. Planning helps you to:
- select the priorities and objectives of the evaluation.
- indicate the kind of methods you need to use.
- decide what you need to do in detail.
- decide the role each person will play in the evaluation.
- indicate how long the evaluation will take and how much it will cost.
- see how one part of the evaluation relates to the others.
- increase skills in planning and organisation.

2.3 MAKING A PLAN TO SUIT YOUR NEEDS

There are many different kinds of evaluation plans. (Sometimes the word 'design' is used instead of 'plan'.) The kind of plan that you choose will depend on the following factors.
- **The objectives of your evaluation.** For example whether it is being carried out to evaluate programme impact, or to provide information to improve programme management and effectiveness.
- **The scope of the evaluation**, that is, whether the programme is large scale or small scale.
- **The people who will be involved and the resources that are available.**

The best way to plan any evaluation is first of all to look carefully at a programme in its own setting. In this way the objectives of the pro-

gramme, the type of people involved, the methods of organisation, and the achievements and problems, can all be more clearly understood, and the real circumstances of the programme used to guide the shaping of the evaluation plan.

In participatory evaluation the evaluation plan should consider carefully the capabilities of the programme staff and participants. The first analysis of the information collected is by programme staff and participants, even if later further analysis may be carried out by computer. So, the evaluation plan and methods have to be clearly understood by all participants.

In order to make this practical a small group of 'evaluation co-ordinators' is usually responsible for the final preparation of the evaluation plan. They co-ordinate the input from other programme participants.

2.4 EVALUATING A MOVING PROGRAMME

Programmes consist of **people** (staff and participants); **structures and material objects** (such as buildings, equipment, vehicles, machines, records, budgets, medicines, supplies, radios); and **activities** (patterns of management, organisation, and action of many kinds).

Some parts of a programme can be seen and touched fairly easily. Some parts take time to become evident, perhaps only through speech or written words. For example, people can say how they see something, or why they behave in a certain way.

A programme varies from day-to-day according to how people feel, the particular things that happen that day. In this sense a programme is 'alive'; it has a 'life' of its own. Unless a programme is short-term (for instance, like a three-month vaccination campaign), evaluation usually takes place while a programme is still 'moving' or in progress.

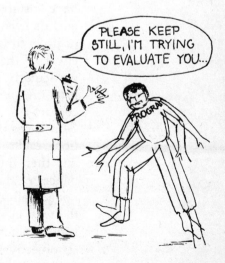

It is difficult to evaluate a programme that is still moving...

Programmes also often exist to give people some kind of service, such as health care or agricultural advice. So evaluation often takes place while the programme continues to serve people. Programmes that have a good system of regular monitoring are already accustomed to finding time for this. However, when evaluation takes place it cannot help slowing down and even slightly disrupting normal programme activities.

The best kind of evaluation plans and methods have to take all this into consideration, and aim to cause the minimum programme disruption.

2.5 EVALUATION OBJECTIVES AND PROGRAMME OBJECTIVES

The objective of most evaluations is to see what progress a programme has made towards reaching it objectives.

However, there are many reasons why it is often very difficult to evaluate programme objectives clearly in this way. The following examples help to illustrate the point.

- Objectives may only have been stated in a very general way when the programme started (for example, to 'relieve suffering' or 'improve lifestyle'). In such cases it is difficult, at a later stage, to turn these objectives into ones that can be easily evaluated.

- Sometimes the programme objectives stated at the beginning may change over a period of time, as they 'evolve' in response to changing conditions, and to a clearer understanding of the problems. For example, a programme that began mainly with nutrition education classes and the objective of 'improving nutrition' found that its objectives also needed to include 'planting vegetables at home' and 'better agricultural practices'.

- Besides official and clearly-stated objectives some programmes also have unstated and unofficial objectives that may be equally important, or even more important, to many participants. If evaluation neglects to look at these it may fail to indicate where some of the effort of the programme has actually been placed. This happens particularly where a programme is being carried out in an isolated location, or where it receives little or poor-quality supervision or contact.

- Sometimes the desire to get on as quickly as possible with evaluation results in brief discussions, study of programme documents and then the listing of specific objectives drawn mainly from the papers of the programme. (The reality of the programme itself is not actually studied until later.) In this way any differences between the way in which the programme itself sees its objectives and the way in which those associated with it (such as a funding agency) see its objectives may be missed.

In evaluation it is helpful if programme objectives are very specific, clearly stated and measurable in some way.

Before participatory evaluation begins it is necessary for those who are going to be involved to come to an agreement about what the programme objectives are.

Sufficient time should be taken for this important exercise as it can reveal differences of opinion, help to clear confused thinking, develop a common purpose between those who will be involved in the evaluation, and provide a better pattern for the future development of the programme.

It is helpful to list programme objectives in order of their importance, if this has not already been done.

Some programme organisers have found it useful to draw a plan or diagram of what the programme is trying to do. This can be done on a chalk board or a large piece of paper.

For programmes that have been in progress for a long time an evaluation cannot usually look at *all* of its goals, so which ones should be looked at – the main ones, the short-term goals, the long-term goals, or those that will improve practice or organisation?

> MANY EVALUATIONS STUDY WHAT
> IS EASY TO STUDY, NOT
> WHAT <u>OUGHT</u> TO BE STUDIED

HOW DO YOU DECIDE WHICH OBJECTIVES TO EVALUATE?
Your decision will probably depend on the following factors.

- Whether the evaluation is being used mainly to look at programme efficiency and progress, or at impact.
- The expectations and needs of policy-makers and funders. For example, do they hope for quick results on which to base policy and planning decisions?
- Whether you have resources such as staff, money and time to carry out a large-scale evaluation.

The programme objectives to be evaluated, and the reasons for this, should be stated clearly or later the criticism may be made that the really important objectives were left out.

The next step is to consider how the objectives are to be evaluated. Sometimes this is not difficult if the objectives have been clearly understood from the start of the programme and if **indicators** are already being used to monitor progress.

2.6 WHY INDICATORS ARE IMPORTANT

An indicator is a marker. It can be compared to a road sign which shows whether you are on the right road, how far you have travelled, and how far you still have to go in order to reach your destination (or objective). Indicators show progress and help to measure change.

Many indicators consist of measurements and are expressed in numbers, such as:

- a **percentage** (part of a total), such as 50 per cent (half) of the farmers in a village use chemical fertilizers.
- a **rate**, such as the infant mortality rate, which is the number of children under one year who die in a year, in relation to 1000 live births in that same year. (It may help to think of a rate as the speed at which something occurs, as well as the amount.)
- a **ratio**, such as the number of teachers in relation to the numbers of children in primary schools in a specific area (for example, one teacher to twenty children).

From experience

In Africa a programme goal was to involve women in co-operative work, like baking bread, to raise family income. The number of women who participated and the amount of bread they sold, were two of the simple indicators used to judge whether the programme was successful.

There are many kinds of indicators; here are some of the most common:

Indicators of availability

These show whether something exists and whether it is available. For example, an indicator of availability in a social development programme might be whether there is one trained local worker available for every ten houses.

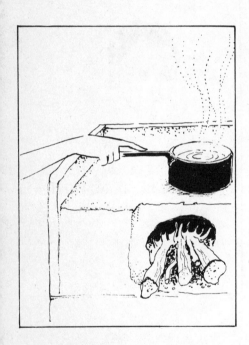

Indicators of relevance

These show how relevant or appropriate something is. For example, an indicator of relevance in a rural women's development programme might be whether new stoves burn less fuel than the old ones.

Indicators of accessibility

These show whether what exists is actually within reach of those who need it. For example, a health post available in one village may be out of reach of other villages in the area because of mountains, flooded rivers, lack of transport, or people's poverty.

Indicators of utilisation

These show to what extent something that has been made available is being used for that purpose. For example, an indicator of utilisation might be how many non-literate villagers are attending literacy classes regularly.

Indicators of coverage

These show what proportion of those who need something are receiving it. For example, an indicator of coverage might be, of the number of people estimated or known to have tuberculosis in a particular area the percentage that is actually receiving regular treatment.

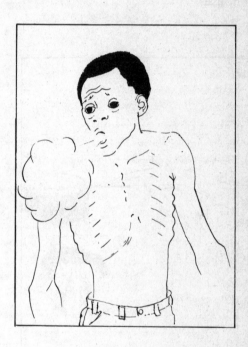

Indicators of quality

These show the quality or standard of something. For example, an indicator of the quality of water might be whether it is free from harmful, disease-causing substances or organisms.

Indicators of effort

These show how much and what is being invested in order to achieve the objectives, such as how long it takes how many men to plant what number of palm trees in a week.

Indicators of efficiency

These show whether resources and activities are being put to the best possible use to achieve the objectives, such as the number, frequency and quality of supervisory visits after introducing bicycles to replace heavy vehicles.

Indicators of impact

These show if what you are doing is really making any difference. For example, an indicator of impact might be, after a campaign against measles, whether the incidence of measles has been reduced.

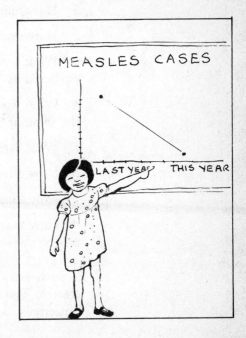

2.7 WHERE INDICATORS ARE NOT CLEAR

In some programmes the objectives, as we have seen, may not have been clearly identified. Without having clear and measurable objectives it is hard to have clear indicators. If you are not quite sure where you are going, how can you assess whether you are getting there?

If programme objectives and indicators have not been clearly defined there is a simple way to help put this right before evaluation starts.

First, programme participants need to look carefully at what they are actually doing and why. They then need to write down what they are doing using separate headings such as 'Training', 'Management', and 'Field Activities'. Then they need to take a closer look at these various parts of the programme. They can do this by asking questions.

Asking basic questions

The example below is adapted from one used at a National Conference on Participatory Evaluation held in 1984 in the Philippines. Participants from twenty-seven community-based health and development programmes chose to look at one kind of training which they called **'Social Awareness Building!'** where people from community level attended 'orientation seminars'.

From experience

Social Awareness Building
Questions

1   How many participants attended the seminar?

2   How many had been expected?

3   What were the educational and occupational backgrounds of the participants?

4   What was the level of awareness of participants at the beginning of the seminar?

5   What were the contents of the seminar?

6   How effective were the different training methods used?

7   How long was the seminar?

8   How many participants had raised their level of awareness by the end of the seminar?

Such basic questions made programme objectives and indicators clearer. The questions helped to reveal more clearly the programme objectives and to suggest appropriate indicators. The answers provided useful information for the evaluation. Some questions were more difficult to answer than others (for example, questions 4, 6 and 8 which dealt with the quality of awareness, learning and effectiveness).

By using a question-and-answer method participants can also begin to see the differences between evaluating **effort**, **efficiency**, and **effect** or **impact**. The first two are often already being monitored regularly by a programme. The third, **effect** or **impact**, is the most important for evaluation. It deals with programme success in reaching its objectives.

Having decided exactly what it is that you want to find out in the evaluation, the next step is to select the best and most appropriate evaluation methods to do this.

2.8 CHOOSING APPROPRIATE EVALUATION METHODS

There are many kinds of evaluation methods. Some are used to evaluate the effects of programmes on people; some help to evaluate programme structure and organisation; and others serve to evaluate the effects of programme activities.

People (commonly-used methods)
- **Physical measurements**, like height, weight, and **medical tests**, for example, those carried out on blood and urine.
- **Verbal questions**, such as those asked in questionnaires, interviews, tests of knowledge and skills, tape recordings, meetings, discussions.
- **Written questions**, such as those asked in questionnaires, tests of knowledge and skills, attitudes.
- **Analysis of existing information**, such as records, reports, diaries and autobiographies (what people write about themselves).
- **Observations**, **photographs and drawings** of customs, practices, procedures.

Programme structure and organisation
As well as the methods used to evaluate people, you can also use:
- **Written information**, such as records, reports, budgets, plans, past evaluations, registers, tests, checklists, minutes of meetings.

- **Verbal or written questions**, such as questionnaires.
- **Interviews**.
- **Observations**.
- **Discussions** and tape recordings.
- **Records of personal work** or work diaries.

Programme activities

The many methods which can be used to evaluate the effects of programme activities include:

- **Measurements of various kinds**, such as areas covered, numbers of people or houses, level of produce, amounts of income, or degrees of participation in programme activities.
- **Physical tests**.
- **Verbal or written questions** such as questionnaires, interviews, surveys, meetings, tape recordings.
- **Observations and pictures**, photographs.
- **Written information**, such as reports and records.

2.9 USING RELIABLE EVALUATION METHODS

A reliable evaluation method is one that can be trusted to give good-quality results. A reliable evaluation method is also one that, if used repeatedly, can give the kind of results that can be compared (if necessary) with one another. This can be done because the method or methods used to obtain the results was the same.

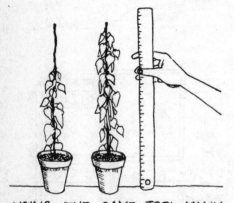

USING THE SAME TOOL MANY TIMES-TO COMPARE RESULTS

For example, if you want to measure the length of a bean, you may use a ruler. Measuring with a ruler is considered to be a reliable method because a ruler does not change itself when it is used to measure different things. However, different people using the same ruler may get different results. So reliability of measurement also depends on the technique used.

Also, if you want to use one weighing scale to weigh many babies, check carefully that the scale remains in good order, or the method you use to weigh the first baby will have changed by the time you weigh the last. If this happens your methods will have become unreliable, thus spoiling any comparison of all the weights.

CHECKING HOW THE TOOL IS STANDING UP TO REPEATED USE

Using rulers and scales is fairly easy. However, what about other kinds of methods, like questionnaires? This is more difficult.

For example, if a questionnaire used to survey family living patterns and conditions is then used three months later to re-survey the same families, the resulting information could look very different. The questionnaire remained the same, but the circumstances changed. For example:

- people may remember the questions from last time (even if they are in a different order);
- people may wish to answer more positively this time to make a better impression; and
- the people carrying out the survey may have changed and they and their families may respond differently to one another.

So, if you try to **compare the results of the first survey with those of the second**, you have to remember that the **changed circumstances of the second survey have affected the results.** You are no longer comparing two things that are exactly equal. If you do not point this out your results will be unreliable.

The importance of careful description.

In evaluation it is important to describe carefully what you are looking at before you begin. If you do not, you may find later that your evaluation results are not reliable.

For example, in describing a rural population as 'farmers', 'skilled manual workers' and 'small traders' you may find it is not a sufficiently careful description because some of the farmers may *also* be traders, and many traders and skilled manual workers also work as farmers.

So, when you say that *half* of the adult working population earns less than a certain amount a year, does that refer to those who *only* trade, or *only* farm, or does it include those who do both?

Unless this is clear the evaluation results may not be reliable as they cannot definitely be said to be true and to relate to the actual circumstances of all the groups.

You may also have chosen for your survey *only* farmers, or *mostly* traders. If this is so it must be pointed out, in order to make your evaluation results clear and reliable.

Reliable evaluation methods and results should produce information, facts and figures which are as true, clear and useful as possible. It is hard, if not impossible, to achieve complete, total reliability with all your evaluation methods. Usually a small amount of error is unavoidable. However, **a large amount of error is dangerous** because it produces results that are not true and that cannot provide a safe basis for drawing conclusions, making plans or making changes.

2.10 WHAT VALID AND INVALID MEAN

When something is said to be valid it is considered to be well worked out, reasonable, based on sound information or opinion. Therefore, when something is said to be invalid it is the opposite.

Evaluation methods which are not of good quality or have not been properly carried out, and evaluation results which are not reliable, are described as invalid, or untrue. There are also other factors which can spoil evaluation and make it invalid. Listing them may help you to avoid them:

Ten ways to spoil evaluation and make it invalid

1. **Assuming that changes are caused only by the existence of a programme**. Changes sometimes happen just because time has passed; for example, people get older, learn more and change their opinions. So change may not just be caused by a programme. Certain changes may have happened anyway, even without the programme.

2. **Ignoring influences outside of a programme.** People are also influenced by many things going on outside a programme, like changes in government, policy, local plans, power groups, opportunities for work, availability of land, what they hear on the radio, what they see in a paper, the building of roads, and so on.

3. **Forgetting that the same evaluation method may give different results** when used by different people. For example, two interviewers ask the same questions, but, one interviewer is patient, friendly and sensitive, and the other is not. The answers they get to the same questions may be very different.

4. **The bad choice of groups for comparison,** such as groups of women from several villages who live at different distances from a water source and have different levels of income. All these facts influence the amount of water that they obtain and how they use it. You cannot, therefore, compare these groups with one another without taking account of these facts.

5. **Loss of interest by programme staff and/or participants** while the evaluation is in progress. If motivation and participation are seriously reduced, this will have some effect on the evaluation.

6. **Repeating tests, interviews, or questionnaires when participants can still remember the questions** which were asked before, or when they may also have other reasons (not understood by the interviewer) for answering differently.

7. **Forgetting that people can respond particularly well just because the evaluation is taking place.** People can be very enthusiastic about something new and want it to be a success. Then real problems or difficulties may be passed over quickly — or hidden.

8. **Claiming that the results of a small-scale evaluation also apply to a wide group of people or to a wide area,** for example, evaluating traditional birth attendants in one African country and then claiming that the results are also true for all traditional birth attendants in Africa. There may be some similarities but there are also many differences according to individual countries, customs, climate, etc.

9. **Planning evaluation badly from the start,** for instance, evaluating a group of families who had attended nutrition education classes to find out how much they had learnt and were practicing, and then claiming that the evaluation results also told you about the nutrition knowledge and practices of other groups of families who had never attended classes. The evaluation plan should have looked at both groups of families, then compared the results.

10. **Using unreliable evaluation methods,** for example, using the same scale to weigh a hundred babies, but not checking the scale regularly. If the scale was not working so well by the time the last babies were weighed the evaluation results were therefore not reliable for all one hundred babies, as the evaluation method had changed during the evaluation.

When evaluation results are valid for just the programme concerned they are said to have **internal validity**, that is, they are valid 'inside' the programme. When evaluation results are valid for not just one programme but for others which are similar, they are said to have **external validity**, that is, they are also valid 'outside' the programme.

Sometimes, even though you may not count every single person who visits every single community centre over a certain period of time, by looking at the total number of people who attend 100 centres over that period you can get a good idea of the average number of people who use each centre. This is called **generalising results** and is a valid way of obtaining useful information.

2.11 MAKING AN EVALUATION PLAN

There are many ways in which this can be done. The particular way in which a programme goes about planning evaluation will depend on what methods of planning and organisation they already use, or wish to try, and who is to be involved. The plan shows how all the different parts of the evaluation fit together to achieve the evaluation objectives.

Whatever the particular planning method chosen, it is likely to include discussions; meetings; making estimates and/or lists; taking decisions; and finally putting the evaluation plan down on paper. An evaluation plan, written or typed, may comprise a few or many pages.

One of the best ways to start planning evaluation may be to draw a diagram of what you want to do.

The accompanying figure shows a diagram that was used to plan an evaluation in Central America. It was called a step diagram and it helped programme staff in a rural area to see more clearly:
• what needed to be done, and in what order; and
• how much time the evaluation would take.

The diagram also included a drawing of the final evaluation report. Most people in the programme area had never seen one before and did not know if it looked like a small book, a large pamphlet or just a collection of papers in a folder.

From experience

Another simple planning method than can help community-level participation in evaluation is a written **Master Plan** which includes all the planning details. This can be drawn up when:
• all those involved are clear as to the objectives of the evaluation; and
• it has been decided how long the evaluation will take, what resources (money, materials) will be involved, and who is going to be involved.

EVALUATION REPORT

Feedback of Results and Putting Them into Practice

A 'STEP' DIAGRAM

PREPARING THE REPORT. DECIDING HOW TO IMPROVE MONITORING AND WHEN TO EVALUATE AGAIN

REACHING CONCLUSIONS WRITING THEM DOWN AND STUDYING THEM

STUDYING THE FACTS FIGURES AND INFORMATION COLLECTED DURING THE EVALUATION

USING THE EVALUATION METHODS CHOSEN SUCH AS QUESTIONAIRES, SURVEYS, STUDYING RECORDS ETC.

COLLECTING MATERIALS AND RESOURCES, BEGINNING THE EVALUATION

CHOOSING EVALUATION GOALS AND METHODS. DECIDING WHO WILL TAKE PART, HOW AND WHEN. MAKING A DETAILED PLAN.

DECIDING TO EVALUTE

One way to begin making a Master Plan is to **decide what are the main parts of the programme that need to be looked at in the evaluation, and then to ask detailed questions relating to them.** (This also helps, as suggested earlier in the chapter, to identify indicators when they are not clear). A Master Plan helps you to:

- **focus on the main parts of the programme** that you want to look at;
- **decide which questions to ask,** according to the evaluation objectives;
- **plan how to obtain the information** to answer them;
- **decide who will do what** in the evaluation, and by when; and
- **plan how to make the best possible use** of material resources.

On the opposite page is an example of part of a Master Plan similar to one used in the participatory evaluation of a health and development programme in the Americas, and in which programme staff had the maximum of six grades of primary education.

By starting with general questions about the country and the region, participants were able to build up a picture that helped them to understand better the setting of their own programme. In this way they could understand the reasons for its difficulties and its achievements.

Evaluation plan

QUESTIONS

A. Introduction
1. Where is the programme situated?
2. What are the characteristics of the country, climate?
3. What are the characteristics of the region, patterns of living, agriculture, employment, education, income, conditions of health?

B. History of the programme
1. When, why, where and how did the programme begin?
2. How has the programme progressed since then? What have been the most important events affecting its development?
3. How many people have been involved as staff, participants, students, patients, groups of farmers, mothers, etc.

C. Programme goals
1. Who chose the original programme goals? Are they still the same today?
2. Which are the most important programme goals at present, and why?
3. Do all those involved in the programme have the same ideas about its goals?
4. What kind of basic information did you have when the programme started, and how was it collected and used?
5. Which of the programme goals are very specific and when do you plan to reach them?

D. Programme effect
(only a quarter of the Master Plan is reproduced here).

Plan

Where to find the answers	How to find and report the answers	Who will do it, and when
1 A map of the country. 2 Written materials. 3 Sources such as radio, school books, newspapers, reports and talking with people who may have information.	1 Copying, tracing, photocopying. 2 Preparation of a two- or three-page report.	1 (Each question was answered and a report made by an individual or a group.)
1 Programme records. 2 Programme records, progress and annual reports, funding agency reports. 3 Programme records and reports, registers, interviews, and personnel records.	1 One-page report. 2 Two- to three-page report. 3 Analysis of records, registers, reports and preparation of report.	
1-5 Programme and agency records and reports. Discussion by programme staff and participants, interviews.	1-6 Analysis and report. Recording and reporting of discussions and interviews and preparation of three-page report.	

2.12 PLANNING THE DAY-TO-DAY DETAILS

There are many different and effective ways of planning an evaluation in detail. Look at your own normal planning, management and monitoring methods and adapt them for use in your evaluation.

For example, a **work calendar** is used in many types of programme for planning the day-to-day activities. It shows what needs to be done, by whom and when.

From experience

Some programmes are using this kind of planning method on a larger scale, for example on a **poster** or a **blackboard**.

This kind of planning method is very useful because it is simple to use, it is inexpensive, and it can be changed when necessary. It is used by programme staff and participants who are literate, but what about

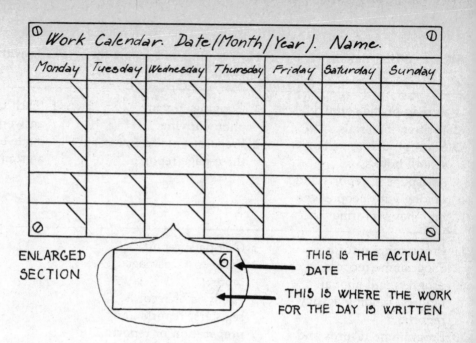

Work Calendar. Date (Month / Year). Name.

Monday	Tuesday	Wednesday	Thursday	Friday	Saturday	Sunday

ENLARGED SECTION

6 ← THIS IS THE ACTUAL DATE

← THIS IS WHERE THE WORK FOR THE DAY IS WRITTEN

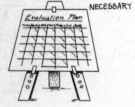

ON A BLACKBOARD THE PLAN CAN EASILY BE CHANGED WHEN NECESSARY

those who cannot read or write? How can they be helped to feel and see that they also have a part to play in an evaluation plan?

One way of doing this is to use colours and/or symbols on the evaluation plan to represent non-literate participants and show their part in the evaluation.

So, planning is a way of trying to see more clearly what you are doing, what else you need to do, and how best it can be done in order to reach your objectives.

EVALUATION PLAN.				MAY.		
Monday	Tuesday	Wednesday	Thursday	Friday	Saturday	Sunday
30 ○△	1 △	2 △	3 ○△	4 ○△	5	6
7 □	8 ○□	9 ○□	10 ○	11 ○□	12	13
14	15	16	17	18	19	20

KEY

Å (NON-LITERATE PARTICIPANTS)

△
□ ← (THE 'KEY' SHOWS WHAT THE SYMBOLS OR FIGURES MEAN)
○

PART OF AN EVALUATION WORK PLAN

(WHICH TELLS YOU WHO IS DOING WHAT AND WHEN)

However, if an evaluation plan is to be really effective it needs to be able to change a little, that is, it needs to be **flexible** so that it can respond to changes in circumstances.

A plan which is too rigid (or inflexible) can cause anxiety and will not, in the end, produce the best kind of evaluation.

KEEP YOUR PLAN
FLEXIBLE -
- LEAVE YOURSELF
'ROOM TO BREATHE...'

2.13 COLLECTING WRITTEN MATERIAL

Planning for evaluation always involves looking at various kinds of written documents relating to a particular programme.

Perhaps the following checklist will help you to decide what you wish to collect for your own evaluation.

1 The original programme proposal which may have been written by a ministry, department, organisation or agency (national, regional, local, or international).
2 Letters and papers relating to the programme proposal.
3 Reports of past evaluations or surveys that may have been carried out in the programme area by other people.
4 A map or drawing of the programme area.
5 A list of present programme objectives, prepared by programme staff.
6 A chart showing staff positions and functions in the programme.
7 Reports of past programme meetings.
8 Regular progress reports (annual and monthly).
9 Other written programme records (like medical records, production records, attendance registers, diaries, and so on).
10 The programme's budget and past financial reports.
11 The budget for the evaluation.
12 Past evaluations of the programme or of similar programmes.

13 Examples of evaluation methods (such as surveys or questionnaires that have been used successfully in programmes like yours).

14 Articles, press cuttings or similar sources of information that mention your programme. This may also include photographic material and tape recordings.

15 Others.

The checklist is long and it is unlikely that you will either need or be able to collect all the documents listed. If you collect what you can, you will have information and facts that are important for evaluation.

Some programmes have been written about a great deal, and much written material exists. (You can probably save time if yours is an 'undiscovered' programme.)

'POPULAR' PROGRAMME

2.14 RESOURCES: WHAT HAVE YOU GOT?

There are many possible resources that you may wish to use in your evaluation. You will already have some of them but probably not in sufficient quantity.

To keep evaluation costs as low as possible:

- use existing resources;
- only buy extra materials that are essential;
- have an evaluation you can afford.

2.15 RESOURCES: WHAT ELSE MAY YOU NEED?

The following checklist may help you to decide which material resources will be the most useful in your evaluation:

Paper

What have you got? What kinds are available? How much does each cost? How can each be obtained and how much will you need? For example, are you going to use questionnaires and how long will your report be?

Is it easier to write on lined paper?

Thin paper can be used to trace the outline of a map.

If A4 size paper (29½″ × 21 cm) is available, it is particularly useful because it is the size that fits best into many copying machines.

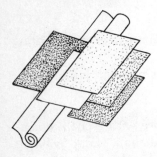

Carbon paper
This is special paper (usually blue or black on one side) used for taking copies of work that is being written or drawn.

Coloured card or thick paper
This is useful for making charts, plans, and covers for personal folders (see below).

These personal folders are used to keep papers like questionnaires and written reports which the owner of the folder is writing during the evaluation.

Personal folders are expensive to buy, but easy to make.

From experience

HOW TO MAKE YOUR OWN FOLDER

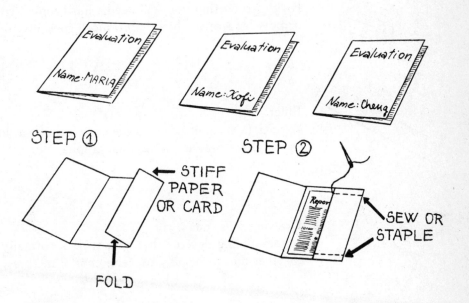

Pencils, pens, felt-tipped pens
Pencils are usually cheaper than pens. Pencil writing can be erased (rubbed out), which makes corrections easier and saves paper.

Felt-tipped pens (known sometimes as felt-tips) of different sizes and colours are useful for making charts, posters and diagrams, and for marking folders, etc.

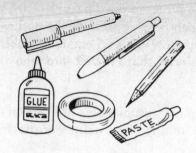

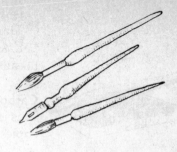

A pen with a very narrow tip or nib is useful for fine, small writing and drawing (for example, on maps).

A fine painting brush may also be useful for use with ink or paint.

Chalk

Chalk (white and coloured) is necessary for use with a chalk board. It is often not very expensive. Where standard chalk is not available there may be local substitutes that can be used instead.

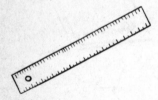

Erasers

Rubber erasers correct pencil writing and drawing easily and clearly. For typed writing you will need a hard rubber eraser, or a white fluid or powder eraser which is produced specially for this job.

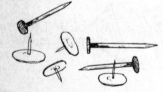

Ruler

A ruler (a straight-edged piece of wood 30 cm long × 5 cm wide) is essential for drawing diagrams, graphs, etc.

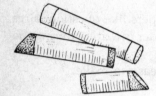

Drawing pins, nails, etc

These are the devices that you would normally use to stick papers together and to display posters, charts, pictures, etc.

Clips, pegs, clipboard

These are the devices that you would normally use to keep papers together.

In the community it is often hard to find a hard, flat surface on which to write. The simple clip board below was made and used to keep papers together on a writing board.

From experience

HOW TO MAKE A WRITING BOARD

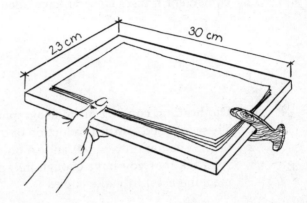

1. Use a thin wooden board or thick cardboard 30 cm × 23 cm (larger than the paper on which you will be writing).
2. A simple 'peg' of wood is used to keep the papers in place on the board.
3. Plastic or water-proof material is useful for keeping rain, dust and insects off the board and papers.

OTHER USEFUL OBJECTS

Scissors, stapler, string or rope
Scissors are used for cutting papers, preparing diagrams, etc.
  A stapler is used for keeping papers together.
  String or rope is useful for hanging up posters and charts.

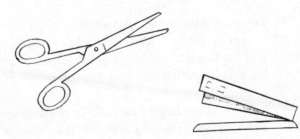

Flip boards
Flip boards and other teaching-learning aids that you normally use are very useful.

LARGER ITEMS

Typewriter and ribbon

Typewritten evaluation reports are the most clear to read and are easily read by others. Do you have a typewriter available? Is there a competent typist? Do you have adequate typing ribbon?

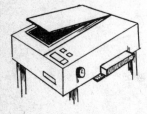

Duplicating, copying or mimeographing machines

These are used for the production of questionnaires, for making copies of the evaluation reports, and so on.

Check that you have enough ink, powder, or spirit (whichever the machine uses) to make copies.

Calculator

A simple and inexpensive calculator helps you to save time and to check your figures and tables. Make sure you have enough batteries of the correct size.

Camera and film

A simple and inexpensive camera may be useful for reporting, for illustrating the evaluation report, or for producing teaching or publicity material. Make sure you have enough film. Black and white film is much cheaper than colour.

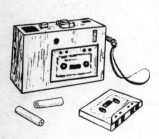

Tape recorder, tapes, batteries

A tape recorder is very useful for recording interviews and meetings, and for assembling material for personal profiles, etc. Make sure you have enough batteries of the correct size and tapes of the correct length.

Some recorders have built-in microphones (for the best sound recording); some have a separate microphone which is plugged into the recorder.

3 Using existing knowledge and records

What does a family need every month? Honduran women analysed their own situation. The main items are corn, beans, coffee, soap and kerosene. Bread is only available in the town

Evaluation does not only mean collecting new information, facts and statistics. It also means making good use of existing knowledge and records of many kinds. This chapter looks at how important information, facts and statistics can be obtained by using and analysing programme records, reports, case studies, profiles, particular incidents, meetings and workshops. It also includes ideas and examples of how maps, pictures and tape recordings can be used in evaluation.

3.1 LOOKING AT WHAT IS HAPPENING

One of the most important steps in evaluation is to look carefully at what is actually happening. Sometimes this is not done in sufficient detail because people appear to be much more interested in collecting new information, facts and statistics. By looking carefully at what is actually happening a deeper and more accurate view of programme realities, achievements and weaknesses will be obtained. This is also important for producing evaluation results and recommendations that are realistic and thus likely to be carried out.

There are many ways in which people can gain a better understanding of what is happening in a programme. Some of these ways may have been used to plan the programme from the beginning (such as making a map of the programme area. Some may have developed as a normal part of good programme management (such as keeping records, writing reports and holding regular meetings). There are also other methods (such as making special observations and using pictures and tape recordings) that you may wish to introduce during evaluation.

3.2 USING YOUR OWN RECORDS AND REPORTS

Records are a way of keeping information about the activities of a programme. There are different types of records depending on the programme activities. Records may show, for example, the amount and type of agricultural production, attendance at literacy classes, the history of an individual patient's health and disease, monthly work patterns of community workers, or administrative matters relating to staff, equipment and supplies. Good records can provide good information for programme management, monitoring and evaluation.

Records often consist of written information kept in folders, files or books, but they may also be kept on tape, or be computerised. They are an important tool in good programme management. They can provide continuous feedback to show what is happening, what progress is being made, and what decisions and changes may be needed.

For records to be useful for management and evaluation they must: be well designed; contain accurate and useful information which is well kept; be economically collected; be appropriately stored; and be accessible when needed.

Unfortunately, some records are like an overgrown sweet potato – only a small part is really useful.

Some programme records are designed by ministries, agencies, organisations, etc. Where these records are not adapted but used as they are at field level, programme participants may have difficulty in understanding them fully. For example, these kinds of record may be designed so that the information fits a faraway computer system. Unfortunately they may not fit all the needs of the programme participants.

Records usually fit into a complete record system. Several kinds of records are often designed for different parts of a single programme. These records may also have to fit into a national, or even international, record-keeping system which is trying to monitor progress.

Regular programme reports written monthly, quarterly and yearly become records of progress. Often they are sent on to the next level of a programme, which may be at district or provincial level. However, all too often those who send them do not get feedback from those levels. In this way record-keeping and reporting become **one-way processes** – they just go up to the next level. For the best kind of programme management and monitoring there needs to be a **two-way flow** – not just upwards, but back again to those who kept and/or who sent the records or reports.

Copies of all records and reports should, if possible, also be kept by those who keep and/or send them. In this way they are kept more 'in the picture', and are better prepared to understand and contribute to participatory evaluation. They are then not just the producers of information; they also share and use that information.

> GOOD RECORDS ARE WELL
> DESIGNED, WELL KEPT, USEFUL,
> ACCURATE AND ACCESSIBLE

3.3 WHAT CAN GO WRONG IN RECORD KEEPING?

Some programme records are not as useful as they could be. For example, they only give information about the people who are participating in a programme, not about the others in the entire area. If you want to know what difference a programme is making, you need to have a certain amount of information about the entire area.

Sometimes little importance or time is given to keeping records. They may be incomplete or inaccurate. They may be out of date, and entries may have been omitted or may not have been transferred regularly to more permanent records.

The information requested may not be the most important for the programme activities — particularly if the record was designed at a different level or some distance away. Ministries and agencies sometimes need to make changes in record-keeping. Unfortunately this may happen without the full understanding of those who are supposed to keep them at local level.

Sometimes those who keep records spend almost more time filling in the records than they do on other programme activities. Keeping a few records well is better than keeping many badly. Where there is great pressure on overworked programme staff and participants to keep many records they have been known to write down, in desperation, anything just to fill in the form! They know that their own performance is being judged partly by their ability to fill in these records and to submit them on time.

Unfortunately record-keeping is sometimes an unpopular activity and is given low priority. Those who keep records need a clear understanding of the value of their own records in order to maintain their commitment to the task of keeping them regularly and as well as possible.

Information which is collected on tape or is computerised can also cause difficulties for participatory evaluation purposes. A great deal of information is collected very rapidly using these methods. If required, a computer can help eventually in analysing a massive amount of information in participatory evaluation, but it is **no** substitute for people taking an active part in the initial analysis of the information they themselves have helped to collect.

Sometimes the way in which information has been computerised makes it difficult to evaluate. When programming a computer to store information it is important to remember that at a later stage some storage methods are going to be better than others for evaluation purposes.

3.4 CASE STUDIES: WHAT THEY CAN SHOW

A case study is a detailed description and analysis of a single event, situation, person, group, institution or programme within its own context. A case study can provide a 'deep' look at something. Case studies have been used for a long time in law, medicine, social work and the social sciences.

Case studies can be used for evaluation in several ways. For example, one or two case studies can be made of national training centres in order to provide good information that can help to give a comprehensive picture of the entire national training programme. Information can be gained by interviewing and testing teachers and students, making observations in classrooms, analysing the content of records and training materials, and describing the centres and their resources. Using a case study method like this often allows the values, attitudes and morale of teachers and students to be seen more clearly than if other more quantitative methods were used.

A good case study method is flexible and able to re-direct its attention to new and important information as it emerges.

Sometimes case studies are used before a large-scale evaluation is carried out. They are used in this way to show more clearly what the objectives of the evaluation should be, which methods will be best, and how they can be used.

Case studies may also be used after an evaluation has been carried out, in order to provide a clearer picture of unexplained or unexpected findings.

3.5 LEARNING FROM PARTICULAR INCIDENTS

In the normal life of a programme certain incidents may occur which affect the programme and its participants. These may be either good or bad. For example, an unexpected grant of money at a certain time may result in further development of part of the programme. On the other hand, a hurricane may devastate a programme area, causing specific effects on the programme. From particular events or **critical incidents** like these there is often much that a programme and its participants can and do learn.

Unlike the case study, which is usually written down, critical incident analysis in participatory evaluation may be a faster process. For example, one person or a group may lead the discussion and analysis of a particular incident. A quick and useful way of recording the process is to use a tape recorder. In this way the benefits can be shared later with others.

From experience

In Brazil a group of village health workers, community leaders, and a visiting medical team held an emergency dawn meeting to discuss why a newborn baby had died of tetanus (a disease which causes convulsions).

They worked out what could be done to help the family concerned and how an untrained traditional village birth attendant could be helped to improve her skills as a midwife so that tetanus did not occur again.

Critical incident analysis in participatory evaluation helps you to:
- take a deeper look at reality;
- share different interpretations of that reality;
- arrive at a greater understanding of the incident;
- learn from experience;
- arrive at conclusions of practical use.

3.6 USING MEETINGS AND WORKSHOPS

A community meeting is a structured assembly involving a large group of people. It usually allows for the discussion of different issues, plans, activities, progress, problems and solutions. In participatory evaluation community meetings can be used for all these purposes. In addition, they are used for the collection and analysis of information, and for the presentation of evaluation results and recommendations.

Community meetings may also involve a visitor or visiting group, the use of a panel or committee, a demonstration of materials and technology, training in specific skills, or displays and exhibitions (of, for example, local agricultural produce).

A workshop is a small or large group of people who meet to discuss, plan and/or produce specific outputs, which may be written, recorded or illustrated. The outputs may also be the production of materials, or skills training. If large numbers of people are involved they may be divided into smaller groups to give better opportunities for individual participation in group discussion. Feedback to the larger group takes place later.

Some workshops are highly structured and have a very specific purpose as, for example, a training workshop. In participatory evaluation, workshops are useful for training people in evaluation methods and skills. Detailed evaluation plans may also be made in this kind of workshop.

Other workshops are less structured and often involve certain key individuals in leadership roles. This kind of workshop stresses the importance of group discussion and the way in which people relate to one another. In participatory evaluation a workshop of this kind may be used on a regular basis during the evaluation period to assist an elected core group in guiding the evaluation. Its function is similar to that of a steering committee.

From experience

In the Philippines, to enable a workshop to run smoothly certain people were elected to play key roles. There was a **facilitator** who was like a conductor of a band of musicians. He helped the music to flow smoothly.

The **process observer** listened to the music and observed the performance of the other musicians. He noted sounds that were out of tune and helped the facilitator by observing group activity and providing feedback to the group on how the discussion was progressing.

The **recorder**, who wrote down the workshop results, taped the music and played it back to the musicians at the end so that they could know how it sounded.

Some useful points to remember

There are some important points to remember when planning a community meeting or workshop. You may find this checklist useful.

1 Give yourself enough time to plan.
2 A calendar of dates helps check day-by-day preparations.
3 Choose a good place and make arrangements/reservations.
4 Choose a good time and let people know well in advance.
5 Inform people of the purpose of the meeting/workshop.
6 Posters, home visits, public announcements, radio, telephone or letters may help to inform people.
7 Think about the size of the group/meeting.
8 Plan exactly who is going to have the responsibility to do what.
9 Plan/prepare handouts/materials to be distributed and decide how this will be done.
10 Plan smaller groupings (if necessary) and feedback mechanisms.
11 Some questions prepared beforehand can help to get the discussions started at the meeting/workshop.
12 If guests/outsiders are to be involved, plan travel/accommodation/briefing/payment/expenses.
13 If the meeting is large use volunteers to prepare the meeting place/direct people/distribute materials.
14 Plan the introduction to the meeting/workshop.
15 Make clear in the introduction the purpose of the meeting/workshop and how it fits into past, present or future events.
16 Prepare/check visual/audio aids/materials before meeting/workshop.

17 Make the introduction brief and plan it specifically for those attending.

18 Ensure that there is a comfortable/pleasant atmosphere. Arrange snacks/drinks where appropriate.

19 Begin and end at more-or-less the stated times.

20 Start with items/topics/issues on which it is easy to get agreement.

21 Allow conflicting opinions to emerge and try either to resolve them or to accept differences of opinion.

22 Summarise the proceedings and outline decisions/next steps/formation of task force/committee. Confirm time and place of next meeting.

23 Try to end on a 'high' or positive note.

3.7 MAPPING FOR CREATIVE LEARNING

Mapping is a structured activity whereby individuals or groups draw or paint graphic representations of the context in which they are living. This may be a whole village, a section of a town or city, a region of a country, or an entire country.

Sometimes maps are prepared at the beginning of a programme or activity; sometimes they are prepared later. They can help to show:

Geographical features, such as mountains, rivers, forests, desert, sea.

Physical features, such as the size of a village, neighbourhood or town, the location of houses by number and type, and the location of public and private buildings such as schools, factories and local stores.

Features which affect lifestyle and well-being, such as water sources, livestock and sanitation facilities.

Communication networks, such as roads, bridges, paths, and distances to the next population centre.

Social structure, for instance, location of leadership, social centres, kinship groupings, neighbourhood boundaries, land boundaries and ownership.

Manpower for development, including the location and number of development agents such as agriculturalists, adult educators, teachers, and health workers.

Development features and resources, such as development centres and organisations, stores for fertilizers and agricultural tools, co-operatives, groups, health centres, health posts and hospitals.

Changes with time. These can be recorded and the map can be regularly updated. Overlays can also be used to show how these changes compare with the original map (see page 136).

Maps may not be familiar to participants at community level. Lines and figures representing 'reality' may be a new idea for them to grasp. If the uses and simple techniques of mapping are introduced carefully, individuals and groups can be helped to participate in creating maps for their own purposes. It is helpful to show a real map made by another group, or a photograph of one.

Maps can give participants a clearer and wider view of where they are living. This can help discussion, analysis, decision-making, planning, management and evaluation. People see and understand things about their own environment that may be new to them.

Mapping as a group activity is not always easy. Different people may have different ideas about who owns what and how something should be presented on the map. This can lead to discussion and analysis of the differences of opinion, but this has to be handled carefully. If it is handled well it can be an important learning process.

Sometimes it may be hard or impossible to reach agreement about differences of opinion. Each programme will need to find its own solution to this problem.

Using small maps

Small-size maps are useful if you need to produce a lot of them. Paper that is about the size of this page is often used. Such maps are easily transported and distributed for learning purposes.

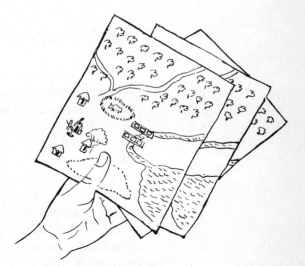

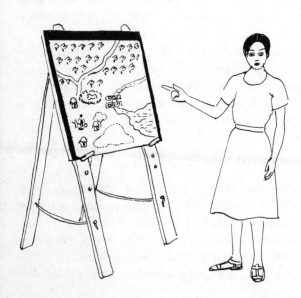

Using larger maps

Larger maps are often drawn or painted on strong paper or cloth. Several smaller sheets of paper can be joined together to get the size you need.

Use paint, ink, dyes or permanent markers for a map which is to last and which will not fade in strong sunlight.

A clear plastic (or similar) covering will protect a paper map from rain, insects, finger marks, etc.

Sticky tape or strips of material pasted behind the folds will make it last longer.

A long protective cloth or plastic bag protects a rolled paper map when it is being carried about.

Frequent use of pins on a paper map can weaken it, so use strong paper or stick cloth on the back of the map.

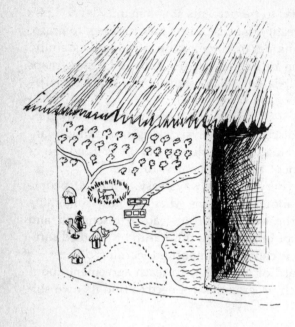

Using maps on walls

Maps can be drawn or painted on plaster or mud walls. Maps inside a building usually last longer. They cannot be moved, but they do provide a permanent visual record.

A community can be involved in making its own map and in monitoring and recording changes as they occur. In this way the map is also a tool for learning.

3.8 OBSERVATIONS: LOOKING AT REALITY

Observation means the act of observing or looking at something. Observation techniques are special systematic ways of observing and have been used for a long time in industry to monitor efficiency in work methods and production. They have also been used to evaluate teacher and student performance in the classroom. Those who were observing either wrote down or tape-recorded their specific observations. Recently, videotape has been used for these purposes.

Anthropologists have also used observation techniques when studying the lifestyle and behaviour of people of different cultures. Sometimes the anthropologists spent many years making observations of this kind. This was called participant observation as the observer also took part (was a participant) in what was happening.

Observation and participatory evaluation

Most people feel that they are constantly seeing and listening as a part of their normal life. This is, of course, true, but such normal skills can be increased and made more useful for evaluation. Simple techniques of systematic observation can be learnt and used by many people.

Observation techniques may be used to look at the results of a programme – for example, the amount and production pattern of rice-fields, or the way a health centre functions and how efficient it is. Observation techniques may be used to look at a part of a programme, such as training, meetings or workshop sessions.

Participant observers need to be well integrated with the people whom they are observing, in order to function effectively. The type of observation in which the observer observes without the knowledge of the people being observed is not in line with the kind of participatory process that is the object of this book. (It is common and legitimate practice in other types of evaluation for an observer to observe without the participants knowing.)

In participatory evaluation, observation can also become a group or team activity.

Different ways of observing

Sometimes a single period of observation will be sufficient to collect the information you need. In this case you have to decide what exactly it is that you wish to observe. For example, if you are observing a meeting you may wish to look at the type of leadership behaviour and the types of participation exhibited by those present.

First of all you make a list of all the different possible types of leadership behaviour participation in which you are interested. You then give them a code number in order to be able to record quickly what you observe during the actual observation period. You may end up with a lot of code numbers. For example, 60 to 100 code numbers have been known to be used in just a five-minute period.

However, fewer numbers can also be used effectively. One observation technique is to record each different observation *once only*, as it occurs. After analysing the information collected you make conclusions for that specific period. This can be repeated, so that several sets of conclusions are obtained for comparison.

From experience

At a twenty-minute meeting participants were given a topic to discuss. The observer then watched the meeting and recorded a single line with an arrow head indicating the direction of each contribution made during the discussion. The result looked like this!

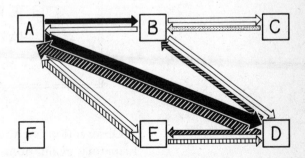

Conclusions

A did most of the talking.

A and D monopolised the discussion.

B answered questions but did not contribute much.

C and B talked to each other occasionally.

E made some contribution (when he could get a word in).

F did not participate, and was not encouraged.

Sometimes specially-prepared, structured guidelines or questions are used during observation. This is called a **directed approach**. Where no such guidelines or questions are used the approach is said to be **undirected**.

Sometimes large amounts of information are collected. If you pre-code before you begin it is easier to analyse the information collected later. If a tape or video recorder is used for observation purposes the information collected also takes time to analyse.

Observation methods can be useful for comparing behaviour between programmes and at different levels of programme activity. They provide a useful means of being able to see unintended, as well as intended, outcomes.

For example, an observer may spend one week living in a slum neighbourhood before a project begins. Then the observer does the same after the project has been operating for some time. This can be a useful way of obtaining a deeper understanding of communities, programmes, groups, and individuals.

Observation methods provide an opportunity to check the validity, or truth, of many verbal statements which people make. They can give a clearer view of the whole process of development and not just its outcomes.

> OBSERVATION DATA MAY
> HAVE MORE DEPTH
> THAN SURVEY DATA

Observation is an important and useful evaluation method in participatory evaluation. The following list of useful tips and problems may help you to improve your own observation methods.

OBSERVATION

Useful tips	Problems
1 Participants need to decide jointly what will be observed.	1 It is difficult to prevent the presence of the observer from affecting the behaviour of those being observed.
2 They need to decide where observations will take place, when and by whom.	2 The actual presence of the observer usually causes changes in normal behaviour.
3 They also need to decide on coding/guidelines/questions.	3 If the observer knows the participant very well this may make it hard for him/her to be objective or unbiassed in his/her observations.
4 If no coding is used they should decide how the information collected is to be analysed.	4 The observations made may be influenced by the role, training and even the personality of the observer.
5 Observers need brief training and support at first, in actual practice.	5 Involving many participants results in many opinions, and many interpretations of the results, all of which takes extra time.
6 After observations have been made the information should be analysed with the participants.	6 Observations that are not recorded immediately will be less reliable.
7 Decisions as to conclusions, feedback and future action should be made jointly.	7 Limiting observation to a specific period does not tell the observer what happens at other times. For example, not all meetings may be like the one he/she has observed.

Good observation can also provide ideas and opportunities for participatory evaluation methods.

From experience

In India it was observed that information was exchanged and opinions formed among women most often as they gathered daily at their bathing place.

Such an opportunity for the exchange of information can be useful in participatory evaluation – for example, when deciding what are the most important questions to ask in a questionnaire, and the best way of phrasing them. Also, it is sometimes the case that sensitive topics, which cannot be discussed by a mixed group of men and women, can be discussed informally and systematically at such a bathing place. It is also a good place to share the latest news on the progress of the evaluation.

3.9 PLACES AND PEOPLE: WRITING PROFILES

A profile is a brief description or outline of something; it helps you to understand it quickly. It can also help you to see something in a wider context. For example, you may be planning to introduce a programme or activity in a certain place. By making a profile of that place and that area you can learn a great deal about how the programme or activity is likely to develop. You can also see how the programme or activity should be introduced and how it will need to be organised to achieve its objectives.

Participation in making such a profile is an important educational experience for those involved. Information for the profile may be obtained from surveys, interviews, meetings, municipal records, etc. The profile is useful for planning, training, orientation, and evaluation at community and other levels.

At community level the final profile will be better shared, not as a document (some people cannot read), but during meetings when the profile can be discussed and when visual aids can be used.

Appendix A at the back of this book contains a profile of a fishing village in the Philipines. The profile was made following a rapid com-

```
┌─────────────────────────────┐
│    ENCOURAGE COMMUNITY      │
│    PARTICIPATION  IN        │
│    COMMUNITY PROFILING      │
└─────────────────────────────┘
```

munity survey during the planning and organisation of a health and development programme.

People themselves need to be more involved in describing and analysing the pattern and conditions of their own lives, and the lifestyle and development of their communities. Sometimes people at community level have never been asked about their own personal life experience. Sometimes they are amazed that anyone else would consider it interesting.

Creating and using profiles of people in participatory evaluation can provide a rich source of evaluation data. It is particularly useful in small-scale evaluations where it may be easier to take the time needed to do this.

How you decide to use information from profiles on people will depend on your evaluation objectives, the scope of the evaluation, the resources available, and of course on the people themselves.

Sometimes many profiles of different people can be analysed to see common patterns, problems and solutions. Sometimes people of different types can be specially selected in a given area. For instance, two women who live in a village, two who live a distance away and two who live in a remote place can be selected. These profiles are then compared and analysed.

Sometimes people have shared similar experiences and they can be encouraged to describe these in profiles. For instance, you can create profiles of people who have lost a family member through death during childbirth. By analysing the profiles people can see how future deaths can be avoided.

```
┌─────────────────────────────────┐
│   NEVER PRODUCE INFORMATION     │
│    NAMING   PEOPLE -            │
│   WITHOUT THEIR PERMISSION      │
└─────────────────────────────────┘
```

3.10 USING PICTURES AND PHOTOGRAPHS

'One picture is worth a thousand words' says a Chinese proverb, and it is true that people often find it easier to learn from what they see themselves. Pictures are often used in schools, in training courses and during publicity campaigns. These may be pictures in books or on posters. They may be drawn in pencil or ink, painted, printed, or silk-screened.

Some of the most effective pictures are photographs. They can be made particularly clear to people when the background details have been cut away and just the main objects or figures are presented.

Sometimes people feel that the production of pictures should be done by those who are specially trained. Of course, some people are better than others at producing drawn or painted pictures. They have special artistic gifts.

However, many people find that they too can produce effective pictures if only they are shown how to master some of the basic techniques. This can release their own artistic talents. Some people are afraid to try. They say "I can't draw". They are then surprised to find that what they *can* produce is quite effective.

Sometimes the materials used to produce pictures are hard to obtain. Paper is scarce or expensive. Pencils, crayons, paints, dyes, etc, are also hard and expensive to obtain.

This is particularly true with photographs. The materials needed to produce just black-and-white photographs are often not accessible to many people. Slides and filmstrips may also be expensive. Moving pictures (film or videotape) are also very effective but they are even more expensive.

Pictures and participatory evaluation

There are many ways in which pictures and black-and-white photographs can be used in participatory evaluation. Their use is particularly valuable where many of the participants are illiterate. Here are some ways in which you may wish to use pictures and photographs.

Pictures	Photographs
Pictures can be used to stimulate discussion and analysis.	A series of photographs can record changes before, during and after a programme.
Large pictures are useful for discussion and publicity; small pictures are better for flash cards, which tell a story.	Photographs can be used to stimulate discussion and group analysis. A story or a profile can be recorded by photographs but this may take a long time to prepare.
Turning evaluation results into pictures helps participants to understand and use the results.	Photographs contribute to the collection of information.

Pictures	Photographs
Pictures can show something that has existed in the past or will exist in the future.	An evaluation report can be made more interesting and effective if photographs are used.
Different people will often see different things in the same picture.	The camera sometimes captures more detail than the eye or pen.
Drawn or painted pictures can be cheaper than photographs and people need less training to produce them.	

Pictures, and particularly photographs, can produce a wide range of reactions in people. Often an emotional response is produced. Pictures can help to raise questions, reveal biases, motivate discussion, provide publicity material, reveal changes, build trust and relationships, provide information, and assist in decision-making.

If presented with a visual portrait of themselves people often begin to see themselves, their lives and their situation in a new way.

From experience

In Peru communities participated in making 'photo-novels' which told stories about a literacy class dealing with water problems in their community and also about different ways of teaching literacy.

In this way the communities took part in the whole process of analysing and evaluating different ways of teaching literacy, and of the experiences of literacy classes in dealing with the problems of bringing water to the community.

When planning and using photography as an evaluation technique it is important to bear in mind cultural and political sensitivies, and the official censorship practices, wherever you are. Try not to use photographs of people without their permission. They may also appreciate having a copy of the photograph for themselves if possible.

The community can participate in deciding on the purposes and plans for taking photographs for evaluation purposes. The extent to which they participate in taking and processing the photographs will depend on many factors, such as technical skill, availability of the appropriate materials, and costs.

PICTURES AND PHOTOGRAPHS
NEED TO BE CAREFULLY
PROTECTED AND STORED

3.11 TAPE RECORDINGS

The cost of tape recorders and tapes has become cheaper in many places (unlike the cost of cameras and film processing, which generally remains quite expensive).

There are many uses to which tape recordings have been put in development projects. These include recording meetings and discussions for analysis later, producing a suitable sound track for a set of slides, and recording information for community and personal profiles.

The main points to consider when planning and making tape recordings are similar to those relating to photography. Cultural and political sensitivities and current censorship practices need particularly to be considered. Do not use a tape recording of someone's voice without his/her permission. Be very sure that people know what the purpose of the recording is and exactly how it will be used.

From experience

In Tanzania, in order to evaluate the effects of literacy on new literates an evaluation method was introduced whereby the new literates themselves described their own experiences. These were recorded by an interviewer.

Guide questions were used to stimulate the dialogue.

In this way the new literates participated in evaluating their own experiences. The tapes were then transcribed, edited, further analysed and the results shared with the new literates.

IN THE OLD DAYS I FELT LIKE A PRISONER BECAUSE IF YOU ARE ILLITERATE YOU ARE LIKE A MAN WHO IS HANDCUFFED.

3.12 WRITTEN MATERIALS: HOW TO USE THEM

In the second chapter we looked at the need to collect written materials, including various kinds of documents relating to a programme or activity (such as programme proposals, past evaluations, regular reports, surveys of the area, programme records, registers, census material, etc).

The exact way in which you use these materials will depend on the availability of resources and time, and particularly on the objectives of your evaluation. Perhaps you have limited objectives or want to look at only a part of a programme. You will then need to decide which materials are to be collected and which parts of them are relevant to what it is you wish to evaluate.

Nevertheless, for the final report of your evaluation it will be necessary to include a certain amount of general background information. In this way your findings will be seen within their proper context.

If the scope of your evaluation objectives is broad it is likely that you will need to use these kinds of written materials more extensively. If what you are evaluating has been in existence for some time, there may be many materials to consider.

However, remember that these important materials are intended only as background to your evaluation. The information, facts, figures, processes and results that you generate yourself during the evaluation will produce your own information. This is new information and should lead to new insights, new decisions and new actions.

> DON'T LET YOUR NEW DATA GET
> BURIED BY EVERYBODY
> ELSE'S OLD DATA...

4 Collecting more information

People's attitude towards a survey can make it good, or bad. Women in Bunkino Faso discuss whether or not they want to start a rabbit breeding project

4.1 WHY YOU NEED MORE INFORMATION

The last chapter looked at the ways in which existing knowledge and records can be used to provide certain kinds of information, facts and statistics for evaluation. However, this alone will not be enough for an efficient and effective evaluation. More information, facts and statistics will also be needed. This chapter looks at the different methods by which these can be collected, such as by surveys, interviews, questionnaires, measurements and tests of various kinds.

One of the simplest ways of obtaining more information is by asking people questions. This happens in a survey or an interview where an **interviewer** asks questions and writes down the answers.

In a village in Thailand a survey team interviewed 333 families to find out more about how people lived; how much money they had and what they spent it on; what level of education they had; who were the leaders in the community; how people communicated with each other; how often they visited the city, and what they thought of it; and how they regarded new practices that they had adopted, like using a small water pump, growing mushrooms for city restaurants, using artificial fertilizers for their crops, using modern health clinics, and rearing a fast-growing type of fish.

4.2 SURVEYS: WHAT ARE THEY FOR?

A survey is the systematic collection of people's self-reported information at a particular point in time. Specific questions are asked mainly in a face-to-face situation, but in some countries such questions may also be asked by telephone.

Surveys are often carried out before programme activities begin, to find out more about an area: its population, the living conditions, the customs and beliefs, the problems and needs. In this case the survey is more correctly called an **assessment** and not an **evaluation**. It is carried out to find out about, and to assess, a situation. Sometimes such a survey is also called a **community diagnosis** or an **appraisal**.

Where surveys are carried out **after** programme activities have been in progress it is better to call them **evaluations** because their purpose was to evaluate the effort, efficiency and effect of those activities.

How do you decide whether you need to do a survey?

The following advantages and disadvantages may help you to decide.

Advantages	Disadvantages
It can provide information and statistics on a large scale and from many people living in a wide area. A lot of information can be obtained in a short time.	Only a little time can be spent with each respondent (that is, the person answering the questions) so the information obtained is limited to what the respondent is willing (or able) to give to the interviewer.
Information from a specially-selected section of the entire population in an area can be used as a basis for making plans for all of the population. So, the information obtained from a few people can tell you something about many more of the people.	The respondents may perhaps have been chosen because they were easier to get to, or more willing to co-operate, and may not be truly representative of the rest of the population.
The evaluation methods used to gather information have to be carefully prepared and standardised (or made similar to each other), so that at the end you will be summing up and analysing results that were obtained in a similar manner and that can be compared with one another.	Using standardised tools, like interviews and and questionnaires, can result in the collection of only superficial information which may be influenced by the respondent's conscious or unconsious desire to please the interviewer, to protect his/her own family or the community, etc. These feelings may cause the respondent to conceal the truth in some way.
Careful study is necessary before the survey begins, in order to determine exactly what information needs to be obtained, and what can be obtained, from whom, how and when.	If a careful study is not carried out and the respondent's way of life and manner of thinking and speaking are not fully understood, then the answers that are given and the information that is collected may be very misleading. For example, at community level people have very particular ways of measuring things. These may not be clearly understood by the interviewer. For instance some people use cigarette tins to fill a basket with maize, or use the position of the sun to measure time.
Many different pieces of information can be collected at the same time. This is useful because it helps to show how one part of the respondent's life (like his/her state of health) relates to other parts of his/her life (like their work, what they eat, what they believe, etc).	Some information, particularly relating to the respondent's past (like the pattern of ill-health during the previous year) may be hard for the respondent to remember accurately. It may be better, in this case, to obtain good information about what happened during the previous three months than poor information about what happened in the previous year.

Advantages	Disadvantages
Information which has never been collected before, even by national census, record cards, tax inspectors, etc, can be collected (for example, from people who do not make use of existing government services).	Surveys are often carried out once, and are not used to start permanent systems for the regular collection and updating of such information. Some expensive surveys are not used once they have been completed.
Other evaluation methods can also be used at the same time, or later, to gather information that can show how reliable the survey information is.	Information that does not seem, to the interviewer, to 'fit' may be ignored. In this way information that is important can be missed.
A large amount of information can be obtained cheaply if unpaid or volunteer staff are used. In some countries secondary or primary school graduates and women's groups have been used successfully.	A large-scale survey is often difficult to supervise and may be expensive because of staff costs and the distances to be covered.

4.3 FIRST STEPS IN PLANNING A SURVEY

The first step in any survey is to decide exactly what it is that you want to find out. In other words, what are the exact objectives of the survey? Some surveys try to obtain far too much information and some of it may never be used properly.

Next you have to decide how you are going to obtain the information, from whom, how and when. At the same time you must consider how the information will be analysed and used.

In participatory evaluation these steps are taken with community-level understanding and participation. Permission to carry out a survey may also have to be obtained from local and regional government officials, landowners, local leaders, etc.

Once there is agreement that the survey is to be carried out it is time to work out the **planning details**. These include the following.

Gathering background information. Gathering background information, like that for the checklist for collecting written material in chapter 2 (page 39).

Training of manpower. Selecting and training those who will carry out the survey.

How many people will you need and for how long?

Will they be paid?

What happens to their normal work while they are involved in the survey?

What kind of qualifications or experience will they need to have?

How will they be supervised?

Who will train them, where and for how long?

Do you need extra people in case some fall sick or have to leave during the survey?

Selecting appropriate survey methods. Choosing and preparing survey methods and materials such as questionnaires, interviews, tests, measuring techniques, and recording instruments.

How precise do they need to be?

Are they reliable?

How quickly can you make/obtain them?

Do you need to use certain survey methods and techniques to gather general information, and others to obtain more detailed information?

Which information can be gained publicly, and which can only be gained privately?

How are you going to record and summarise the information you get?

Will those who give information expect some kind of reward?

Estimating costs. Estimating the costs of the survey.

Will personnel expect extra pay for extra work?

Will you have to pay others who are involved in the survey?

Estimating timing. Choosing when to do the survey and estimating how long it will take.

What are the distances and costs involved?

Factors such as the seasons, planting or harvest time, local markets, festivals and holidays have to be considered or people may not have the time or interest to participate in the survey.

Will you need to visit a person, a family or a group more than once to fill in a questionnaire or to get more information? If so, this takes extra time.

All the various steps in planning and carrying out the survey will need to be clearly explained to all those who will be involved.

Does the community understand exactly what part it will play in the different stages of the survey?

Others. These will depend on the circumstances and context of a particular survey.

The way in which the community sees the purpose of the survey and the part that it will play in it will influence the way members of the community answer questions. People's attitude towards the survey can make it either a good survey, or a bad survey.

There are many ways of preparing people for a survey. Some ways may take days, and some may take weeks if they involve meeting community leaders and organising group meetings. In the following example a community development worker had been preparing the people for a whole year.

From experience

I CAN'T PROMISE YOU MONEY OR JOBS. I'M HERE TO LEARN HOW WE CAN WORK TOGETHER.

In Zaire a community development worker spent a year living in a certain area. He spent hours talking with people about their problems and helping them to spray their houses to kill termites, bedbugs and mosquitos. He planted a garden, began a demonstration soyabean plot and raised rabbits.

The survey in Zaire was presented to the people as an opportunity for them to participate with the worker and his colleagues in planning development activities (not evaluating them). The worker had also prepared for the survey in another way. He had drawn maps of each of the seven villages which were to be surveyed. This made it easier to plan the details of the survey because the households could be numbered on the map, and particular households chosen or 'sampled', to be included in the survey.

4.4 USING DIFFERENT TYPES OF SAMPLING

Sampling means looking closely at part of something in order to learn more about the whole thing.

If you want to know how a pot of food tastes, take a spoonful.
You don't need to eat the whole pot!

Why do you need to sample when you do a survey?

In most cases it is not possible to include **all** people, or households, or farmers, in a survey because the population is too large, there is not enough time or enough survey staff to see everyone, or it would be too expensive.

Many times it is not necessary to include all people or households (these are called sampling units) in a survey. By sampling or systematically selecting certain people or households you can get a good and reliable idea of all the people or all the households.

A CAREFULLY CHOSEN SAMPLE CAN
PROVIDE INFORMATION ABOUT
THE WHOLE COMMUNITY

From experience

Choosing what kind of sampling to use

The way in which you choose a particular method of sampling will depend on the purpose of your survey, and who will be involved. There are two main ways in which sampling is carried out.

TITLE: HOW BIG A SAMPLE SHOULD YOU TAKE?

The following table may help you to decide - ①

Total number in group	Suggested number in sample	Percentage
100	15	15
200	20	10
500	50	10
1000	50	5

① From "Field Programme Management, Food and Nutrition. A Training Pack."
FOOD AND AGRICULTURE ORGANIZATION, Food Policy and Nutrition Division 1982

TITLE: A SIMPLE WAY TO SAMPLE FOR ASSESSMENT OF MALNUTRITION

If you want to know how many children under 5 years old are malnourished, the number of children you must measure depends on how many people live in the community. Here is a list that will help you know which houses to visit in the community.

People in Community	Children in Community	Children to Measure	Houses to Visit
100	20	20	all houses
500	100	100	all houses
1,000	200	200	all houses
2,000	400	200	every 2nd house
5,000	1,000	200	every 5th house
8,000	1,600	200	every 8th house
10,000	2,000	200	every 10th house
20,000	4,000	400	every 10th house
50,000	10,000	400	every 25th house

"Finding the Causes of Child Malnutrition" A Community Handbook for Developing Countries, J.E. Brown and R.C. Brown, Teagle and Little, USA 1979

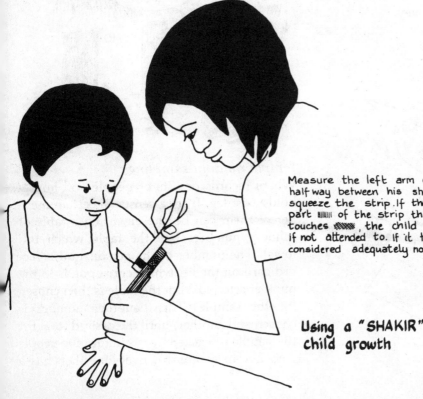

Measure the left arm of a child aged 1-5 years, halfway between his shoulder and his elbow. Do not squeeze the strip. If the black line touches this part ▥ of the strip the child is malnourished. If it touches ▨, the child may later become malnourished if not attended to. If it touches ▤, the child can be considered adequately nourished.

Using a "SHAKIR" strip to monitor child growth

PURPOSIVE SAMPLING

This method involves using your own judgement to choose, for a particular purpose, exactly who will be included in your sample. For example, you may decide to choose only a specific group of villages or people (such as farmers), or a particular neighbourhood.

OBJECTIVE SAMPLING

With this method you start by identifying, naming or numbering **all** the villages/houses/people/families/record cards, and you then give each an equal chance of being chosen for the sample. This is called making a **sampling frame**.

Then, from the frame, you choose who will actually be chosen for the final sample.

This is also called **probability sampling** because all start off with a probable, or equal, chance of being chosen for the sample.
You may need to use more than one method of sampling in the same evaluation. Here are some of the most common sampling methods.

Systematic sampling

With this method every person/house/record card is given a number. You then select systemically every fifth, tenth, etc, person/house/record card and include them in your sample. In this way you obtain the sample size that you need for the survey.

Simple random sampling

Where records or lists of people and households exist (eg, from a census) a certain number of them can be chosen, using a table of random numbers (see the table which follows). The number of the person/house/record card on the list which corresponds to the number selected from the table is then chosen for the sample. Then, another number is chosen and another, until the desired total for the sample is reached (for example, 100 people who live in a suburb). Everyone then has a

chance of being included in the sample.

However, there may be no adequate census information for rural areas, or for slum areas of cities where people move in and out very frequently.

Stratified random sampling

The sample is chosen from different layers or **strata** of a population or section of a community, like nurses, farmers, or fishermen, in order to examine them in more detail during the survey. A table of random numbers can again be used, as for the simple random sampling method.

Multi-stage random sampling (or sampling in stages)

Here the samples are selected using simple random sampling, but at different times or stages.

For example, you may start with all (350) primary schools in a region and choose just 300. Then you may want to choose just the children (7000) who have enrolled in the first class in all 300 schools. From these you may then want to choose 3000 for your final sample.

Cluster sampling

This is where the people/houses/records are chosen in groups or **clusters**, and **not** on an individual basis. At first houses are chosen at random, then other houses are drawn into the sample by going to the **nearest** houses to those chosen, and continuing until the desired sample size is reached.

You can sometimes use this type of sampling where lists or the results of a census are not available.

It is a method that can also be cheaper, and one that can be more easily understood by minimally trained survey workers.

Quota sampling

In this method the survey worker is given a certain number of interviews to be carried out or a **quota** to complete. He/she may go to the market and question people who are willing to talk until the necessary quota sample has been completed.

This method relies a lot on personal judgement – who is willing to talk and why, etc. Information can thus be biassed.
Respondents are **not** selected at random.

The table of random numbers which follows has been prepared so that the numbers do not follow one another in the normal way. They have been mixed up so that when you are sampling you can choose many numbers in a way that gives an equal chance of being chosen to all the people/houses/record cards etc, that have already been numbered. There are 250 numbers in the table below.

Table of random numbers

It does not matter where you begin selecting numbers in the table. You can close your eyes and place a finger or pencil on the table and begin at whatever number the finger or pencil touches.

TITLE: EXAMPLE OF RANDOM NUMBERS USED IN SAMPLING

```
10 27 53 96 23 71 50 54 36 23 54 31 04 82 98 04 14 12 15 09 26 78 25
28 41 50 61 88 64 85 27 20 18 83 36 36 05 56 39 71 65 09 62 94 76 62
34 21 42 57 02 59 19 18 97 48 80 30 03 30 98 05 24 67 70 07 84 97 50
61 81 77 23 23 82 82 11 54 08 53 28 70 58 96 44 07 39 55 43 42 34 43
61 15 18 13 54 16 86 20 26 88 90 74 80 55 09 14 53 90 51 17 52 01 63
91 76 21 64 64 06 91 13 32 97 75 31 62 66 54 84 80 32 75 77 56 08 25
00 97 79 08 44 37 30 28 59 85 53 56 68 53 40 01 74 39 59 73 30 19 99
36 46 18 34 94 75 20 80 27 77 78 91 69 16 00 08 43 18 73 68 67 69 61
88 98 99 60 50 65 95 79 42 94 93 62 40 89 96 43 56 47 71 66 46 76 29
04 37 59 87 21 05 02 03 24 17 47 97 81 56 51 92 34 86 01 82 55 51 33
```

This table forms part of a larger table of random numbers given in "Statistical tables for biological, agricultural and medical research" by R.A. Fisher and F. Yates.

The following example shows how a sampliing frame was made and used in a rural survey.

From experience

In an African survey households occupied by tax-paying adults in seven villages were numbered on a specially-prepared map. These numbers were then written on small pieces of paper and mixed in a basket. Different members of the community then took turns to draw the numbered papers out of the basket. After drawing the first number in each village a coin was tossed to decide whether to interview the head male or female in each household. After this an equal number of males and females were chosen alternately.
By using this simple sampling frame one hundred households (or 1 in 3) were chosen for the final sample.

In the same survey, where there was more than one wife in the household each wife was given a number, and one wife randomly selected for interview. If a household head was absent (for example, away looking for work) when the interviewer called, another household was randomly selected. One household head was found to be deaf, another blind, one in mourning, two very ill and one had a sick child. In these cases other households were selected randomly to make up the full sample needed.

This kind of replacement is sometimes called **substitution sampling**.

HOW YOU SAMPLE WILL DETERMINE THE QUALITY OF YOUR SURVEY RESULTS

Sampling is not always easy. Sometimes you may have to choose between collecting a lot of information based on an imperfect sample, or less information based on a more carefully chosen sample. The latter may be more useful than an enormous amount of information that is not so reliable.

4.5 HOW BIAS CAN SPOIL SAMPLING

Bias in sampling means unfair influence or prejudice. When you decide to evaluate a programme or part of a programme (or carry out a survey before starting a programme), the very act of choosing is biassed or influenced by the reasons you have for making that particular choice. For example, certain villages or neighbourhoods may be easier to work in than others, so they may be selected mainly on that basis. Your sampling frame has already become partly biassed by that reason.

In order to avoid bias in evaluation you must know where it exists or is likely to occur. If bias occurs, evaluation results will be unreliable and often invalid. Simple ways to avoid bias include the following.

- If you are using a census as a sampling frame, try and make sure it is as accurate and complete as possible.
- Remember that some administrative boundaries may not reflect cultural differences (such as tribal characteristics, language, etc). For example, there may be dozens (or even hundreds) of different tribes or groups and dozens of local dialects in the same country.
- Give the best possible training to those who will be carrying out the survey/evaluation.
- Try to allocate sufficient money, time, and resources.

4.6 QUESTIONNAIRES: DECIDING HOW TO USE THEM

A questionnaire is a group of written or printed questions used to gather information from respondents who will provide answers to the questions.

In this way information can be obtained on what individuals, families or groups do, think, possess, expect, feel, want, need, plan or have experienced.

The questions can be asked in one of two main ways described below.

Open-ended or free-response questions. The respondent answers these questions in his/her own words and at whatever length he/she chooses.

This way of asking questions can be particularly good for determining people's feelings and attitudes.

Fixed-choice or fixed-response questions. The respondnet is asked to choose one or more answers from those provided.

This way of asking questions is good for gathering facts and is often used where a lot is already known about the respondent or the area.

This enables a sufficiently wide variety of possible answers to be provided on the questionnaire.

However, if not used skilfully this kind of questioning could force a respondent to give an opinion that he/she really didn't have. In cases like this it is important to provide a 'don't know' answer as well.

People answer questionnaires either by writing the answers down on the questionnaires themselves in the spaces provided specially (**self-report method**), or by answering the questions as the interviewer asks them (**interview method**). (In some countries people may be asked to answer these kinds of questions over the telephone.)

In participatory evaluation the level of literacy is one of the factors that will influence whether and how the self-reporting method can be used. Perhaps the following table, which shows some differences between the two methods, can help you to decide which method will be best for your own purposes.

THE SELF-REPORT METHOD	THE INTERVIEW METHOD
Cheaper to use. You do not need to pay for interviewers to see every respondent.	May be more expensive. Takes up more interview time.
Questionnaires can be distributed by people with minimal training.	Interviewers have to be trained, which takes time and money.
Questionnaires can be distributed to a large number of people.	It may take longer for respondents to be interviewed than for them to fill in a questionnaire themselves.
Respondents can answer in their own time, and at their own pace.	The time and place of the interview may be decided jointly, but the speed of the interview is usually determined by the interviewer.
Respondents may not have to sign their names (ie, they can remain anonymous), so may feel more free to answer truthfully.	The respondent can also remain anonymous, or not give his/her name, if desired.
Questionnaires are identical, so respondents get the same questions in the same order.	The interviewer usually asks the same questions in the same order and records the answers him/herself.
Many answers can easily be recorded quickly (like using ticks, simple words or by ringing numbers) **but**: (see the next point, below).	The interviewer can explain questions which are not clear, probe for more information, or check answers which are not clear.

THE SELF-REPORT METHOD	THE INTERVIEW METHOD
The information obtained is limited to specific questions so you may not find out why people answer that way, or what else they think.	The interviewer meets the respondents, and sees the circumstances in which answers are given and how respondents feel about their answers.
It is hard to know whether the answers are reliable. Perhaps the respondent is just guessing, he/she has ticked the wrong box or may be he/she does not really understand the question. It is usually difficult and expensive to check answers.	The interviewer's personality/appearance/ attitude, etc, may influence, unintentionally, the way that answers are given.
The best method for seeking mostly quantitative information.	
Questions are standardised (that is, they are the same) but the answering conditions are not; the answers may be provided at different times of day or when the respondent is tired/distracted/short of time/ bored.	
Respondents may feel that both questions and answers reflect the interests and needs of other people but not their own.	

IN AN INTERVIEW THE RESPONDENT DOES NOT NEED TO BE LITERATE

There is another way in which questionnaires can be used during an interview. It is called the group questionnaire method and is described below.

Group questionnaire method

In this method the interviewer records the answers of not only a single respondent or family, but of a whole group in one place. Normal printed or written questionnaires may be used in the group method.

The interviewer explains the questions, then assists the respondents to fill in the answers. Completing the questionnaire then becomes a group activity.

Alternatively the interviewer may display the set of questions on a chalkboard or large sheet of paper. He/she explains the questions, then assists the respondents to provide answers. This time, however, the answers are recorded on the chalkboard or paper.

In the group questionnaire method the answers given can often be checked immediately. For example, neighbours can often confirm whether the information is true or not. Respondents can see for themselves how the results are forming. Illiterate respondents can take full part in the method, and in analysing and discussing the results. It is also a group learning process.

The disadvantages of the group questionnaire method include the necessity to avoid questions that may be of a very personal private nature (for example, in mixed sex groups, questions about contraceptive practices).

Usually the size of the group also influences the scope and length of the questions and how long it takes to answer them. It is important to leave sufficient time during a group questionnaire meeting for people to make brief comments on both the questions and the answers. It is sometimes difficult to stop people getting 'away from the point' during such discussions. Also, leave time for a break for refreshments.

The best conditions for using a group questionnaire method are where community-level groups have already been formed, have become accustomed to working together, and can trust each other and the interviewer.

From experience

A chalkboard is used to record the answers to evaluation questions during a community meeting. Each family is given a number.

4.7 THE ART OF ASKING QUESTIONS

Deciding which questions you need to ask in a survey and/or questionnaire is not always an easy task. There are always many questions that you could ask but only some of them will be important for providing the information you need for your evaluation. Do not start to evaluate until you are sure that you know what the right questions are.

In the following example a nutrition programme ran into trouble because the right questions were not asked before the programme began.

From experience

A nutrition team started classes to show mothers how to pound dried fish and how to add it to their babies' normal diet of porridge. However, the mothers did not have enough money to buy dried fish in the market. They really needed to make and sell baskets to get money. They also needed to join together in order to buy fish at a cheaper price. The classes failed because the main problem was that of not having enough money to buy fish.

When you know exactly what you are trying to find out in your evaluation, then you can start to identify the main questions that you need to ask. However, in order to answer these main questions you may also need to ask several sub-questions.

Identifying main questions and sub-questions

In the following example a health programme wanted to evaluate their activities. Their main evaluation question was: 'How efficient are existing health services and how effectively are they functioning?'

With this main question there were many possible **sub-questions** such as:

- Who used the health services and for what reason?
- Who needed to use the services, but did not, and why?
- What problems did the services and users encounter, and why?
- How could these problems be solved?

These sub-questions helped them to find the best way to ask the right questions in order to get useful information for evaluation:

The health services themselves – where they were; how they functioned; who staffed them; what kinds of equipment, resources and funds were involved; how many people were seen daily, by whom, for what and how long did they have to wait; what treatment was given; and how long did it all take?

Health service users as groups in the community – how many of them used the services, when, and what for; whether groups such as lepers were involved, and if so, what percentage of them sought care; how often users came for treatment and when; whether the same person received several treatments on one visit, and then came back for more treatment for the same illness or a different illness; who did not use the services; and what were people's normal traditional health beliefs and practices in their homes.

The people who use the health services (patients) – how and when they felt the need for care by the services, or how and when they used traditional treatment in their own communities; whether the patient had recovered after traditional treatment or had been referred (sent for more treatment) to the health service; how the patients saw and felt about their own illness, and about past health care they had received (like vaccinations); and the reasons why the patients used (or did not use) the health services.

The context (reality) surrounding the services and patients – the characteristics of the area such as climate, type of land, season; transportation and communications; leadership patterns; kinship groups; social and economic patterns, disease patterns.

HELP THE COMMUNITY TO TAKE PART
IN DECIDING WHICH QUESTIONS
TO ASK AND HOW

81

There are always several ways in which the same question can be asked. The aim is to ask clear questions which help the respondent to answer and to provide information.

From experience

These examples from Africa show how several carefully-chosen and clearly-presented questions helped respondents to give the best information.

TITLE: EXAMPLES OF GOOD - AND BAD QUESTIONS

These are bad questions	These are good questions
Do people raise small animals?	How many chickens does your family have this year? How many goats? How many rabbits?
What foods are usually given to little children?	What foods do you give to your child?
At what age do children stop getting their mothers' milk?	At what age did your child stop getting your milk? (If she doesn't know, ask more questions. Did the child have any teeth then? Could he walk then?)
What does your family usually eat?	What did you eat since this hour yesterday? What did your husband eat? What did your little children eat? What did your older children eat?

"Finding the Causes of Child Malnutrition" A Community Handbook for Developing Countries, J. E. Brown and R.C. Brown, Teagle and Little, USA 1979

BEGIN BY LEARNING,
LISTENING AND TALKING
WITH THE COMMUNITY

The following general guidelines to asking questions may help you.

General guidelines to asking questions

1 **Do not begin with difficult/sensitive questions**. Put these near the end so that if the respondent decides not to answer these, you do not lose his/her willingness to answer earlier questions.

2 **Do not make respondents feel they ought to know the answers.** Help them by saying "perhaps you have not had time to give this matter much thought?" Maybe they can find the answer later.

3 **Respondents may not have the answer.** Even though they would like to co-operate, respondents may not have the answer. Perhaps they just do not know, cannot remember, cannot express the answer well in words, have no strong opinion, or are unfamiliar with answering questions. Also, they may even be unreliable or untruthful.

4 **Decide carefully whether you should avoid emotional or sensitive words.** Using words like 'greedy', 'oppressed' or 'immoral' may seem to imply a judgement. Such words can cause bias in the answers. Respondents may be reluctant or nervous to give answers. However, if you are looking for truthful answers you may need to use such words.

5 **Avoid making assumptions.** Do not ask questions like "How many grades did you complete in primary school?" Perhaps the respondent had no chance to go to school.

6 **Do not use confusing questions.** Avoid asking questions like "would you prefer your child not to be vaccinated?" Keep it simple and positive. Ask "do you wish your child to be vaccinated?"

7 **Different ways of asking the same question.** These may be needed by the interviewer in order to be able to adapt the questions to different respondents.

8 **Use both direct and indirect questioning.** For example, asking a parent about an older child's health is not the same as asking the child about his/her own health. Older children can often provide important answers, but it is necessary to get their parent's or guardian's permission first, before questioning them.

The care with which you plan and design your questionnaire will influence the quality of the information you obtain. The following basic steps may help you.

4.8 BASIC STEPS FOR EFFECTIVE QUESTIONNAIRES

1. **Decide exactly what you need to find out**, then write out the questions.

2. **Keep questions short and clear**, not more than twenty words. If the question deals with more than one idea, use several shorter

questions instead of one long one. Underline or emphasise the main words or phrases in some way.

3. **Keep the language clear and simple**, using words and phrases in common use. Do not use slang or jargon, unless these are considered clearer than other words. Make sure questions cannot have more than one meaning to the respondent.

4. **Avoid words which are not exact**, words like 'generally', 'usually', 'average', 'typical', 'often' and 'rarely'. If you do not, you may get information which is unreliable or not useful. Use exact words with one meaning and pronunciation.

5. **Decide how the questionnaire will be completed**. Will it be filled in by the respondents themselves, by an interviewer, or as a group activity?

6. **Then plan the questionnaire carefully**, choosing only important questions. Arrange them in the best order with those that are easiest to answer, or those that are more general, first. Asking personal details such as age can be left to the end when a good relationship has been established between interviewer and respondent. Take care that the order of the earlier questions does not influence the answers to later questions.

7. **Make the questionnaire attractive**. Plan how to set it out clearly with sub-headings, spaces, etc. Make it look easy for a respondent or interviewer to complete. Keep it short – a very long questionnaire may alarm respondents.

8. **Make sure the answer to one question relates smoothly to the next**. For example, if necessary add "if yes ... did you?" or "if no ... did you?".

9. **Decide how the answers will be recorded and analysed**. For example, the answers can be **coded** which means they are given a number or code so that later it is easier and faster to summarise and analyse them all.

10. **Leave space for recording 'no response', 'no opinion', 'don't know'**, etc. Do not leave blanks when filling in answers on a questionnaire. Later these are difficult or impossible to understand when you are trying to analyse the answers.

11. **Give exact instructions to the interviewer or respondent on how to record answers**, such as explaining exactly where to write the answers, tick a box, circle a number, put a mark on a scale, etc.

12. **Allow enough space for recording answers**. Perhaps the respondent or interviewer will need to write more on the back of a page or on a separate sheet of paper.

13. **Mark each page of the questionnaire clearly**, using a heading or a number. If the pages become separated they can then easily be put together again.

14. **Mark each questionnaire clearly**, giving each respondent/house/group an identifying letter or number. One way of doing this is by using boxes and numbers like this: 1 8 3 6 This means that inter-

viewer number 18 completed this thirty-sixth questionnaire. The interviewer should also fill in the day, month and year in which the questionnaire was completed.

15. **Plan how the questionnaire will be introduced** to the respondents. Train interviewers to explain the exact purpose of collecting the information and the ways in which it will be used. For example, respondents may be nervous about admitting how much property, how much land or how many animals they own if they fear it may result in heavier taxation. They may not even want their name on the questionnaire.

16. **Train the interviewers to introduce themselves and to behave carefully.** They may need to carry an official letter/badge/card to identify themselves. Make sure they wear the correct clothes and behave according to the cultural customs of the community/area/country.

17. **Thank the respondents for answerng the questions.** Immediately after the interview, thank the respondents and acknowledge their contribution in the final results of the evalution.

18. **Decide how respondents will take part in summarising and analysing answers.** This will depend on many factors. A community or group meeting may be organised for this purpose.

19. **Decide how respondents will share the information obtained and in what form,** for example, at a community or group meeting, in a radio broadcast, on a tape recording, in a newsletter, etc.

20. **A sheet of instructions is useful for interviewers.** This gives additional explanations about the questions, how to ask them and how to record the answers.

21. **A questionnaire must be pre-tested** or tried out in practice to see

how well it works, and what changes may be necessary, before it is used on a wider scale.

Leave time to accept food and drink if it is offered. Accepting hospitality is important but it can become a problem where people are very hospitable. Constantly stopping to accept drinks, food or fuit takes time and can be a strain on the interviewers. In order to overcome this kind of problem the interviewers taking part in a survey in Sarawak joined with representatives of the local community in providing and preparing a midday meal which they all shared. In this way everyone was happy. Everyone had given and received hospitality.

4.9 THE IMPORTANCE OF PRE-TESTING

What is a pre-test and why is it necessary? A pre-test is a means of trying out or testing the evaluation method that you are planning to use before you actually use it in the evaluation.

You can pre-test all kinds of evaluation methods but the particular types with which we are concerned here are questionnaires and interviews.

When a questionnaire is pre-tested it is tried out on a number of respondents who are as similar as possible to those who will be interviewed in the evaluation. The purpose is to find out whether the questions are well presented, clearly understood and easy to answer, and do not cause anxiety, embarrassment, resistance, etc.

Also, a pre-test helps to show how long it will actually take to interview all the individuals/families/groups involved and to indicate the best times for interviewing.

A pre-test usually results in changes being made to the questions, their wording, their sequence, the length of the questionnaire, etc. Some questions may even be removed and others added. After these changes are made the questionnaire needs to be re-tested again. The pre-test is the last opportunity to make changes before the evaluation itself.

If you fail to pre-test properly your entire evaluation may be spoilt.

From experience

Mtu
Ni Afya
Man is health

In Tanzania, during the evaluation of a radio-based health education programme, a questionnaire containing 25 questions was tried out on 75 adults in urban and rural areas. Unclear or weak questions were removed leaving a final total of 13 questions.

The questionnaires were finally answered during study-group meetings, under the leadership of normal group leaders supervised by district adult education officers.

It is important to supervise a pre-test very carefully and to use both experienced people and people who have only basic training for this task.

A pre-test is NOT the time to train new interviewers. However, if you use *only* the most experienced programme staff, your overall good result from the pre-test may hide problems that might appear later when you use people with less experience and training.

Pre-testing CAN help to show which interviewers will eventually be the most suitable for that kind of work. It helps the interviewers themselves to see how they need to behave, which techniques they need to use, and how respondents actually do behave and respond in a real interview situation. They see how the questionnaire or other evaluation methods actually work in practice. They learn how to record their observations, criticisms and suggestions. They also learn how to be more confident, and how to solve different problems that might arise.

Interviewing is one of the most important techniques used in evaluation.

4.10 INTERVIEWING: AN ESSENTIAL SKILL

An interview is a face-to-face meeting between two or more people where an interviewer asks questions to obtain information from one or more respondents. In addition, an interviewer is also able to observe and form impressions about the respondents.

There are two main types of interview: the **individual interview** and the **group interview**. These different types of interview are described in more detail below.

THE INDIVIDUAL INTERVIEW
With this type of interview there is one interviewer and one respondent. It is used to:
- obtain information;
- find out about attitudes, and interests;
- assess knowledge and skills;
- help select people for training or promotion;
- assess performance;
- give advice about problems and stresses;
- find out about reactions to programmes; and
- provide a better basis for the preparation of questionnaires.

THE GROUP INTERVIEW

With this type of interview there is one interviewer and several respondents.

This kind of interview is used to:

- obtain information;
- find out about attitudes and interests;
- assess programme performance;
- determine reactions to a programme;
- find out how people think and act as a group;
- identify and find solutions to problems;
- provide a better basis for the preparation of questionnaires.

Structured and unstructured interviews

An interview may be either **structured** or **unstructured**. Both types are described below.

STRUCTURED INTERVIEW

A structured interview is one in which you know exactly what you want and where you want to go (like two people paddling the same canoe, at the same time, at the same place and in the same direction towards the opposite bank).

In the structured interview the interviewer uses one questionnaire, or a list of questions or topics. He/she then structures or organises the interview to try and obtain certain specific information from either one or several respondents.

The way in which the interview will be conducted and the content of the interview has been worked out in advance.

The specific questions are asked in a specific order. Visual aids are also often used to obtain information or to obtain the answers to questions, and are helpful where respondents may not be literate. These aids may be in the form of pictures, display cards, drawings, photographs or objects.

Sometimes a few additional **open-ended** (or **free-response**) questions are included. The respondent can then add extra information if desired.

The structured interview is sometimes easier for less skilled staff, and for participants who are interviewing respondents, to handle.

UNSTRUCTURED INTERVIEW

An unstructured interview is one in which you know the general direction in which to go but you will take time getting to an agreed point (like two people in a canoe who do not paddle, who let the canoe take its own course, but who still aim to get to the other bank).

In an unstructured interview the interviewer does NOT **use a questionnaire**. In this way the content of the interview and the exact way that it will be carried out cannot be planned in detail in advance.

The interview is more like an ordinary conversation "Tell me," the interviewer may say, "what do you think about . . ." or "we are interested in finding out whether the programme should be continued as it is or needs to be changed. What is your opinion?" These kinds of questions are called **open-ended** (or **free-response**). The respondent is free to answer or reply in his own way, in his own words, and at his own speed.

The unstructured interview is very flexible. The interviewer can adapt his/her next questions to the actual answers that the respondent gave to earlier ones. The respondent's main interests may guide the way the interview progresses.

The interviewer may also follow-up one of his/her questions during the interview by asking more about the particular answer that the respondent gave. This is called **probing** (or **digging deeper**) and needs some skill if it is to be done well. Sometimes people are reluctant, at first, to talk about sensitive and private matters like personal wealth, corruption, normal sexual practices, etc.

The interviewer tries to probe in order to be able to form, gradually, a clearer picture of what is really happening.

The timing, place and manner of the interview are usually chosen by the interviewer. The unstructured interview requires a more skilled interviewer if it is to produce useful results. In general, the more structured the interview and the simpler the questions the less interviewing skills the interviewer needs.

Hundreds and thousands of people have been interviewed successfully during **rapid surveys**. An example of the type of survey form and questions used for interviews and physical examinations during the type of rapid survey known particularly in Asia as research and development, is presented in Appendix B at the back of the book.

THE AMOUNT OF "STRUCTURE" YOU NEED
DEPENDS ON THE INFORMATION SOUGHT
AND THE INTERVIEWER'S SKILLS

4.11 SELECTING AND TRAINING
   INTERVIEWERS

Many different types of people have been used as interviewers, including office clerks, government census officials, rural school teachers, agricultural field workers, community development workers, secondary school students, public health nurses and village women.

Teachers have been found to be particularly good at interviewing as they often know their community well, and are respected by that community. They also have the education and experience to understand, after brief training, how to use the evaluation methods chosen.

What kind of person will make the best interviewer?

What are the main points to consider when selecting people for training as interviewers? Perhaps the following points will help you to decide.

AGE

In some places it may be difficult for younger people to question older ones. For example, in parts of Africa a man under 25 is still considered to be a young man. Young interviewers may not have the status or confidence to ask questions of their elders. On the other hand, where secondary school children have been trained to conduct simple interviews they have been very successful.

GENDER

In many places it has been found that women are better for interviewing other women.

In Pakistan, however, local minimally-literate Moslem women were used to interview women in their own communities. Unfortunately they failed to get some of the information needed as their new roles were not well accepted in their own communities. Nevertheless, they did gain much private and personal information of a kind that would not have been given to men or to people from outside their communities.

BACKGROUND AND POSITION IN THE COMMUNITY

Sometimes people from outside a community do collect information fairly easily because people are accustomed to giving information to people like doctors, officials, etc. If the interviewers are from the same community they may find it difficult to avoid tribal or group pressures, influences from their own families and kinship group, or pressures from local leaders.

It is sometimes better to have interviewers from a different community in the same area. Familiarity with the community and the area may tend to make interviewers feel that they know all the answers already and they may record them from knowledge and observation, instead of asking the chosen questions.

EDUCATIONAL LEVEL
The level of education required by the interviewer depends on the purpose of the evaluation and the kind of evaluation methods being used. If the answers are to be recorded in writing the interviewer needs to be at least basically literate. If a tape-recorder is being used to record respondents' answers, then literacy is not of primary importance.

SOCIO-ECONOMIC LEVEL
Sometimes those with a lot of formal education may have lost touch with life at community level or they may never have experienced it. For example, in some countries university students who come mostly from the urban upper classes may find it difficult to interview successfully people of a different social class or dialect.

However, these problems can be overcome. In Ghana, for example, university students were used to interview rural people during a survey. In this case some of the students themselves had either come originally from rural areas, had attended school there, or had spent part of their holidays in rural areas. All the students were received without any problems. Rural people were happy and even flattered that the university-trained interviewers were so friendly and willing to share the benefits of their own education with people at community level.

From experience

In Ghana the rural people tried to find special, comfortable chairs for the university-trained interviewers. However, the interviewers stopped them, and used the normal type of chairs or simply sat on the cement step in the doorway. The people commented "When people have learned so much how are they not more proud? Our own secondary school boys are proud, but look at these people. We can learn a lot from them."

PERSONALITY, ATTITUDES AND GOALS

The best interviewers are naturally friendly, polite, tactful, sensitive, intelligent, and not too timid or forceful, or too talkative. A well-balanced person is needed — one who has common-sense and self-confidence, is reliable, is patient, attends to details, is honest, is enthusiastic, is understanding and can control his/her own feelings (and hide them when necessary). They must want to do the work and not just do it because, for example, they have no other work or have nothing better to do.

PHYSICAL HEALTH

An interviewer needs to be in good health. Interviewing can be hard, tiring and even dangerous. Interviewers have been killed by falling off horses, or rescued from angry villagers, or nearly blinded by acid, or afflicted by the sun or floods.

In one country interviewers had to crawl on their knees up a steep path to reach a particularly isolated home during a survey.

LANGUAGE

Do the potential interviewers speak the language or dialects of the people? Will it be necessary to use interpreters?

RELIGION AND CULTURAL CUSTOMS

The religion of the interviewer may affect his/her ability to understand, be acceptable to, or even to question certain respondents or groups of respondents about certain topics. Religious beliefs and customs may also influence the way an interviewer should behave and dress. For example, in some societies women cannot be interviewed by men, and vice versa. Women interviewers may have to cover their heads, wear long sleeves, avoid wearing trousers, avoid drinking alcohol if offered, etc.

EXPERIENCE AND EMPLOYMENT

Many types of people have been used successfully as interviewers, such as teachers, clerks, students, government officials, school children, community leaders, farmers, community health workers, etc. Often they have worked for a salary, but sometimes they have been unpaid volunteers.

Looking at good and bad interview methods

By selecting and training the right kind of people to be interviewers there is a good chance that the interviews in your evaluation will serve their purpose. However, even good interviewers need good questions in order to obtain good information.

In the first of the three examples that follow you can see what happens when questions are difficult or not clear to the respondents. In the second example you can see two ways of carrying out the same interview – the good way, and the bad way.

From experience

In Africa an interviewer had difficulty in questioning an old woman during a survey of seven villages in Zaire. The interviewer wanted to find out about common attitudes towards family size.

It was hard for the old woman to think or answer beyond her own life experience and she did not see the point of thinking about family size in relation to other families in the village or to the village as a whole. In the end the interviewer got little useful information.

Reproduced from 'Approaches to Appropriate Evaluation', by kind permission of the American Council of Voluntary Agencies for Voluntary Service, April 1978.

Interviewer: "In life these days, it is good to have how many children? A few children? Or many children?

Woman: "Snort . . . can't you see my white hair?"

Interviewer: "Yes, but I don't think I understand . . ."

Woman: "I have white hair. Do you think I would be able to give birth again? Go ask my daughter over there. She is still giving birth, but my womb is closed."

Interviewer: "In life these days, it is good for people like your daughter to have how many children? A few children, or many children?"

Woman: "It is good to give birth."

Interviewer: "Yes, but to a *few* children or to *many* children?"

Woman: "Do I look like God? Do you think I am God? . . . huh!"

Interviewer: "Excuse me but I don't think I understood."

Woman: "Whether you give birth to few children or to many children, it is the will of God."

From experience

Mrs Mulenga is an interviewer who is trying to get information for a government survey on nutrition. Mrs Keri is a village woman who is trying to answer her questions. There are two ways in which the same interview can be carried out – a good way and a bad way, as shown below.

Bad Interview*

Mrs Mulenga: Good morning, Mrs Keri. The government needs information about how you people feed your children, so I would like to ask you some questions.

Mrs Keri: I'll try to help you but as you can see I'm rather busy. I have to go to the market in a few minutes.

Mrs Mulenga: Well I'm afraid I must have this information today and I can't come back later.

Mrs Keri: What can I tell you? I'm only a humble person.

Mrs Mulenga: That's alright, we really know what's going on, but the government has to check on it from time to time.

Mrs Mulenga: Now I suppose you feed your children mainly on maize porridge without anything added?

Mrs Keri: Well, I do my best, but at this time of the year there is hardly any food to be found around here.

Mrs Mulenga: I'm sure there are some things to be had somewhere, but wait a minute while I write that down.

Good Interview*

Mrs Mulenga: Good morning, Mrs Keri, I wonder if you could help me. I'm asking all the mothers in the village about the foods they use for feeding young children. Might I ask you too?

Mrs Keri: I'll try to help you but as you can see I'm rather busy. I have to go to the market in few minutes.

Mrs Mulenga: I appreciate that you're busy Mrs Keri with so many fine children to care for. I'd gladly come back at a more convenient time, but unfortunately I've got to get the information today. The questions won't take a minute.

Mrs Keri: What can I tell you, I'm only a humble person?

Mrs Mulenga: Well, can I start by asking what's the main food you feed your children?

Mrs Keri: Maize porridge.

Mrs Mulenga: Thank you. And do you ever add anything to it?

Mrs Keri: Well, I do my best, but at this time of the year there is hardly any food around here.

Mrs Mulenga: I know it's a problem isn't it? I've got two children myself. Can you tell me if there are any other foods that you regularly give to your young children?

Mrs Keri: Chick peas, pumpkin.

Mrs Mulenga: I haven't got much time. Perhaps you could tell me what foods you eat which have a high protein content.

Mrs Keri: I'm sorry, I don't understand what you mean.

Mrs Mulenga: Well, never mind. How much money does your husband earn every month?

How do you think Mrs Keri felt, and how much information did Mrs Mulenga get?

Mrs Mulenga: Thank you very much indeed. That information was most useful. I'm very grateful. Oh, one final question. Could you please tell me what job your husband does?

Mrs Keri: Bus driver.

Mrs Mulenga: Excellent. Thank you again Mrs Keri. I'll say goodbye now. Goodbye.

How do you think Mrs Keri felt, and how much information did Mrs Mulenga get?

*Adapted from 'Mrs Mulenga Tries Interviewing', Hanbout 41, *Field Programme Management: Food and Nutrition*, (A Training Pack), Food and Agriculture Organisation, Rome 1982.

4.12 RECORDING THE ANSWERS

At the same time as you plan how to ask questions and obtain information, you will need to plan exactly how you will record the

answers. If you do not you may be left with hundreds (or even hundreds of thousands) of answers that may be wasted, because you did not plan how to handle them.

There are many different ways of recording answers. For example, you can use checklists, two-way questions, multiple-choice questions or ranking scales.

Checklist

With this method the question is asked and the respondent is asked to **check** or mark one answer from a list of possible answers.

Q. Which of these learning aids did you use during the course?

☐ posters ☐ role playing

☐ flip chart ☐ field trips

☐ tape recordings ☐ visiting speakers

☐ slides ☐ other, please specify

☐ demonstration

A good checklist must contain all the possible answers and allow space for the respondent to add more information if he/she wishes to. If it does not, you may get a response that is wrong or that contains errors because the respondent has been forced to check only the answers you have offered him, not what he/she really wishes to reply.

Be careful to ensure that the answers offered do not overlap with one another. Each one must be different and separate. Make sure your checklist is well balanced, well ordered and not too long or biassed. Poorly prepared checklists are one of the most common faults in many questionnaires.

Two-way questions

These are question that require the respondent to choose only one of two possible answers. Both possible answers are stated, but only **one** should be chosen. For example:

Q. Do you think the community should provide cement for the new community centre?

☐ Yes ☐ No

Sometimes, instead of 'yes' and 'no' the words 'agree' and 'disagree' are used.

With two-way questions the respondent is not given an opportunity to say why he/she answers in that way. However, he/she may find it easier to reach a decision more quickly.

You can also leave space for a 'no opinion' answer or an 'uncertain' answer. For example:

Q. Do you think the community should provide cement for the new community centre?	Agree	Disagree	Uncertain

Multiple-choice questions

These are useful where there are several possible answers and you want to make sure that the respondent is aware of all of them. There are different ways of setting out these kinds of questions. Here are two examples:

Do you feel that on the last refresher course the workers:

☐ made more progress in learning

☐ made less progress

☐ made the same progress at last time

☐ not able to say

What part of the course did you find most useful for your future work in the community?				
	very useful	useful	not very useful	useless
1. Discussions				
2. Practical Sessions				
3. Field Trips				
4. Visiting Speakers				

Make sure that the answers you offer relate to only one idea at a time, do not overlap, are well balanced and are not biassed. Below is a **bad** example, where the possible answers are confusing and overlap. (It is hard to check just one answer. Try it yourself.)

Q. How does the new agricultural course compare with the old one?

☐ The new one is better, needs little alteration

☐ The new one is better, but needs some alteration

☐ The new one is better, but needs a lot of alteration

☐ The new one is not as good as the old one

Place all your answers, or response-boxes, spaces for ticks, etc, in one column at one side of the page. This helps respondents to answer in the right place, and to avoid missing any questions.

Open-response questions

How do you record open-response information? Open-response information is obtained when you ask respondents open-ended or free-response questions like "what do you think of the new Community Centre?" and allowing them to answer in their own words and at their own length (which may be very long).

HOW DO YOU SUMMARISE AND ANALYSE SUCH INFORMATION?

Information from open-response questions can be summarised and analysed in one of the following ways. You can:

1 **Produce a short summary** of what each person says, containing what you feel are the main points of interest.
2 **Read at least a quarter of all the responses** that you get to the question, then write down the main points most frequently mentioned. You then read all the responses and record how many times those points were mentioned by the respondents and by which respondents, etc. Or, you can divide the piles of responses into those favourable or against something, or those with various degrees of enthusiasm about something. You can use quotations from the actual responses to emphasise certain points when you are writing the results of the survey.

   Arrange for several people to look through your different piles of responses, using the same method you used. In this way you can see whether someone else also considers the responses to be in favour, or against, something. This helps to prevent bias, because more than one person has come to the same decision independently.

3 **Give each respondent a number** and then, using method 2 above, you can also give the main points numbers, so that your information can then be summarised, coded, and analysed by number (numerically).

You also need to find out why people respond as they do. This can provide important information about the various individuals and groups in the community.

If you use open-response questions be absolutely clear about what you are trying to find out.

Scales

One way to ask questions about people's opinions and attitudes, or how they think and feel, is to use **scales**. A scale is a way of arranging things in a regular order from high to low, like a ladder or a scale of musical notes.

In evaluation there is a special way of classifying something according to different degrees or levels. There are several different types of scales used to evaluate how a respondent feels about something. The three described below are the **ordered scale**, the **agreement scale** and the **opposite scale**.

THE ORDERED SCALE
The ordered scale consists of several statements that give an idea about how people might feel about something. Each statement is given a special number so that when respondents have marked their chosen statements the results can be summarised easily.

Statements about facts are not included because people might find it difficult to disagree with facts. So only statements about opinions are included.

Respondents are asked only to mark the statement with which they agree, and to leave the others.

Example of an ordered scale
☐ The slide show was useful for our work here
☐ The slide show was too long
☐ The presenter explained the slides well
☐ Making a set of slides is too expensive for us
☐ The presenter did not really answer our questions about the slides
☐ The slides had been arranged in the best way

There are some useful points to remember when you want to make and use an ordered scale like the one above. These are described below.

How to make and use an ordered scale
1 First you need to collect a large number of statements (about 100) that represent a wide variety of opinions (for example, from interviews with respondents).
2 Write each on a separate piece of paper.
3 Ask several people (if possible, people of a similar type to the respondents) to sort the papers into **eleven** piles. The first pile will be very favourable opinions, the middle ones will be **neither favourable or unfavourable** and the last piles will be increasingly **unfavourable**.
4 Throw out any statements that are not clear and that may have a double meaning.
5 Decide which is the middle opinion and take a set of statements (not more than 25) which extend from **favourable** to **very favourable**.
6 Give numbers to the statements in this set.
7 When you use these statements to construct your questionnaire, they must **not** be in logical order according to the numbers you have given them. They must be in a **random** order which does not follow logically. **Do not indicate which number has been given to any statement**.
8 The respondents answer the questionnaire by indicating if they **agree** or **disagree** with the statements. The scores (sums of numbers) are then added so that you can see the results more clearly.

THE AGREEMENT SCALE
An agreement scale is rather like an ordered scale because it is also made from a set of opinion statements. However, this time each respondent is asked to show, not just whether he/she agrees or disagrees with certain statements, but **how strongly** they agree or disagree.

An agreement scale looks like this:

SA	A	U	D	SD
strongly agree	agree	undecided (don't know)	disagree	strongly disagree

(This pattern can also be used for other evaluation methods besides the attitude agreement scale.)

How to make and use an agreement scale
1 **First you need to collect a large number of statements** (about 60) that represent a wide variety of opinions about the attitude you wish to look at (for example, from interviews with respondents).

2 Then ask several people who are of a similar type to the respondents (as many as possible) to respond to those statements, using the five-point scale (from strongly agree to strongly disagree).

3 Give each of the five points a number from 1 to 5, such that, for instance, 1 will denote strongly agree and 5 will denote strongly disagree. **Note carefully** whether the statement is unfavourable and if the highest number (5) will indicate agreement, or if the statement is favourable and number 5 indicates disagreement.

4 Add up the score for each respondent, according to the numbers they indicated on the scale.

5 High scores and low scores can then be seen for each statement.

6 Look carefully at the result for each statement and analyse what it means.

7 Keep those statements (about 20) that provide a good range of attitudes among the respondents.

8 Make your questionnaire by listing your final statements in **random** order.

9 When the final respondents have answered the questionnaires, the sum of all the results can be added according to what the respondents indicated.

Make sure you get good statements to use in your evaluation.

THE OPPOSITES SCALE

This scale is made by using selected words (descriptive words, or adjectives) in relation to other words that mean the exact opposite of the first words. The proper name for this scale is a **semantic differential** scale. **It uses the differences between the meanings of words such as 'right' and 'wrong', 'fast' and 'slow', 'new' and 'old', 'boring' and 'interesting', 'clear' and 'confusing'.**

Seven points are given so that the respondent can indicate his/her opinion or attitude on the scale between the words. Several words may be used at one time to get information from respondents on one topic. For example, you may want to find out what people in an urban neighbourhood think about cigarette smoking. In this case respondents are asked to put a dot or a tick on just one of the points along the scale between the words, like this:

Cigarette smoking is:		
good	_ _ _ _ _ _ ∠	bad
not healthy	∠ _ _ _ _ _ _	healthy
cheap	_ _ _ _ ∠ _	expensive

This type of scale is useful for determining opinions and attitudes where people are likely to have strong feelings about something but may not have thought about it very deeply.

However, the scale will only give a very general idea about what, and how strongly, people feel about something, unlike the other scales which provide more in-depth information. Also, some people have difficulty working out just how strongly they do feel and where they should put their mark on a seven-point scale.

How to make and use an 'opposites' scale

1 Decide what you wish to evaluate.
2 Choose the pairs of words you need (**10 if possible**).
3 Give a number from one to seven to each of the points between the pairs of opposite words. (Give 1 to negative responses and 7 to favourable responses.)
4 Write what it is you are evaluating at the top of the scale (eg, cigarette smoking). If you use more than one object (what you are evaluating) keep the pairs of words on the scales below the objects in the same order each time.
5 To make sure that people are thinking carefully as they use the scales, do **not** put all the positive words on one side of the scale. Put some on the opposite side.
6 Tell respondents how and where to mark the scales. You need then to respond quickly so that their first thoughts, opinions and attitudes can be obtained.
7 Add up the scores using the numbers given to each of the points. A respondent's general score for the object (for example, cigarette smoking) is the average (middle) of the score for responses on all the scales for the object. So, you take the numbers indicated by the mark on *each* of the scales and add them up. You then divide them by the number of scales. The answer is the respondent's average score.

You can also take all the numbers on the same scale for different respondents (for example, cigarette smoking is 'healthy' or 'unhealthy', add the numbers, and divide by the total number of respondents. This will give you an average result for that particular scale.

4.13 SUMMARISING AND ANALYSING ANSWERS

In participatory evaluation an important objective is that staff and participants take part, not only in collecting information, but also in summarising and analysing the information obtained. There are two main ways in which this can be done: it can be done either by **hand** or by **machine**.

Summarising by hand

There are several ways in which information can be summarised by hand. These include using a **tally sheet**, or a **summary sheet**.

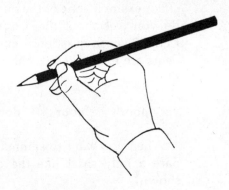

TALLY SHEETS

These are specially-prepared sheets of paper which show all possible responses and are useful for summarising and analysing some types of information, such as production figures, attendance figures or medical records. For example, two questions in participatory evaluation might be "how many patients have been seen in the last four months?" and "what ages were they and what was wrong with them?"

Using a tally sheet, a single stroke can be used to record each patient visit by age and symptomatic diagnosis (such as diarrhoea, cough or fever).

This is a particularly good method of summary and analysis where many non-literate participants are involved. When the tally sheet is prepared at a meeting or by a group, the pattern of the result emerges in a way in which everyone can see. Paper or chalkboard can be used for tally sheets, too.

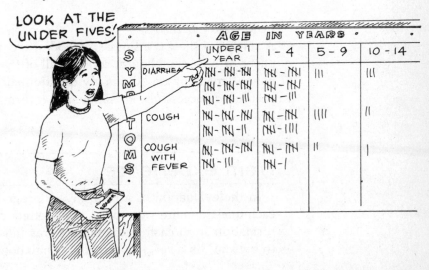

From experience

You can also use a tally method to summarise information about people's attitudes.

For example, one of the questions in a questionnaire might be "what do you feel about the activities organised by the new Community Centre?" Each question is given a special letter to identify it. Respondents are then asked to check just one box as they answer each question.

very poor   **poor**   **don't know**   **good**   **very good**

When you want to summarise and analyse the results you can prepare a tally sheet like the one below (only a section of which is shown).

Question	1	2	3	4	5
	(very poor)	(poor)	(don't know)	(good)	(very good)
(A)	11111	11111	11111	11111	11111
	11	11	111	11111	1111

Using these methods to summarise your information helps you to see exactly how many (and what percentage of) people responded in a specific way to specific questions. At the end you can say, for example, that on average, half (or 50 per cent) of the respondents agree or disagree with a particular question. However, using this method you do lose the individual answers from each different respondent.

If you want to see clearly how each respondent answered, you may wish to use a summary sheet.

SUMMARY SHEETS

A summary sheet is a simple method of recording, on a large sheet of paper or on a chalkboard, some or all of the responses to a questionnaire (depending on how many questionnaires were involved). It has been used successfully to summarise information on a population of 700.

From experience

In the evaluation of a rural health programme in central America each questionnaire was coded using letters of the alphabet. Then information from each questionnaire was filled in vertically, from top to bottom, on a specially-prepared chalkboard. The information was then analysed by 'reading' it horizontally, from left to right. Finally, the results were added and made into averages and percentages.

If you have graph paper (which is paper that has been printed with squares or boxes), this is useful.

This way of summarising information is sometimes called a **people-item-data roster** because it sets out clearly in lines (**or rosters**) information (**data**) as it relates to certain aspects (**items**) of the individual people.

TITLE: USING A CHALKBOARD AS A SUMMARY SHEET

QUESTIONS	A	B	C	D	E	F	G	H	I
Age	29	28	21	19	19	23	30	25	
Primary Grades Completed	3	2	0	3	3	2	1	2	
Age at Marriage	17	19	19	17	16	20	18	15	
Number of Living Children	5	7	2	2	3	1	6	7	
Number of Years as Promotor	5	2	4	3	2	5	5	5	

QUESTIONNAIRES

This is a section of the chalkboard:
The data from each questionnaire is filled in downwards;
Then the data is summarized and analyzed by reading it across horizontally from left to right.

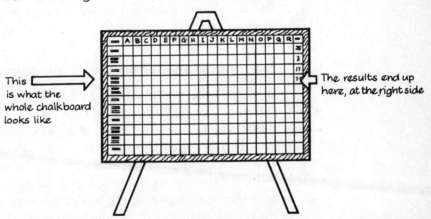

This is what the whole chalkboard looks like

The results end up here, at the right side

When you have hundreds of questionnaires, you will need to use the same chalkboard many times to summarize and analyze the data. Be careful that you <u>write down the results each time</u> the board is used.
At the end <u>all the results are added together</u>.

TITLE: USING A SUMMARY SHEET WHEN THERE ARE
HUNDREDS OF QUESTIONNAIRES

The questions are written here

The final results are written here

GROUPS RESPONSIBLE FOR ANALYSIS →	A	B	C	D	E	TOTALS AND PERCENTAGES
GROWS						
RICE	95	97				
CORN	30	40				
VEGETABLES	85	80				
FRUIT	32	40				
OTHER, WHAT?						
KEEPS						
CHICKENS	96	94				
DUCK	80	82				
PIG	60	55				
BUFFALO	80	75				
OTHER, WHAT?	GOAT-2	COW-3				
FISHING						
SEA	20	23				
RIVER	40	45				
POND	4	0				

Each column contains the answers from 100 families

1 Each group analyzes 100 questionnaires using the agreed design on the chalkboard which corresponds to the questionnaire design.

2 One or two people are elected to fill in the results from each group on to the chalkboard.

3 Finally, all the results from all the groups are summarized and analyzed on the right side of the chalkboard.

If you are scoring with numbers you can easily see individual scores. Be careful with the 'don't know' answers or your average results may not be correct in the end.

Summary and analysis by machine

In participatory evaluation the initial summary and analysis of the information collected is carried out by programme staff, with selected participants. This works well if the evaluation is not on a large scale and there is not an enormous amount of information (as would be the case from a nation-wide programme) to be summarised and analysed.

Where there is an enormous amount of information, staff and participants in each part of the programme can carry out the initial summary and analysis of the information for their own part, that is, for their local programme. The information can then pass on, with their summary and results, up to the next level (perhaps district or provincial level) so that it can be added to the information from the other parts of the entire programme. Machines such as calculators and computers will probably be used eventually to further summarise and further analyse all the information.

Where this happens staff and participants in local programmes play only one part in the summary and analysis of the information collected during the evaluation. They participate in summarising and analysing the information relating to their own part of the large-scale programme. If they can take a more active part in a large-scale evaluation, they achieve a deeper understanding of that programme and get a better idea of their own part in it.

When there is a lot of information to be summarised and analysed, computers are often used.

In participatory evaluation the aim is to encourage people to use the personal mini-computer which each person has, right inside his/her own head – their own brain. It does not need batteries. Just keep it active and polished for best use.

COMPUTERS

When computers are going to be used in summarising and analysing evaluation results the answers or responses are given numbers or codes as, for example, before respondents answer a questionnaire. Later these numbers can be transferred to specially-prepared coding sheets, a part of one of which is shown below.

TITLE: A SECTION OF A COMPUTER CODING SHEET

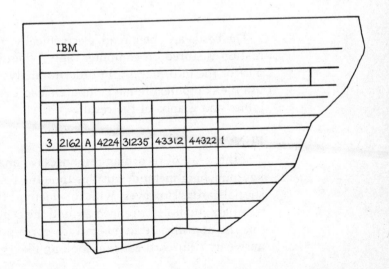

Then the numbers on the coding sheets are recorded by being punched onto special cards. This is called **key punching**. A hole is made in a particular place to denote where a certain number occurs. So, the responses from just **one** respondent might end up looking like the computer card below. The dark holes represent the responses given. You may need to use more than one card for a single respondent.

Sometimes you can punch information directly from a questionnaire, if it has been coded a certain way. For example, the code 1(20-22) tells you where in the columns on the card to punch the hole.

A typical card has 80 rows of numbers and the meaning of each row has already been worked out using a **codebook** written by a **data analyst** who is a specialist in analysing this kind of information.

TITLE: EXAMPLE OF A COMPUTER CARD

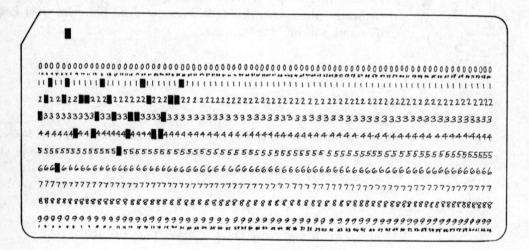

The cards are then 'read' electronically by computer and the information is stored on computer tape. When you want to look at all or part of the information, in order to analyse it in different ways, you use the computer. Some computers can even construct and print out tables and graphs of the results.

PUNCH CARDS

Another way of recording responses for analysis is by again using the **key-punching method**, but this time the responses are punched on to special cards. However, with this method the cards have all the code numbers and holes arranged around the edges of the cards. You punch out the appropriate numbers that correspond with the respondent's answers. Your card ends up looking like this:

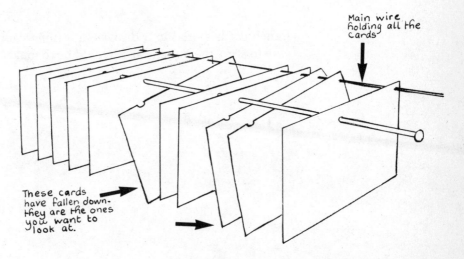

The purpose of recording answers in this manner is so that if all your cards are stored correctly, one behind the other, there is a quick and easy method of drawing out all the cards which certain respondents answered in a particular way. For example, you may want to know how many respondents raise chickens.

You simply take a long rod, a piece of wire, a stick, a knitting needle, or anything which fits the holes exactly and then push it through the hole on the first card that corresponds to the responses you are looking for. (The first card has all the possible responses that

Main wire holding all the cards

These cards have fallen down. They are the ones you want to look at.

were listed on the questionnaire.) In this case it is the responses dealing with who raises chickens that are required. Then, when **all the cards are held up** (by the central rod, wire, stick or knitting needle) **only some cards will fall down**. These particular cards will fall because they have a hole punched out in the place corresponding to the particular answer you want to look at, that is, who raises chickens.

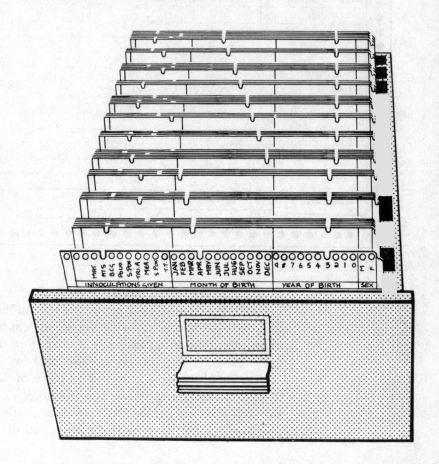

Punch cards stored in a drawer in a filing cabinet. Another effective way to store the punch cards would be to make a special box for them.

5 Reporting the results of evaluation

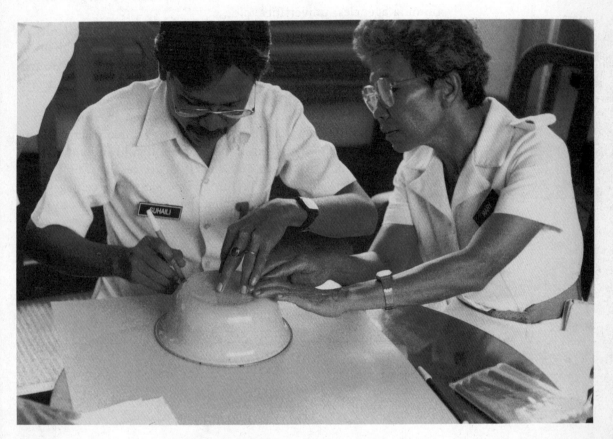

A bowl makes the best circle for a pie chart being prepared by district health staff in Sarawak, Malaysia

This chapter looks at the many ways in which evaluation results need to be presented. These include written and verbal reports, and many ideas for presenting simple statistical data and information in tables, graphs, charts, pictures and recordings, so that they can be clearly understood by a wide range of people.

Some simple guidelines are included to help increase confidence in the handling, analysing and presenting of numerical evaluation results.

5.1 PARTICIPATION IN REPORTING

Reporting the results is one of the most important and most interesting parts of an evaluation. All too often evaluation results are reported only by staff, researchers and experts; people at community level usually take little part in deciding what the results are and how they will be reported. Many written evaluation reports are full of complicated statistics and difficult words. They are not intended to be understood by those outside of ministries, departments, organisations, funding agencies, universities, etc.

In participatory evaluation programmes staff and participants go through all the stages of planning and carrying out an evaluation. They are then ready to report the results of what they have found. They are also better able to see programme strengths and weaknesses, and to decide which plans need to be made for future action.

In an evaluation some results will be presented in writing, some numerically and some in spoken words. For example, there may be brief reports which have been prepared by different individuals and groups. There may be survey and questionnaire results. Some of the numerical results will need to be turned into simple percentages.

Exactly who does what in reporting the results will depend on the purpose and methods used in each evaluation. It will also depend on the capabilities of the participants. With brief training some participants at community level can also analyse and report evaluation results numerically. However, it is essential that they understand the meaning behind such results and that the presentation does not become merely an exercise in adding up numbers.

```
GET THE MEANING
   NOT   JUST
   THE NUMBERS
```

5.2 WHAT RESULTS ARE EXPECTED TO SHOW

Evaluation results are expected to show:
- what a programme has been trying to do;
- what actually happened;
- where there are differences or gaps between the programme plans and what happened;
- the reasons for these differences or gaps;
- what needs to be done about them.

When planning how to report results, go back to your original evaluation objectives. Then think about the different groups or 'audiences' with whom you plan to share the results. Your audiences may range from ministries and funding agencies to community groups. Each one may have a particular interest in certain aspects of the results. This can cause problems in producing the kind of evaluation results that will be useful to everyone.

One answer to these problems is to present the results in different ways. The difficulty, however, is that there may be limited resources to do this. Some of the ways are not expensive (like sharing evaluation results at a community meeting by giving a talk and using a chalkboard, posters, charts, maps, etc). Short printed information sheets or 'handouts' may also be useful, if the resources for these are available.

Summative and formative results

What is needed is to present the best information, facts and figures to the different audiences in the most useful way?

For example, ministries and agencies often need **summative** information which 'sums up' the results in the form of a written report. They usually have a particular interest in programme effectiveness and impact, in order to be able to make decisions on whether to continue funding, whether their present policies are working, and how they can share positive experiences so that other programmes can also benefit. They need results which 'sum up' what has happened.

Programme participants also need summative results so that they can see whether all their effort is efficient and effective. They also have to plan for the future development of their programme.

Formative results show how the form, or shape, of a programme is evolving. These results are also needed by programme participants, ministries and agencies on a more regular basis. They can be obtained by regular programme monitoring. Such monitoring procedures need to be built into a programme, preferably at the time it begins. They can provide constant feedback to guide programme development.

5.3 PREPARING A WRITTEN REPORT

Sometimes ministries, agencies and organisations provide outlines for reporting evaluation results. These are often designed to suit their own needs, and not those of programme staff or community-level needs.

Some evaluation results, as we have seen, may also be written in a form and style suited to universities, agencies and publication in journals. Although it is useful and important to be able to share evaluation results in this way, the needs of programme staff and participants themselves should be more carefully considered when preparing a written report.

General points

There are some general points which you will find useful whatever the type of report you are writing and whatever the audience. These are listed below.

KEEP IT SHORT

Very long reports tend to be used less than short ones. Who has time to read a long report?

KEEP IT CLEAR

The report is supposed to be read and understood. Avoid very technical words and jargon. Use simple, clear, familiar, and precise words wherever possible.

USE SHORT SENTENCES

Try to use not more than 20 words (and if possible less than 16) in each sentence. Use positive sentences. Do not put a lot of ideas in one sentence.

PLAN SPACING AND LAYOUT

For a clearer 'layout', break up the text into short paragraphs to help the reader. Present only one idea in each paragraph.

USE SUBHEADINGS

These help people to remember what they read and make the report more interesting.

EMPHASISE KEY POINTS

Use larger letters, underline changes in type style, and use stars (asterisks), dots, boxes, etc, to emphasise key points in the report.

USE A 'RUNNING COMMENTARY'

In a wide margin beside the main text of the report present the key points from the text in the form of a running commentary.

USE LISTING AND CHECKLISTS

Information can be presented more concisely and absorbed more easily if it is presented in list form. It also saves space, and the reader's time.

AVOID LONG FOOTNOTES
Present additional information or references very briefly. Try not to use footnotes.

EDIT YOUR REPORT CAREFULLY
If possible leave a day between completion of the report and its final editing. This will be very helpful as it will allow you to take a fresh look at it.

LISTEN TO TAPE RECORDINGS
If possible record part or all of the report on tape and listen to it. Then you can make any final changes.

KEEP COSTS LOW
Use inexpensive and locally-made materials. A thick cover or folder will be necessary if the report is going to be handled by many people.

SUBMIT ON TIME
Ensure that the report is presented on time, particularly if the results are to be used for decision-making.

From experience

The following extract is from an evaluation report from Central America:

> "An original evaluation objective had been to analyse all available pro-gramme records of treatments and registers of births and deaths over the past five years in selected communities, in order to find out about patterns of morbidity and mortality (disease and death). However, this was found to be impossible. Some records were not available for certain months and even whole years. The task of analysis was further compli-cated by the recording of illness according to symptom only and by the cause of death frequently being recorded as 'suddenly' or 'tragically'. The first generally referred to a 'heart attack' and the second to one of the frequent killings in the area. Also many of the infant deaths in the area went unrecorded in isolated communities. These deaths often occurred as a result of abortion or tetanus.
>
> What the evaluation did identify by small-scale analysis of selected rec-ords and registers was the high disease rate in the 'under-five' and 'five to fourteen years' age groups. By using a simple method of recording the cases as single strokes — one per patient — from the records onto a large 'master-score' sheet by 'age' and 'specific diagnosis', a strongly visual pattern appeared which could be instantly interpreted. This method of visual presentation was of particular interest to participants who were not literate".

Using some of the general points already outlined this extract can be improved and presented more clearly, as follows.

EVALUATION OBJECTIVES

To analyse available records   Programme treatment records
over 5 year period   Registers of birth
                                      Registers of death

The purpose of the analysis was to look at **pat terns of morbidity and mortality** (disease and death).

PROBLEMS ENCOUNTERED

Some records not available for months/years.

Some illnesses only recorded by symptom, for example 'suddenly' (heart attack) or 'tragically' (local killing).

Many infant deaths not recorded in isolated communities (often due to abortion or tetanus).

EVALUATION METHOD

A very large sheet of paper was prepared. Two classifications were used: AGE and DIAGNOSIS. The information from ten communities over a three-month period was recorded as single strokes (one per patient). A strongly visual pattern then emerged and this could be clearly interpreted by participants, some of whom were not literate.

RESULTS

High disease rate in children under five years

High disease rate in 5-14 year olds

Programme staff and participants state clearly the need for more action regarding the improvement of child health.

5.4 WHAT THE REPORT NEEDS TO CONTAIN

Front cover

Title, name and location of programme.
Names of those who carried out the evaluation.
Names of those with whom programme is linked, such as ministries, agencies, etc.
Period covered by the report.
Date report completed.

Summary

A brief one- or two-page overview of the report is useful for busy readers and those who wish to study it in more detail.

Explain the purpose of the evaluation; for whom it was carried out; how; where; when; major results; conclusions; and recommendations. Write the summary last.

A 'question-and-answer' style, or a specially-designed diagram or table of the information, may be useful.

List of contents

A list of contents in clear, logical order will help the readers find sections of special interest to them.

Background information

This puts the programme into perspective and shows its origin, objectives and evolution.

Explain briefly when, why and how a programme began, who was involved by type/age/group/training/number, etc.

Which were the priority objectives?

Which were the main activities and resources involved?

The length of this section will be depend on the objectives of the report and the space available. It can be drafted early on in the evaluation. Programme proposals, plans, reports, minutes of meetings, memos, etc, can be used to provide information.

Ensure this section does not overlap with other sections (for example, manpower and resources.

Different opinions may have to be 'ironed out' or presented as they are.

Purpose of evaluation and methods chosen

Explain the purpose of the evaluation and state the intended audiences.

Be clear about what it is **not** intended to do.

Explain briefly the reasons for the particular evaluation plan and the methods used to obtain the information.

Include samples of methods used where necessary (for instance, questionnaires in an appendix).

Mention problems of manpower, finance, physical resources, and political context (where appropriate). This can be drafted at the planning stage.

Outcome of using the methods

Where and how were the evaluation methods developed and tested before use?

How was the information collected and by whom, and which methods were used?

How reliable and valid did they prove to be?

Include any timetable or evaluation schedule in an appendix.
Include information about how staff and participants were trained to use the methods.
Also mention unintended results, if appropriate.

Results of data collection and analysis

After analysis of the facts, figures and information collected, tables, graphs, test results, etc can be prepared and included.
You may also want to include typed examples from tape recordings, illustrations or photographs. These can often convey a particular point which cannot be expressed in any other form, for example, numerically.
Briefly describe the methods you used to analyse the information, either with the results or at the beginning of the section.

Conclusions

These may include the following:
To what extent have programme objectives been achieved?
Which aspects of the programme (such as planning, management, monitoring training, field activities, etc) are strong, and which need to be strengthened?
Have human and material programme resources been used efficiently?
How has the programme changed with time?
What are its financial costs and benefits?
What predictions can be made for the short-/long-term future of the programme?
Most important of all, what effect or impact is the programme having?

Recommendations

On the basis of your conclusions what course(s) of action are proposed?
How are these to be implemented, by whom and when? List your recommendations.
This may be the part of the report which some people read first. It may be the only part which they read. Identify the priority recommendations.

> "EVALUATING" YOUR OWN
> EVALUATION ADDS
> WEIGHT TO YOUR RESULTS

5.5 OTHER WAYS OF USING WRITTEN EVALUATION RESULTS

Sometimes you will need to use only part of an evaluation report, for example, in the form of a news-sheet or for training purposes. You may need to write a memorandum (memo) for an organisation or for your superior. You may wish to give a press release to a local news-paper or to a radio programme.

For these purposes you need to provide only a one- or two-page report, and you will have to select very carefully what the pages are to contain. Give the report a large clear title saying **exactly** what the information is about. Then use the basic questions what? why? who? when? and where? in order to present the information clearly. High-light the main message, use sub-headings, and include visual material if possible.

Try out what you have produced before using it. If the meaning is not **immediately** clear, the report is useless. Busy people will probably ignore it.

5.6 MAKING A VERBAL REPORT

Even where there has been participation in planning and carrying out an evaluation, not all of those involved will know all of the results. An elected group of staff and participants will probably have been given the task of putting all the results together.

One way of sharing the evaluation results with a large number of participants is to have meetings during which results are discussed. The specific results may be prepared by different individuals or groups.

When preparing the presentation remember the following points.
Keep it short — Do not give people too much information; just help them to remember the main points.
Think what they need to know — Remember their own needs and interests and prepare your presentation to suit them.
Emphasise key points — It helps to use visual materials, posters, quo-tations, tables, graphs, tapes, photos, slides.
Encourage participation — Question-and-answer sessions, a panel of selected people, or socio-dramas can all help in the presentation and sharing of the evaluation results.
Encourage people to express their views — Discussion of results may result in conflicting views. Coping with these is an important part of a participatory approach.
Listen and be tactful — Try to maintain a good atmosphere and good relationships between people, especially if they have differences of opinion.

From experience

Using socio-drama for feedback of results. In Peru, village women acted out a socio-drama to feed back results about crafty coastal merchants selling over-priced food to highland women who could not understand Spanish or maths. The coastal merchants took advantage of the highland women's ignorance of the real price of the food.

5.7 USING NUMBERS WITH CONFIDENCE

A few decades ago people used to expect, and to produce, evaluation results that were mostly in the form of words, opinions, estimates, and even guesses. More recently people have been demanding, and producing, evaluation results more in the form of numbers and statistics. This is particularly the case where decisions (often large-scale) have to be made about business, economics or development. Numbers and statistics usually provide a better basis for making important, and often expensive, decisions.

Evaluation results may consist of numbers, and these often help to show more clearly what is being examined. The information can be better understood and more easily used. When numbers are analysed and statistics are produced a more scientific approach is said to be taking place in evaluation.

In participatory evaluation basic mathematical skills, such as making additions, subtractions, divisions, multiplications and basic percentages, are needed by those who are co-ordinating the evaluation.

Some people are a little frightened of numbers, particularly at community level where people may have had little or no schooling. Help people to understand the purpose and value of numbers and statistics. Help them, where necessary, to participate in using numbers with confidence.

Different kinds of statistics

The word **statistics** means facts which have been systematically collected and organised in a special way, and presented in the form of numbers. These facts may relate to people, things, events, etc. They may exist now, have existed in the past or be predicted for the future.

For example, you can count the population of a country in a national census. This enables you to produce statistics which will show the size and type of the population in that country. Or, using the same numbers from the census, you can compare them with the estimated population of that same country 50 years ago and make a statistical estimate (if exact figures are not known) that the present population is 20 per cent larger today. Or, you can estimate what the population of that country is likely to be in 20 years' time.

There are two main types of statistics. **Descriptive statistics** describe something and **analytical statistics** analyse something.

DESCRIPTIVE STATISTICS
Descriptive statistics often describe large quantities and situations. For example, if you read that the **ratio** or rate of doctors to the population is 1:50 000 (one doctor to fifty thousand people) you can see that there are too few doctors available for the large population.

ANALYTICAL STATISTICS
Analytical statistics enable a conclusion to be drawn from the numbers. For example, you may read that 80 per cent of all doctors are located in towns in a country where 90 per cent of the population live in rural areas. You can see that most doctors live in urban areas and that most rural people live far from the services of doctors.

A special language is used in statistics. For example, 'f' is used to denote the frequency or amount of times that something occurs in a given period. In participatory evaluation, where the aim is to keep technology and terms simple you will have to decide yourself whether, or how extensively, you wish to use the language of statistics. Sometimes the terms can be made simple and easy to understand and use. Where they cannot, you must decide on your own course of action.

The main types of statistics that you will find useful in participatory evaluation are **percentages**, **averages** and **frequency distributions**.

PERCENTAGES

A **percentage** means a part of something in relation to its whole, which is normally taken to mean 100 (or 100 per cent).

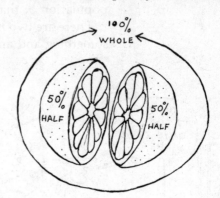

**PERCENTAGES COMPARE
ONE NUMBER WITH ANOTHER**

How to calculate a percentage

Divide the number of people or things in a group by the total number in that group and multiply by 100. Look at the example given below.

Example

Total number of people in the village = 300
Total number of people in the special group (for instance, total number of women in the village)   = 60
Therefore, percentage of women in the village

$$= \frac{60}{300} \times 100$$

$$= 20 \text{ per cent}$$

Sometimes you are given a percentage and you need to know how many people or things are represented by that percentage.

How to change a percentage into a number

Divide the percentage by 100 and multiply by the total number of people or things given. Look at the example given below.

Example

Sixty per cent of the 20 farmers are using the new fertilizer. So, how many farmers are using the new fertilizer?

Percentage of farmers using fertilizers

$$= \frac{60}{100}$$

Therefore, total number of farmers using fertilizer

$$= \frac{60}{100} \times 20 = \frac{1200}{100}$$
$$= 12$$

AVERAGES

The **average** or **mean** of a group of numbers is the sum of those numbers divided by the total number (N) of those numbers.

The average is usually near the middle of all the numbers you are looking at.

How to calculate an average

Add all the numbers together, then divide the answer by the total number (N) of the numbers you had originally.

Example

Ten children attend a clinic one morning. Their ages are 5, 7, 5, 3, 6, 8, 6, 4, 4, 2. What is the average or mean age of the children?

Number (N) of children   = 10
Sum of their ages   = 50

Therefore, the average age is $\dfrac{50}{10}$ = 5 years

**AVERAGES HELP YOU TO COMPARE
DIFFERENT GROUPS OF NUMBERS
USING JUST ONE NUMBER FOR
EACH GROUP**

This is important where you have a very large quantity of numbers.

However, be wary of averages which relate to very large quantities. They are sometimes not as reliable as averages which relate to a smaller quantity of numbers.

The **range** of a group of numbers is the difference between the highest and lowest numbers you are using. The first step in organising your numbers is to look at the way in which they are spread or how large the range is between the highest and lowest number.

FREQUENCY DISTRIBUTIONS

The **frequency** with which something occurs means the number of times that it is repeated at specific intervals.

Where you have a lot of numbers you can use a **frequency distribution** to see how often something happens.

General guidelines on making a frequency distribution

The guidelines given below will help you to make a frequency distribution from a large quantity of numbers.

1 **Organise your numbers into groups** — Arrange your numbers into groups to include the whole range of numbers from the largest to the smallest.

2 **All groups need to be the same width (equally wide) for comparison** — If you have more than one group, make sure the groups are the same width so that you can compare the numbers in the different groups (for example, measurements of children from several clinics).

3 **Avoid overlap** — Make sure the groups do not overlap. Each number should belong to one group only.

4 **Record your numbers using the selected groups** — Organise your own numbers according to the groups. For example, record and count how many children fall into the selected groups.

5 **Add and check your results** — Add up and check your results. The total should be the same as the number of measurements that you started with.

6 **Turn your results into a frequency table** — You can now turn your frequency distribution into a table with a title describing what the measurements are.

A common method of making a frequency distribution is the **population pyramid**, which is described below.

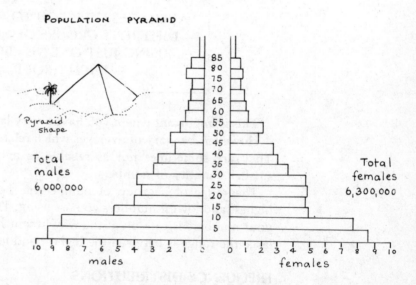

The population of a country by age and sex

Population pyramid

One way to obtain a clear idea of how the population of a village, district or country is made up is to use a population pyramid. This shows you the frequency of, for instance, the age groups and sexes in the population. It is important for planning and evaluating development, especially that of the health, social and educational services.

In a national population census all the people in a country are counted and their age, sex, normal place of residence and other characteristics are recorded. Then the percentage of people falling into each **five-year group** for males and females is calculated. From this a population pyramid can be made.

You can see from the population pyramid that the shape is due to high birth rates, together with high death rates, in every age group.

On this page is a chart which was used to study and evaluate the pattern of illness at community level in a rural area of Central America. This was a simple way of looking at the frequency distribution.

From experience

TITLE: ANALYSIS OF 1600 PATIENT ILLNESSES IN 12 COMMUNITIES OVER 4½ MONTHS

	0 – 1	2 – 4	5 – 14	15 – 24	25 – 34	35 – 44	45 – 54	55 – 64	65 +
FEVER	llllllll llllllll lll	llllllll llllllll	llllllll llllll	llllllll	llllllll llllll	llll	llllll	ll	llll
ROUND WORMS	llllllll llllll	llllllll llllll llllll llllll	llllllll llllll llllll	llllllll	llllllll	llll	llll	lll	l
DIARRHOEA	llllllll llllll llllll llllll	llllllll llllll llllll	llllll llllll	ll	llllll	l	lll	ll	l
FEVER & COUGH	llllllll llllll l	llllllll llllll	llllllll llllll	llllll	llllllll	llllllll	llllll	lll	ll
COUGH & COLD	llllllll llll	llllllll ll	llllllll ll	lll	lll	llll	llll	lll	ll
MALNUTRITION		llllllll	llll	ll	ll	ll	lll	l	
ANAEMIA & WEAKNESS	ll	llllll	llllll	llllll llll	llllllll llll	llllllll llll	llllll	llll	llll
*	ll	llll	llll	lll	ll	l	l	l	

(Data recording continues downwards for a further eight types of illnesses)

A rural health programme in Central America wanted to evaluate its work over the past five years. One method used was to analyse the pattern of illness in selected isolated communities. In this way, those in the programme (many of whom were not literate) could see more clearly just who was ill and with what disease. For example, it could be seen that the children under five years old were the ones who were sick most frequently. The programme then made plans to develop their health activities to help children under five years of age.

The extract on the previous page is only part of the large form that was actually used and which had been made of a number of small pages stuck together.

Common mistakes when handling numbers

In order to be useful numbers must be clearly understood and correctly handled. Sometimes they are not. Common mistakes when handling numbers are listed below.

Taking good numbers but interpreting them badly. You get the wrong message, like being told that all houses in a district have thatched roofs, then discovering that the sample only looked at half the villages and, in fact, some of the other villages contained houses with aluminium sheet roofs.

Using sources which are biased. If it is not clear exactly who has supplied the numbers, and for what purpose, people may suspect that there could be hidden motives in what they read or are told. This can be like the political candidate who only tells of the positive things that his party has done, or is going to do, in order to win votes. He does not mention the negative things.

Using good sources but applying poor reasoning. In this way the final analysis, the final statistics and the final point of view presented will not be valid or reliable. One example might be: presuming that poor field performance by a number of newly-trained managers is due only to failure in selecting good candidates and not trying to see whether there was a something missing in the training that they received.

Understanding how people normally count and measure things in communities

Everyone counts things; it makes no difference whether they went to school or not. For example, the boy looking after his goats counts them to make sure that they are all in for the night. The woman keeps a special jar or tin for measuring the rice which she gives regularly to a local community centre. The old, traditional midwife places different coloured beans in different bowls to record the number of deliveries that she has attended and whether they were normal deliveries or not.

From experience

A farmer in the Philippines places a grain of corn in a tin for every rod of tobacco leaves that he plans to sell to the tobacco merchant. Then he counts the grains of corn so that he knows how many rods he has and how much money he should receive.

Try asking a fisherman in a remote area 'How far is it along the river to the next big town?' He will not usually give you an answer in kilometres. He will probably tell you 'half a day' or 'two days by canoe'. He estimates the distance by the time it takes to get there.

Ask a slum child who does not have a watch what the time is, and he will probably look at the sun before giving a fairly accurate estimate of the time. He calculates time by the sun's position, or perhaps by whether he feels hungry (unless he feels hungry most of the time).

A patient who needs to take a tablet four times a day also needs help in deciding exactly when is the best time to take it. For example, this may be when she gets up in the morning (often before 5 am), before she eats at midday (around 11 am), when she comes home from the fields (around 5 pm), and finally, before she goes to sleep (often 10 pm).

It is very important to know how people normally count and measure things. These normal methods can then be built on, and skills and confidence increased for participatory evaluation. Some normal methods are, in fact, very ancient. For example, in China a special wooden counting frame or abacus with rows of beads has been used for centuries. Other methods are much more informal and simple, such as those already described.

At community level, people are often afraid of numbers, particularly if they have had little or no formal education. For those with a

127

basic grasp of arithmetic, such as may be gained from attending a few grades of primary education, some new skills and abilities can be developed gradually.

Generally, it is better to rely on mental arithmetic skills than on a calculator to increase self-reliance. However, if a reliable calculator is easily available people with basic arithmetic have already shown how fast and efficiently they can use it for evaluation purposes. Many people at community level take great pride in keeping regular records and accounts of their work. Some already prepare simple statistics.

Take a step-by-step approach when you help people to develop skills and confidence in handling numbers. Never 'flood' people with numbers, tables, graphs that they cannot understand.

Help people to be unafraid of numbers.

Help middle-level workers to use numbers

Most people managing development programmes are already familiar with handling numbers. Such skills are normally being used to plan and monitor the work. Sometimes the numbers relate to large-scale programmes; sometimes the programmes are much smaller. Usually numbers are used to make regular reports to the next level 'up', such as district or provincial level. From these levels the numbers are again used to report to national level. Numbers are also used in preparing reports for funding agencies or organisations.

These different levels also **receive** numbers in the form of statistics, such as those in reports from ministries, agencies and organisations. For example, a ministry report may give details of the situation in the entire country or in the local area where the programme is situated. In this way the local programme can be compared with other, similar

128

programmes. The work of that programme can also be seen in a wider context.

Middle-level workers often need help to increase their skills in using numbers and statistics. They also need to develop approaches and skills that will help people at community level to develop their own abilities and skills in using numbers and statistics.

5.8 USING TABLES AND GRAPHS

During evaluation a large amount of information, facts and figures are collected. These then have to be organised, analysed and presented so that their meaning can be clearly seen. One clear and concise way to do this is to prepare tables and graphs. These can be used in the evaluation report, as handouts for further study or at meetings, or as visual material from which to make posters, slides, etc.

Not all information can be easily presented in the form of tables and graphs. Some information is better presented in written form.

Tables and graphs

The main advantages of tables and graphs are that they:
- help to show key information quickly;
- make it easier to show comparisons;
- show patterns and trends;
- take up less room.

POINTS TO REMEMBER WHEN PRESENTING TABLES AND GRAPHS

1   Each table/graph needs a **full title** which explains what exactly it is about (who/what/when/where). Use capital letters for the word TABLE, then give it a number.
2   Give **full, clear labelling**. Use capital letters for headings, in boxes and at the beginning of important words.
3   **Titles** and **labels** should be *outside* the frame or box which surrounds the information.
4   Provide a **key** to explain symbols.
5   List your **information sources**, such as how, where, when and by whom the information was obtained, so that others can check its reliability or obtain further information if needed.
6   Provide **footnotes** where necessary, giving additional comments, highlighting specific points, making connections or comparisons between different pieces of information, or explaining why information is missing.
7   Any **accompanying text** must describe and discuss key results.
8   Always include a **date** with the day, month and year.
9   Using **asterisks** like this * can help to highlight important results.

10 Use **black lettering on white paper** as it is easier to photocopy. Use shading, continuous lines, dots, crossed lines etc, to show differences.
11 Point out **one idea at a time**. Several presentations may be needed to show different ideas.
12 Be sure about **exactly** what it is you want to show.
13 Choose the **best method** for your purpose, for example, graphs to show trends, and bar charts to compare differences between similar information.
14 **Propose conclusions carefully.** They must apply to all the information from which they come. Do not make extravagent claims that are not supported by the information in the table.

5.9 PREPARING TABLES

Both words and numbers can be presented in tables. For example, programme plans, activities or statements of progress can be listed, and then made into a table. Figures relating to programme finances, production figures, or the incidence of diseases are often made into tables. Test results can also be presented in tabular form.

Some tables present only a few items of information. For example:

TITLE: TABLE WITH A FEW ITEMS OF INFORMATION

Development of health facilities in Tanzania, 1961-78

	1961	1965	1969	1971	1973	1978
Rural health centres	22	40	50	87	108	220
Dispensaries	975	1236	1362	1436	1515	2308
Hospitals	98	109	121	123	123	151

Sources: Chargula and Tarimo (1975); Tanzania Ministry of Health (1980).

The next table presents many different kinds of information. In Kerala, in India, a survey of what people ate was made among housewives at various income levels. The objective of the survey was to find out what differences education and income made to the diet of the families concerned.

The table shows that the level of education did not appear to make a difference to the number of malnourished persons in the very low income households. Their main problem was that there simply was not enough money to buy food for everyone. However, above the lowest income level education did appear to make a considerable difference.

TITLE: TABLE WITH MANY ITEMS OF INFORMATION

Average per capita caloric intake per day and proportion of calorie-deficient persons classified by monthly income and education of housewife.[a]

	Household income per month (Rupees)				
Education of housewife	Below 100	100 to 250	250 to 500	Above 500	All classes
Illiterate	1577 (93.9)[b]	1365 (97.7)	1575 (83.8)	— —	1471 (93.6)
Literate but below SSLC[c]	1432 (94.9)	1994 (70.5)	2213 (59.2)	2512 (43.2)	2108 (54.1)
SSLC and above[c]	— —	— —	2292 (35.3)	3062 (0.0)	2861 (9.2)
All classes	1513 (94.3)	1761 (80.6)	2088 (62.0)	2728 (26.2)	2010 (66.5)

[a] Source, Diet Survey, p. c-11, Centre for Development Studies. Trivandrum (1973/1974).
[b] Figures in parentheses are percentages of calorie-deficient persons to the total within each cell.
[c] SSLC = Secondary School Leaving Certificate (i.e. high-school graduate).

In participatory evaluation one of the objectives is to produce certain tables that can also be understood at community level. Where the level of literacy is very low, tables with words and basic numbers can sometimes be turned into symbols or pictures. This helps people to see, understand and remember the evaluation results.

From experience

In the Philippines health and community development workers used leaves of different colours to make a simple poster. They cut shapes from the leaves to represent different health statistics. In this way people at community level could easily understand, remember and plan for action on the basis of the meaning of the statistics.

The leaf 'cut-outs' do not last as long as other materials, such as paper, but they are easily available, cost nothing and will last for several days. They are useful for meetings, workshops or training sessions.

Sometimes, just one part of a table can be turned into a picture or

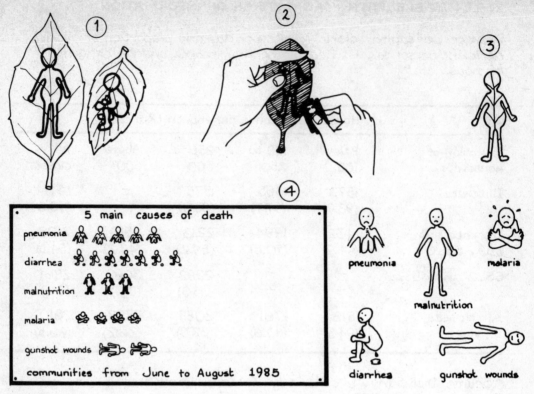

① ② ③

④

	5 main causes of death
pneumonia	
diarrhea	
malnutrition	
malaria	
gunshot wounds	
communities from June to August 1985	

pneumonia

malnutrition

malaria

diarrhea

gunshot wounds

Figure No.

TITLE: USING LEAVES TO PRESENT STATISTICS

a poster. This helps people to focus on that particular piece of information, and in this way they can absorb the message more easily.

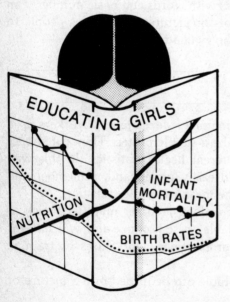

The picture shows that there is a connection between the education of girls and the health and growth of children. When girls are educated infant death rates fall. Child nutrition improves. Birth rates fall. The message is: 'better education for girls improves child health and child spacing'.

In the picture opposite the message is about the spacing of carrots. If you plant the carrots too close together they do not get a chance to grow large.

This message also applies to having children. If you have them too close together, they may not have a good chance of growing up.

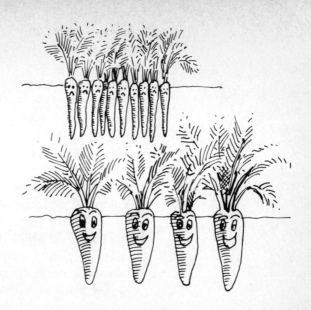

5.10 PRESENTING SIMPLE GRAPHS

A graph is a good method of presenting evaluation results clearly and effectively in a small space. The most common type of graph is the **line graph**.

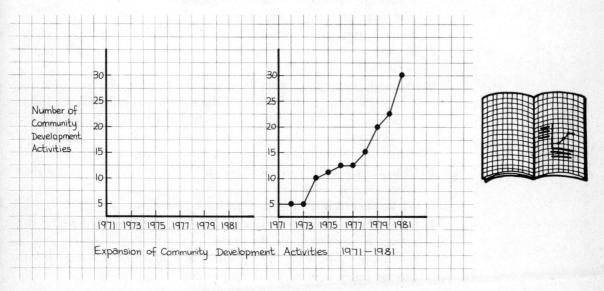

MENARA PROJECT, EASTERN PROVINCE

Figure No.

TITLE: A SIMPLE LINE GRAPH

133

Special paper printed with squares, called **graph paper**, may be available. This makes the drawing and presentation of graphs easier, but such paper is only available in a few places.

However, a type of squared paper that *is* often available in many places is the type used in squared arithmetic exercise books for schools. This is useful for drawing and presenting small graphs, or a number of pages can be stuck together to make a large graph.

The use of squared paper helps you to obtain more exact measurements when you are making your graph. Once you have got a correctly-drawn graph on the smaller squared paper then it is much easier to enlarge it on large paper, even if the paper is not squared.

POINTS TO REMEMBER WHEN MAKING A GRAPH

1 **Give a clear, complete title**, especially where the information shown is only a part of the total amount. Every graph should be self-explanatory, that is, it should explain itself. The title can be placed above or below the graph.
2 **'Read' the graph from left to right**, to understand it best.
3 **Figures for the horizontal scale** should be placed at the **bottom**, leaving the top of the graph clear. For example, indications of time are usually placed horizontally.
4 **Figures for the vertical scale** are usually placed **on the left** of the graph (but they may also be on the right). Frequency is often placed on the vertical scale of a graph.
5 **Use clear lettering and numbering**.
6 **Keep it simple** and use as few lines as possible.
7 A **zero point** must be shown at the bottom left point of the vertical scale.
8 A **break** in the graph may be necessary because of a lack of space (there may not be room for all the figures to be included). However, a graph with a break like this will be particularly difficult for participants at community level to understand.
9 **Equal** increases on the scales must represent **equal** numbered units.
10 **Indicate scale divisions**, and the **units** into which the scale is divided, clearly.
11 **Make curved lines darker than background ones**.
12 **It may help to have a vertical line** linking each point shown on the curve. It helps to guide the eye.
13 **Use a key** to show clearly the different characteristics of the information being presented on the graph.

Histograms

When you have to present limited and precise information in the form of numbers you may want to use a **histogram**. This is a type of graph which shows the frequency of something. Unlike a **'bar chart'** (which is described later) a histogram has *no spaces between the sections or 'cells'*. You cannot use a '**scale-break**' on a histogram. The horizontal scale shows the particular characteristic being presented; the vertical scale shows the frequency with which that characteristic occurs.

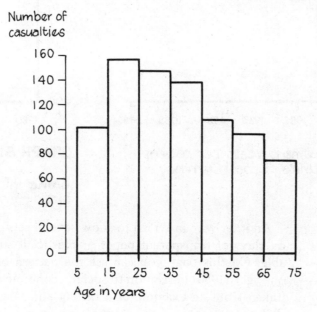

Number of casualties

HISTOGRAM

Frequency of Fatal Fire Casualties in Urban Areas in Relation to Age in one year.

Age in years

5.11 USING GRAPHS TO SHOW PROGRESS

Simple graphs can be used to show several different results, or sets of information, at the same time. They can also show whether changes have occurred, and when. In this way you can see trends.

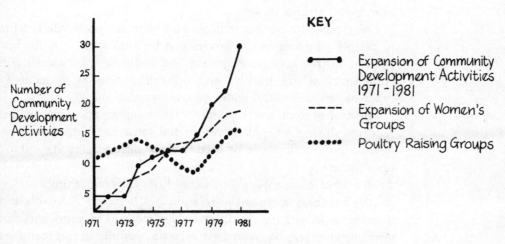

Number of Community Development Activities

KEY

●——● Expansion of Community Development Activities 1971 – 1981

- - - - Expansion of Women's Groups

●●●●●● Poultry Raising Groups

GRAPH showing several kinds of information

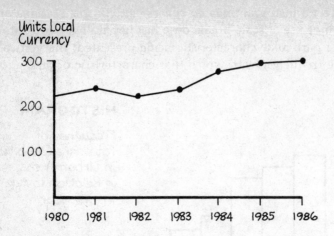

GRAPH A: Treatment costs per patient in Units of Local Currency

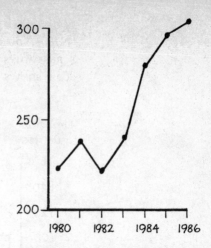

GRAPH B: Treatment costs per patient.
Same information as A — **but** different presentation.

Another way in which to show several sets of information is to use **overlays** of transparent paper or plastic, if such materials are available. On this page you can see the pattern of common diseases for one year (1980) in relation to social, economic and seasonal variations (taken from an example of a fishing and farming community in the Philippines). The visual symbols or simple drawings make the presentation more interesting and suitable for sharing at community level.

5.12 OVERLAYS: WHAT THEY CAN SHOW

Overlays can also be used very effectively during surveying and mapping. The accompanying illustration shows an urban neighbourhood as mapped after a survey.

The type of housing is indicated by different patterns. The number of people who live in the houses can be indicated by a dot for each person. In this way development and health workers learn with the community where healthy and unhealthy housing is located. The types of sanitation and water supply are also shown.

The transparent overlay shows the number and type of illnesses reported during a rapid survey of the same neighbourhood. Several transparent overlays can be used to show different results and to build up a picture.

This kind of mapping can show how different things are related to one another, such as the relationship between ill health and bad housing or insanitary conditions. This method of using survey mapping and overlays has seen used very successfully in Indonesia and the Philippines.

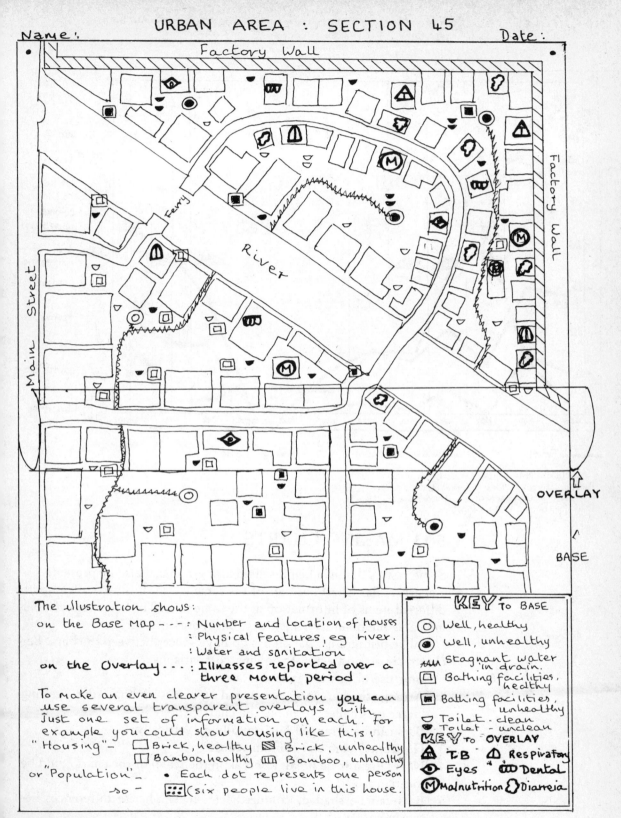

The illustration shows:

on the Base map - - - : Number and location of houses
: Physical features, eg river.
: Water and sanitation

on the Overlay . . . : **Illnesses reported over a three month period.**

To make an even clearer presentation **you** can use several transparent overlays with just one set of information on each. For example you could show housing like this!

"Housing" - ☐ Brick, healthy ◩ Brick, unhealthy
☐ Bamboo, healthy ▥ Bamboo, unhealthy

or "Population" - • Each dot represents one person
- so - ⚅ (six people live in this house.

KEY TO BASE

◉ Well, healthy
◎ Well, unhealthy
〰 stagnant water in drain.
▣ Bathing facilities, healthy
▩ Bathing facilities, unhealthy
▽ Toilet - clean
▼ Toilet - unclean

KEY to **OVERLAY**

△ TB △ Respiratory
◈ Eyes ⠿ Dental
Ⓜ Malnutrition ⬡ Diarrhea

Adapted from original idea by Dr G. Nugroho used in Indonesia.

137

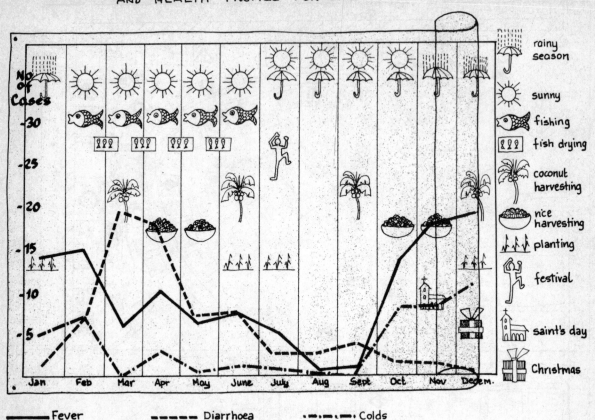

TITLE: OVERLAY SHOWING COMMUNITY SOCIO-ECONOMIC AND HEALTH PROFILE FOR ONE YEAR

———— Fever   - - - - Diarrhoea   ·—·—·— Colds

Adapted from presentation in
'Research and Development (R+D) Project
Carigara Catchment Area (CCA), Leyte.
Philippines 1977-1982.

5.13 MAKING CHARTS

Some results that can be presented as a graph can also be presented as a chart. A **Bar Chart** has bars of the same width. It is used to compare different items of information at the same time. The length of each bar indicates the quantity which that bar represents.

Unlike histograms, bar charts *do* have spaces between the bars. Bar charts are a good way of showing comparisons.

Some useful tips to remember are:

1 **Arrange the bars in either ascending or descending order,** (getting larger or smaller) to make the chart clearer.
2 **Bars can be arranged horizontally or vertically.**
3 **Horizontal bars can contain words.**
4 **Never use a scale break** (a break in the scale) or the chart could be misinterpreted.
5 **Bars can be shaded, coloured,** etc, to emphasise differences between bars.

6 **Precise numbers may be placed over the specific bar** to indicate the number of cases on which each result is based.

7 **Label bars** at the bottom and to the left of the chart.

8 **When making comparisons** it is optional to leave a space between bars in the same group, but it is *essential* to leave a space between each group of bars.

9 **Provide a key.**

10 **Give a clear title**, showing information such as who, what, when and where.

11 **A second result can be shown** by putting a second bar behind the first bar.

12 **Make the chart interesting** where possible by using symbols, figures of people, etc.

In the **Horizontal Bar Chart**, which is described below, you can follow the progress of an income generating project over a period of one year.

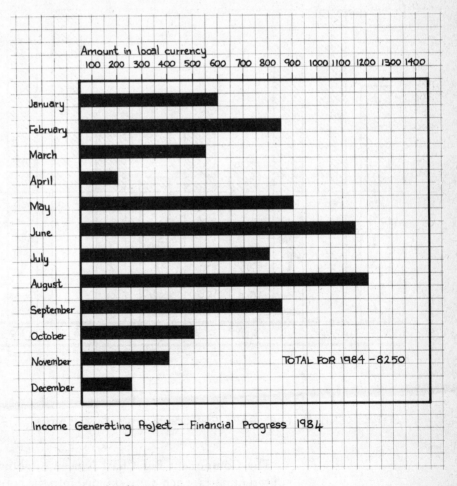

Figure No.

TITLE: HORIZONTAL BAR CHART

In the **Vertical Bar Chart**, which is described next, you can see the number of people who attended adult literacy classes in a certain area during a period of one year.

On this chart you can also see a second piece of information. You can see the pattern of harvesting and planting during the same year. The main crops are rice and coconuts.

You can see the relationship between harvesting and attendance at literacy class. During the months of February and August, for example, many people attend literacy classes; these are the months between planting and harvesting.

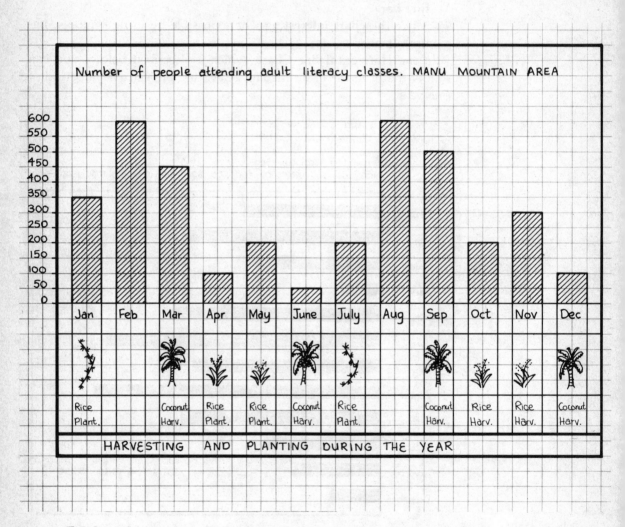

TITLE: VERTICAL BAR CHART FOR COMMUNITY DISCUSSION

The **Component Bar Chart** is used to show comparisons between different parts. Each bar is divided into the appropriate components or sections. Several different results can be shown on the same chart.

In the following example you can see what percentage of children were immunised against childhood diseases such as measles, whooping cough, and polio, in a certain district. There were three types of families in this district. The first lived in large villages, the second in small villages or large farms, and the third in small farms which were very isolated.

You can see that the children who were adequately, or fully, immunised against these diseases came mostly from the large villages and the families who had higher or middle incomes. The children who lived in the small, isolated farms were either not fully immunised (they did not receive all the doses necessary) or did not receive any immunisation at all.

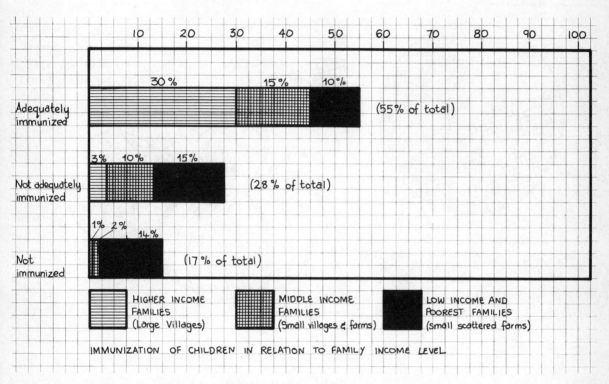

TITLE: COMPONENT BAR CHART

A **Pie Chart** is used to show the different parts of a whole in relation to one another. This kind of chart is circular and named after a pie (a baked dough case which often contains fruit, meat or fish).

To use a pie chart effectively in participatory evaluation it is best to liken the chart to a common round object. A melon, an orange, a coin are all shapes that have been used successfully at community level. The advantage of using examples like this is that the real object to which the chart is likened can actually be cut so that the message or idea can be more clearly illustrated.

The clearest pie chart is one that is divided into the least number of segments. A half (or 50 per cent) is easy to understand at community level; so is one quarter and three quarters. One tenth may also, in some cases, be easily understood. However, as the divisions become smaller or more complicated their meaning may be very difficult to understand at community level.

In the following example you can see how a pie chart was used to illustrate the progress of the polio campaign for young children.

TITLE: **PIE CHART**

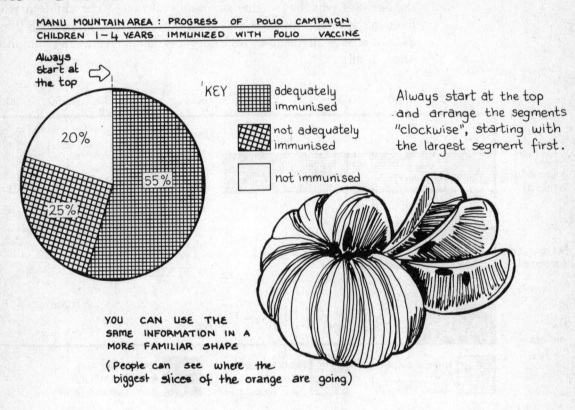

MANU MOUNTAIN AREA : PROGRESS OF POLIO CAMPAIGN
CHILDREN 1-4 YEARS IMMUNIZED WITH POLIO VACCINE

Always start at the top ⇨

KEY
adequately immunised
not adequately immunised
not immunised

20%

55%

25%

Always start at the top and arrange the segments "clockwise", starting with the largest segment first.

YOU CAN USE THE SAME INFORMATION IN A MORE FAMILIAR SHAPE

(People can see where the biggest slices of the orange are going)

USE FAMILIAR OBJECTS
TO MAKE A
"PIE" CHART

Different kinds of **Map Charts** can present evaluation results visually in a way that helps people to learn and to plan for further action. In the examples given below the first map shows the infant mortality rate (death rate of children under one year of age) in different regions in Ghana. On the second map the same information has been presented in a different way. By using various patterns it is possible to see at once which areas of the country have the highest infant mortality rates and which have lowest.

Infant mortality rates, Ghana 1976.

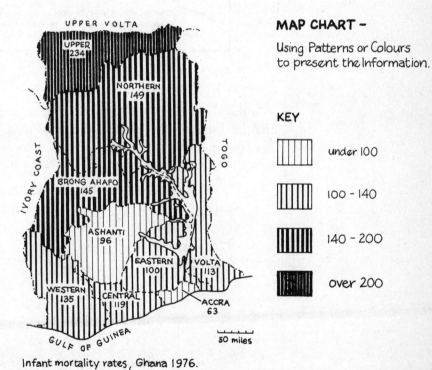

Infant mortality rates, Ghana 1976.

MAP CHART –

Using Patterns or Colours to present the Information.

KEY

▦	under 100
▦	100 – 140
▦	140 – 200
▦	over 200

One problem with using map charts at community level is that many people may not have seen a map before. In such cases the whole idea of a map, and what it is supposed to show, has to be explained first.

The **Geographic Co-ordinate Chart** is also based on a map. It is a good way of showing the location of diseases or other information that you wish to present so as to show people the location and extent of something.

In the following example people can see clearly where cases of animal rabies were reported, and in which villages of a certain area, during a period of one year. Each black dot represents one village which had one or more cases of animal rabies.

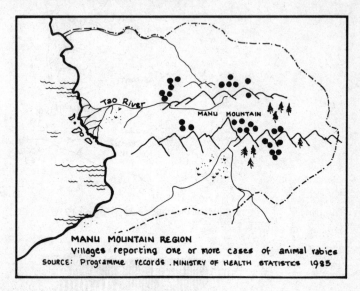

MANU MOUNTAIN REGION
Villages reporting one or more cases of animal rabies
SOURCE: Programme records . MINISTRY OF HEALTH STATISTICS 1985

Figure No.
TITLE: GEOGRAPHICAL COORDINATE CHART

In the next example the chart shows an entire country, not just one area or district. Each black dot represents a children's welfare clinic. The first map shows how few clinics there were in 1968. The second map shows how the clinics had increased by 1972.

DEVELOPMENT OF COMPREHENSIVE CHILD CARE SERVICES IN MALAWI

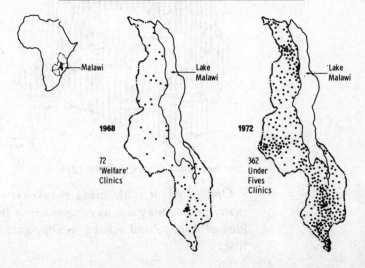

144

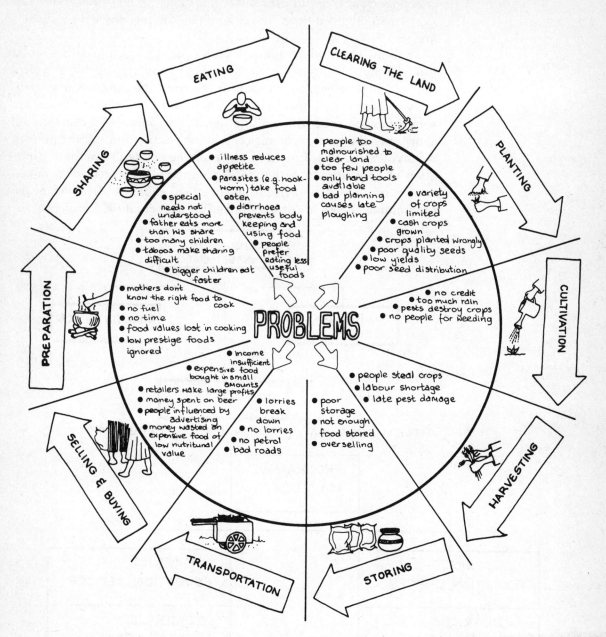

Adapted from material in the training pack on 'Field
Programme management, Food and Nutrition', Food and
Agriculture Organization, Rome.

The **Flow Chart** shows separate parts of a sequence linked to one
another. It also shows which way the intended 'flow' is supposed
to go. For example, a flow chart can show how a crop is produced
and finally reaches a market. It may show the 'flow' of out-patients

through the different parts of a clinic. It shows movement. It shows a process as it was planned, or as it functions in reality.

A flow chart is useful in evaluation for identifying problems or 'barriers' to an intended flow. In this way you can see where the problems are.

The flow chart which follows shows the steps or linked parts of a food-supply system to a typical local community, and some typical barriers or problems which spoil or interrupt the flow of the system.

Two charts, the **Organisational Chart** and the **Personnel Chart** are sometimes confused with one another. An organisational chart should show only the name of an office/division/section but *not* the personnel involved or their function. The example below shows the organisation of a nutrition programme. A Council of Management is linked to a nutrition team and also to the practical administrative part of the programme. These in turn are linked to the actual field projects.

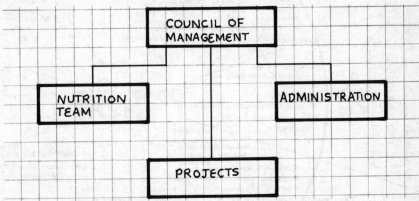

TITLE: ORGANISATION OF NUTRITION PROGRAMME

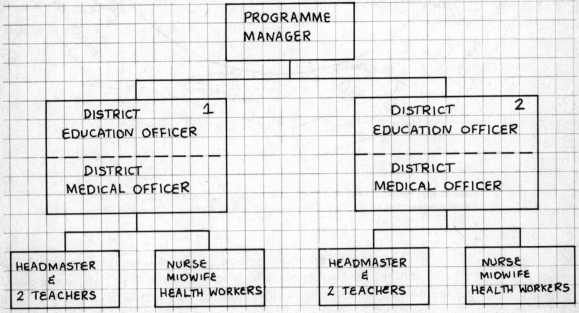

TITLE: PERSONNEL CHART

The personnel chart below shows the people who are involved in an integrated district development programme. A Programme Manager is linked to district education and medical officers. These people are then linked to teachers and health workers at district and community levels.

Special-Purpose Charts can include many imaginative ways of presenting evaluation results. For example, a programme may want to present an analysis of the exact way in which its money has been spent over the past year. The special-purpose chart below shows how one programme spent its money.

In order to make the chart even clearer and more useful for non-literate participants the information on such a chart could also be turned into simple pictures (for example, a chalkboard, a trainer, tools and seeds, staff holding their salaries, transportation, etc).

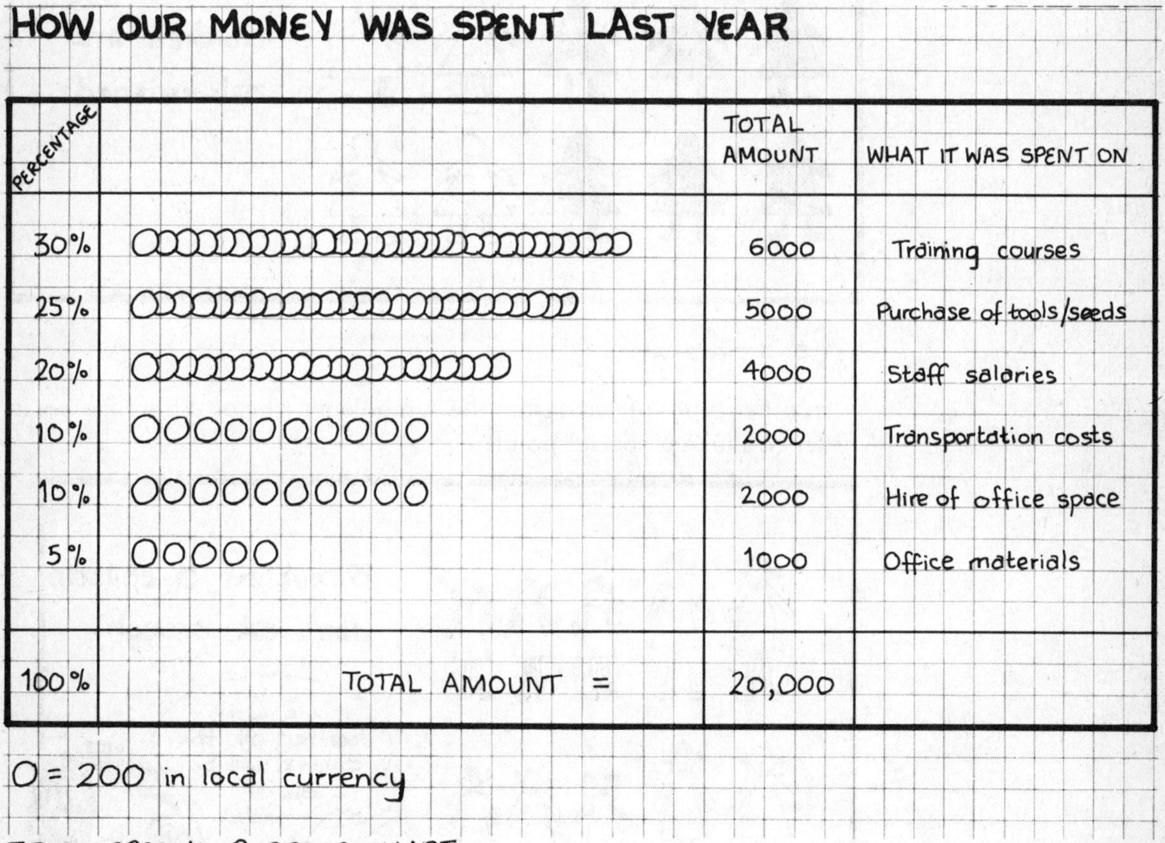

HOW OUR MONEY WAS SPENT LAST YEAR

PERCENTAGE		TOTAL AMOUNT	WHAT IT WAS SPENT ON
30%	OOOOOOOOOOOOOOOOOOOOOOOOOOOOOO	6000	Training courses
25%	OOOOOOOOOOOOOOOOOOOOOOOOO	5000	Purchase of tools/seeds
20%	OOOOOOOOOOOOOOOOOOOO	4000	Staff salaries
10%	OOOOOOOOOO	2000	Transportation costs
10%	OOOOOOOOOO	2000	Hire of office space
5%	OOOOO	1000	Office materials
100%	TOTAL AMOUNT =	20,000	

O = 200 in local currency

TITLE: SPECIAL PURPOSE CHART

5.14 TURNING RESULTS INTO PICTURES

The **Pictogram** is a type of bar chart that uses a series of symbols or pictures to present the data. Each symbol may represent a single person or a particular unit of information. One symbol may also represents several people or units of information. The system which you decide to use depends on how much information you wish to present.

In some pictograms, like the one below, the symbols are all the same size. Each symbol (in this case a symbol shaped like a human figure) represents one child. In the special purpose chart described in the last section and entitled 'How Our Money Was Spent Last Year', each symbol shaped like a coin represented 200 units of local currency.

TITLE: PICTOGRAM

In other types of pictogram the symbols may be of different sizes in order to make a special point.

TITLE: PICTOGRAM USING DIFFERENT SIZES

Using **Cartoons** to make a particular point can be very effective. However, it generally requires a special skill and a little training to produce good results. Cartoons overstate or exaggerate a point in order to emphasise it. People appear as caricatures, and not as they really are. If they have a big nose, for example, they are drawn with an even bigger nose.

Some evaluation results can be turned into cartoons. People will remember something that is interesting and amusing.

The cartoon below is adapted from one which appeared in a Central American newspaper. It shows the corruption of the peasant leader of a peasant organisation. Now that he is successful he enjoys money, owning land, having expensive clothes, jewellery, wine and women. He and his lifestyle are no longer useful to or typical of the peasants. He has now become another burden around their necks.

Cartoons often illustrate a point which is political and/or controversial. If you use cartoons like this remember that not everyone is likely to agree with them.

5.15 PRESENTING PHOTOGRAPHIC RESULTS

Earlier we saw how photography can be used as an evaluation method. Photographs are also a good way of presenting some kinds of evaluation results. If the budget is adequate, slide presentations and filmstrips can also be made. The advantage of photographic or slide presentations over written results is that they can be shared with illiterate groups at community level.

In Central America the results of a survey on basic household expenditure were turned into a photograph. This was then used to stimulate group discussions about poverty and nutrition, and to plan for income-generating activities.

From experience

In 1977 the average annual income of a family of five in one Central American country was officially stated to be about $140. From a basic household expenditure survey carried out during a participatory evaluation, the average rural family of six was found to need a minimum of four times the average annual income for just basic foods. At certain times of the year, between harvests or if there was a bad harvest, the families just went hungry if they could not borrow food from family or friends.

This information helped the programme to see the urgent need for income-generating activities, a better system of land distribution, the need for agricultural equipment and training, and cheaper basic foods and household items. In the photograph at the beginning of chapter 3 (p45) you can see what a family of six needs in order to be able to survive for one month. The main items are corn, beans, coffee, salt and sugar. Rice, flour, macaroni, dried meat, eggs, cheese, a few vegetables and fruit, matches, soap and kerosene, are also shown. Bread is usually only available in towns.

5.16 TAPE RECORDINGS

The use of tape recordings as an evaluation method was described earlier, and their use as a method of helping you to improve your evaluation report was also discussed.

In participatory evaluation an important objective is to involve people at community level actively in the analysis and presentation of evaluation results. There are several ways in which a tape recorder can be used to help you do this.

By making a tape recording of selected evaluation results you will have a tape that can be used for several purposes, such as to:
• provide information for further analysis;

- feed back evaluation results to large gatherings or smaller groups;
- stimulate group discussion of evaluation results;
- provide publicity material, for example, to a local radio station or a newspaper;
- train or update programme personnel;
- keep a record of a particular situation for comparison at a later date.

In the following example health and development workers met to discuss the results of a participatory evaluation of traditional birth attendants. They listened to a tape recording made by the illiterate birth attendants whom they had trained. The birth attendants had already analysed their own work during the past year. A tape recording was made during their meeting.

TITLE: USING TAPE RECORDINGS IN EVALUATION

6 Using your evaluation results

This last chapter looks at the ways in which evaluation results need to be used and by whom. Different ways of sharing results are suggested, including the use of newsletters and pictures. Good evaluation depends partly on good monitoring, supervision and programme management, and a well-thought-out information system. The importance and uses of baseline information are outlined, and ideas and examples are included for strengthening programme action in these ares.

A traditional birth attendant (left) and a community health worker (right) meet regularly with an assistant district health officer (seated on the step) and a local leader to monitor progress of development activities in Thailand

6.1 RESULTS: USING THEM, OR LOSING THEM

Some evaluation results have taken as long as a year to write up and report. In these cases much of the information was analysed by computer. Unfortunately, by the time the evaluation results were available they were already out of date and thus less useful to the programme concerned.

Don't take too long writing the results of the evaluation .....
they may be out of date.

In participatory evaluation one of the objectives is for staff and participants to join together in producing the evaluation results. In this way both staff and participants are better able to assess programme progress and to take decisions concerning future action.

EVALUATION RESULTS ➜ DECISIONS ➜ ACTION

If evaluation results are to be useful they have to be shared with those who can make use of them. They are not useful if they are just 'filed and forgotten'. Evaluation reports should not gather dust on shelves in offices. They should result in more effective development programmes. But who is to get them and how? What do the evaluation results mean? How can the recommendations of the evaluation be put into practice?

6.2 WHO GETS THE RESULTS, AND HOW?

Before an evaluation begins it is important to ask "Who is this evaluation for?" In most cases there will be several groups involved. Each one will have particular needs and expectations regarding the evaluation results.

WHO NEEDS TO GET THE RESULTS, WHY AND HOW

Audience	Role in evaluation and follow-up	Which results they need to get and why	How they can get them
Community not directly involved in programme	Takes a small part (eg, answering questionnaires).	Summary of results to create interest/support for programme.	Meetings. Discussions. Mass media. Newsletters. Pictures.
Community directly involved in programme	Takes a part in planning and carrying out evaluation.	Full results and recommendations so that they can help to put them into action.	Through participation in evaluation. Meetings. Study of results. Mass media. Newsletters. Pictures.
Programme staff	Responsibility for co-ordination, facilitating community decision-making and action.	Full results and recommendations to be able to put them into action.	Through participation. Meetings. Study of report.
District-level departments agencies, organisations	Receive information and/or specified active role. Disseminate lessons learnt. Support future action.	Full results or summary only for analysis of lessons learnt and policy decision-making.	Full report or summary (1-2 pages). Discussions with evaluation co-ordinators. Mass media.
Regional level.	Same as district level.	Same as district level.	Probably summary only. Discussions. Meetings..
National-level ministries, agencies, organisations	Receive information. Disseminate lessons. Support future action.	Full results or summary for analysis of lessons learnt and policy-making.	Summary. Discussions. Meetings.
External funding agency	Receive information. Disseminate lessons. Support future action.	Full results for analysis of lessons learnt and policy-making.	Full report plus summary discussions.
International agencies. UN development agencies	Receive information. Disseminate lessons. Support future action.	Full results or summary for analysis of lessons learnt and policy-making.	Probably summary only. Discussions. Meetings.

Adapted from 'Flow of Information Matrix' by Peter Van Brunt, Save the Children Federation

Evaluation results should be used:

- to improve programme organisation and management;
- to improve planning;
- to assist decision-making;
- to assist policy-making;
- to indicate where action is needed;
- to indicate where further research is needed;
- to provide materials and indicate approaches for training; and
- to provide information for publicity.

```
DECIDE WHAT YOU WISH
     TO  SHARE
  AND WITH  WHOM
```

An evaluation that has taken a detailed look at a programme will have a whole range of results. It may not be to the advantage of the programme for *all* these results to be shared with everyone. For example, some programmes may wish to keep private the exact details of their funding or expenditure, or even the specific names of individuals and places. The actual context of each programme will indicate what can safely be shared, and with whom. Decide what you wish to share and what it is safe to share, and then prepare the information and materials accordingly.

6.3 SOME APPROPRIATE WAYS TO SHARE RESULTS

A full evaluation report will probably be distributed among programme staff, perhaps to some community-level participants, and to selected ministries, departments, organisations and agencies. Because of the cost of production only a carefully-specified number of full reports are likely to be produced.

Other forms in which selected evaluation results can be shared with a wider audience include information sheets (or handouts), meetings, discussions, posters, chalkboard presentations, drama, tape recordings, slides, film-strips or video recordings. The latter may be too expensive, or unavailable for many programmes.

Using a newsletter

On the following pages are extracts from a regular newsletter which was used to feed back the results of a participatory evaluation of an international children's programme. The eight-page newsletter was relatively inexpensive to produce and was mailed to the countries around the world that had Child-to-child programmes in progress. The programmes themselves had participated in providing information for the evaluation. In this way initial analysis of the programme information and activities was carried out by the programmes themselves.

CHILD-to-child programme

c/o Institute of Child Health, 30 Guilford Street, London WC1N 1EH.
Telephone 01-242 9789

NEWSLETTER 4
SPECIAL EVALUATION ISSUE September 1982

CHILD-to-child is an international programme designed to teach and encourage older children and especially school children to concern themselves with the health and general development of their younger brothers and sisters. Simple preventive and curative activities as well as games, play and role-playing can be taught to the children in school, so that they may pass ideas on in the family or community environment. Initiatives and encouragement from government and other official sources help support teachers and older children in their activities.

This Newsletter describes briefly an evaluation of the programme commissioned in 1981 to see how far CHILD-to-child has spread; who is involved in its organization; what ideas and practices have been most often used and why; what plans are being made for the future.

With a world-wide programme but limited funds it was clearly not possible to set up interviews and the evaluation was carried out by means of postal questionnaires mailed to all groups known or believed to have established local CHILD-to-child projects.

219 replies were received. Of these 113 described existing programmes. 43 sent reports, letters, articles and photographs. In this way they took a central part in the evaluation and the sharing of their knowledge and experience was invaluable in achieving an over-all assessment of CHILD-to-child.

Many of the correspondents asked for 'feedback' of the evaluation results. This Newsletter records the main results of the evaluation and so provides this feed-back.

Extent of CHILD-to-child

An idea of the number of countries to which CHILD-to-child has spread is given on page 3.

There are at least ONE AND A HALF MILLION CHILDREN, older and younger, involved around the world.

In action:

In Mexico health workers drew fang and teeth marks of poisonous snakes on the arms of school children.

Then these older school children taught the younger children the same lesson, and what to do in case of a snake bite.

Who were the children involved?

Over half (54%) of the children were school children.

But NEARLY 20% OF THE CHILDREN DID NOT GO TO SCHOOL - AND WERE UNLIKELY EVER TO DO SO.

The remainder were described as scouts, guides or members of other youth groups.

Favourite Activities

Learning about Nutrition
Diarrhoea and Dehydration
Health and Hygiene Sessions
Accidents and First Aid
Weighing and Immunization
Using the Shakir Strip
Looking at the Neighbourhood
Teeth
Eyes
Feeding small Children
Playing with small Children
Health Scouts
Learning about Relationships
Learning about Family Planning
Gathering information on Families
Budgeting family needs
Planting Trees
Playing with children with Handicaps

Why they liked these activities

"Care of children with Diarrhoea" — *It was simple and practical - they learnt new technology to use at home" (India)*

"Teeth" — *They examined the teeth of the family at home and reported to the class" (Philippines)*

"Puppets" — *They are fun" (Mexico)*

"Story telling" — *Because children are illiterate" (India)*

"Scouts" — *They feel involved and feel they render important services" (Sudan)*

What did they do?

Of the 17 CHILD-to-child Activity Sheets, the following were reported to be the most frequently used.

Care of children with Diarrhoea	35
More Healthy Food	15
Accidents	10
Our Teeth	8
Toys and Games	6
Shakir Strip	6
Our Neighbourhood	5
Handicapped Children	5
Health Scouts	5
Let's find out how well children See and Hear	3
Caring for children who are Sick	2
Our Babies Growing Up	2
Playing with Younger Children	2

How it was done

Games
Role-Playing
Practical Activities
Dancing and Singing
Puppets
Contests and Quizzes
Making Toys
Filmstrips, TV and Radio
Drawing and Painting
Exhibitions
Festivals
Rallies
Making Books
Making Posters
Telling Stories
Having a Library

Adapting Activity Sheets

Only 25 reports said that sheets had been used as they were received.

36 said they had been both translated and adapted to suit local conditions.

Activity sheets have been translated into Spanish, French, Arabic, Filipino, Hindi, Indonesian, Portuguese and Swahili.

Who's been involved?

The diagram opposite shows the people who have been involved in setting up CHILD-to-child projects in many different countries.

Some programmes have been started with only a copy of a newsletter as guidance.

At least 35% of those involved have worked on a VOLUNTARY BASIS.

Parents and community leaders have been involved. They have provided food or accommodation, taught songs, published articles or local newsletters .... helped children to put knowledge into practice.

2

What adults were involved?

Country	Nurses	Doctors	Prim.Teachers	Health Educators	C.D. Worker	Nutritionist	Sec.Teacher	Comm Worker	C.H.W.	Soc.Worker	Womens groups	Day care Worker	Nurse Students	T.B.A.s	Pre-school Teacher	Midwife Students	Theatre groups	Youth groups	Young farmers
Australia			●				●												
Bangladesh	●	●	●							●									
Benin					●														
Bolivia	●	●	●	●				●											
Brazil	●	●	●	●		●	●	●	●	●	●	●	●	●			●		●
Chile	●	●	●	●	●	●													
Columbia			●																
Dominican R			●																
Ecuador	●					●													
El Salvador	●	●	●					●											
France		●					●												
Fiji			●	●				●	●										
Gambia			●	●															
Guatemala	●		●			●			●										
Grenada	●	●		●						●									
Honduras				●								●							
Indonesia	●	●	●	●	●		●					●		●					
Israel			●																
India	●	●	●	●	●	●	●	●	●			●			●	●	●		
Jamaica	●	●	●	●															
Kenya	●	●		●						●									
Korea	●	●			●				●	●									
Kuwait	●	●	●					●											
Liberia			●	●			●												
Lebanon	●																		
Mexico			●	●				●											
Nepal										●									
Nicaragua	●									●									
Nigeria	●	●	●		●					●									
Pakistan	●		●		●										●				
PNG	●	●	●	●												●			
Paraguay	●		●																
Peru					●						●								
Philippines	●	●	●	●	●	●	●		●										
Rwanda	●		●			●			●										
Singapore	●	●		●		●													
S.Africa	●	●			●				●										
Sri Lanka	●	●	●	●		●	●												
Sudan	●	●		●		●	●												
Syria			●																
Tanzania	●	●	●	●															
Thailand		●	●																
Togo			●		●														
Tonga	●	●																	
Uganda		●						●											
Zaire	●	●	●			●									●				
Zambia	●	●																	
Zimbabwe	●	●	●								●							●	●

3

Using pictures

An effective way of sharing evaluation results at community level is to turn the results into pictures.

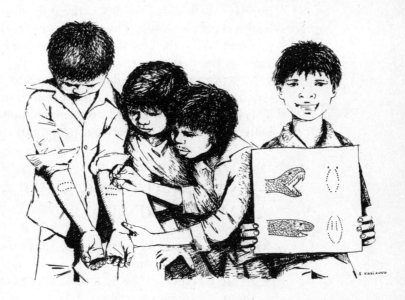

This is good way of stimulating a discussion. It is also useful where many participants may be illiterate. Photographs, slides, posters, drawings and cartoons can all be used to share and discuss evaluation results.

From experience

Adapted from a sketch by A. Kroeger and used in participatory evaluation of primary health care programmes with four Indian populations in Ecuador

In Ecuador, South America, evaluation results were turned into picutures and discussed with sixty programme participants and staff. These included community health workers from four different Indian groups, rural doctors, other health service staff, and university staff.

The picture shows a family seeking help from a health centre on the Sunday Market day, which is the only day they come to town. The health centre is closed. The staff do not work on Sundays. The 'result' pictured is that the best time for the people to seek treatment is not the same as the best time for health centre staff.

Most programme evaluations indicate that there is a need to strengthen the system of regular programme monitoring being used. This is important for good programme management and will provide better information for the next programme evaluation.

6.4 STRENGTHENING REGULAR PROGRAMME MONITORING

Monitoring means keeping track of day-to-day programme activities. Monitoring helps you:
- to see whether all the action is being planned and directed towards the programme objectives;
- to assess what progress is being made and if the time available is being used well;
- to see whether good standards are being maintained;
- to see whether manpower and materials are being used effectively;
- to identify any differences between knowledge and practice, and to plan training accordingly;
- to facilitate recognition of good performance in order to identify people for promotion and/or further training;
- to identify problems and possible solutions.

By using a carefully-planned and systematic method of regular monitoring you can assess programme strengths and weaknesses, and see where improvements are necessary.

Monitoring and record-keeping

Monitoring involves record-keeping and regular assessments (both written and verbal). Some programmes have weekly and/or monthly meetings as part of their monitoring system, but if such meetings are to to be really useful they must be more than brief informal discussions. They need to be linked closely with a carefully-thought-out system of record-keeping and reporting. Good monitoring is partly dependent on good record-keeping.

Good record-keeping relies on programme participants regularly and systematically recording important facts and information about their own work. Sometimes records are well designed and can be very useful for monitoring. Unfortunately, as we have seen earlier in this book, even good records are sometimes not kept well enough to be useful in this way. For example, they may only be kept from time to time, or be incomplete, or they may not be dated, or they may not even be kept at all.

6.5 MONITORING AND INFORMATION SYSTEMS

A programme needs a monitoring system that can provide good information. Good monitoring should provide regular information of activities in progress in the same way as a moving picture. (A census or a survey provides a picture of a situation at a particular time; this is static or 'non-moving' information.)

The different ways in which information is collected and used make up an entire **information system**. A good information system should provide the right kind of information needed for making sure that a development programme is going in the right direction, in accordance with the programme objectives.

Sometimes information systems try to provide too much information. Some of it may not even be correctly analysed or used. Sometimes people involved in development programmes want to try to obtain 'perfect' and very precise information. This can take a lot of time and money. Sometimes it is simply not possible. Often 'less perfect' yet reliable information can be used very effectively.

```
ONLY COLLECT INFORMATION
RELATING TO
YOUR OBJECTIVES
```

When planning and using monitoring and information systems it is important to consider:

- exactly what information will be needed;
- who will use this information, and how. (Users may include practitioners, managers, researchers, trainers, policy makers and the public at many different levels, from national to community level);
- how those who collect the information will have a part in analysing and using it;
- how different types of information will need to be presented in different ways;

- how new types of information will be included and used as they become available;
- how and when the efficiency of the monitoring and information system will be checked;
- how improvements can be made, where necessary.

The main uses to which development programmes, particularly large-scale programmes, put information are: policy making and planning; monitoring and managing practice; identifying needs, problems and solutions; training; organisation of personnel; and evaluation.

THE KIND OF INFORMATION NEEDED
The following is a list of the kind of information needed for:

Policy — Information on size, distribution, ages, sex, and growth patterns of population in the community, area and country. Socio-economic realities at these levels, such as money available and from what sources.

Practice — Information on services and programmes by type; scale; availability; how accessible they are and to what extent those for whom they are intended actually use them; systems of distribution of material resources and supplies; communications networks; financial costs relating to services and programmes; and physical infrastructure (eg, training centres, distribution centres, hospitals, health centres, technical and research institutions, schools, colleges, etc.)

Personnel, production and management — Information on personnel by type; number; levels (including community, level); location; ratios to one another and population; their urban-rural distribution; annual increase; management; training; and projected needs, etc.

Problem identification and solution — Information by type, scale, cause, priority, potential for solution. The areas to be considered include: food; shelter; agriculture; health; education; employment; marketing; communication systems; geographic and climatic features; administration; management and planning; patterns; and trends.

Many programme evaluations reveal that not enough good 'baseline' information has been collected.

6.6 IMPROVING BASELINE INFORMATION

Baseline information is the kind of information collected, preferably, before a programme begins. It is often obtained through surveys or a national census.

Sometimes such information has not been collected at the beginning, particularly where programmes began some time ago. In such cases it may be collected later.

Why is such information important?

Baseline information provides a base of foundation that can be used to understand better what the situation was like before a programme started. It also provides essential information for identifying priority needs and problems, and for indicating the kinds of programme plans and activities that are needed. In addition, it provides a base for regular assessment of how a programme is changing and progressing.

Why community involvement is important in collecting baseline information

One of the objectives in participatory evaluation is to help the community understand how baseline information can help them. They can take part, for example, in deciding what information is needed, which questions need to be asked, how the information can be collected, and how to analyse and use it. This can be an important community learning process. Communities are usually more interested and committed to future action plans that are based on information which they themselves have participated in collecting and analysing.

BUILD YOUR PROGRAMME
FROM A
STRONG BASELINE

What kind of information do you need to collect for a baseline?

This depends on the kind of activities (such as agriculture, community development, health, or education) in which you are involved. The following example is from a national organisation of community-based health programmes in the Philippines. The organisation worked with the health programmes to decide what baseline information was needed in order to strengthen the programmes and to make them more effective.

From experience

Demographic
How many people live in the community, how are they related to one another, and how old are they? How many people are there in an average family?

Causes of morbidity and mortality (disease and death)
What are the most common diseases and causes of death by age and sex groups? This will help you to see, for example, how many children die before they are one year old and why; and how many women die from complications which occur during their pregnancy and during childbirth.

Structure of society, socio-economic conditions, leadership
What are the main means of livelihood, who are the poorest families, who are the leaders, and what is the basis of their leadership? What are the costs of common commodities such as salt, kerosene, fertilizer and fishing nets?

Food supply, diet, weaning conditions
What do families normally eat, are there any shortages, how is weaning carried out, how much malnutrition is there and in which groups (such as the children under five years old, and pregnant women)? What livestock do they have?

Cultural patterns, common beliefs and habits
What do people believe and how does their behaviour affect health, disease and development?

Environmental factors and causes of ill health
What water sources are there and to what use are these put? Do comfort rooms (latrines) exist and are they used? Do health hazards, such as stagnant water, exist? Do vectors of disease, such as rats, exist? What are the methods of garbage disposal used?

Use of health services: referral, frequency and methods of use

What is the availability of health centres and trained staff, what are their distances from the community, what are the methods of referral? How are services used and for which conditions? What is the availability of medicines and sources.

Self-care, community service

What do families normally do when they are sick? What is the availability and use of home treatment, such as herbal remedies? To what extent are community resources such as *hilots* (traditional midwives) and other traditional practitioners used?

Educational level

How many grades were attained in which levels in school? What further education or training exists at community level?

Existence of community-level groups and organisations

What types of group activity are there, such as associations, Green ladies (women's clubs), cooperatives, religious groups and parent-teacher associations?

Contact with development agencies

What contact is there with government or non-government development agencies?

Social and religious life

What are the main social and religious events in the community?

Where evaluation results show that better baseline information is required, programme staff and participants can co-operate in planning how this can be done. They then collect and analyse the information necessary to make their programme more effective.

Another frequent evaluation result is that programmes find that their methods of supervision are not as good as they need to be. They often find that supervision needs to be improved at all levels.

6.7 PROVIDING SUPPORTIVE SUPERVISION

Supervision is an important part of programme activities. Unfortunately, in some programmes it can be the weakest part. Sometimes there is little or only poor quality supervision so that the workers at levels closest to, and including, community level (often called the field workers) feel neglected, isolated or unsupported. On the other hand, too much supervision can make such workers resent the attitudes, regulations, form-filling and management styles of programme staff.

Supervision is **not** just a matter of checking on work and giving instructions. it is an important part of effective monitoring.

There are many ways in which supervision can be carried out. The best way is for the supervisor and the workers being supervised to take enough time to share and discuss experiences, problems and progress.

THE BEST SUPERVISOR PROVIDES SUPPORT WITHOUT TAKING CHARGE AND WITH SKILL, UNDERSTANDING AND PATIENCE

Who makes the best supervisor?

Those who trained the field workers in the first place are often the ones who make the best supervisors for such workers. An important part of good supervision is trust and friendship.

In some countries primary-school teachers have been trained to supervise community health workers. They make good supervisors as they learn just the necessary amount of health knowledge, and they have their own teaching skills which they can pass on to the health workers.

An experienced field worker like a community-based worker can also be a good supervisor of other community-based workers. He/she knows, at first hand, the realities and problems of the work. In some

166

places this kind of supervisor can be used to organise an entire network of field workers.

Where the supervisor has not taken part in training the field workers whom he/she is supervising, it can be difficult, at first, for both the supervisor and the worker. Also, supervisors sometimes feel that they have little interest in supervision.

The field worker may also feel that a supervisor does not understand his/her needs, problems and working conditions. Supervision then becomes largely a matter of submitting reports and records, and collecting different kinds of supplies. With this kind of supervision there is little exchange of experience, advice and information.

The cartoon below shows the kind of rapid supervision where the field worker does not even get a chance to say "Good morning" let alone make any comments or ask questions.

What is good supervision?

1 Supervisors and worker/s in a relationship of partnership.
2 Shared responsibility for mutually-agreed objectives and working methods.
3 Good teamwork, with frequent meetings at which all view points can be expressed.
4 Clear and agreed job descriptions for all involved.
5 The giving of praise where it is due and the opportunity for promotion and/or further training.
6 Discussion of mutual progress, problems and plans.
7 Realistic decision-making and planning, according to need, priorities and available resources.
8 Awareness of responsibilities and possible problems in the personal lives of one another.
9 Reaching agreement wherever possible during discussion, or if not, agreeing to differ.
10 Where conflicts arise, listening patiently to all points of view separately, before trying to resolve them together.
11 Avoidance of public criticism, even where it may be justified.
12 Avoidance of favouring some workers in preference to others.
13 Fair distribution of mutually-agreed tasks.
14 Careful joint planning of the work plan with objectives that can be measured or clearly evaluated.
15 Giving advice and instructions that are clear, relevant, feasible and practical.
16 Using the opportunity to share and learn new facts and skills.
17 Providing regular opportunities for workers to meet each other, to prevent feelings of isolation and to encourage learning.
18 Provision of learning materials such as manuals, pamphlets, newsletters and visual aids where possible.

19 Recognition that the supervisor also learns from, and with, the field worker.

How often is supervision needed?

This will depend on:
- how much support the field worker normally receives from community/team/other workers.
- distance and cost (how far it is, and what it costs for a supervisor to visit a worker or for a worker to visit a supervisor).
- reimbursement of costs (whether the worker is being paid for the journey and by whom, and how long the worker is away from work).
- seasonal factors (for example whether it is planting or harvesting time, or the rainy season).
- length of visit (whether the visit is for a few hours, overnight or longer).
- normal workload (whether the worker needs more frequent advice or supplies, and also how much time the supervisor has, if supervision is only a part-time activity).

6.8 TAKE TIME TO EVALUATE YOUR OWN EVALUATION

Evaluation is hard and often painful work. This is because it requires those who are associated with a particular programme to be very honest with themselves and with each other. This is not always easy.

They also have to learn how to use a range of new intellectual and technical skills and to take on new roles and/or alter existing ones. They have to spend long hours looking in great detail at what they are doing and why. They may also have to travel long distances and/or work in very difficult conditions, according to the context of their own programme. From all these experiences a programme and its participants will learn a great deal. Participatory evaluation is also an educational process.

Take time to evaluate your own evaluation. Be critical of your own approach, methods and results. In this way, not only can you improve your own evaluation abilities but, by sharing your experiences with others, they can learn from them too.

Evaluation strengthens decision-making

During evaluation many decisions are made. Some relate to the way in which the evaluation will be organised and carried out. Some relate to the results of the evaluation and the ways in which these will be used.

Through participatory evaluation the whole foundation of decision-making can be strengthened. For example after evaluation decisions can be made on the basis of better information and statistics, and on a clearer understanding of the role, performance, weaknesses and strengths of a programme and its participants in that particular context.

Real partners in evaluation

New methods of participatory evaluation are developing around the world all the time, because it is a dynamic and growing process. More and more people are realising that they need these kinds of evaluation approaches because they stand the best chance of producing more self-aware, self-sustaining and self-directed development programmes, both small-scale and large-scale.

A participatory evaluation approach enables a very wide range of people to make their own individual contributions in the same evaluation process. In this way they become real partners in development, sharing decisions, planning, implementing and analysing results to see whether what they are doing can be improved for the benefit of people at community level.

Appendix A

MAKING A COMMUNITY PROFILE

A profile is an outline or a brief description. The purpose of making a community profile is to be able to obtain a fast 'picture' of a community which is as accurate as possible. A community profile should:

- summarise information;
- present results and figures clearly;
- be useful for planning and monitoring.

It will help to remember the questions who? where? when? what? and why? when making a profile.

The following community profile is of a fictitious village in the Far East. Most of the data, however, is from real villages and was collected from several sources during rapid 'Research and Development' surveys carried out jointly by development workers with the active participation of the communities concerned. They used the kind of survey form shown in Appendix B.

AN EXAMPLE OF A COMMUNITY PROFILE

Name of community . . . . Telok
District . . . . Mayan
Responsible for profile . . . . (names)
Position . . . . (of people responsible)
Date completed . . . . (day, month, year)

1. General description of the district

(This tells you about the area in which the community is situated, its **location, size population size, main features, commercial patterns, communications systems**, etc.)

The district of Mayan, with a population of 22 000, is situated 70 km from the provincial capital. It is bounded on the east by a river, on the south and west by mountains and on the north by the sea. The district extends along the bay.

The main town of Mayan has a population of 10 000 and is situated at the western end of the bay. It contains local government officials and representatives of the departments of agriculture and education. There is a thirty-bed hospital, a secondary school, a church, a temple, several general stores, a small pharmacy and a market place.

An unpaved road connects the town with the provincial capital. There is a public bus which travels once a day between the town and the capital. There is also a telephone link. The town has had electricity for ten years. An unpaved road leads 20 km around the bay to the village of Telok.

2. Agricultural patterns and seasons

(This tells you about the **land**, **agricultural patterns**, **climate**, and **seasons**.)

Coconut palms have been cultivated on the coastal strip, behind which rice paddies extend to the foot of the scrub covered mountains 2 km away. A little sugar cane and coffee is grown, largely for domestic consumption. The dry season is from February to June, with heavy rains from November to January. Rice is harvested twice a year and coconuts four times a year. During heavy rains the road to Mayan may be flooded for some weeks.

3. Description of the community

(This tells you about the community, its **location**, **size**, **population size**, **local features**, **commercial patterns**, **communications systems**, etc.)

The village of Telok is situated beside the bay and on two sides of a small river. The original settlers were fishermen from the mainland. The village extends 1 km back from the bay and contains 118 houses packed closely together. There are 1001 inhabitants, of whom 15 per cent are under fifteen years of age. The average family size is eight. (You may wish to make your own population data into a 'pyramid' showing the sex and age of the whole population.)

The village contains three general stores, one temple, one chapel, a primary school, a meeting hall and a football ground. There is a ferry twice a week to Mayan and there are a small truck and four motorcycles in the village. The truck carries passengers to Mayan once a week. There has been an electricity supply for two years and half of the houses have electricity.

The leader of the community is appointed by the government and is assisted by a committee of four which includes the school teacher, a store owner and two community representatives. There are no women on the committee. There is a Parent Teacher Association, religious associations and a women's club.

4. Ethnic, cultural and religious information

About 800 members of the population are the original inhabitants of the area, 150 members belong to a group which arrived fifty years ago and 51 belong to another racial group which arrived more recently. (In your profile add the names of the races.) The religions of the population are: native 750, Christian 200 and Buddhist 51. There are several religious festivals each year. During one of these fishermen make yearly offerings to the sea spirits who are believed to control the sea resources.

Many people attribute ill fortune or ill health to the anger of a local spirit who sometimes appears in the form of a big monkey, especially when the moon is full.

The educational level in Telok is as follows:

Educational level	Parents	Children
No formal education	107	0
Primary school	108	160
Secondary school	21	182
High school	nil	nil

6. Socio-economic information

(This tells you about the **occupational patterns**, **sources of income**, **marketing patterns**, etc.)

The main sources of income are fishing and agriculture, with rice and coconuts as primary products. The bay and river are good fishing grounds. Bamboo and rattan are plentiful.

A few residents are employed by the government. The majority are engaged in fishing, farming, vending and carpentry. The table below shows the pattern of employment.

Occupation	Family head	Percentage
Fishing only	30	25.4
Fishing/farming	65	55.0
Rice and vegetables	10	8.4
Employees	5	4.2
Others	8	7.0
	118	100.0

The livelihood of the fishermen is intermittent unless they have trawling nets. Most fishermen work from fishing boats which go out in good weather or on moonless nights. In trawling half of the profit goes to the boat owner and the rest to the crew. Where the profits of a catch are shared there are different ways of dividing the catch according to who owns the boat and the type of work done by each member of the crew. The fish is sold mostly in the town of Mayan, with a small amount being consumed locally.

The coconut products are also sold in Mayan, but the rice produced is consumed locally. A few vegetables and fruit trees are grown. Ninety-one families keep poultry (77 per cent), fifty-seven keep ducks (48 per cent) and thirty-two keep pigs (31 per cent). Most livestock are kept free-range or unfenced.

The annual cash income, expenditure and balance of the families of Telok is estimated to be as follows:

a) INCOME

Annual income	under 1000*	under 2000	under 3000	under 5000	Total
Families	47	51	18	2	118
Percentage	40	43	15	2	100

*1000 units of local currency is equivalent to 240 US dollars.

b) EXPENDITURE

Annual expenditure	under 1000	under 2000	under 5000	Total
Families	56	62	0	118
Percentage	47	53	0	100

c) BALANCE BETWEEN ANNUAL INCOME AND EXPENDITURE

Expenditure in relation to income	Total no. of families	Percentage
Expenditure *above* income	31	26
Expenditure *below* income	87	74
Total	118	100

The cost of common consumer goods, such as salt, kerosene, soap and sugar has risen sharply over the past year.

7. Environmental situation

At the moment there is no piped water supply in Telok. All water for drinking, cooking or washing purposes is obtained directly from the river. Ninety houses were found to have adequate domestic drainage, but 28 houses had stagnant water nearby. Of the total 118 houses, 85 had clean surroundings but 33 had garbage littering the yard. Garbage disposal was as follows:

METHOD OF GARBAGE DISPOSAL

Method	Families	Percentage
bins	36	31
burning	47	40
pits	35	29
Total	118	100

Most families used river water to flush their pit latrines (the pour flush method).

METHOD OF HUMAN WASTE DISPOSAL

Method	Families	Percentage
pour flush	85	72
pit latrine	14	12
river	8	7
fields	11	9
Total	118	100

Some of the latrines were not in good condition and many were not clean.

8. Health situation

The leading health problems, according to the results of the two-day survey and discussions with the community, were as follows:

diarrhoea
intestinal worms
eye diseases
fever and cough

diseases of the teeth
 and mouth
belly pains
skin diseases
muscular pains
accidents

headaches
tuberculosis
malnutrition
measles

The immunisation of children under seven years of age against diphtheria, whooping cough, tetanus and measles was as follows:

IMMUNISATION STATUS OF CHILDREN UNDER SEVEN YEARS

Status	Children	Percentage
completely immunised	30	21
not immunised	47	33
incompletely immunised	65	46
Total	142	100

Of the total population of Telok, 399 were women between 15 and 65 years old. Between them they had had a total of 702 pregnancies. Of these, 37 women reported less than 10 pregnancies and 41 reported between 10 and 20 pregnancies. Twenty-six women reported that they had not received medical check-ups before delivery, but 52 reported one check-up and 17 had received two check-ups.

Last year a woman died in childbirth when the road to Mayan was flooded and the sea was too rough for passage. It should be noted that some of the women, between the ages of 50 and 65, had been delivered long before the hospital opened in Mayan ten years ago.

TYPE AND NUMBER OF DELIVERIES REPORTED

Type of delivery	Number of deliveries
delivered by trained midwife	49
delivered by untrained midwife	616

There are two traditional midwives in Telok but they have not yet received the training which it is planned will be extended from the provincial hospital 70 km away. There is also a herbalist.

In Mayan there is a physician, a nurse, a nurse-midwife and a dental health assistant. Telok hopes to send two villagers to the hospital to train as community health workers. A team from the hospital visits Telok every two months to carry our curative work and vaccinations.

Few families in Telok plan their family size or use contraception. Having children is regarded as being a sign of wealth, especially by those who do not own properties such as land.

(This kind of community profile can be adjusted to your own situation and needs, and more information can be collected on agriculture, land owner-ship, health conditions, educational needs, leadership patterns, economic realities, etc.)

Appendix B

SAMPLE COMMUNITY SURVEY FORM

DAY/MONTH/YEAR _____ FAMILY CODE NUMBER _____ FULL NAME OF INTERVIEWER _____

ADDRESS: _____

FAMILY DATA									
FULL NAME (HEAD OF THE FAMILY FIRST)	SEX	AGE	RELATION TO HEAD OF FAMILY	CIVIL STATUS	EDU-CATIONAL BACK-GROUND	OCCU-PATION	ETHNIC BACK-GROUND	RELIGION	REMARKS
1.									
2.									
3.									
4.									
5.									
6.									
7.									
8.									
9.									
10.									

HEALTH DATA (Please examine everybody)

	PHYSICAL EXAMINATION																					(FOR ADULT FEMALES)									
	HEAD	EYES	EARS	LIPS	TONGUE	TEETH	HEART	LUNGS	LIVER	SPLEEN	SKIN	BONE	FEVER	COUGH	PAIN	DIARRHOEA	TB	GASTRO-ENTERITIS	MALARIA	MALNUTRITION	BRONCHO-PNEUMONIA	INTESTINAL PARASITES	PREGNANT NOW	NUMBER OF PREGNANCY	NUMBER BORN ALIVE	NUMBER OF ABORTIONS	NUMBER OF CHILD DEATHS (UNDER 15)	AGE OF CHILD (0-6)	CAUSE OF DEATH	AGE OF CHILD (7-15)	CAUSE OF DEATH
1.																															
2.																															
3.																															
4.																															
5.																															
6.																															
7.																															
8.																															
9.																															
10.																															

WHAT DO YOU DO WHEN SOMEONE IS SICK AT HOME?

	CHW	BHT	RHU	PUBLIC HOSPITAL	PRIVATE HOSPITAL	HILOT
Simple illness						
Seriously ill						
Emergency Care						

HOW DO THE SEASONS (ie, WET, DAY) AFFECT WHAT YOU DO?

WHAT MEDICINES DO YOU USE? HERBAL/WESTERN

ENVIRONMENTAL DATA

HOUSE

Quality
- good ☐
- bad ☐
- (dirty, dark, condition, etc)

Walls
- wood ☐
- brick ☐
- concrete ☐
- other ☐

Yard
- clean ☐
- dirty ☐
- no yard ☐

WASTE DISPOSAL

Sanitation
- pit ☐
- pour flush ☐
- bushes ☐
- river ☐
- other ☐

Garbage
- bury ☐
- burn ☐
- throw ☐
- collected ☐

WATER

Quality
- good ☐
- bad ☐

Type
- tank ☐
- well ☐
- spring ☐
- river ☐
- faucet in house ☐
- shared faucet ☐
- distance to faucet ☐

Maintenance
- good ☐
- bad ☐

Under House
- clean ☐
- dirty ☐

Roof
- zinc ☐
- tile ☐
- thatch ☐
- other ☐

Animals
- penned ☐
- not penned ☐
- penned under house ☐

Electricity
- yes ☐
- no ☐

178

SOCIO-ECONOMIC DATA

AGRICULTURE	Value of Produce	Income from Trading	LIVESTOCK	Value of Produce	Income from Trading	FISH	Value of Produce	Income from Trading	OTHER PRODUCE	Value of Produce	Income from Trading
Rice ☐			Chickens ☐			Sea ☐			Handicraft ☐		
Corn ☐			Ducks ☐			River ☐			Hunting ☐		
Potatoes ☐			Pigs ☐			Lake ☐			Herbal Medicine ☐		
Vegetables ☐			Buffalo ☐			Fish Pond ☐			Other goods or Services What? ☐		
Fruit ☐			Cows ☐								
Other What? ☐			Goats ☐								
			Other What? ☐								
TOTAL FOR YEAR											

Is the head of the family SELF-EMPLOYED FULL-TIME all the year ☐ SELF-EMPLOYED PART-TIME ☐ EMPLOYED BY AN EMPLOYER FULL-TIME ☐ EMPLOYED BY AN EMPLOYER PART-TIME ☐ OCCASIONALLY EMPLOYED BY AN EMPLOYER ☐ NOT EMPLOYED ☐ ?

179

What is the estimated ANNUAL EXPENDITURE for the family?

FOOD	
CLOTHING	
SCHOOL	
LIGHT	
WATER	
TRANSPORT	
RENT	
MEDICINES/HEALTH	
FERTILIZER	
SOCIAL	
OTHER-WHICH?	

TOTAL INCOME FOR YEAR =
TOTAL EXPENDITURE FOR YEAR =
DIFFERENCE IN AMOUNTS =

Appendix C

GUIDELINES FOR DETERMINING CURRENT POPULATION

If you do not have up-to-date census figures for your health area, the chart below can help you estimate the current population.
- First, find out what the population of your health area was at the last census, and find out how many years ago that census was taken.
- Then, find out the annual growth rate for your country. (If you do not know what it is, ask your district supervisor.)
- Now, use the chart.

Read down the left column of the chart until you come to the number that is the same as the number of years since the last census.

Follow that row across the chart until you come to the column representing your country's annual growth rate. Note the number at that point.

Multiply that number by the population of your health area at the time of the last census. This will give you the approximate current population.

Number of years since last census:	Annual growth rate			
	1%	2%	3%	4%
1	1.010	1.020	1.030	1.040
2	1.020	1.040	1.061	1.082
3	1.030	1.061	1.093	1.125
4	1.040	1.082	1.126	1.170
5	1.051	1.104	1.159	1.217
6	1.061	1.126	1.194	1.265
7	1.072	1.149	1.230	1.316
8	1.082	1.172	1.267	1.369
9	1.093	1.195	1.305	1.423
10	1.105	1.219	1.334	1.480

EXAMPLE

In the Bornu Area, the population at the time of the last census was 23103. That census was taken in 1980 and it is now 1984. The annual growth rate for the country is 2 per cent. To compute the current population:
- Read down the left column of the chart to the number "4" (because the census was 4 years ago).
- Follow that row across to the column under 2 per cent (the annual growth rate). The number at that point is 1.082.
- Multiply 1.082 by 23103 (the population at the time of the last census), and you will get the approximate current population, which is 24997.

NOTE: When computing current population, take into consideration any factors that might make the growth rate of your area different from that for the entire country (for example, nomads moving into the area, or people leaving because of a drought).

Courtesy of WHO: "Evaluating Vaccination Coverage: Training for Mid-Level Managers", WHO Expanded Programme on Immunisation.

Glossary

Definitions of some of the words and concepts used in this book.

Access The opportunity to obtain or use something.

Accessibility The extent to which something that exists can be reached by those who want or need it.

Accountability The extent to which a person (or group) is responsible for, and accounts for, something.

Action-oriented records Records which are designed and kept in such a way that they show what actions should be taken.

Approach A specific and chosen method of advancing or proceeding.

Appropriate technology Technology that is suitable for the purpose for which it is intended.

Assessment A process (which may or may not be systematic) of gathering information, analysing it, then making a judgement on the basis of the information. Sometimes used to mean the same as 'evaluation'. In this book it is used to mean something which takes place before a programme begins.

Attitude The feeling and/or point of view which a person (or group) has (or reveals by behaviour or verbally) relating to people, events, opinions or theories.

Availability The extent to which something exists and is available.

Average The sum of a group of measurements divided by the total number of measurements.

Barrier Something which bars advance or prevents access, such as an obstacle on a path or rigid ideas which prevent new ideas being absorbed.

Baseline information Information, consisting usually of facts and figures, which provides a basis for planning programme development and evaluating progress.

Baseline measures Measures taken before something begins, in order to have a basis for comparison when evaluating progress later.

Behaviour The total reaction of an individual (or group) which can be observed. (Thought and understanding are types of 'internal behaviour' that can not be observed directly but can be concluded from observing other behaviours.)

Bias Something which influences, distorts or prejudices.

Biassed sample The result of an incorrect method of taking a sample (so that the sample is not representative of the population from which it is taken). Bias can also be the result of making incorrect interpretations or conclusions, giving an incorrect result.

Birth rate The number of births per 1000 population per year.

Budget The annual estimate of financial resources and expenditure needed or available with respect to a country, organisation, programme, group or individual.

Calculate To try to find out and foretell something using mathematics.

Calculator A machine or set of numbered tables used to calculate something.

Cartoon Usually an amusing drawing or series of drawings, with or without words, designed to make a special point.

Case study An intensive and detailed analysis and description of an event, programme, situation, condition or organisation in the context of its environment.

Catalyst A person who begins and/or makes change possible.

Census The official numbering, counting and analysis of the population of a country.

Chart A specially designed set of visual information (eg, diagrams or numbers), usually on large or small sheets of paper.

Checklist A specially-constructed list which allows a check to be made of the contents which are listed.

Collective test A test that can be administered to a certain number of persons at the same time.

Communicate To convey or transmit information or feelings to an individual (or group).

Community A group of people living in the same locality and sharing some common characteristics.

Community development Collective action to improve a community's material and non-material life, usually in collaboration with government and non-governmental development agencies.

Community diagnosis A method of systematically assessing community needs, usually before a programme begins.

Community involvement The active involvement of the community in planning and operating development activities. (Now used especially in the health sector to imply greater community participation in development activities and especially in decision-making.)

Community participation The active participation of the community in development activities.

Community worker A person who has been trained

to work with one or more communities in order to achieve some aspect of development.

Community health worker   A resident of a community who has been trained to provide certain kinds of health care to that community.

Competence   The ability required to take on certain chosen roles or functions.

Computer   An automatic electronic machine for storing or processing information in the form of facts, figures or symbols.

Content analysis   A structured method by which the whole and parts of something are examined, analysed and described, often to help in developing measuring instruments like questionnaires.

Control group   A specially-selected sub-group of people who purposefully do not receive the same treatment, input or training, etc, as the whole group, in order that differences between the sub-group and the main group can be measured and evaluated.

Correlation   The relationship or connection between two scores or measures.

Cost-benefit analysis   A systematic process by which the benefit of decisions and actions are compared to their costs, usually financial.

Cost effectiveness and efficiency   A process by which the effects and/or efficiency of decisions and actions are compared to their costs, usually financial.

Coverage   The extent to which something is 'covered'. In health terms this means the extent to which those who need something are actually receiving it.

Criteria   The plural of 'criterion'.

Criterion   A standard by which something may be judged or evaluated (for example, a set of scores that have been selected as the best way of measuring performance or success).

Critical incident analysis   A structured method of examining in detail something that has happened or the way that a person (or group) has behaved.

Curriculum evaluation   Evaluation of a training programme or course of study, particularly the teaching texts, materials, length of course and teaching methods.

Data   Facts and information collected for a special purpose.

Death rate   The number of deaths per 1000 population per year.

Demographic survey   A survey which examines and measures a population by age, sex, birth and death rates, etc.

Design of evaluation   The entire plan of an evaluation showing its methods and timing, and how different parts fit together to achieve its purpose.

Deviation   The amount by which a score differs from some selected reference value (eg, a point considered 'normal').

Diagnostic test   A test used to 'diagnose' or identify specific causes of something like an illness, or areas of weakness or strength in education, or a particular type of insect or condition which is destroying crops.

Diagram   A visual presentation showing a process or showing the features of an object, using lines, drawings, symbols, etc.

Diary   A daily record of events, usually written in a book.

Distribution   The setting out of numbers in the form of tables extending from high to low, or from low to high, showing the number of individuals or items that fit into specific groups.

Education   A process of systematic instruction and learning.

Effectiveness   The state or quality of being effective in relation to certain objectives (for example, is what is being done reaching the objective?).

Efficiency   The state or quality of being useful and productive in relation to certain objectives (for example, is it the best way to do something?).

Effort   The attempt to achieve something particular (for example, how much work, time, resources are being put in?).

Epidemiology   The study of health and disease in a population.

Episode   A single occurrence of something, like an episode of illness.

Estimate   To make an approximate judgement or forecast.

Evaluator   A person who carries out evaluation or enables evaluation to take place.

Explicit   Something that is stated in a clear and precise manner so as to leave no doubt as to its meaning.

Factor   A circumstance, fact or number which contributes to a result.

Factor analysis   A process in which circumstances, factors or numbers are analysed to explain common characteristics and/or differences between the factors.

Failure   Lack of success in performance in reaching specific objectives.

Feedback   To return and share information (eg, evaluation results) with those who participated in the evaluation.

Flow chart   A chart which shows the separate parts of something and the way in which these parts are linked to one other.

Formative evaluation   The type of evaluation which aims to help the development of programmes in a way that they can use as they proceed.

Frequency   A measure of how common something is or the times at which it is repeated at certain intervals.

Frequency distribution   A method of assessing and analysing how often something occurs, or a method of presenting a series of numbers by dividing them into groups and counting the number in each group.

Geographic co-ordinate chart   A chart based on a map which shows the location of specific data and how frequently it occurs.

Goal   A point marking the objective of effort, ambition or destination.

Graph   A method of presenting data by positioning it in relation to a horizontal and vertical axis.

Guidelines A set of principles and practices which guide or direct something.

Health centre A centre which carries out specified promotive, protective, preventive, diagnostic, curative and rehabilitative activities, mainly for outpatients (but it may have inpatient beds).

Impact The effect of something on an object or on the objectives of a programme.

Incidence rate The number of times that something occurs in relation to a whole (eg, the number of times an illness occurs in a total population).

Indicator Something which provides a basis for measuring progress towards objectives. It may relate to number or qualitative factors. An indicator is like a 'marker' which shows what progress has been made and how much progress is still expected.

Individual test A test that is given to only one person at a time.

Information Items of knowledge (eg, facts and/or figures).

Information system A whole system of connected parts that aims to organise and classify facts and figures for a specific purpose.

Infrastructure A collective term for fixed installations (like buildings, roads, etc.)

Integration Joining one or more parts of something together to form a whole, usually to achieve better functioning.

Interview A face-to-face meeting where an interviewer aims to obtain information and/or impressions about the person or group being interviewed.

Interviewer Person who meets an individual or group for the purpose of carrying out an interview.

Item A single question or exercise, usually in a test.

Item analysis The process of evaluating single test items by any one of several methods.

Job analysis A method of identifying and defining the duties, requirements and conditions of jobs in a systematic way.

KAP survey A survey which measures Knowledge, Attitudes and Practice (KAP) in a individual (or group) in relation to a specific purpose.

Knowledge The range of information gained by experience of an individual or group.

Lay reporting The collection of information, its use and transmission to other levels of a reporting system by non-professional people.

Learning The process of acquiring knowledge, skills and experience. The process may be systematic and formal (as in school), or informal (as in learning from life's experiences).

Line graph A graph drawn by connecting points on a graph using straight lines.

Longitudinal study A study which looks systematically at the same people, programme, community, etc, over a long period of time.

Machine scorable A questionnaire or test that can be scored by means of a machine (eg, a computer or a calculator).

Management The process of planning, organising, operating monitoring and evaluating all the inter-related parts of a system (eg, a programme or business).

Map chart A chart based on a map which shows specific information using various kinds of design and layout.

Mapping A structured activity where individuals or groups make a graphic representation of either a part or the whole of the context in which they are living.

Matching item A method of testing knowledge or performance by giving two choices (like two lists), and requiring the correct matching of listed items.

Mean (*See* Average.) (The word 'mean' is sometimes used instead of the word 'average'.)

Measure To examine the extent or quantity of something by comparing it with a fixed unit or object of known size.

Median The central position or number which divides numbers or measurements into two equal parts when they are arranged in increasing or decreasing order.

Method error A result that can not be repeated or is invalid because of changes in the method or instrument used.

Model A simplified description of a system showing the parts, how they fit together and their purpose. It may be either written or drawn, or may be a version produced as an example.

Monitor The systematic and continuous following, or keeping trace, of activities to ensure that they are proceeding according to plan.

Motivation A feeling of desire to do something. Lack of motivation means a feeling of not caring or having no interest in doing something.

Multiple choice question A method of testing knowledge or performance where several possible answers are presented and only one (usually) can be selected.

Multiple response item A method of testing knowledge or performance where several possible answers are presented and only one (usually) can be selected from the code given.

'N' The symbol commonly used to represent the total number or numbers of measurements given.

Needs assessment A process by which needs are identified and priorities decided upon.

Norm A set standard of development or achievement.

Objective test A test where the scoring is designed so that there is no possibility of differences of opinion about whether responses are right or wrong (unlike tests where different scorers may give different marks according to their own assessment).

Observation techniques Systematic evaluation methods for observing people, events and/or their contexts.

Observer A person who watches but does not participate in what is being watched.

Oral test   A test where an examination or assessment is made by questions being asked in a face-to-face situation.

Organisation chart   A chart which names the parts of an organisation (eg, offices, divisions, sections), but not the people involved, or their function.

Overlay   To lay one thing over another (eg, a transparent sheet over a sheet of paper).

Participation   A process in which an individual (or group) decides to take part in specific decision-making and action, and over which he/she may exercise specific controls.

Participatory evaluation   A systematic evaluation process in which participation is sought in initial decision-making, planning, implementation, summary and analysis, and in the use of results.

Participatory research   A research process where participants take a part in the different stages of the process (eg, decision-making, planning implementation, and production of results.)

Percentage   The number of people with a particular characteristic in a group, divided by the total number in the group and multiplied by 100.

Performance   A test which measures the extent to which a person or programme has achieved a set objective. It usually involves concrete equipment or materials.

Personnel chart   A chart which shows the names and/or functions of different people, usually those in a programme or organisation.

Pictogram   A type of bar chart which uses a series of symbols or 'pictures' to present data.

Pie chart   A circular chart used to show the different parts of the whole in relation to one other.

Plan   A proposal which indicates the times and places of intended proceedings, which outlines or details the methods by which something is to be done.

Policy   A document containing an agreed course of action about how something is to be done.

Population pyramid   A histogram of a population which shows age groups for each sex and which has a broad base, becoming narrower towards the top.

Pre-coded records   Survey records in which all responses (answers or results) are given a code before the survey begins.

Prerequisite   Something required as a previous condition.

Pre-test   To test something (like a questionnaire) before using it. Also, to test the knowledge of people before they acquire additional knowledge, so that their newly-acquired knowledge can be 'measured' against what they already knew.

Prevalence   The percentage (or rate per 1000 or 10 000) of the population with a special characteristic (eg, a disease).

Primary health care   Essential health care made accessible at a cost which a country and community can afford, with methods that are practical, scientifically sound and socially acceptable.

Priority   Something which is selected as being of first importance.

Profile   An outline or short written or printed description.

Progress   To move forward or onward.

Prognosis   A test or prediction of future success or failure in a specific situation, field or subject.

Programme   A plan decided in advance, usually with fixed objectives, methods, sequence and context.

Programmed learning   A method of learning where there is a system of questions with an immediate check on the answers. The right answer is needed in order to answer the next question.

Quality   The degree of excellence or standard of something.

Quantitative   Something measured or measurable by, or concerned with, amount or quantity and expressed in numbers or quantities.

Questionnaire   A group of written or printed questions used to obtain information from individuals (or groups).

Random numbers   A table of numbers constructed in such a way that the numbers 0 to 9 occur in an irregular way and with equal frequency. It is used in sampling to give all people or items an equal chance of being selected.

Random sample   A method of selecting members of a population (or other items) in such a way that everyone (or everything) has an equal chance of being included in the sample.

Range   The difference between the lowest and highest numbers or measurements in a group.

Rank ordering   The process of arranging numbers, people or measurements according to a chosen standard (eg, arranging the scores that people obtain in a test).

Rate   A proportion, expressed in numbers, between two sets of things [eg, a bus moving at a rate of 10 miles an hour or the rate of doctors (1) to nurses (20)].

Ratings   Assessments made by an individual on an established scale, like an attitude scale.

Ratio   A relationship expressed in numbers between two amounts of similar magnitude and determined by the number of times one contains the other as a whole or as a fraction (eg, a ratio of 1 to 5 is the same as 20 to 100).

Recall item   An item (like that on a questionnaire) which requires the examinee to supply the correct answer from memory.

Recognition item   An item requiring the respondent to recognise or select the correct answer from among two or more given answers (similar to a multiple choice question).

Recording   A method of collecting information regularly, in the form of words, figures or symbols, for a particular purpose.

Register   A record set down regularly in writing.

Relevance The extent to which something is appropriate for a particular purpose.

Reliability The extent to which something can be relied on and trusted to be of consistent quality when used repeatedly.

Replication An attempt to do again what has been done before.

Report An account (written or verbal) which is prepared or presented for a particular purpose.

Representative sample A sample which is chosen so that it truly represents the whole population from which it comes.

Research A systematic method of scientific study which usually seeks to discover new facts or examine old ones.

Respondent A person who answers or replies.

Risk factor A factor which may cause a person to get a disease or problem.

Sample A part of a whole selected to represent that whole (eg, a sample of the population).

Sample survey A survey of a sample of a specific population.

Sampling The process and techniques of studying part of something to gain information about the whole (like a population) and the particular methods of analysing the information collected.

Scale A continuous series of selected values in which numbers, measurements or attitudes can be ranged in order to assess them with respect to the whole.

Scientific evaluation Evaluation which is systematic and objective, which is capable of drawing conclusions and of making realistic predictions.

Score The number of points obtained in relation to a specific measure.

Screening test A simple, cheap and fast way of identifying people with risk factors or the first symptoms of a specific disease.

Side effects The unintended outcomes of a particular event or incident.

Skill A structured way of looking at something. Expertise or practiced ability in doing something.

Special purpose chart A chart which presents data in various ways for a special purpose.

Standard score A general term relating to a variety of corrected scores in which an average score is used for convenience, comparability, etc.

Standard weight for age The average weight of children from a standard population in a given age-group (eg, a standard based on Harvard students is commonly used).

Standardised records Records in which the same information is collected on all people, animals, items, etc and is recorded in the same way.

Statistical analysis A systematic method of studying and drawing conclusions from statistics.

Statistics Numerical facts which are systematically collected, organised and presented in a special way.

Success The favourable outcome of an undertaking in relation to its objectives.

Summative evaluation The type of evaluation concerned with evaluating or 'summing up' the overall achievements of a programme.

Supervision The process of overseeing the performance or carrying out of specific actions and/or responsibilities.

Survey A structured way of looking at something.

Survey methods The techniques and procedures used to obtain information, often about a human population.

Systems analysis A structured and systematic method of looking at a system to assist decision-making, especially when making choices between alternatives.

Table The laying out of facts and numbers in an orderly fashion, usually in columns and rows, so that they can be more easily understood.

Tally sheet A sheet on which information is recorded using a scoring system based on a fixed number of marks or symbols which relate to people, events, goods produced, etc.

Tape recording A reproduction on magnetic tape of sounds which can be 'played back' on a tape recorder.

Target A specified objective.

Task analysis A systematic way of looking at work which is being performed in relation to a specific purpose.

Teaching The process by which a student is assisted to understand and absorb information or skills.

Technology The science of practical or industrial arts.

Test A series of questions, exercises or other means of measuring the skill, knowledge, intelligence capacities or aptitudes of an individual (or group).

Tester error A test result that can not be repeated, or is invalid because of changes in the way the test was given.

Trend The specified general direction of something.

Use rate The number of persons using a service per 100, 1000 or 10 000 of the population during a specific time period.

Utilisation The extent to which something that has been made available is being used, preferably for specified purposes.

Validity The extent to which something is reliable and actually measures or makes a correct statement about that which it claims to.

Values A set of values that an individual (or group) has which, together with personal characteristics, group norms, etc, often determine behaviour.

Variables The varying characteristics of something that is being looked at or measured.

Video A method of recording and displaying photographic images on a television screen.

Workshop A specific small (or large) group meeting where available resources are used to discuss, plan or produce specific outputs which may be written, recorded or illustrated.

References for further reading

ABBATT, F.R: "Teaching For Better Learning: A Guide for Teachers of PHC Staff". WHO, Geneva, 1980.

ACTION: "Project Evaluation Handbook" (Vol. I) and "Program Monitoring Handbook" (Vol. II) in 'Assessing Performance: A Reference Series for the Field', ACTION, Washington, 1981.

AID: "Design and Evaluation of AID-Assisted Projects", Agency for International Development, Washington, November 1980.

AMERICAN COUNCIL OF VOLUNTARY AGENCIES FOR FOREIGN SERVICE: "Evaluation Sourcebook for Private and Voluntary Organizations", ACVAFS 200 Park Avenue South, New York, NY. 10003, 1983.

AMERICAN COUNCIL OF VOLUNTARY AGENCIES FOR FOREIGN SERVICE, Technical Assistance Information Clearing House: "Approaches to Appropriate Evaluation" (a report on a series of workshops on evaluation), April 1978.

AMONOO-LARTSON, R. et al: "District Health Care: Challenges for Planning Organization and Evaluation in Developing Countries", Macmillan Press, London, 1984.

ANDERSON, S.B. et al: "Encyclopaedia of Educational Evaluation", Jossey Bass, 1976.

ANNEL, M: "Evaluation — A Tool or a Burden", Salubritas, July 1980 (3 pages).

BACHRACH, P: "Evaluating Development Programmes: A Synthesis of Recent Experience", (Occasional Paper No. 3, 1977). OECD Development Centre, 94 rue Chardon Lagache, 75016 Paris, France.

BARK, L: "Evaluation: Obstacles and Potentials", *International Journal of Health Education*, 23/3, 1980 (pp. 142–149).

BENNETT, C: "Up the Hierarchy", *Journal of Extension*, March-April, 1975 (Agricultural Impact Evaluation).

BENNETT, F.J. (Ed.): "Community Diagnosis and Health Action: A Manual for Tropical and Rural Areas". Macmillan Tropical Community Health Manuals, 1979.

BENNETT, F.J: "Community Diagnosis: Its Uses in the Training of Community Health Workers and in Primary Health Care in East Africa", *Israel Journal of Medical Sciences*, 17, 1981 (pp. 129–137).

BHOLA, H.S: "Evaluating Functional Literacy", Training Monograph 1979. (Available in English, French, Spanish, Arabic.) International Institute for Adult Literacy Methods, P.O. Box 1555, Tehran, Iran.

BROWN, J.E. and BROWN R.C: "Finding the causes of Child Malnutrition". A community handbook for developing countries produced by Task Force on World Hunger, Presbyterian Church of the U.S, 341 Ponce de Leon Avenue NE, Atlanta, Georgia 30308, USA, 1979.

CHAND, A.D. and SONI, M.I: "Evaluation in Primary Health Care: A Case Study From India", in MORLEY D. et al: "Practising Health For All" 1983 (pp. 87–100).

COHEN, J.M. and UPHOFF, N.T: "Rural Development Participation: Concepts and Measures for Project Design, Implementation and Evaluation", Cornell University, Rural Development Committee Monograph Series No. 2, 1977.

COLE KING, S: "Approaches to the Evaluation of Maternal and Child Care in the Context of Primary Health Care", WHO, Geneva HSM/79.2, 1979.

COOKE, T.D. and REICHARDT, C.S. (Eds.): "Qualitative and Quantitative Methods in Evaluation Research", Vol. 1, Sage Research Progress Series in Evaluation, Sage Publications, Beverley Hills, California, 1979.

COUNCIL FOR PRIMARY HEALTH CARE: *Proceedings* of First National Conference on Participatory Evaluation of Community Based Health Programmes, Cebu, Philippines, 1984. C.P.H.C. Third Floor Belen Building, 1787 Mabini Street, Malate Manila, Philippines.

COUVERT, R: "The Evaluation of Literary Programmes", UNESCO, 1979.

CLARKE, N: "Assessing Progress", Reports Magazine, World Education, 1980 (pp. 18–19).

CLARKE, N. and McCAFFERY, J. (Eds.): "Demystifying Evaluation", World Education, 144 Sixth Avenue, New York, NY 10019, USA, 1977.

CROSS, L. et al: "Self Survey — Towards a New Approach to Conducting Surveys in the Developing World", Philippine International Institute of Rural Development, 1980. (Also available as condensed article in *Rural Reconstruction Review*, 1981.)

CRUICKSHANK, B. et al: "Epidemiology and Community Health in Warm Climate Countries", Churchill Livingstone, Edinburgh, UK, 1976.

DEVELOPMENT COMMUNICATION REPORT: (issue on Evaluation), Number 29, January 1980, 1414 22nd Street NW, Washington DC 20037, USA.

DJUKANOVIC, J. and MACH, E.D. (Eds.): "Alternative Approaches to Meeting Basic Health Needs of Populations in Developing Countries", WHO, Geneva, 1976.

EDWARDS, N. and LYON, M.H: "Community Assessment: A Tool for Motivation and Evaluation in Primary Health Care in Sierra Leone" in MORLEY D. et al: "Practising Health For All", 1983 (pp. 101–113).

ETHERINGTON, A. "Conscientizing the Evaluator", Participatory Research Project, (paper prepared for Commonwealth Specialist Conference on Non-Formal Education for Development, New Delhi, 1979) (11 pages).

F.A.O: "Guide for Supervisors of Fieldworkers" Food and Agriculture Organization, Food Policy and Nutrition Division, F.A.O, Rome, 1982.

F.A.O: "Field Programme Management: Food and Nutrition — A Training Pack" Food Policy and Nutrition Division, F.A.O, Rome, 1982.

FEUERSTEIN, M.T: "Evaluation As Education — An Appropriate Technology for a Rural Health Programme", *Community Development Journal*, 13/2, 1978.

FEUERSTEIN, M.T: "Evalution By The People", International Nursing Review, 25/5, 1978, pp. 146–153.

FEUERSTEIN, M.T: "Participatory Evaluation — An Appropriate Technology for Community Health Programmes" *Contact*, (bulletin of the Christian Medical Commission), 55, February 1980, CMC, Geneva.

FEUERSTEIN, M.T: "Mobilization for Primary Health Care: The Role of Adult Education", *Convergence* (the international journal of Adult Education), 15/2, 1982 (pp. 23–34).

FEUERSTEIN, M.T: "Participatory Evaluation: By, With and For the People", University of Reading Rural Development Communication Bulletin (issue on Evaluation), April 1982, (pp. 18–23).

FEUERSTEIN, M.T: "Talking With the Community", *World Health Magazine*, June 1983, WHO, Geneva.

FINK, A. and KOSECOFF, J: "An Evaluation Primer", Sage Publications, 1978.

GIDEON, H: "Making the Community Diagnosis", *Contact* (bulletin of the Christian Medical Commission), World Council of Churches, Geneva, 1977.

GORDON, G: "Evaluation of Nutrition Programmes", Institute of Development Studies, University of Sussex, Brighton, England, 1975.

GUBA, E.G. and LINCOLN, Y.S: "Effective Evaluation: Improving the Usefulness of Evaluation Results Through Responsive and Naturalistic Approaches", Jossey Bass Publishing, San Francisco, 1981.

GUILBERT, J.J: "Educational Handbook for Health Personnel", WHO Offset Publication No. 35, WHO, Geneva, 1977.

HALL, B. et al: "Evaluation, Participation and Community Health Care: Critique and Lessons", 1979. International Council for Adult Education, 29 Prince Arthur Avenue, Toronto, Ontario M52 1B2, Canada (16 pages).

HALL, B: "Mtu Ni Afya — Tanzania's Health Campaign", Clearinghouse on Development Communication, No. 9, 1978.

HAMLIN DE ZUNIGA: "Evaluation as an Educational Process in Rural Health Programs in Guatemala", 1980 (unpublished).

HAMILTON, D. et al: "Beyond the Numbers Game — A Reader in Educational Evaluation", Macmillan Educational, 1977.

HARPER, W.M.: "Statistics", Second Edition M and E Handbook Series, Macdonald and Evans, Estover, Plymouth PL6 7PZ, UK, 1971.

HATCH, J: "A Record-Keeping System for Rural Households", Michigan State University Working Paper No. 9, 1981, (21 pages).

HAYES, S.R: "Measuring the Results of Development Projects", UNESCO, 1959.

HENDERSON, R.H. and SUNDARESAN, T: "Cluster Sampling to Assess Immunization Coverage: A Review of Experience with Simplified Sampling Method", Bulletin of World Health Organisation, 60/2, 1982 (pp. 253–260).

HURSH, G. and ROY, P. (Eds.): "Third World Surveys: Survey Research in Developing Nations", Macmillan, India, 1976.

INSTITUTE OF PRIMARY HEALTH CARE: "Health Worker Record System", Davao Medical School Foundation, Mindanao, Philippines, 1982.

INTERNATIONAL COUNCIL FOR ADULT EDUCATION: "Our Own Health: The Role of Adult Education in Community Involvement in Primary Health Care", ICAE, 29 Prince Arthur Avenue, Toronto, Ontario M52 1B2, Canada, 1983.

JELLIFFE, D.B: "The Assessment of the Nutritional Status of the Community", WHO Monograph Series No. 53, 1966, WHO, Geneva.

JOHNSON, M: "No Need to be Confused", Vibro, No. 18, 1978, Yayasan Indonesia Sejahtera.

KASSAM, Y: "Illiterate No More — The Voices of the New Literates from Tanzania", Tanzania Publishing House, P.O. Box 2138, Dar es Salaam, Tanzania, 1979.

KATZ, T.M: "Guidelines for Evaluation of Training Programmes for Health Personnel", WHO, Geneva, 1978.

KINDERVATTER, S: "Striving for an Ideal: The OEF Participatory Evaluation System" (mimeographed), Overseas Education Fund, Washington, 1982.

KORTEN, D.C: "Community Organization and Rural Development: A Learning Process Approach", *Ford Foundation and Asian Institute of Management*, *Public Administration Review*, Sept–Oct, 1980.

KNOTTS, B.E: "Participatory Evaluation: An Educational Process for Social Development Action", dissertation prepared for Agricultural Extension and Rural Development Centre, Reading University, UK, 1979.

KROEGER, A: "Participatory Evaluation of Primary Health Care Programmes: An Experience with Four Indian Populations in Ecuador", *Tropical Doctor*, 12, 1982 (pp. 38–43).

KROEGER, A. and BARBIRA-FREEDMAN, F: "Culture, Change and Health: The Case of South American Rainforest Indians", *Medizin in Entwicklungs landen*, 76 Seiten 1982, Verlag Peter Lang, Frankfurt Main, West Germany.

KROEGER, A. and Luna: "Atencion Primaria de Salud in Latinoamerica" Pan American Health Organization, Washington (forthcoming).

KUMEKPOR, T.K: "Fact Finding from Rural People", Current Research Report Series No. 1, Department of Sociology, University of Ghana, 1971.

KWANZA, E.V. et al: "Perception and Comprehension of Health Education Visual Aids by Rural Ghanaian Villagers" *Ghana Medical Journal*, No. 11, 4, 1972 (pp. 387–96).

LEWIS, O: "Medicine and Politics in a Mexican Village", pp. 403–34 in PAUL, D.B: "Health Culture and Community", Russell Sage Foundation, 6th reprint, 1969.

LITSIOS, S: "The Principles and Methods of Evaluation of National Health Plans", *International Journal of Health Services* 1/1, 1971 (pp. 79–85).

LYONS MORRIS, L. and TAYLOR FITZGIBBON, C: "The Program Evaluation Kit", Sage Publications, Beverley Hills, California, USA, 1979.

MACAGBA, R: "Health Care Guidelines For Use in Developing Countries", World Vision International, 919 West Huntingdon Drive, Monrovia, California 91016, USA, 1977.

MALHOTRA, P. and PRASAD, B.G: "A Study of Morbidity Among Children Below Five Years of Age in an Urban Area in Delhi", *Indian Journal of Medical Research*, 54.3, 1966 (p. 277).

McCUSKER, J: "Epidemiology in Community Health", Rural Health Series 9, African Medical and Research Foundation, P.O. Box 30125, Nairobi, Kenya, 1978.

MILLER D: "Project Tracking System", Wheaton Illinois, MAP International, November 1980.

MISSLAP, M.A. et al: "Women's Studies — Evaluation Handbook", National Institute of Education, US Department of Health, Education and Welfare, December 1979.

MORLEY, D. and WOODLAND, M: "See How They Grow: Monitoring Growth for Appropriate Health Care in Developing Countries", Macmillan Tropical Community Health Manuals Series, Macmillan Press, London, UK, 1979.

MORLEY, D., RHODE, J. and WILLIAMS, G: "Practising Health For All", Oxford University Press, Walton Street, Oxford, OX2 6DP, UK, 1983.

NEUMANN, A.K. et al: "Education and Evaluation in an Integrated MCH/FP Project in Rural Ghana: The Danfa Project", *International Journal of Health Education*, 19.4, 1976 (pp. 233–244).

NEWELL, K.V. (Ed.): "Health By the People", WHO, Geneva, 1975.

OBERG and RIOS in PAUL, D.B: "Health, Culture and Community", Russell Sage Foundation, reprinted 1969.

OVERSEAS EDUCATION FUND: "Improvement of the Socio-Economic Conditions of Low-Income Women Aged 25–50 Through the Strengthening of the Union of Moroccan Women", (duplicated report of OEF Participatory Evaluation Approach), 1982.

PAGADUAN, M. and FERRER, E.M: "Working As Equals — Towards a Community Based Evaluation System", *Community Development Journal*, 1812, April 1983 (special health issue), (pp. 146–158).

PAN AMERICAN HEALTH ORGANISATION: "Medical Auxiliaries" (Delivery of Primary Care by Medical Auxiliaries, Techniques of Use and Analysis of Benefits Achieved in some Rural Villages in Guatemala), PAHO, Washington, 1973 (pp. 24–37).

PARLETT, M: "Evaluation as Illumination: A New Approach to the Study of Innovatory Programmes", in HAMILTON, D. et al. (see earlier reference).

PATTON, M.Q: "Qualitative Evaluation Methods", Sage Publications, Beverley Hills, California, USA, 1980.

PYLE, D.F: "Framework for Evaluation of Health Sector Activities by Private Voluntary Organizations Receiving Matching Grants", AID, Washington, USA, 1982.

RAM, E: "Realization of an Integrated Health Services Programme in Rural India", *Contact* 44, Christian Medical Commission, Geneva, 1978.

RAO, P.S. et al: "Methods of Evaluating Health Centres", *British Journal of Preventive and Social Medicine*, 26, 1972 (pp. 46–52).

RIPLEY, R.M. (Ed.): "Studies in Transactional Education", McCutchan Publishing Corporation, Berkeley, California, USA, 1973.

ROEMER, M: "Evaluation of Community Health Centres", Technical Report Series Number 528, WHO, Geneva, 1973.

ROSS, D.A: "The Village Health Committee — A Case Study of Community Participation from Sierra Leone", *Contact*, No. 49, 1979, Christian Medical Commission, Geneva.

ROSSI, P.H. and FREEDMAN, H.E: "Evaluation: A Systematic Approach", Sage Publications, Beverley Hills, California, USA, 1982.

SAUNDERS, D.J: "Visual Communication Handbook", United Society for Christian Literature, Butterworth Educational, Guildford and London, UK, 1979.

SCOTNEY, N: "Health Education", Rural Health Series No. 3, African Medical and Research Foundation, P.O. Box 30125, Nairobi, Kenya, 1976.

SCRIVEN, M: "Pros and Cons About Goal Free Evaluation" in 'Evaluation Comment', Vol. 3, 1972 and "Goal Free Evaluation" in 'School Evaluation: The Politics and Process', edited by E.R. HOUSE (pp. 319–28), McCutchan Publishing Corporation, 1973.

SELLITZ, C. and JAHODA, M. et al: "Research Methods in Social Relations", Methuen and Co, London, UK, 6th reprint, 1977.

SIDDAL, S: "Getting the Message Across" (A Step-by-Step Guide to Making Health Service Noticeboards and Displays Interesting and Effective), Health Education Service (Avon), Room 48, Central Health Clinic, Tower Hill, Bristol, UK (22 pages).

SIMMONS, D. (Ed.): "Charts and Graphs — Guidelines for the Visual Presentation of Statistical Data in the Life Sciences". Institute of Medical and Biological Illustration, 27 Craven Street, London WC2N 5NX, UK. Published by M.T.P. Press Ltd, Falcon House, Lancaster, 1980.

SMITH, N.L. (Ed.): "Field Assessments of Innovative Evaluation Methods", New Directions for Program Evaluation Series No. 13, Jossey Bass Publishing, San Francisco, USA, 1982.

SMITH, N.L. (Ed.): "New Techniques for Evaluation" *New Perspectives in Evaluation*, Vol. 2, Sage Publications, Beverley Hills, California, USA, 1981.

SOLIDARIOS: "Numero Especial: La Evaluacion de Projectos de Desarollo Social" in *Solidarios* No. 18, July-September, 1981 (issue on Evaluation and Participation in Latin America). (In Spanish only.) Solidarios AP 620, Santo Domingo, Dominican Republic.

SOUMELIS, C.G: "Project Evaluation Methodologies and Techniques", UNESCO, Paris, 1977.

STEUART, G.W. et al: "Workshop in Evaluation of the Educational Component of Public Health and Medical Care Programs", University of California, USA, 1965.

STROMBERG, J.S: "Some suggestions for Improving and Applicability and Utilisation of Evaluation Assessments", paper prepared for Panama Conference 'Measurement of Impact of Nutrition and Related Health Programmes in Latin America: A Conference on Methodology', WHO, Geneva, 1977.

STRUENING, E.L. and GUTTENTAG (Eds.): "Handbook of Evaluation Research" (Two Volumes), Sage Publications, 1975.

SUAREZ, F. and CALATRONI, M.T: "Evaluacion de Programas de Accion Social", Centro InterAmericano Para El Desarollo Social, (mimeographed), undated.

SUCHMAN, E.A: "Evaluative Research", Russell Sage, reprinted 1974.

SUVA, E.G: "Experiment in Manila", (Research and Development Survey Methods), World Health Magazine, WHO, Geneva, July 1983 (pp. 5–7).

SWANTZ, M.L: "Participatory Research as a Tool for Training", *Assignment Children*, UNESCO, No. 41, 1978 (pp. 93–109).

UNDP: "Rural Women's Participation in Development", Evaluation Study No. 3, United Nations Development Programme, New York, June 1980.

U.S. DEPARTMENT OF HEALTH, EDUCATION AND WELFARE: "Descriptive Statistics, Tables, Graphs and Charts", Public Health Service, Center for Disease Control, Atlanta, Georgia 30333, USA (Publication 00-1834), undated.

WEISS, C: "Evaluation Research", Methods of Social Science Series, Prentice-Hall, New Jersey, USA, 1972.

WEISS, C.H: "Evaluating Action Programs: Readings in Social Action and Education", Allyn and Bacon Inc, Boston, USA, 1972.

WEISS, C.H: "Evaluation Research: Methods of Assessing Program Effectiveness", Prentice-Hall, Englewood Cliffs, New Jersey, USA, 1972.

WERNER, D. and BOWERS, B: "Helping Health Workers to Learn" (a Book of Methods, Aids and Ideas for Instructors at Village Level), Hesperion Foundation, P.O. Box 1692, Palo Alto, California 94302, USA, 4th Printing, 1983.

WORLD HEALTH ORGANISATION (WHO): "Development of Indicators for Monitoring Progress Towards Health for All by the Year 2000" Health For All Series, Number 4. 1981. 1211, Geneva 27, Switzerland, WHO.

"Health Programme Evaluation", Health For All Series, Number 6. WHO, Geneva, 1981.

"Planning and Evaluation of Health Education Services", Technical Report Series Number 409, WHO, Geneva, 1969.

"Research and Development (R & D) Project Carigara Catchment Area (CCA), Leyte, Philippines 1977–1982, WHO Western Pacific Regional Office, Manila, Philippines.

"Statistical Indicators for the Planning and Evaluation of Public Health Programs", Technical Report Series Number 472, WHO, Geneva, 1971.

"Evaluation of Environmental Health Programms", Technical Report Series Number 528, WHO, Geneva, 1973.

"Glossary of Terms Used in the Health For All Series, Nos. 1– 8", WHO, Geneva, 1984.

"The Place of Epidemiology in Local Health Work", WHO Offset Publication No. 70, 1982, (available in English and French).

"Methodology of Nutritional Surveillance", Technical Report Series Number 593, WHO, Geneva, 1976.

"Document AFR/NUT/84: Rapid Village Nutrition Survey Technique", WHO, Brazzaville, 1977.

"Guidelines For Training Community Health Workers in Nutrition", WHO Offset Publication No. 59, WHO, Geneva, 1981.

"On Being in Charge: A Guide for Middle Level Health Workers in Primary Health Care", WHO, Geneva, 1980.

"Background Paper on the Use of Epidemiology at the Periphery of Health Care in Developing Countries", Division of Strengthening of Health Services, SHS/79.1, WHO, Geneva (available in English and French).

"Report of Meeting Held in Geneva 5–9 March 1979 on the Use of Epidemiology at the Periphery", SHS/79.2, WHO, Geneva (available in English and French).

Background Paper on Measurement and Coverage", SHS/79.4, WHO, Geneva (available in English).

"A Review of Primary Health Care Development", SHS/82.3, WHO, Geneva (available in English).

"National Assessments of Health Care Coverage and of its Effectiveness and Efficiency", SHS/83.7, (available in English).

WHO: "Evaluating Vaccination Coverage: Training for Mid-Level Managers", WHO Expanded Programme on Immunisation.

Index

and decision making, 168–9
large scale, 23, 72
methods, 19–44, 117
objectives, 22–3, 153
participatory, 7–12, 55; meaning
  of, xi; National Conference
  1984, 28; stages in, x; types
  of, 11–12
partnership in development
  type, 12
planning for, 19–44
qualitative, 7
quantitative (aspects), 6–7
reasons for, 2–4, 12–14, 153
reporting results, 111–151
resources, 40–44
self-evaluation, 168
small scale, 72
and studying specimens, 11
time for, 16–17, 20
understanding, 1–18
use of results, 152–159
Evaluators:
  expert, 7–9
  external, 9–10, 15, 17
  internal, 9–10
Expectations:
  from evaluation, 13–14
Experiences:
  sharing, 3
  see also Results: sharing

F
Facilitator:
  in workshop, 50
Flexibility:
  in interviewing, 89
Flip boards, 44
Flow chart, 145–146
Folders, 41
  how to make, 41
Frequency distributions, 123–124
  guidelines for making, 124
  table, 124
  use of, 124
  see also Population pyramid

G
Geographic co-ordinate chart, 144
Graphs
  line, 133–134
  paper, 134
  presentation, 129–130
  as progress indicators, 135

statistical, 129
  see also Histograms
Group learning process, 79

H
Handouts:
  for information, 113
Health
  and interviewing, 92
Histograms, 134–5

I
India:
  information exchange, at
    bathing place, 57–58
Indicators, 23–8
  accessibility, 25
  availability, 25
  coverage, 26
  efficiency, 27
  effort, 27
  impact, 27
  quality, 26
  relevance, 25
  utilisation, 26
Information:
  analysis of, 50
  background, 63, 67, 117
  baseline, 162–5; type of, 164–5
  biassed, 74
  collation, 2, 50, 56, 64–109
  kind of, 162
  sources of, 37, 129
  systems, 161–2
  use of, 161
  written, 29
Interviewers, 65, 79, 84
  age of, 90
  qualities of, 90–91, 94–95
  selecting, 90–95
  training of, 85, 87, 90–95
Interviews, 37, 65, 86
  group, 87, 88
  individual, 87
  methods, 93–95; in
    questionnaires, 77–78
  probing in, 89
  structured, 88
  techniques, 87–95
  un-structured, 88, 89
Invalid evaluation, 32–34

M
Manpower:

training, 67
Maps, 37, 75, 136
  charts, 142–147
  in creative learning, 52–54
  problems of, 43
  as records, 46, 52–53
  large size, 53–54
  small size, 53
  wall maps, 54
Material resources, 17
  see also Writing materials
Measurements, 65
  at community level, 126–128
Meetings:
  community, 50–52; planning of,
    51–52
  for monitoring, 160
  in programme management, 46
  for reports, 119
  see also Workshops
Methods:
  choosing, 29–30
  of evaluation, 20
  reliability, 30–32, 33
Mimeographing machines:
  use of, 44
Monitoring:
  improvement of, 2
  of programmes, 113, 160–162
  regular, 22
  and supervision, 166
  system, 12, 161–162

N
Newsletter:
  as information, 155–158
Numbers:
  familiarity with, 128
  see also Random numbers

O
Objectives:
  of evaluation, 20, 63
  long term, 14
  and results, 112–113
  in sampling, 72
  short term, 14
  of surveys, 67
  unofficial, 22
Objectivity:
  in evaluation, 9
Observation, 54–58
  directed approach, 56
  participant, 54–55

PLEASE SEND YOUR COMMENTS/ SUGGESTIONS ON HOW THIS BOOK CAN BE IMPROVED

1. How has the book helped you in your work? . . . .
. . . .

2. Is the book well organised?   YES ☐   NO ☐

3. Could you find what you wanted easily?   YES ☐   NO ☐

4. Did you use the steps suggested for participatory evaluation?
   YES ☐   NO ☐
   Or, did you select certain parts for use?   YES ☐   NO ☐
   If yes, which? . . . .

5. Which parts of the book were least useful, and why? . . . .
. . . .

6. Is the language clear?   YES ☐   NO ☐
   If no, which words were not clear? . . . .

7. Did you find any errors in the book?   YES ☐   NO ☐
   If yes, which? . . . .

8. Did you use the List of Contents?   YES ☐   NO ☐
                     Index?   YES ☐   NO ☐
                     Glossary   YES ☐   NO ☐
                     Appendices   YES ☐   NO ☐

9. Did you find the illustrations useful?   YES ☐   NO ☐
   Did you find the photos useful?   YES ☐   NO ☐

10. Should any illustrations be removed next time?
    YES ☐   NO ☐
    If yes, which? . . . .

11. Should any photos be removed next time?   YES ☐   NO ☐
    If yes, which? . . . .

12. What difficulties did you encounter in using the book, and why?
. . . .

13. What else should be included in the next edition? . . . .
. . . .

14. What should be left out in the next edition? . . . .
. . . .

15. Have you any other suggestions/comments for improving the
    organisation of the book? . . . .
. . . .

THANK YOU FOR YOUR VALUABLE SUGGESTIONS/COMMENTS

YOUR NAME . . . .
ADDRESS/COUNTRY . . . .
. . . .
OCCUPATION . . . .
PRESENT POSITION . . . .

PLEASE RETURN TO: DR. MARIE-THERESE FEUERSTEIN
49 HORNTON STREET
LONDON W8 7NT
ENGLAND

SOLOMON LUTNICK

The American Revolution
and the
British Press
1775 - 1783

UNIVERSITY OF MISSOURI PRESS

COLUMBIA • MISSOURI

Copyright © 1967 by
The Curators of the
University of Missouri
Library of Congress Catalog
Card Number 67-15812
Manufactured in the United States of America

for Jane

Preface

FOR ALMOST TWO CENTURIES scholars have been probing into the era of the American Revolution. Countless historians have covered in detail almost every action of all the major and of many of the minor figures and events on both sides of the Atlantic for the period between 1775 and 1783. Yet, one of the greatest available mines of information is still largely unworked; there have been no serious studies of the American Revolution and the British press. Dora Mae Clark's *British Opinion and the American Revolution*, published in 1930, which mentions the bias of some English newspapers, and Fred Junkin Hinkhouse's dissertation on the press and the Revolution from 1763 to 1775, published in 1924, are the only books dealing with the subject. However, Clark's work does not concentrate on the press, and Hinkhouse's ends just when the fighting war begins. Thus, it has been my aim to fill a small but conspicuous gap in our knowledge of the War of American Independence. This study, then, will not rewrite the history of the American Revolution. Rather, it will attempt to explain the Revolution—and British reaction to it—as viewed by a press three thousand miles and over six weeks distant from the major scene of action.

My emphasis is upon newspapers and magazines. While citing letters, manuscripts, memoirs, and secondary sources, I have tried never to lose sight of the fact that a study of the press should center about the press. Thus, if I ignore some major occurrence in

America, it is because the press, lacking information, ignored it. If I give as much prominence to falsehood as to truth, it is because the British public read and, to a large extent, believed this falsehood. And if this study appears at times to disregard the findings of scholars of the Namier school, who have demonstrated that the structure of British politics consisted of small but powerful factions covering the parliamentary spectrum with "Old Tories" on the extreme right, the pro-American "Republicans" on the extreme left, and a host of other groups filling in the middle shades, it is because the press frequently ignored these distinctions. Thus, the North ministry was considered Tory, despite the fact that Lord North considered himself a Whig. *Whig* was usually a newspaper synonym for all the Opposition, regardless of how diverse and unorganized were the elements that comprised this opposition.

Attempts to measure the influence of the newspapers and magazines of this era can readily frustrate students of history, journalism, and public opinion. Most editors and printers were relatively minor figures who left us few manuscripts or memoirs. Robert L. Haig, in his detailed study of the *Gazetteer,* could not even uncover who edited the newspaper between 1776 and 1779. Yet, the importance of publications about whose owners and editors we know very little cannot be denied. Newspapers and magazines were oftentimes Britain's only source of news. They had come in large part to replace political periodicals and pamphlet literature as the main reading matter of literate Englishmen. When something significant happened in Middlesex, men in Yorkshire were reading about it within a few days; when something significant happened in America, all London usually knew of it a few hours after official word was received by the Government.

It must be borne in mind, while considering the period, that George III and the North ministry had very little trouble managing Parliament between 1775 and 1782. The King's measures were so certain of passing through the House of Commons with a handsome majority that he could afford to ignore popular opinion. Although George III insisted that the latest London and American newspapers be delivered to him as soon as they arrived, if the London press ever influenced him directly it was only to make him more intransigent in his policies concerning

America. The Opposition press's task, then, was clear: It had to convince a London populace that needed little convincing and a country populace that frequently saw eye to eye with its King that the war in America could not and should not be won. Further, it had to convince Englishmen that a government that acted without regard to the will of its citizens was on the road to disaster. What the press said, and how and why it said it comprise the major part of this study.

The late Professor Moses Coit Tyler prefaced his *History of American Literature* with the remark that it would have been easier to write his book without illustrative quotations than with them. While of the same view, I believe, too, that because this mine has never been seriously worked, this study requires some concise quotations for illumination. Rather than sprinkle *sic* throughout the book, I have corrected only the obvious typographical errors and have kept the original spelling and usage. With seventeen regularly published newspapers saying different things at the same time (and vice versa) and with the story of the war in America and British reaction to it requiring at times a topical and at times a chronological pattern, I have chosen on occasion to provide the reader with bearings. All daily newspapers carried either *daily* or *morning* in their titles. All other papers, whether morning or evening, were tri-weekly, unless otherwise noted. They were published invariably on Tuesdays, Thursdays, and Saturdays, which were the three main post nights. The date cited for a tri-weekly publication is the earliest one on the masthead; for example, the *Evening Post* for June 16-18, 1779, is cited as the *Evening Post,* June 16, 1779. In a study so replete with dates the author believed this small mercy would be appreciated by the reader.

Professor Richard B. Morris and President Robert D. Cross of Hunter College read the manuscript and made countless suggestions for its improvement. Dr. Harold C. Syrett of the State University of New York Graduate Center and Professor Joseph Raben, my colleague at Queens College, also contributed many telling suggestions. I should like also to record my debt to the librarians in the North Library and the Manuscript Division of the British Museum, the New York Public Library Rare Books Room, the William L. Clements Library of The University of Michigan, the Columbia University Library, and the Paul Klapper

Library of Queens College. The many extra courtesies extended to me by these people made the research for this book over the past decade much more a pleasure than a chore.

S.L.

Queens College
April, 1967

Contents

The British Press

Without newspapers our Coffee-houses, Ale-houses, and Barber shops, would undergo a change next to depopulation; and our Country Villagers, the Curate, and the Blacksmith, would lose the self-satisfaction of being as wife [to] our First Minister of State.[1]

B‍Y 1775 Englishmen were being exposed to a flood of written opinion, fact, and rumor concerning public questions. Regularly published newspapers and magazines were mailed from London to countless county homes, posted in taverns, public houses, and coffeehouses, and peddled in the streets of the cities. Many of these publications had been founded in the previous two decades upon commercial rather than political principles, and their sponsors consisted primarily of printers, booksellers, and editors, with a sprinkling of investors as diverse as David Garrick the actor-producer, Caleb Whitefoord the wine merchant, and James Christie the auctioneer. London's most famous printer, William Strahan, earlier Benjamin Franklin's friend and associate and now a firm supporter of the North ministry, was a major stockholder in five different publications, all of which were profitable and all of which expressed different political views.[2]

[1] *Lloyd's Evening Post*, July 24, 1780; *Chronicle*, July 25; *London Magazine*, August, 354-56. This article was written by "W.C."

[2] For Strahan's vast newspaper holdings, see British Museum (hereafter cited as BM), Strahan Papers, Add. MSS 48805-7.

The Seven Years' War had created a market of readers avid for any journal that could present the news in a fresh and interesting fashion. Lured by the hope of huge profits, many entered the field, and because war encourages newspaper sales, a large number succeeded.[3] Troubles with America and the ensuing revolution again stimulated newspaper circulation. The total number of papers sold throughout the kingdom increased steadily from 1775 to 1782, while failures became less frequent. The Stamp Tax figures demonstrate that the average daily sale of all seventeen London papers in 1775 was 41,615. Despite the imposition of an extra half-penny tax per copy in 1776, the circulation of the seventeen papers had risen by 1780 to 45,422.[4]

It must be remembered that at this time the average Englishman was at best semiliterate and could ill afford the nearly 3d. per day for his morning or evening newspaper. He consequently read (or had read to him) most of the day's publications in his favorite coffeehouse, which supplied this service to its patrons. A man reading a newspaper aloud in a coffeehouse was a common sight, and newspapers generally were not discarded "until the print wore off." So, in judging the effective number of readers (and listeners) of a publication, we may note that as early as 1711 Addison thought twenty readers for each paper sold was a modest computation. Sixty-five years later one copy of a newspaper was published daily in Great Britain for every one hundred and fifty persons. Thus, we can readily understand why Edmund Burke insisted that "newspapers are a more important instrument than is generally imagined; they are a part of the reading of all; they are the whole of the reading of the far greater number."[5] Knowing this, Burke and many other of London's leading politicians used the newspapers whenever they planned a swift, effective, and inexpensive appeal to the public.[6]

---

[3] *Lloyd's Evening Post* and the *Chronicle* were founded in 1757. The following year the *Public Advertiser* and the *Universal Chronicle* went into business. In 1759, the *Public Ledger* brought out its first issue, and two years later the *St. James's Chronicle* followed suit. See Appendix for a list of London newspapers, their editors, dates of founding, and circulation estimates.

[4] Alexander Andrews, *History of British Journalism*, I, 220: "In 1777 the circulation of papers throughout the kingdom was 13,150,642; in 1778, 13,240,059; in 1779, 14,106,842; in 1780, 14,217,371; in 1781, 14,397,620; in 1782, 15,272,519." See also Arthur Aspinall, "Statistical Accounts of the London Newspapers in the Eighteenth Century," *English Historical Review*, 63 (1948), 201-32.

[5] Quoted in F. Knight Hunt, *The Fourth Estate: A History of Newspapers and of the Liberty of the Press*, 226.

[6] Wilkes Papers (Clements), September 17, 1779, Wilkes to Petrie.

Englishmen may have been semiliterate in 1776, but in respect to politics they were far from ignorant.

Limited only by hazy libel laws, the British press published almost whatever it pleased.[7] Journalism had evolved so swiftly in the eighteenth century that the laws could not cope with editors shrewdly intent on their circumvention. The English treason acts, for example, dated back to a fourteenth-century statute of Edward III and were much too archaic for use in the control of newspapers. Juries knew that under a treason statute even a minor journalistic offender could receive severe punishment, and, consequently, they were reluctant to bring in a verdict of guilty. Although some editors still feared prosecution under the sedition or criminal libel laws, litigations were so long and costly as to discourage the Attorney General's meager staff from prosecution.[8] Further, attempts to harass the press backfired more often than not. When, in 1775, Parliament ordered copies of *The Crisis* sequestered and burned by the common hangman, people rushed all over London and paid premium prices for a publication that was previously unknown to them.[9]

The most effective weapon government could muster against the press in the eighteenth century was financial. Parliament made its first fiscal attempt to control printed matter in 1712, and the reaction was immediate. Defoe, in his *Review*, warned that an excise would not suppress criticism of the Government, but would drive it underground, and printers, publishers, and papermakers joined in the protest. This levy, which exempted publications of more than six sheets, clearly was aimed at the four-sheet newspaper press. If its real intent was suppression rather than revenue, it was successful, for it killed off more than

[7] By 1776 the Tudor and Stuart prohibitions, printing monopolies, and license systems had long been abolished; even George III had reluctantly surrendered his authority to control the press. See Frederick Seaton Siebert, *Freedom of the Press in England, 1476-1776*, 300.

[8] The single series of suits emanating from John Wilkes's famous *North Briton Review*, Number 45, cost the Government over £100,000 and was eventually lost on all counts. See H. R. Fox Bourne, *English Newspapers*, I, 172. By 1770 the Government had all but ceased prosecutions under the criminal libel statutes. Edmund Burke hoped that H. S. Woodfall's acquittal in January of that year would teach the Commons not to start petty wars with individuals. However, persons within government continued to sue newspapers for personal, rather than criminal, libel. In 1771, John Miller, printer of the *Evening Post*, at the suit of Lord Sandwich was confined in the Fleet Prison on a charge of "personal libel."

[9] *St. James's Chronicle*, March 6, 1775.

half of London's newspapers.[10] By 1714 even a journal as re-
nowned as *The Spectator* had succumbed. An advertising tax,
added to the stamp duties of 1712, made publication impossible
for many other prints, but objections from prominent literati of
the caliber of Addison, Swift, and Steele were in vain.

Primarily for purposes of control, Walpole, under George I,
increased the stamp duties once again; Pitt, needing funds to finance a war with France in 1757, raised the newspaper tax an
additional ½d. on all editions of four pages or less. The stamps on
a four-page newspaper were now 1½d., plus 2s. per advertise-
ment. This tax was fatal to fifteen marginal periodicals in 1757
and to six more in 1758.[11] By padding their papers to six sheets
per edition, editors of marginal publications could avoid this new
tax and pay only 3s. per edition, as did book publishers. The need
to fill the extra two pages encouraged the appearance of lengthy
political essays, which soon found favor with author, editor, and
reader.

In the spring of 1776, Lord North, sensing the increased
popularity of many anti-Ministry newspapers, tried to curtail
newspaper circulation by placing an additional duty upon the
press. Editors were horrified at this latest attempt to silence
them.[12] So long as "a certain fat Lord" [North] was quoted as saying, "If the people of England were so fond of reading lies in the
newspapers, they ought to pay for it exorbitantly,"[13] the press,
especially that of the Opposition, could be expected staunchly
to defend both its prerogatives and its independence before the
public. But when, in 1782, the North Government was replaced
by the Rockingham and then the Shelburne ministries, the new
and ostensibly more liberal Whig governments made no attempt
to repeal the heavy stamp duties levied upon the press by Lord
North.[14] There seemed to be bipartisan agreement that a tax on
newspapers was a simple and convenient way of raising money.

10 Siebert, *Freedom of the Press*, 312, 314. It must, however, be noted that the
existence of newspapers was so tenuous in the first half of the century that almost
half the publications on the street failed every year even before the passage of this
bill.

11 Siebert, 321.

12 *Morning Post*, April 26, 1776: "After this step we need not wonder if we
see the *Minister's edict* for the total suppression of every other print in Great
Britain except his own partial *Gazette*." See also *St. James's Chronicle*, October 12,
1775: "To enslave the Colonies, and subvert the Freedom of the Press, are the two
darling objects of the present hopeful administration. . . ."

13 *Gazetteer*, March 23, 1776.

14 Arthur Aspinall, *Politics and the Press*, 66.

Although heavy taxes limited profits, they did not operate as an effective control over the periodical press. The larger publications, well financed by a joint-stock company arrangement, could not be intimidated, and the scores of marginal publications that had been discontinued quickly reappeared with new names and with new backers, but with the same old ideas and editorial personnel:

> For as soon as morning dawns with roseate hue
> The "Herald" of the morn arises too,
> "Post" after "Post" succeeds, and all day long,
> "Gazettes" and "Ledgers" swarm a noisy throng,
> When evening comes she comes with all her train
> Of "Ledgers", "Chronicles", and "Posts" again,
> Like bats appearing, when the sun goes down
> From holes obscure and corners of the town.[15]

In fine, freedom of the press was not absolute in England during the era of the American Revolution, but the press said what it wanted to say; if freedom of expression was not legally guaranteed, it was not overtly taken away; and while an occasional jail sentence was considered a common occupational hazard for a newspaper editor,[16] legal prosecutions from either Parliament or the Attorney General's office never drove an important newspaper or magazine off the streets during this period.

In the five years before the outbreak of hostilities at Lexington, John Wilkes and a group of Opposition newspapers, ably supported by London's Lord Mayor, had successfully opened the richest field for all journalists: the proceedings in Parliament. Both houses had tried to maintain their time-honored prerogative of secrecy, but with the London populace supporting its mayor and press, Parliament retreated. One realistic member of the Commons reportedly advised his colleagues: "The best thing you can do with the press is to let it alone. It may publish some very bad speeches; but it is impossible that it can publish very much worse speeches than some that are made in this House,

---

15 George Crabbe, *The Newspapers,* 23.

16 For a description of James Perry's incarceration, see Henry Angelo, *Reminiscences,* II, 273.

and many of them are very much better."[17] The Commons has, in effect, acted upon this advice ever since. Parliament, by 1775, would confine itself to libel charges based upon imputations on the character of a member.[18]

In January, 1772, William "Memory" Woodfall (brother of Henry Sampson Woodfall of the *Public Advertiser*) commenced his reporting, which soon became legendary, of the transactions in the Commons. Since note-taking was still forbidden, Woodfall employed his phenomenal powers of recollection (or imagination) and was able to publish in his *Morning Chronicle* detailed accounts of the speeches delivered the previous day. He did not risk fine or imprisonment by attributing a speech directly to its speaker; his camouflaging of such names as Burke and Chatham as b--ke and ch--ham was no real disguise, yet it was considered legally protectible.[19] While Parliament sat, over half of the column space of the newspapers not given over to advertising was devoted to its debates. Woodfall's competitors thought highly enough of the accuracy of his reporting to freely plagiarize his words, and both the friends and foes of the North ministry agreed that Woodfall's summations were quite accurate.[20] It was more than coincidence that on November 21 and 22, 1777, five different London newspapers (the *Morning Chronicle* included) used exactly the same paragraph to sum up a speech by John Wilkes condemning the war in America.

Parliament, however, was not without weapons in its dealings with the press. At the motion of a member, the lobbies and galleries of either house could be cleared of "strangers," but this action was rarely taken. During the entire time of the American Revolution both the press and the public had almost free ac-

---

[17] Quoted in Charles Pebody, *English Journalism and the Men Who Have Made It,* 65. See also John Lord Campbell, *The Lives of the Lord Chancellors,* V, 93: "Alexander Wedderburn, when asked if a speech attributed to him in the newspapers was correct, is reputed to have made this reply: 'Why, to be sure, there are in that report a few things which I did say, but many things which I am glad I did not say, and some things which I wish I could have said.'"

[18] *Lord's Journal* (1770-73), XXXIII, 198, 200; (1774-75), XXXIV, 324, 330, 331; (1776-79), XXV, 575, 685, 692, 696.

[19] As late as December, 1778, *Gentleman's Magazine,* which by this time opened each issue with a "Summary of Proceedings in the Last Session of Parliament," still utilized this technique for stating names. The newspapers had abandoned this system by 1776 and were identifying each speaker fully.

[20] Historical Manuscripts Commission (HMC), Carlisle MSS, Report XV, Appendix VI, February 28, 1781, Anthony Storer to Carlisle. See also February 1, 1781, George Selwyn to Carlisle; and Wilkes Papers, BM Add. MSS 30872, no. 30: "My speech is given with tolerable exactness in the London Evening Post of last night."

cess to Parliament's chambers.[21] When Colonel Henry Luttrell complained in the Commons of the *Morning Post's* unfair treatment of Parliament, General Henry Seymour Conway "ridiculed the idea of shutting up the House because some men were abused in the newspapers." The Colonel, whom the Commons had awarded John Wilkes's seat in the contested Middlesex election of 1769, conceded that he "should not like to take on himself the odium of shutting the doors, and dropped his complaint."[22] Despite occasional expulsion of reporters, newspapers continued to quote the proceedings of both houses with disturbing accuracy.[23] The cliché, "informed sources close to government," had not yet entered the newspaperman's vocabulary, but when the *Gazetteer* claimed that sources of *"friendly aid* and confidential *intercourse"* were used when the galleries were cleared for reasons of "state secrecy," it was known that members of Parliament were supplying reporters with the information that closed doors denied them.[24] In November, 1776, the King made it known that he, too, was reading in the newspapers the parliamentary proceedings, which heretofore had been closed to him for fear of a breach of privilege.[25] The government erected a press gallery in 1831, finally admitting that journalists were entitled to observe and to report the proceedings of the British legislature.

Aside from reporting on the parliamentary scene, news-

---

[21] The June 13, 1781, issue of H. S. Woodfall's *Public Advertiser* apologized for the inadequate coverage of the preceding day's debates in the Commons. Its reporter came to the House one hour before the opening of the session, but the gallery was so crowded he could not enter. A substitute had to be found among those already admitted.

[22] *Horace Walpole's Journal of the Reign of George III, 1771-1783,* J. Doran, ed., II, 185, 186, dated 29 January 1778.

[23] *Gazetteer,* March 11, 1778. See also October 30, 1780. In March and November, 1775, and again in April, 1776, when Edmund Burke moved his famous resolutions for conciliation with America, the Opposition, led by Charles James Fox and John Wilkes, fought for the free admission of the press. When, on April 30, 1777, the Opposition again moved to alter the order for the exclusion of strangers, Richard Rigby, speaking on behalf of the North ministry, concluded that the only good that could result from the presence of strangers in the gallery would be printed speeches "in newspapers of all sorts." This was a blessing the North ministry clearly was prepared to do without, for the motion was easily defeated. See *Parliamentary History of England,* T. C. Hansard, ed., XIX, 205-11.

[24] *Gazetteer,* November 20, 1777. See also Peter D. G. Thomas, "The Beginning of Parliamentary Reporting in Newspapers, 1768-1774," *English Historical Review,* 74 (1959), 631-32, discussing the *Evening Post's* reports of the debates in Parliament when the doors were closed to strangers.

[25] Richard Pares, *King George III and the Politicians,* 200n.

gathering was, in the main, a secondhand affair. No periodical could afford to send correspondents to the Colonies or even to the Continent. Despite this handicap, editors kept their reading public relatively well informed. Much news was obtained from communications printed in the Government's official organ, the *London Gazette*. Heavily relied upon also were scraps of information supplied the editor by his friends in government, letters from Englishmen abroad (usually submitted free by the author's family), translations of articles from foreign newspapers, and—of special value by 1775—letters, pamphlets, newspapers, and proclamations from the Colonies in America. In addition, most large metropolitan newspapers had at least a half-dozen part-time essayists and reporters on their payrolls who wrote on everything from affairs of state to local gossip culled in coffee-houses frequented by important persons.[26] Before he became editor of the *Gazetteer* in early 1783, James Perry was paid one guinea per week for his contributions to the *General Advertiser* and an additional half guinea for helping the *Evening Post*.[27] He rounded out his income with free-lance pamphlet work.

News was so scarce that filling the columns of a four-page, four-column newspaper that came out daily or tri-weekly was indeed difficult, and editors did not overlook the myriad rumors and reports that passed across their copy desks. The reader consequently came to expect truth, half-truth, and often complete falsehood in the paragraphs of his newspaper. The press, the leading agency for disseminating news, was therefore widely mistrusted by its intelligent (and loyal) readers, regardless of political affiliation. "I am accustomed to think little of newspapers," wrote Samuel Johnson, who contributed to them.[28] Horace Walpole admitted, "It is true, most things are in the newspapers now as soon as they happen," but, he added, "so are ten thousand things that have not happened," and he concluded by pitying posterity, which he believed would not be able to discern a thousandth part of the lies of two of the Ministry's most prominent penmen, James Macpherson and Henry Bate.[29]

26 Robert L. Haig, *The Gazetteer, 1735-1797*, 178, 179, lists ten names on the *Gazetteer* payroll in 1780.

27 "Memoir of James Perry," *European Magazine*, 74 (1818), 188-90.

28 *The Letters of Samuel Johnson*, R. W. Chapman, ed., II, 482.

29 *Letters of Horace Walpole*, Paget Toynbee, ed., XII, 207, 261. See also 399: "Our newspapers are grown such minute registers of everything that happens, and still more of everything that is said to have happened, . . . if they do get hold of truth, they are sure of overlaying it by blunders. . . ."

Lord Camden, one of the leaders in Parliament of the Opposition also wrote, "The newspapers are so poisoned with falsehood, that I find it utterly impossible to distinguish the truth."[30] His words were echoed by John Wilkes, who, despite being one of the heroes of the London press, believed that the only way printers could fill "so many columns of so many newspapers" was to "print a lie one day and contradict it the next."[31]

The reader expected from his monthly magazine, which ostensibly had time to sift through the events of previous weeks, a more accurate, sober, and detached analysis. Most magazines, which in content often resembled monthly newspapers,[32] tried to fulfill this expectation. *Gentleman's Magazine,* for example, was certain to preface each yearly edition with a statement affirming its fair course. It even opened its 1778 volume with the boast, "We have adhered so strictly to impartiality, that our labours may justly be considered as something more than a brief chronicle of the times—they are authentic materials for future historians." Ralph Griffith, founder of the *Monthly Review* and its publisher from 1749 to 1803, was an excellent example of a politically impartial magazine editor. Although always in the eye of an intellectual hurricane (Oliver Goldsmith quarreled with him, and Tobias Smollett attacked him in the *Critical Review*), he saw no reason why political views should influence literary and artistic criticism. In spite of Griffith's warm friendship for Benjamin Franklin and his hearty disapproval of the Tory Government that waged war upon the American Colonies, the reader could seldom discern this bias from the pages of the *Monthly Review.*[33]

Many contributions to London's periodical press were made by major literary figures who, unfortunately for the historian, chose to publish anonymously. Although James Boswell has been identified as the author of a series of seventy essays that appeared regularly (1777-1783) in the *London Magazine,* and Smollett, Johnson (who had been on the royal payroll since 1762), George Colman, William Cowper, and Oliver Goldsmith

---

[30] *Augustus Henry, Third Duke of Grafton, Autobiography and Political Correspondence,* William R. Anson, ed., 292.

[31] Wilkes Papers (Clements) II, 194, January 3, 1780 (?).

[32] Mary Elizabeth Craig, *The Scottish Periodical Press, 1750-1789,* 33, states that *Scot's Magazine* and the other Scottish periodicals were "nothing more than a compilation of extracts from current newspapers, magazines, and books."

[33] Benjamin C. Nangle, *Monthly Review,* 11.

also have been identified, most of the writers are exceedingly difficult to recognize. The name of "Regulus," the anti-Ministry author who contributed over one hundred letters to the *Gazetteer* between 1775 and 1779 (and who was paid £160 for his services), is still unknown.[34] It may be that journalism still carried the disreputable connotation attached to it in the Walpole period of wholesale corruption of the press, or perhaps men feared the possibilities of law suits or of political repercussions. At any rate, it was clear that everybody—from Lord Sandwich to Benjamin Franklin to John Wilkes—used the press for the swift and effective dissemination of ideas, and with few exceptions the efforts of newspaper contributors to avoid discovery have been successful.[35]

All of Britain's great periodical press was published in London. The city editions circulated with such rapidity that they rendered the influence of the smaller provincial journals almost completely negligible. If a country reader desired ready knowledge of affairs in America or on the Continent, he was forced to subscribe to one of London's newspapers. His only other choice was to wait for his local publication, usually printed weekly, to copy the news from the city papers.[36] Any newspaper that failed to give its readers adequate coverage of the events on the other side of the Atlantic would have had difficulty surviving. James Donaldson, editor of the *Edinburgh Advertiser*, tried desperately to keep his publication going during the war years, but he could not provide the latest news from either America or Europe as swiftly as the London press. On July 11, 1782, as sales fell and Edinburgh readers waited for delivery of the metropolitan publications, Donaldson went out of business. In his closing issue he noted that his paper, "circumscribed as it has been in the historical de-

---

34 Haig, *Gazetteer*, 151, 152.

35 It is known that James Scott was the author of the "Anti-Sejanus" letters that were written in the interests of Lord Sandwich against the Earl of Bute. It is also known that John Horne Tooke was the influential "Another Freeholder of Surry." The identity of "Junius," the most feared and respected letter writer of the century, is still clothed in doubt. For the scores of pseudonyms that Franklin used in his letters to the press, see *Benjamin Franklin's Letters to the Press, 1758-1775*, Verner W. Crane, ed., xxvii-xxx. For Wilkes's payments to "Philo-Wilkes" see BM Add. MSS 30872 (ff 285), John Wilkes General Correspondence, VI, 63, 64.

36 Pebody, *English Journalism*, found, "In its main features the provincial press is of necessity a reproduction of the press of the metropolis." See also Mildred A. Gibb and Frank Beckwith, *The Yorkshire Post*, which states that this paper in 1777 received its news chiefly from the London journals.

partment, is ill calculated to satisfy a curiosity so ardent or an anxiety so natural at the present momentous crisis." The paper resumed publication a year later when news from abroad was no longer of such active interest to the Scottish reader. When it came to coverage of the American war, the British press both in London and the provinces was a publish-or-perish institution.

Since the Tories were strongest in the country, they controlled few powerful organs of public opinion, while the Opposition-oriented elements of the great city spoke to all Britain. A student of the provincial press has concluded recently that the country newspapers, by copying the political news from London, "educated their readers in the significant national issues, and helped to form a centralized almost national public opinion."[37] And this education had a distinctly Whiggish hue. The North ministry, therefore, was to be plagued by an overwhelmingly Opposition press from the first news of the Battle of Lexington to the day, seven years later, when it was finally driven from power, to the applause of this hostile press.

[37] G. A. Cranfield, *The Development of the Provincial Newspaper, 1700-1760,* vi.

CHAPTER I

Politics and the Press

Looking back over the blunders that allowed a civil war eventually to grow into a world conflict in which almost all Europe was arrayed against Britain, John Fielding's *Courant*, on August 11, 1781, denounced those few remaining Englishmen who were still "so destitute of principle" as to claim the "virtue" of political impartiality. "In this hour of ministerial turpitude," it asserted, "every honest man cries out shame upon . . . those creatures and those prints, that affect an impartiality." Most newspapers, however, deviated from their pledges of impartiality, and the war in America was reported by a London press hostile to the North ministry long before news of Lexington and Concord forced Englishmen to choose sides in their civil war.

George III and his supporters could find little comfort in the London newspapers. Their impressive roster of opponents included the *Middlesex Journal*, which had been founded by William Beckford, the "patriot" Lord Mayor of London, "in order to write more bitterly against the government"[1] and which now passed into the hands of supporters of Lord Camden; James Dodsley, who established his *Annual Register* in 1759 in conjunction with Edmund Burke;[2] and John Wilkes, who received support from the pages of the *General Advertiser* and the *Public Ledger*, among others. In fact, not only was the London press in the hands of the Opposition, it was in the hands of the most

1 Alexander Andrews, *History of British Journalism*, I, 182.
2 *Cambridge History of English Literature*, X, 324.

12

radical elements of the Opposition. John Almon, for example, whom Horace Walpole knew and regarded as " a rogue" and who was connected with the interests of both Lord Temple and John Wilkes, was a leader in the press's struggle to report parliamentary debates. Almon had been prosecuted, back in February, 1765, for publishing a letter on libels that defended Wilkes and his famous *North Briton*. He now used his *Evening Post* as a vehicle for directing a stream of almost treasonous invective at both Crown and Ministry, and opponents of governmental policy (including three members of the Burke family)[3] found his standard a convenient rallying point. Almon had innumerable correspondents who volunteered the information that filled his columns. Governor Pownall, Lord Camden, and Thomas Townshend were regularly in touch with him, and because he was generally regarded as "the favourite Publisher of Tracts on the Popular and Patriotic side,"[4] he never lacked for information and opinion hostile to the Government. In July, 1773, Almon's printer, John Miller, was tried by a special jury before Lord Mansfield for accusing Lord Sandwich of selling a place. He was found guilty and was fined the immense sum of £2,000.[5] The *Evening Post* had long held a bitter score to be settled with the Government.

In 1776 William Woodfall sold his interests in the *Packet* to a group of partisan Whigs, led by Alexander Chalmers, whose anti-Administration sentiments soon were reflected in the editorial bias of the newspaper. At the same time William Parker, slow to forget some earlier encounters with the Government, likewise discharged much venom in the columns of his *General Advertiser*. The *Gazetteer, Courant, St. James's Chronicle*, and scores of lesser journals, too, contributed support to the Opposition from 1775 to 1782. The Ministry's difficulties were compounded by the fact that most "moderate" and "neutral" publications also demonstrated definite hostility. For example, the "neutral" *Town and Country* magazine's most frequent contributor was Thomas Chatterton, who was thought a more out-

[3] In his *Biographical Anecdotes*, II, 347, Almon stated that the articles signed "VALENS" that appeared in his *Eevening Post* from October, 1775, to the end of 1776 were written in collaboration with the Burkes. For Almon's involvement in the trials of Junius, see Robert R. Rea, *The English Press in Politics, 1760-1774*, 174-87.

[4] BM Add. MSS 20733, numbers 6, 17, 29, 111.

[5] *Horace Walpole's Journal of the Reign of George III, 1771-1783*, John Doran, ed., I, 253.

spoken democrat than John Wilkes. And Henry Sampson Wood-fall's *Public Advertiser,* considered one of the most sober and respected publications of the era,[6] with a daily circulation of over three thousand copies and a subscription list that included almost all the members of Parliament and the King, by 1781 also reflected anti-Ministry sentiments.[7]

Unfortunately for London's Opposition press, the Marquis of Rockingham, the most powerful leader of the Opposition, thought almost as little of public opinion as did his monarch. Although the radical London press demanded a change in the Ministry and Rockingham stood to profit most from this change, there was no direct connection between the Marquis and the London editors. As long as Rockingham saw no need to alter the system of parliamentary representation that the city radicals thundered so heavily against, there could be little political rapport between the ostensible head of the Opposition in Parliament and the Opposition press.

Rockingham's lieutenants, however, concerned themselves with public opinion. In 1782, Dennis O'Bryen (or O'Brien), a noted propagandist, wrote Charles James Fox, asking to be appointed his press manager. O'Bryen called Fox's attention to the fact that there were 25,000 papers published every day in London. Allowing ten readers to every copy, he concluded that 250,000 was the reading class of the community, and they could be reached and influenced.[8] Fox took O'Bryen on, and, working mostly in the *General Advertiser,* which he edited for William Parker, O'Bryen saw to it that at least once daily this newspaper praised Fox's politics, abilities, or humanity. Fox, however, never overrated the importance of newspapers. He believed crucial subjects should first be treated in pamphlets or in a series of letters and only afterwards in newspaper paragraphs. Charges such as "secret influence at Court" he thought fit for paragraphs, but the complexities of foreign politics he wanted explained in detail "before any paragraphs alluding to them can be understood by one in a thousand."[9]

    [6] H. R. Fox Bourne, *English Newspapers,* I, 195; A. S. Collins, *Authorship in the Days of Johnson,* 256; Charles Pebody, *English Journalism and the Men Who Have Made It,* 75.
    [7] See *Public Advertiser,* January 10, 18, March 10, 30, 1781, for "nonpartisan" attacks on the Ministry and on Lord North and Lord Sandwich.
    [8] Burke Papers (Sheffield), 1782, 1, 211/1056.
    [9] BM Add. MSS 47580, folio 131, Fox to Fitzpatrick, dated November (or December), 1785.

Edmund Burke wrote regularly for James Dodsley's *Annual Register*, and his large and talented family also helped place puffs and longer articles favorable to him in the newspapers. On March 13, 1779, appeared the first issue of a short-lived Opposition publication, *The Englishman*. Sponsored by Richard Brinsley Sheridan and apparently financed by the Duchess of Devonshire, this twice-weekly newspaper came to include some of the finest satirical essays of the era. Sheridan signed his own contributions "D," while Fox's essay in the March 14 edition was signed "Z." Richard Tickell, who was Sheridan's brother-in-law, and Richard Burke also were major contributors. On June 2, however, the final issue of the entertaining but unprofitable *Englishman* was published. Sheridan was now busily penning *The Critic*, and in late 1780 he would enter Parliament from Stafford. Thanks again to the Duchess of Devonshire, he would keep his seat for twenty-six years, while becoming not only one of England's outstanding playwrights, but after 1783 one of its most important newspaper managers.[10] So, while Rockingham remained uncommunicative, three of his most ardent supporters saw to it that at least a semblance of a united Opposition appeared in the press.

In an attempt to counter these measures and bring public opinion over to its side, the Ministry not only badgered Opposition publications,[11] but it also hired writers and paid publishers in order to place its point of view in many of the leading journals. The idea of hiring writers or even of purchasing a complete newspaper operation for the purpose of establishing a Government "house organ" was not new to eighteenth-century Englishmen. Robert Walpole, while First Minister, had made an art of manipulating public opinion (in 1742 the Committee of Secrecy discovered that over £50,000 of Secret Service funds had been paid to pamphleteers and to Treasury newspapers in the last decade of his administration),[12] and Professor Namier has demonstrated that Newcastle, in the reign of George II, paid £4,000 to the hired journalists and pamphleteers who comprised his "propaganda department."[13] By 1774 John Almon had charged

---

10 An adequate account of *The Englishman* is in Walter Sichel, *Sheridan,* I, 592-95. For Sheridan's later career as a manager of the press for the Foxites, see Lucyle Werkmeister, *The London Daily Press, 1772-1792.*

11 *Chronicle,* February 13, 1777; *Morning Post,* May 2; Robert L. Haig, *The Gazetteer, 1735-1797,* 162.

12 Arthur Aspinall, *Politics and the Press,* 67.

13 Louis B. Namier, *The Structure of Politics at the Accession of George III,* 229.

that the Ministry was repeating its technique of a decade earlier (the Administration of the Earl of Bute) in order to deceive the nation by hiring writers and newspapers and by printing immense numbers of pamphlets that were sent through the mails, free of postage and expense, to every part of the kingdom. Almon accused, among others, the hired pens of Samuel Johnson, James Macpherson, William Knox, and Israel Mauduit of "deluding and duping" the nation as to the true state of affairs in America.[14] At the same time, Thomas Townshend attacked Lord North in the Commons because of the pensions bestowed by the King "on those notorious Jacobites" Samuel Johnson and John Shebbeare.[15] On October 3, 1775, "DETECTOR" made it clear in in the *Morning Post* that liberty of the press, one of England's "greatest blessings and dearest privileges," was in jeopardy because "needy and profligate writers," hired by the Administration, were subverting this liberty by writing "with a pensioned hand" rather than with honest and honorable political motives. "DETECTOR" also gave the alerted reader some of the pen names used by the most prominent "ministerial scribblers." Five years later "BRITANNICUS," writing in the *Public Advertiser,* made the same charges.[16] Both of these anonymous authors did not know, but would not have been surprised to learn, that John Robinson, North's Secretary to the Treasury, was indeed paying printers and authors for the publication of anti-American tracts.[17]

Dr. John Shebbeare and the playwright Hugh Kelly were two of the most prolific penmen for the Government. Shebbeare had been a professional propagandist since the 1750's, turning out almost a hundred books and pamphlets and probably ten times that number of letters and articles to newspapers and magazines. "A confirmed Jacobite," he had stood in the pillory in the reign of George II; he now enjoyed a pension in the reign of George III. The *Public Ledger* attacked him so violently in July and August, 1775, that Shebbeare published a 179-page defense late in the year. In so doing, however, he confessed that he was on the pension list for services rendered with his quill. Within a few months he brought out a 212-page challenge to Richard Price's pro-American essay, *Origin, Progress and Establishment of National So-*

---

[14] John Almon, *Anecdotes of the Life of William Pitt, Earl of Chatham,* II, 108, 109.

[15] *Walpole's Journal,* I, 307, 308.

[16] *Public Advertiser,* October 16, 1780.

[17] BM Add. MSS 48803, William Strahan's Quarto Ledger, 1768-1785, IV.

ciety. On July 24, 1776, the *Morning Post* vigorously attacked Shebbeare for propagating a "most dam--ble parcel of lies!" and for forgetting that, like a weathercock, he became useless the moment he was "fix't."[18] William Mason, writing as "Malcolm Macgregor" in 1777, referred to Shebbeare as

> The same abusive, base, abandoned thing
> When pilloried or pensioned by a king,

while Smollett depicted him as "Ferret" in *The Adventures of Sir Launcelot Greaves*. On April 24, 1777, Almon's *Evening Post* warned its readers that Shebbeare again was poisoning the ink of the pro-Ministry press.

Kelly, too, was an old hand at writing short essays and political paragraphs for the press. He was so acidulous a critic of the drama that in the 1760's he was called "the scourge of the theater," and reaction to his opinions necessitated his wearing a sword while walking through the streets of London. After penning a moderately successful sentimental comedy, Kelly became a lawyer in 1774. But he never ceased attacking the parliamentary Opposition, which presently was to get its revenge. Kelly's comedy *A Word to the Wife* was condemned in the London press not so much because it was a poor play, but rather because it was the creation of a bitter political foe.[19] When he died suddenly in March, 1777, the *Chronicle* used its entire first page and a full column of its second to pay homage to a literary figure whose great contribution was more in the service of his Ministry than in that of his craft. Mrs. Kelly and the children received, of course, a handsome pension from the Crown.[20]

It was impossible to determine exactly how many colleagues Kelly and Shebbeare had on the royal payroll. The Opposition *Evening Post* ran a series of articles with biographical sketches of the men it was certain were being paid well "for the daily letters and paragraphs which they insert in the several newspapers . . . telling the nation idle tales about the conquest of America." Sir John Dalrymple (like Shebbeare a "notorious Jacobite"), Samuel Johnson ("a pedant in letters, a brute in manners, and a jacobite in principle"), and William Knox (the "ignorant,

---

[18] The *Morning Post*, July 15, 1783, stated that Shebbeare's pension was £300 per annum.

[19] *Memoirs of the Life of David Garrick*, Thomas Davies, ed., II, 133-38, 142, 143.

[20] *Chronicle*, April 1, 1777.

illiterate, petulant and arrogant Under Secretary to Lord George Germaine") were among the foremost of this "mercenary band of *hired* writers, or rather assassins, whom Ministers keep in pay, to daily whitewash their proceedings," according to the *Evening Post*.[21]

The exact amount expended through the Secret Service Fund, the pension and place lists, and the King's and Minister's private accounts was not known. The *General Advertiser* was certain that huge sums were being spent by the Ministry to have its point of view expressed so that Englishmen could be "deceived, duped, and seduced into an opinion that this unhappy, wicked, and self-destroying war against America, was a right measure."[22] Horace Walpole charged, late in 1781, that James Macpherson, whom he detested, "had a pension of £800 a year from Court for inspecting newspapers, and inserting and deleting what lies he pleased." Macpherson had also been a Jacobite, and while he quarreled bitterly with Johnson over the authorship of the poems of Ossian, North considered him "a most laborious and able writer in favor of Government." His *Short History of the Opposition During the Last Session*, published in 1779, North considered "the best defense of the American war." In writing to the King in March, 1782, North credited Macpherson with producing "almost all the good pamphlets on the side of the Administration."[23] Macpherson had been on the private list of pensioners before North came to office in 1770, and his pension of £500 per year had been supplemented by a sinecure as Secretary to the Province of West Florida that paid him £300 annually. Besides writing tracts and placing pro-Ministry squibs in the newspapers, Macpherson kept busy appealing to important members of the Government for additional place and preferment for himself and for his relatives.[24] He repeatedly sought a seat in Parliament, and it was granted him in 1780.[25] He was sent to the Commons from

21 *Evening Post*, October 14, 1778.

22 *General Advertiser*, November 20, 1777.

23 *Correspondence of King George III*, Sir John Fortescue, ed., V, March 26, 1782, North to King.

24 On February 13, 1779, Macpherson wrote Charles Jenkinson, asking for promotion of a relative who was a lieutenant in the army; on July 11, 1781, he again sought preferment, this time for another relative. See Liverpool Letterbook, BM Add. MSS 38306 nos. 109, 148.

25 For Macpherson's plea for a seat in Parliament and for his intervention concerning certain military promotions, see HMC, Abergavenny MSS, 10th Report, 27, dated 18 December 1779, and 30, dated 28 April 1780, letters to John Robinson.

the Government borough of Camelford, in Cornwall. Although he sat in Parliament until his death in 1796, he never spoke. But if, as Smollett said, one good writer was equal to twenty placemen, Macpherson earned his keep. His pen constantly pricked the Opposition, and his effectiveness can be gauged by the amount of vituperation his works brought down upon him and by the fact that his regular requests for favors were as regularly heeded. The highly biased Walpole was certain that Macpherson, along with Joseph Galloway ("an American renegade") and the "still more infamous Bate," were a triumvirate of editorial "profligate abuse."[26]

The Opposition, of course, stoutly maintained that its columns were uncorruptible. John Horne, who in 1777 was imprisoned for criminal libel because he accused the British of committing murder at Lexington and Concord,[27] asserted in 1782 that an assistant editor of the *General Advertiser,* a loyal Foxite who earned four guineas a week, turned down a pension of £400 per annum "with scorn, and persevered through a long career of opposition, until he at length obtained wealth, celebrity, and independence." Horne lamented that he was not at liberty to disclose the name of his subject and thus to document his assertion beyond doubt.[28]

On occasion the anti-Ministry forces, too, were accused of seeking favorable treatment in the press. In fact, the *Morning Chronicle* reported an "equally strange and incredible" rumor that the American Congress had voted $1,000 to the printer of an evening paper "for the spirit with which he and his correspondents had maintained their side of the question."[29] Later, "DETECTOR AMERICANUS" attacked London's "several hireling American newspapers," which, he declared, were edited by a "hired host who

---

[26] *Walpole's Journal,* II, 483.

[27] For the trial of John Horne (he presently added *Tooke* to his name), see John Horne (Tooke), *The Trial of John Horne, Esq., for Libel.* The British Museum has Horne's copy, with his marginal notes and comments. See also *Morning Chronicle,* November 20, 25, 1777; *Gazetteer,* November 25; *St. James's Chronicle,* November 25. The loyal *Morning Post* did not report the trial.

[28] *Memoirs of John Horne Tooke,* Alexander Stephens, ed., II, 483.

[29] *Morning Chronicle,* September 14, 1776. Arthur Aspinall, in *Politics and the Press,* 68, noted that most newspapers in the 1780's and 1790's received less than £200 per year from the Secret Service Fund, as did most "newspaper hacks" who wrote for the Ministry. These amounts seem too meager to have swayed any newspaper's editorial viewpoint. They probably were expended by the Government for favorable coverage of a particular issue.

forge lies against the land of their nativity."[30] He could not document these charges, however, because Congress gave no indication that it had any interest in bribing English publications. Curiously enough, the French were not accused of bribing the press to accomplish their political ends. Aside from one clever letter by Caron de Beaumarchais to the *Morning Chronicle* on May 6, 1776 (he had found a lady's mantle and was certain she was the most "alert beauty" in Britain—which he defined as being England, Scotland, and Ireland—but not America), it appears that France did not attempt to influence British public opinion via the press. The American cause in the British press, notwithstanding the letters of Benjamin Franklin, Charles Lee, or a few others, was championed by a group of radical London editors whose only reward was the downfall of the North ministry of George III. Conviction, political opportunity, petty faction, or downright disgust with the Government may have driven many editors into the camp of the Opposition, but none sold themselves to the cause of America.

The story of the war in America could not be told impartially. Because the Government could—and did—at pleasure withhold some official accounts and distort others, its versions of the news were regularly attacked by the Opposition press, which maintained that its own sources either entirely contradicted the official versions of the news reported in the *London Gazette* or else illuminated some glaring, and usually embarrassing, governmental omissions.[31] The Secretaries of State were responsible for the publication of the *London Gazette*, and any profits that accrued from its sales were deemed perquisites of office and were duly shared between them.[32] It was the task of the American Department to select the news and dispatches from the Colonies that were to be published. From the day in 1770 when he was appointed as Under Secretary of State for America to 1782, when

30 *Morning Chronicle*, January 3, 1778. On March 6, this newspaper copied from a forged "American Gazette" being circulated in London's West End the story that the editors of the *Public Ledger* and the *Evening Post* were granted medals by America for their pro-American "inflammatory puffs and impudent representations."

31 *St. James's Chronicle*, July 30, 1775; *Middlesex Journal*, August 1, 1775, and May 7, 1776; *Morning Chronicle*, July 12, 13, 1776.

32 Margaret M. Spector, *The American Department of the British Government, 1768-1782*, 84-85.

the Shelburne ministry abolished the position, William Knox chose the official items of war news Englishmen were permitted to read.[33] Knox knew more about America than did most of his contemporaries in the Government. From 1757 to 1761 he had been Provost Marshal of Georgia. For the next four years he was the London agent for Georgia and East Florida; he was removed from that position by the Colonies for writing a pamphlet defending the Stamp Act. While Knox's reputation as a propagandist was enhanced in 1775 with the publication of *The Claim of the Colonies to Exemption from Taxes imposed by Authority of Parliament, examined,* he rarely published anything subsequently. There is no evidence that Knox ever wrote to or for any newspapers or magazines while serving in the American Department, but the extreme confidence placed in him by his superior, Lord George Germain, rendered Knox vulnerable to the Opposition, which was certain that he was regularly writing to the press in defense of the Ministry and its American policies.

Knox and the *London Gazette* made certain that good news from the Colonies traveled fast, but, as one editor asserted, when bad news was to be disseminated, "it was some days before the accounts are sufficiently garbled, to be laid before the public; and it is generally some weeks before half the truth is really known."[34] As soon as rumor of an important action in America spread, readers waited for the next edition of the tri-weekly *Gazette* or for a *Gazette Extraordinary,* and if no clarifying information appeared in the royal publication, they assumed that "the news was of such a nature as the Ministry thought improper to be published."[35] The Opposition press regularly advised its readers to distrust the "nonsense and falsehoods" of the *London Gazette.*[36] The *Westminster Journal* called the *Gazette*'s compilers "dealers in Fustian" who were busy building castles in air,[37] while the *General Advertiser* argued that the American gazettes were now far more

[33] HMC, Knox Papers, September 25, 1777, Germain to Knox; see also August 22 and October 31, 1777, and December 29, 1780, when Germain wrote Knox: "I suppose you will publish in the Gazette on Saturday. . . ." See also Knox Papers not calendared in HMC (Clements) November 13, 1777, Germain to Knox. For Knox's pamphlets, see Almon's *Biographical Anecdotes,* II, 12-15.

[34] *Morning Post,* September 20, 1776.

[35] *Evening Post,* December 3, 1776.

[36] *Evening Post,* September 10, 1776, November 1, 1777. The *Morning Post,* July 5, 1776, printed a letter that stated that the *London Gazette* and the Poet Laureateship were to be consolidated into one office because "they both speak the language of fiction." See also *Courant,* May 15, June 16, 1781.

[37] *Westminster Journal,* February 21, 1778.

accurate than their London counterparts.[38] At best, it was believed the journal that was "Published by Authority" could be
counted upon to deliver only a highly biased version of affairs
in America; even editors loyal to the North ministry occasionally
found it necessary to criticize the "absurd" reports carried in the
Gazette.[39]

Yet, however untrustworthy these official reports, they eventually proved to be more nearly accurate than the conflicting
information that appeared in London's other publications.[40] One
letter writer declared, in May, 1775, that the daily accounts in
the public newspapers were so little founded in truth that not
one article in twenty could in the least be depended on.[41] Three
months later another wrote that not one account in ten could be
relied upon.[42] Despite this reputed improvement in so brief a
period, wild conjectures continued to appear during the war
years. An unidentified correspondent, commenting to the *St.
James's Chronicle* on the most absurd rumors propagated by the
Ministry—the conditions of hunger that led the American troops
to eat one another, the Washington-Mrs. Gibbons tale, and the
murder of the American Commander by his own sentinels—concluded that of the many advantages derived by England from
the American war, "the great improvement in the Art of political
Lying is not the least considerable."[43] So long as accounts of this
kind flooded the newspapers and magazines and so long as both
sides accused one another of inventing these accounts, the *London
Gazette* could be used to advantage by all editors. The Ministry's
prints adhered closely to its official accounts of the proceedings
in America, while the Opposition press assumed that anything
printed in the "Royal Lying Gazette" was often far from the truth.
Gentleman's Magazine, studying scores of "spurious accounts"
of the war that were circulating throughout England, accurately
concluded in late 1777 that it was no easy matter to distinguish
truth from falsehood.[44]

38 *General Advertiser*, October 8, 1779: "Good God! how we are changed, the
vain bombast of France has taken possession of Britain and the old rough honesty
of Britain has fled to America!"

39 *Morning Herald*, January 18, 1781.

40 The pro-Ministry *General Evening Post*, December 16, and the Opposition
Gazetteer, December 19, 1777, agreed that the *London Gazette*'s version of the
battle at Saratoga was both accurate and impartial.

41 *Gazetteer*, May 17, 1775.

42 *Gazetteer*, August 18, 1775.

43 *St. James's Chronicle*, January 2, 1777.

44 *Gentleman's Magazine*, October, 1777, 501. See also May, 1776, 231.

Aside from the *London Gazette*, in mid-1776 the *General Evening Post*, a moderate and well-respected tri-weekly newspaper,[45] was the only important London publication a Tory could buy with confidence. From the very beginning of the difficulties in America this newspaper proclaimed its impartiality, but the tone of the majority of its letters, paragraphs, and introductory remarks convinced the reader of its Tory predilections.[46] However, when provoked by what it believed to be ministerial error, the *General Evening Post* asserted its political independence. When rumor of an additional impost upon newspapers prompted a petition from the London Association, this paper praised the association's action against the "PRESENT MINISTERIAL TYRANTS," who were "striking against the EXISTENCE OF A FREE PRESS." But it warned other publications that with freedom came responsibility, which many were rejecting by filling "the public prints with panegyrics upon rebellion and libelous aspersions upon the conduct of men who are labouring to secure our rights and properties."[47]

Lloyd's Evening Post, which sold best in the more conservative provinces, was the only other London newspaper to support the Ministry. The *Post* was a tri-weekly tabloid that had been set up in 1757 by a group of eleven partners (including four printers, two of whom were William Strahan and Richard Cave, owner-editor of *Gentleman's Magazine*) as an imitation of the more successful *London Chronicle*.[48] As early as March, 1775, it came out strongly against the American "Sons of Sedition." On April 3 it stressed the "absurdity and downright lunacy of our making the smallest concessions to the rebellious colonists!"[49] It continued to reflect the Ministry's stand throughout the war. The *Packet* called *Lloyd's* a "motley medly of soporific dullness" that not only plagiarized from the morning press, but—still worse—it transcribed stories "however incredible, ill-founded or flagrant, and propagated them with malevolent delight" if they happened to favor the Ministry. It recommended that *Lloyd's* be used as wrapping paper.[50]

[45] John B. Nichols, *Literary Anecdotes of the Eighteenth Century*, IV, 466-67.

[46] *General Evening Post*, June 22, 1775, February 27, October 12, 1776. On January 26, 1776, "Epigram" blamed the Whigs on both sides of the Atlantic for commencing this "most wonderful dispute twixt royalty and Vermine. . . ."

[47] *General Evening Post*, July 28, October 7, 1775. For a later loyal view, see November 23, 1779.

[48] Strahan Papers, BM Add. MSS 48893, pack 1.

[49] *Lloyd's Evening Post*, March 24, April 24, and April 26, 1775.

[50] *Packet*, June 1, 1778; *General Advertiser*, January 26, 1779.

In mid-October, 1776, London's two Tory publications received reinforcement from a most unexpected quarter. Without warning, the Reverend Henry Bate's *Morning Post,* the gossip-column newspaper with the largest circulation in Britain, consummated the most important editorial revolution of the decade when it converted from an independent anti-Ministry policy to one of a firm defense of the North Government.

Bate began his improbable career as curate to the Reverend James Townley, Vicar of Hendon. It was through Townley, who wrote the popular farce *High Life Below Stairs,* that Bate became friendly with David Garrick. While editing the *Morning Post,* which he did from its inception in 1772, Bate soon became a dramatist in his own right. In 1775 Garrick produced his comic opera *The Rival Candidates* at the Drury Lane, and in 1779 *The Flitch of Bacon* was staged there. Garrick also reviewed plays and wrote of the theater for Bate.[51] Bate's escapades, both in and out of the theater, involved him in at least four duels. He also criticized men in his *Morning Post* with what John Taylor called a "sportive severity"; he was tried at King's Bench for adultery; and he behaved generally as though he was trying to supply copy to all gossip columnists of the contemporary press. Yet Bate was both respected and feared for the power of his pen, and his purchase by the Government demonstrated that the Ministry was not oblivious to the importance of publicizing the official version of the war in America.[52]

Aside from an occasional letter attacking the minority or the Americans,[53] the *Morning Post* gave no prior indication that it was to become London's leading Tory journal. While never in sympathy with the American cause,[54] the *Morning Post* had for-

51 James Boaden, *David Garrick's Private Correspondence,* II, 197-98, 225-26, dated December 25, 1776, and June 11, 1777. For the many letters between Garrick and Bate, see David M. Little and George M. Kahrl, *The Letters of David Garrick,* III, *passim.*

52 When North settled his accounts with George III in April, 1782, Bate and Macpherson were the only editors or authors on the pension lists. See Fortescue, *Correspondence of King George III,* V, 465-72.

53 *Morning Post,* May 26, 1775, "Political Looking Glass" attacked "the degraded" Lord Camden and his followers. See also January 13, 1776, for an attack upon the Americans.

54 *Morning Post,* August 24, 1776, compared the Americans to the ancient Romans, who built an extensive empire by thieving and robbing. It considered the "transported pickpockets, reprieved felons, the refuse of prison and jails," etc., which, it stated, comprised the American population, as trying to emulate the Romans upon whom Heaven smiled for so long.

merly been one of the Government's outstanding critics. It had discounted Lord North for being "no Prime Minister but merely an office creature confined to the treasury,"[55] while complaining that American affairs were "too ridiculous to laugh at." It believed the Administration's impotence was "inexcusable" and its military talents were "well adapted to convert a flower into a thistle."[56] Moreover, the *Morning Post* had maintained that the Ministry was so divided that only a Chathamite coalition could save the day. Reporting that a recovered and healthy Chatham would soon be leading the House of Peers "as gallantly as ever" and that this unexpected intelligence had a more distressing effect on the Government "than their whole train of American miscarriages put together,"[57] the *Morning Post* in early 1776 adequately demonstrated that it preferred a change in the Ministry.

The *Morning Post*'s attacks upon the parliamentary minority and the American "rebels" began on October 15, 1776. Suggesting that political opposition be stifled with bribes, it reported that Lord Rockingham was ready to abandon "Poor Edmund" Burke and come over to the Government and that Charles James Fox had "fixed his price with administration."[58] Militarily, "the cowardice of the panic-smitten Yankies, at Long Island" reflected credit on Lord Sandwich, who had told the Ministry's critics in Parliament that the Americans "never would face a body of the King's troops, like soldiers or men."[59]

The Opposition assumed, and Tories rarely denied, that the sudden shift in allegiance of the *Morning Post* was purchased with the promise to Bate of an immediate pension and perhaps an eventual peerage.[60] By contemporary standards, Bate was paid a small fortune. For a while he received a pension of £200 per annum, but in 1781 Lord North settled all of Bate's claims upon the Government for £3,250, which was duly taken from the Secret Service account under the head of Pensions and Preferments.

[55] *Morning Post,* September 27, 1775.

[56] *Morning Post,* October 20, 1775, January 20, 1776. See also March 20, October 19, November 7, 1775, and January 16, 1776.

[57] *Morning Post,* February 27, 1776.

[58] *Morning Post,* October 15, 17, 1776.

[59] *Morning Post,* October 21, 1776.

[60] *General Advertiser,* June 18, July 10, 1778, February 18, 1780. See also *Public Ledger,* November 17, 1778, and *Gazetteer,* December 12, 1778. Bate, in the *Morning Herald,* November 22, 1781, admitted he was pensioned by the Government. See also the *Poetical Review,* published anonymously in London in 1780, for a poem condemning Bate for getting a position in return for selling "a Kingdom and his Freedom too."

In defense of this large expenditure, North wrote the King that Bate kept his newspaper "open for all writings in favour of Government" and that "to do Mr. Bate justice, he was a very constant, diligent, zealous and able, though perhaps too warm a writer on the part of government."[61] The King refused, however, to be privy to this agreement. North made it clear that David Garrick had represented the Ministry in the transaction, but George III washed his hands of the deal by writing North that Bate's preferment represented "an article that never was stated to Me, and therefore for which I cannot stand indebted the £3250 to that worthless man, Mr. Bates. . . ."[62] The *Morning Post* had few friends even amongst its sponsors. No evidence indicates that George III ever called for a copy.

Few doubted that Bate was earning his pay. Under his care the *Morning Post* tampered with some facts, withheld others, and generally brought the tone of its politics down to the sex-and-spice level of its social columns. Respectable Englishmen of all political persuasions detested, feared (and frequently read) the *Morning Post*. Samuel Johnson would not allow Boswell to give Bate credit for possessing any merit, although the Doctor did admit that Bate had courage, a quality always respected "even when it is associated with vice."[63] Horace Walpole considered "the vile author of the Morning Post" to be "the worst of all scandalous libellers,"[64] while the Earl of Carlisle, writing to George Selwyn, a Tory member of the Commons, mentioned in reference to the *Morning Post* that "your maxim is to despise the nonsense; mine is, not to read it."[65]

Opposition editors believed the "Reverend Trumpeters Morning Post" so flagrant in its perversion of truth on behalf of the Ministry that only "exposure paragraphs" could counterbalance the harm being done by Bate. The *General Advertiser* frequently began columns with a quotation from the previous issue of the *Morning Post*, usually labeling the column "the ministerial lie of yesterday." The article would proceed to print a "factual" refuta-

61 Fortescue, *Correspondence of King George III*, V, 471, dated 18 April 1782.

62 Fortescue, *Correspondence of King George III*, VI, 7, dated 5 May 1782.

63 James Boswell, *Life of Johnson*, G. B. Hill, ed., revised by L. F. Powell, IV, 296-97.

64 *Walpole's Journal*, II, 427, 464. See also *Letters of Horace Walpole*, Paget Toynbee, ed., IX, 440; XI, 185.

65 John Heneage Jesse, *George Selwyn and His Contemporaries*, III, 165-66.

tion of the ministerial pronouncement.[66] The *Packet* also corrected misinformation found in "that vile receptacle of ministerial subterfuge,"[67] while the *Public Ledger* of December 11, 1778, entitled one corrective article "Ministerial Trash in the Morning Post of yesterday." This column quoted a dozen remarks and then corrected everything in them, from Bate's grammar to his "lying politics." The *General Advertiser* vowed to continue its crusade against the *Morning Post* so long as it continued "by command, patronage, and bribe" to poison the channels of public information. It was horrified at the report (proven false) that Bate not only claimed the pension of £300 made available by the death of David Hume, but that he had it raised to £400 for doing nothing more than "lying, puffing, and abusing for the ministry."[68] The *Packet* was still more violent in tone. Affirming that Bate, an "impudent slave" in the pay of "Jemmy Twitcher" (Lord Sandwich),[69] was daily driven to barefaced inconsistencies in order to earn his *"unhallowed"* bread,[70] it expressed the hope that he and the ministers he served would eventually be brought to the block.[71] That a statement so crude did not bring the editor of the *Packet* to the bar is eloquent testimony of the freedom—and license—of the press.

At first the *Morning Post* ignored most of these attacks, but by the summer of 1778 Bate was leveling countercharges against his assailants. On July 25 he referred to "an impudent falsehood published by the republican printers"; on July 30 he labeled the

[66] *Morning Post*, June 18, 1778. Cf. *General Advertiser*, January 19, June 19: "The ministerial lie of yesterday was, that Sir Henry Clinton has attacked General Washington and defeated him. There is no vessel arrived." See also *Evening Post*, June 23, August 29, 1778; *Public Ledger*, September 22, 25, November 17, 19, 20, December 29, 1778.

[67] *Packet*, July 3, September 25, October 12, 23, November 13, December 28, 30, 1778.

[68] *General Advertiser*, July 10, 15, 25, 27, 29, August 7, 22, 23, 24, 25, 28, 29, October 5, 1778, *et passim*.

[69] Jemmy Twitcher, a character in Gay's *Beggar's Opera* had "peached" upon Captain Macheath. Sandwich acquired this nickname in 1765 when he led the prosecution against John Wilkes, a former friend. "This treachery made him, perhaps, the most unpopular man of his time. . . ." *The Private Papers of John, Earl of Sandwich, 1771-1782*, G. R. Barnes and J. H. Owen, eds., I, xi.

[70] *Packet*, July 13, 1778. See also *Evening Post*, October 14, affirming that the Tory admiral, Hugh Palliser, negotiated the "purchase matter" between Sandwich and Bate.

[71] *Packet*, July 20, 1778. On August 26, the *Packet* requoted from other newspapers the "logical rumour" that Bate, "scavenger in ordinary to the ministry," would be made a member of Parliament. See also article in July 24 issue, affirming that he would probably be made a bishop. Bate was made a baronet in 1813.

Opposition journals "the traiterous papers"; on August 8 he condemned "a certain morning paper that is too *contemptible* to be named"; and by August 25 the *Morning Post* was engaged in a newspaper war when it attacked the *Public Ledger* for being "a wretched, contemptible, republican print." The term *republican* was to join *patriot* as an epithet of opprobrium in the columns of the *Morning Post*. Bate endeavored to discredit his adversaries by associating them with radical movements and by rarely using the violent language so often found in their columns. His comments affirming that the *Public Advertiser* "was remarkable for the staleness of its intelligence" and that the *Public Ledger* was "founded in falsehood"[72] were mild indeed compared to the invective Bate's enemies used to describe him and his journal.

The widespread knowledge that the *Morning Post* could be counted upon to disseminate the latest ministerial "closet talk" made it important even to its enemies. Often a hint that the "propagators of rank treason" presently would be punished caused Opposition editors temporarily to mend their ways. The *Public Ledger's* notorious and anonymous "CURTIUS" gained such renown for his remarks about both the Ministry and the *Morning Post*[73] that on December 1 the *Public Ledger* apologized for omitting "CURTIUS's" previously advertised "Letter to the King" because, it declared, however true the charges, truth alone "might not guard the publication from attack."

The Opposition expected that even Bate's most loyal followers eventually would discover the frauds perpetrated upon them and cease purchasing the *Morning Post*.[74] But Bate, relying upon the mammoth circulation of his paper (he boasted it was about 5,000 daily, but it was probably closer to 3,500),[75] remained unperturbed. Confident that there would always be an audience for the type of scandal and gossip that filled his social columns, he knew his reading public could be counted upon to purchase his newspaper from conviction, habit, or curiosity. He was helped also by semiofficial support from the Government, which tried to make certain that the *Morning Post* was the only newspaper sold at

---

72 *Morning Post,* March 6, 9, 30, May 1, 1779.

73 *Public Ledger,* November 17, 18, 1778. "CURTIUS," describing Bate as "an unhappy deserter of his God, and scourge of his country" who was "the mere entrance into the Augean Stable of the State," thought it expedient to "sweep away the nuisance from the door before taking notice of the filth and ordure within. . . ."

74 *Packet,* September 25, 1778; *General Advertiser,* January 30, 1779.

75 *Morning Post,* October 26, 1778.

military encampments.[76] Although the Opposition press regularly announced that it was nibbling away at the *Morning Post*'s circulation,[77] for years Bate was quite secure. So long as the interests that supported him made good profit, why should he be replaced? The *Morning Post* had been founded as a business venture by the bookseller John Bell, with about ten other partners, and the investors recognized that its immense success was due in no small measure to the controversial parson who catered so capably to the tastes of his large reading audience.

Bate's political judgments were not the same as those of most of the *Morning Post*'s owners. In late 1776, when he had first brought the paper over to the side of the Ministry, his employers (who included Alderman Thomas Skinner, a noted member of the London radical movement) attempted to dissuade him from his position. Bate called them a "parcel of cowards," and he eventually forced Joseph Richardson, the only bachelor among the owners, to defend his honor. Neither Alderman Skinner nor the other owners felt disposed to take the field against Bate. Upon wounding Richardson slightly in the right arm, Bate apparently vindicated his challenge; he was not removed from his position nor were the *Morning Post*'s politics changed.[78]

On February 25, 1780, Bate overstepped the bounds of legal propriety when, in a column titled "Queries," his newspaper stigmatized as a rebel and a traitor the Duke of Richmond, a prominent leader of the Opposition who was most unpopular with the Ministry (Charles Jenkinson wrote John Robinson that "if there were two Dukes of Richmond in this country, I would not live in it").[79] The Duke immediately pressed charges at King's Bench, and Bate, convicted of atrocious libel, was in August sentenced to prison for twelve months.[80]

[76] *General Advertiser,* January 11, 1779.

[77] *General Advertiser,* January 1, 4, 30, 1779. See also July 9, 1778, for an earlier claim that its circulation was rising at the expense of the *Morning Post,*

[78] For details of Bate's career, see *Memoirs of James Stephen,* Merle M. Bevington, ed., 288-95; James Boaden, *Memoirs of the Life of John Philip Kemble, Esq.,* II, 38; and the chapter on Bate in John Fyvie, *Noble Dames and Notable Men of the Georgian Era.*

[79] HMC, Abergavenny MSS, Jenkinson to Robinson, July 21, 1780.

[80] *Morning Post,* September 26, 1780; *Morning Chronicle,* October 30. The Duke, addressing Lords, alluded to Sandwich's close connection with Bate and said that "those who either employed or rewarded the nefarious wretch were ten times more infamous, than he was himself." *The Parliamentary Register; or Proceedings and Debates of the House of Lords, 1780,* XV, 296-98. After his conviction, but before his incarceration, Bate continued to insult and challenge the Duke. *Walpole's Journal,* II, 464.

After his conviction, but before his actual confinement (justice had to be postponed for almost a year while the jails that the mobs destroyed during the Gordon riots of June, 1780, were rebuilt), Bate again quarreled with the proprietors of the *Morning Post*, this time over the heavy expenses of his trial. The proprietors maintained that Bate's indiscretion was a personal one, and hence he was personally liable. Bate, of course, maintained that his trial was incurred in the line of his editorial duties and, hence, his employers should finance the costs of litigation. Bate presented his side of the story in the *Morning Post* of September 25, 1780. He stressed his opposition to the desire "to sacrifice the paper to republican purposes." Rather than so do, he wrote, he had agreed to sell his share of the paper for five hundred guineas. But, Bate charged, the proprietors of the *Morning Post* had now cut their offer to three hundred fifty guineas, thus reneging on their agreement. There followed in the same issue a rebuttal by the proprietors. They agreed to pay Bate his price, with the understanding that the parson would retire to the country. Once discovering that Bate was contemplating a new daily newspaper aimed at competing with the *Morning Post*, they offered him the face value of the stock, which was three hundred and fifty guineas. Further, Alderman Skinner, Richardson, John Bell, and Jeremy Hargrave, the majority stockholders, assured their readers that Bate had been absent from his duties more often than not for the past two years and that the printer rather than the editor had been running the publication for this period. In short, the owners were confident that the *Morning Post* would continue to flourish without Henry Bate.

The *Morning Post*'s scandal stories had alienated so many important people that even Bate's powerful and influential friends (Garrick had recently died) were unable to have his sentence reduced, let alone to secure a pardon for him. Additional libel suits added to his woes, so that Bate was frequently called from his cell to defend himself against new charges. He had served ten months, commencing in June, 1781, before Richmond finally obtained a pardon for him.[81]

Any pleasure Bate's conviction may have given either his former employers or the Opposition was short-lived for, while fighting his prison sentence, he joined with a group of prominent supporters of Sandwich to plan a new newspaper that, it was hoped,

81 *Morning Chronicle*, November 24, 1781; *Walpole's Journal*, II, 541.

would serve not only as a defender of ministerial policy, but also as a semiofficial organ of the Government. In October, 1780, the *Morning Herald* was created to meet these specifications. Completely dissociating itself from the gossip-column press, it endeavored to cater to a class of supporters of the Ministry who demanded a journal more sophisticated in approach than the *Morning Post*. In fact, the *Morning Herald* boasted that its rapidly rising circulation was at the expense of the *Morning Post* and that the latter newspaper was "as inferior to the *Morning Herald* in point of sale, as we flatter ourselves it is, and ever will be, in point of conduct."[82] But the *Morning Herald* made few converts to the ministerial cause. Many of Bate's readers shifted over from the *Post,* and though there were now two major Tory dailies in London, the second was achieving most of its circulation through inroads on the first.

As expected, the *Morning Herald* not only praised all ministerial actions, but before it was two months old it undertook a vigorous attack against the "republican prints."[83] Thus, it was not long before Opposition editors lumped the *Morning Herald* and *Morning Post* together as "wretched hirelings of a yet more wretched administration"[84] and attacked these "ministerial profligates" and the readers who were gullible enough to be duped by the "abominable nonsense" of the two loyal morning dailies.[85]

In June, 1781, John Fielding purchased the *Courant,* a fast-failing anti-Ministry newspaper. In his first edition the new owner-editor announced his belief that, since "the generality of the Morning Prints are subservient to Ministerial Purposes, an Independent Paper will be honored with the patronage of the most respectable part of the Community."[86] But to Fielding, as to many of his contemporaries, *independent* meant *anti-Government,* and the *Courant* continued the attacks, commenced years earlier by the previous owner John Cooper, against "the HIRELING RUF-

---

82 *Morning Herald,* November 8, 1780. See also December 2: "The sale of this paper is now more extensive than that of the *Morning Post* ever was, at its most prosperous period . . . any person may be convinced of the fact, who will give himself the trouble of enquiring at the Stamp Office." See also January 5, 1781, and *Gentleman's Magazine,* March, 1824, 273-76, for comments on the two newspapers that Bate edited during the era of the American Revolution.

83 *Morning Herald,* December 18, 1780.

84 *Courant,* January 9, 1781. See also November 6, 1780. Cf. *Morning Post,* November 9, 1780.

85 *Courant,* December 23, 1780.

86 *Courant,* June 4, 1781.

FIANS of the ministerial prints."[87] Stressing that the *Morning Herald* had been "patronized and pensioned into existence by a nefarious and callous hearted administration," the *Courant* summed up its views of the new Tory newspaper by calling it both a "wretched farrago of nonsense and contradiction" and a "prostituted paper."[88] Employing a regular series entitled "List of Lies Political in the Ministerial Papers during the course of last week," Fielding quoted the "lying paragraphs" of the loyal dailies and, after correcting the untruths, printed a running tally of the results.[89] He soon announced that the popularity of the *Courant's* anti-Ministry position had pulled its circulation "well above" the thousand mark for each issue,[90] which assured it a prosperous future. The loyal newspapers were quick to respond. Asserting that the "patriotic republican prints" were prostitutes that opposed any ministry whatever, the *Morning Herald* warned Englishmen that these domestic enemies caused more trouble in the Empire than did the Americans, French, and Spaniards combined.[91]

Despite general newspaper opposition to the Government and its "pensioned organs," there was almost no direct cooperation between the publishers of anti-Ministry prints. Opposition editors did not consider themselves members of an organized political party, and they demonstrated no reluctance when afforded an opportunity to condemn or expose one another. The *Public Ledger*, for example, wished "a few of the miseries" of destruction and waste being suffered in America upon H. S. Woodfall of the *Public Advertiser* because he published a scheme suggested "by one of the ministerial crew" for forcing the Colonies to come to terms by setting fire to their towns and harbors and laying waste the country.[92] The *Public Ledger* likewise attacked the "licentiousness of the press" when it implied that Almon's *Evening Post*, one of the most violent anti-Ministry publications, would upon occasion accept money for the insertion or deletion of paragraphs

---

[87] *Courant*, August 6, September 18, 1781. See also March 11, 1782.

[88] *Courant*, August 29, 1781.

[89] *Courant*, September 25, 1781: "Total of lies: In the *Morning Herald*, 15; in the *Morning Post*, 10; List of lies the same as last week: 25." See also *Courant*, October 8, 17, 23, *et passim*.

[90] *Courant*, August 6, September 8, 1781. The sale of one thousand copies per edition of a tri-weekly newspaper was generally considered the profit-making point.

[91] *Morning Herald*, October 9, 18, 1781.

[92] *Public Ledger*, September 22, 1778.

that would spare the reputations of "the culprits in high life."[93]

Although on the offensive editorially, the Opposition feared being placed on the defensive legally. If an editor was brought before the bar by the Government, the Opposition immediately closed ranks and supported him, for they knew that if one were successfully attacked, the others might well be next. For this reason only, Henry Bate, before going to jail, took satisfaction in announcing that William Parker, printer of the *General Advertiser* and one of Bate's worst tormentors, was, in 1779, sentenced to Newgate for one year for contempt of Lords. Parker was convicted because of his acerbic comments in a special handbill that defended the acquittal of the Whig admiral, Augustus Keppel, who was court-martialed for alleged negligence in combat with French fleets during the summer of 1778.[94] Parker, whose newspaper columns regularly contained attacks upon the Government and its subsidized press,[95] was certain that his prosecution stemmed directly from these attacks, and he continued to give the Ministry no peace. After converting his cell into an editorial office, he managed the *General Advertiser* from Newgate.[96] In February, 1780, while still in prison, Parker vigorously supported the crusade for the passage of Sir George Savile's motion to compel the Government to produce its pension lists. The *Morning Post*, as expected, opposed the bill.[97] The *General Advertiser* used two full pages to list the name of every man who helped defeat this motion "in order to distinguish who are placemen, contractors, pensioners, etc.,"[98] and Parker's attacks upon the Ministry and its "prostitute morning paper" became still more pronounced.[99] So long as he was allowed to write for his own news-

[93] *Packet,* February 23, March 17, 1780; *Morning Chronicle,* February 28, October 30.

[94] *Morning Post,* March 9, 30, May 1, 1779.

[95] *General Advertiser,* January 7, 9, 20, 26, 1779. Parker, incidentally, named his next son Augustus Keppel Parker.

[96] On October 22, November 3, 5, December 30, 1780, while hammering away at the point that Bate and Lord Chief Justice Mansfield were in collusion (thus ensuring his conviction), Parker publicized the fact that his room, ten yards by seven in size, was one of the smallest in the prison. Eventually he gained his point; the *Morning Post* announced on February 17, 1780, that Parker had been moved to larger quarters. The additional space gave him enough room to establish almost his entire editorial operation within his prison walls.

[97] *Morning Post,* February 24, 1780.

[98] *General Advertiser,* February 29, 1780.

[99] *General Advertiser,* March 10, 14, 21, 24, 27, 30, 1780.

paper from his cell, his imprisonment was indeed a hollow victory for the Government.

On March 20, 1780, Parker's *General Advertiser*, still boasting of its extensive and increasing sale, absorbed the insolvent and anti-Ministry *Public Ledger*. Thomas Brewman, in his final statement as editor and publisher of the *Ledger*, affirmed that he had "tried to destroy the corrupt administration," and he now believed he could help do so more effectively by serving on the staff of a larger, more influential publication.[100] Brewman was convinced that Parker had succeeded in making the *General Advertiser* one of the most important Opposition journals in England.

In spite of all efforts by the Ministry, the press was as hostile to the Government in 1781 as it had been five years earlier. Although the *Morning Herald* had given the Tories some additional strength, no other pro-Government publications were undertaken during the American Revolution, and only one Opposition publication came over to the Government. William Woodfall's *Morning Chronicle*, which previously had balanced its paragraphs in such a way as to demonstrate that, while not wishing the American cause well, it was opposed to the Ministry that appeared to be blundering into a defeat in America, threw its support in mid-1778 behind the Ministry, once France became the major enemy. Its columns were always open, however, to hostile opinions.[101] In summing up his father's position, William Woodfall, Jr., wrote that he was "a friend to government and a moderate man in politics."[102] The Opposition press never forgave the *Morning Chronicle* for deserting its ranks. By 1781 the abuse that had been reserved for the *Morning Post* and the *Morning Herald* was heaped also upon the *Morning Chronicle*.

Unfortunately for the King's friends, the London press, adequately supported by rising circulation and advertising revenues, was not for sale. And this fact did not augur well for the Ministry of George III.

---

[100] *General Advertiser*, March 20, 1780.
[101] *Morning Chronicle*, November 23, 1778.
[102] BM Add. MSS 20733, Almon Correspondence, 147, dated August 12, 1782 or 1792.

CHAPTER II

The Beginnings: Boston and the Improper Americans

THE DIVERSE ELEMENTS of the British press were certain that Boston, queen city of the Massachusetts Bay Colony, was the heart of the troublesome uprisings in America. The Tea Party of December, 1773, had given this town such prominence that England now took careful cognizance of all that occurred there. When, in March, 1774, Lord North rose in Parliament and called the Bostonians "the ringleaders of all the riots in America for seven years past,"[1] his words were not seriously challenged. Few recalled the irate Rhode Island citizenry's burning the *Gaspee* just two years before. Fewer still could name a southern colony that had had the temerity wantonly to destroy government property. None could name another city in America that had caused so much difficulty for both King and Parliament. Whether one argued for or against the Colonies, London's initial premise was clear: Boston was not only the economic hub of New England, she was also America's political center.

New England's reputation as a land that allowed the Church to dominate politics led Englishmen to believe that Bostonians, encouraged by a clergy that had long been "stirring up the people

---

[1] *Gentleman's Magazine*, March, 1774, 140. See also *General Evening Post*, July 24, 1775, for an article entitled "O Rare Boston Loyalty," questioning the patriotism of Bostonians as far back as 1772.

to sedition by their inflammatory sermons,"[2] apparently received from their pulpits more political infidelity than religious instruction. As the Puritans had constantly opposed the establishment of an Anglican episcopate in America, was it not to be expected that they would embrace the rebel cause rather than ally with a King whose faith was a constant thorn in their ecclesiastic sides? The alleged violence of these dissenters knew no bounds. "A Boston Saint" informed readers of the *Gazetteer* that a loyal militia officer was deprived of his virility on the advice of a Congregational deacon, while the *Morning Chronicle* announced that the Puritans had introduced the auto-da-fé in America.[3] Small wonder, then, that the British were forced to send troops to restore order, protect the innocent, and restrain the turbulent in rebellious Boston, "where all the authority of legal government had been long extinguished by the tyranny of a rabble instigated by factious leaders."[4] On September 29, 1778, after reviewing the proceedings in America for the past three years, the *Morning Post* accused the dissenting pulpits of having "done more towards exciting the flames of rebellion than all the other causes united."

Although by 1774 Samuel Adams and John Hancock were well known in Boston for their labors in support of rebellion, it was not until the following year that Englishmen read detailed accounts of the two leaders of America's "unnatural revolt."[5] Adams and Hancock were brought to the attention of all Britain in July, 1775, when a widely publicized proclamation of Thomas Gage, Governor General of Massachusetts, reached London. It castigated the Bay Colony's "incendiaries and traitors" for conducting the "infatuated multitudes" into activities of avowed rebellion. It also charged that Bostonians had, among other things, suppressed truth, engaged in the "grossest forgeries, calumnies and absurdities that ever insulted human understanding," and had

---

2 *Morning Post*, October 23, 1776. The author, identified as "An Officer at Boston," accused "Channing and Cooper" of being leading pulpit patriots. On June 7, 1779, this newspaper reported that a "Rev. Mr. Peters" was another rebel leader. Peters, who had recently died, had left England after he was discovered to have two wives, Bate informed his readers. See also July 2, 1776, and the *Evening Post*, September 14, 1775, for attacks upon the Presbyterian ministry.

3 *Gazetteer*, March 14, 1775; *Morning Chronicle*, July 29.

4 *Scot's Magazine*, March, 1776, 125. See also *London Magazine*, November, 1774, 563, and *Annual Register*, 1775, 49, for earlier accounts of Boston's violent and "obnoxious" conduct.

5 The "House of Hancock" received scattered commercial notice in the press in 1773 and 1774. Hancock and Adams were infrequently noted in these years in a political sense.

even prostituted the press, "that distinguished appendage to public liberty." In spite of these many offenses, Gage was willing to forgive all of His Majesty's refractory subjects except two, Adams and Hancock, whose offenses he considered of too flagrant a nature "to admit of any other consideration than that of CONDIGN PUNISHMENT."[6]

Publication of a general pardon for all rebels save two produced a stream of controversy in the British press. Was the American revolt of such a nature that it would collapse with the arrest of two New England leaders? Most editors believed not. A perusal of British publications in 1774 and 1775 would belie any idea that only a handful of men in Boston were responsible for the tumultuous state of American politics. Scores of American names marched across the pages of the London press; the "Pennsylvania Farmer," John Dickinson, for example, was widely praised for his "spirited and sensible" works in defense of American rights and than quickly forgotten as his warmth for the colonial cause cooled and his writing disappeared from both English and colonial publications.[7] Others, like the "moral and virtuous" Virginian Benjamin Harrison, were severely castigated for the immorality they cloaked in the garb of respectability[8] and were never again mentioned. With so many names, facts, and dates arriving from America, editors, in order not to omit anything that might prove important, included everything, adding but a bare outline or commentary. For example, Dodsley had little idea of the importance of Patrick Henry when his *Annual Register* reported that the people of Virginia were "assembled in arms to a considerable number, under the conduct of a Mr. Henry." An additional report on the next page that "resolutions of Governor Dunmore condemn Henry, but his conduct is vindicated and applauded" by Virginians completed the *Annual Register*'s coverage of his activities from 1774 to 1776. Whether Henry was as important an American leader as Benjamin Harrison was left for the reader to decide.

[6] *Gentleman's Magazine,* July, 1775, 331; *Scot's Magazine,* July, 373; *Annual Register,* June, 384.

[7] *London Magazine,* 1774, Supplement. The *Morning Post,* June 7, 1779, described Dickinson as "too irresolute and pusillanimous to be a dangerous partizan on either side."

[8] *Scot's Magazine,* September, 1775, 499, asserted that Harrison was "busy DEBAUCHING all the pretty girls in his neighbourhood, on purpose to raise a squadron of whores to keep his old General warm during his winter quarters."

Still it was clear, from continuing reports, that in every colony the Hancocks and Henrys were receiving wide support. *Scot's Magazine,* as early as November, 1774, published "Thoughts of a Traveller upon our American disputes," which concluded that the colonials, being generally freeholders with "a loose form of government," were so "bold, licentious, and republican" that they "often awed and forced their betters into many disagreeable resolves and compliances by their dangerous spirit of insurgency."[9] Dodsley's *Annual Register* concurred, reporting the growth of colonial militias so spirited that "persons of family and fortune who were not appointed officers were serving with alacrity in the ranks." Even the Quakers, forgetting their cherished principles of forbearance and nonresistance, were forming themselves into companies at Philadelphia, the sympathetic Dodsley added.[10]

While reporting the broad base of American discontent, it was apparent to the press that Adams and Hancock were indeed in great measure to blame for fostering the unrest in the Colonies. The *Gazetteer,* comparing the Tea Party to Britain's Jacobite rebellion in 1745, noted only one major difference: "Instead of Charles Stuart at the head of Highland Clans, Sam Adams now led a banditti of hypocrites against Great Britain."[11] Similar assertions in one form or another were widely reiterated.

Although Samuel Adams was known to be the guiding force behind the rebellion in Massachusetts, John Hancock received much more notice in the British press. This was to be expected. The House of Hancock was one of the largest and formerly one of the most reputable American firms. A great merchant's embracing the cause of rebellion would naturally provoke a storm greater than would the conversion of a hitherto little-known politician. While devoting more space to Hancock than to Adams, the press thought Adams the more important leader. *Scot's Magazine,* quoting a letter culled from an Edinburgh newspaper, "giving an account of the politics in America," summed up:

John Hancock, a counsellor under the late administration, a man of property, is the ostensible leader of patriotism. He is a man of irreproachable honesty and benevolence, but of weak ambition; and

9 *Scot's Magazine,* November, 1774, 590. See also December, 637.

10 *Annual Register,* 1775, 141.

11 *Gazetteer,* April 2, 1775. See also *London Magazine,* August, 1774, 384, for "Harlequin's" defense of Dickinson, Hancock, Adams, and Putnam as "the defenders of their country, the asserters of the rights of mankind—and the immortal champions of liberty."

is a generous dupe to another of deeper designs, who is Samuel Adams, a man of cunning and abilities, but of no reputation. He was formerly connected with the town taxes; in which capacity he is alleged to have cheated the town of Boston of no less than £2,000, and is now principal delegate to the Grand American Congress.[12]

The *Morning Post*'s "American correspondent" agreed, but added that Hancock, now realizing his mistake, abhorred his association with "the rebel and crafty pettifogger Adams," who completely dominated him.[13]

Hancock's abilities were seriously questioned, and many believed he was more to be pitied than punished. Upon learning of his election to the presidency of the Continental Congress, James De Solis, writing in the *Chronicle*, assumed that the Bostonian was awarded this position by virtue of his extreme wealth, "which they say at Boston, one of his ancestors himself accumulated chiefly by smuggling. The sum qualifies him for cat's-paw to the Congress."[14] "An Officer of distinction on Long Island," quoted in the *Morning Post*, concluded that, of all the troublemakers in America, "the arch rebel Adams stands most conspicuous," but for Hancock the "Officer" had much compassion. Hancock's crimes resulted from "the machinations of that traitor [Adams]." He was "lamented by several of the King's best friends, who, no doubt, will use their endeavours to procure for him the royal clemency, in case of a reconciliation," surmised the "Officer,"[15] whose opinions closely reflected those held by American Tories at that time. Peter Oliver, Daniel Leonard, or any of a score of loyalists could easily have penned the appraisals of Hancock and Adams that were printed in the British press.

A merchant whose reputation and fortune already were sacrificed to the cause of American liberty was, of course, suspected of ulterior motives. *Town and Country* magazine maintained that all Americans were risking enslavement by pinning their faith on a character as suspect as Hancock,[16] while two newspapers predicted that Hancock and James Otis would become America's

12 *Scot's Magazine*, April, 1775, 176, "The American Leaders characterized in a letter from an Officer at Boston to an Officer of Edinburgh."
13 *Morning Post*, August 21, 1776. See also June 7, 1779, for an article describing Hancock as "a mere stalking horse under the direction of Adams" and Adams as an embezzler and hypocrite who made "religion the vehicle of rebellion, and faith the groundwork of faction."
14 *Chronicle*, November 30, 1775.
15 *Morning Post*, October 23, 1776. See also *Scot's Magazine*, September, 1775, 499
16 *Town and Country*, October, 1776, 526.

Lord of the Treasury and Chancellor of the Exchequer and would divide the spoils accordingly.[17] Surely the leaders of the Continental Congress had no interest but their own at heart. Only five of them were men of appreciable property, asserted the *Chronicle,* as it surmised that men in financial predicament were seldom scrupulous about the means of mending their fortunes.[18] The opinion that personal gain and glory was the motivation behind most American leadership pervaded the press in 1775 and 1776.[19]

Hancock symbolized for Englishmen the rebellious American spirit. Thus we find *Hancock, rebellion,* and *America* used interchangeably in stories about the Colonies. And of course Hancock was vilified for the cause he represented. One poet, for example, in the widely printed "Expedition to America," implored General Wolfe to rise from his tomb and

> In injured Hamlet's awful form array'd!
> Stalk pale and terrible round HANCOCK'S bed,
> And harrow up his soul with conscious dread;

The poet then asked Hancock:

> And dost thou dare, Ambition's paltry slave,
> With rebel-hoardes the bloody flag to wave,
> To seize with impious hands the rich domain
> Unnumbered millions were misspent to gain?[20]

He concluded by ordering the Bostonian and his fellow rebels to drop "the snaky crest and hiss no more,/ But prostrate, mercy undeserv'd implore."

Samuel Adams' *Boston Gazette,* "official organ of the rebellious Americans," fared no better in the British press than did his "coconspirator." As early as May, 1774, *Scot's Magazine,* in printing excerpts from the *Boston Gazette,* derided this "specimen of the rhetoric and courage of some good and wise people in the province of Massachusetts Bay."[21] By early 1776 all London was

---

[17] *Public Advertiser,* July 27, 1775. See also *Lloyd's Evening Post,* same date, which accused Otis and Hancock of "perjuring themselves with joy . . . for the good of the New Jerusalem." Otis' partial insanity, which by this time rendered him all but useless to the American cause, was unknown in London.

[18] *Chronicle,* March 7, 1776.

[19] *London Gazette,* October 21, 1775. See also *Gentleman's Magazine,* October, 478. *Lloyd's Evening Post,* January 26, 1776, incorrectly noted that John Adams was Samuel Adams' brother, when it maintained that place and pension seemed to be the driving force behind the Adamses in America and Franklin in England.

[20] *Gentleman's Magazine,* April, 178; *Scot's Magazine,* April, 1776, 214.

[21] *Scot's Magazine,* May, 1774, 250.

aware that the *Boston Gazette* was Adams' personal vehicle for propaganda. "The Weekly Dung Barge," as it was called by New England loyalists, was roundly condemned in Britain for being "so totally defective and dissatisfactory, that it seems to have laid a foundation for every other error and contradiction relative to this business."[22]

However reliable its sources, the press was judging the actions of Hancock and Adams from a distance of three thousand miles and, frequently, a time lapse of two months. The difficulty of obtaining news swiftly often obstructed England's view of these men. But, fortunately for British editors, the impediments that shielded most Americans did not protect all, for in the midst of London in 1775 dwelled Dr. Benjamin Franklin, perhaps America's most prominent son and surely her foremost European press agent. The rebellion was not a child of his imagination. At first it seemed that he did not take the uprisings seriously, but when he adopted the colonial standard he gave to it the weight of his renown and reputation. The English public might at first know little and care less about an Adams or a Hancock who, after all, were well removed in time and space, but they could not refrain from investigating the relationship of this philosopher-scientist-statesman to the cause of American independence.

Late in 1772 Franklin, while a colonial agent in London, had procured the ten famous "Whately Letters." Six were written by Governor Thomas Hutchinson of Massachusetts Bay when he was Chief Justice of that colony from 1767 to 1769; the other four were written by Andrew Oliver, Hutchinson's brother-in-law and later Lieutenant Governor of the Bay Colony. Originally sent to Thomas Whately, a member of both the Grenville and North ministries, the letters were certain to create an immediate storm if placed in the proper hands in Boston, since one of them asserted that "there must be a diminution of what are called English liberties" in Massachusetts if the Empire was to be preserved. Perhaps wishing to add coals to the fire of American dissatisfaction, Franklin sent them to Speaker Thomas Cushing of the Massachusetts House of Representatives, swearing Cushing to secrecy. In June, 1773, Samuel Adams read them before a closed session of the House and later had copies made and published in the *Boston Gazette*.[23]

22 *Annual Register*, 1776, 162.
23 *Encyclopedia of American History*, Richard B. Morris, ed., 81-82.

In comparison with much of the language used by the contemporary press on both sides of the Atlantic, the contents of the letters were indeed mild. Through the *Boston Gazette*, however, Adams was able to magnify their importance. The adverse publicity given this correspondence throughout the colony resulted in a cry for the impeachment of Governor Hutchinson and Lieutenant Governor Oliver. On January 26, 1774, the Privy Council reviewed Franklin's impeachment petition, presented on behalf of the already widely distrusted Massachusetts Bay Colony. This petition, it seems, would have long lain neglected as had its precursors, had not Franklin, by acknowledging that he was the source through which Adams received the Whately letters, "given an opening to his enemies to load him with unmerited abuse."[24] Before denying the request for the removal of Hutchinson, the Privy Council heard Solicitor General Alexander Wedderburn denounce Franklin as "a man without honour" and compare him to a thief. The Council presently removed Franklin from his position as Deputy Postmaster of the American Colonies. Wedderburn's harsh attack upon him probably did more to make the Philadelphian a rebel than did any of Samuel Adams' machinations.

Franklin was soon dispatching a steady stream of letters to the *Public Advertiser, Public Ledger, Gazetteer*, and London *Chronicle*. William Strahan of the *Chronicle* and H. S. Woodfall of the *Public Advertiser* were among the American's closest friends in London, and there is no record of the rejection of any of Franklin's letters to a newspaper. Despite his use of forty-two different signatures for his letters, readers were able to recognize many of the contributions as Franklin's, and his many friends facetiously referred to his house as "the Craven Street Publicity Office," because it was London's center "for the dissemination of American facts and opinion."[25] Besides writing to the press, Franklin arranged for his longer articles and the works of other prominent Americans to be reprinted and mailed to the homes and offices of countless influential Englishmen. These modest expenditures for propaganda were charged to his Massachusetts account, and the Bay Colony readily paid them.

Even after Wedderburn's attack Franklin was still extremely

24 *Annual Register,* 1774, 86.

25 Crane has discovered seventeen of Franklin's letters in the British press in 1774. *Benjamin Franklin's Letters to the Press,* Verner W. Crane, ed., 240-78.

popular. *Scot's Magazine,* in May, 1774, had commended his "brilliant discourse in which he stated that the only effectual way of composing the present differences was to put the Americans precisely in the situation they were in before the passing of the Stamp Act."[26] This issue also opposed his removal from the Post Office, and it printed a letter from an unnamed American who wrote that Franklin "had signally served the cause of America." The author concluded that Franklin "should be placed above a dependence on the caprice of an unrighteous ministry . . . and should be placed in the grateful arms of his applauding country-men."[27]

Frankliniana appeared everywhere in the press.[28] In addition to his contributions to political discussions in the newspapers, the science sections of the magazines made constant reference to his experiments and speculations,[29] and by early 1775 his renown was at its zenith. This popularity, however, was short-lived. In March there appeared in almost every London journal "an inflammatory letter supposed to be Dr. Franklin's," which stirred up a new storm of controversy. The letter claimed that Britain, among other misdeeds in America, was "growing rich by rapine." After condemning its "wicked and treasonable" contents, the press assumed that, unless proof to the contrary was furnished, the blame of authorship must rest with Franklin.[30] Although he did not write the letter, Franklin never disclaimed its authorship, so the blame fell upon him. The fact that he presently left Britain for America added circumstantial evidence to the case against him. A few editors remained unconvinced of his "seditious principles," but as articles praising him became more frequent in the American press, hitherto pro-Franklin editors in Britain fell into line and helped contribute to the downfall of his good name. The technique of quoting American praises of the man in order to lower him in the estimation of Englishmen was a simple but

26 *Scot's Magazine,* May, 1774, 248-51.

27 *Scot's Magazine,* May, 1774, 248-51.

28 Franklin's death (he actually died in 1790) was regularly reported. The *Morning Post,* April 23, 1781, characterized him as "an evil genius" with "principles of a perfect Machiavellian," who, among other misdeeds, was "Whitefield's constant attendant."

29 *Universal Magazine of Knowledge and Pleasure,* January, 1775, 23, in a typical article printed "sundry letters between Dr. Franklin, Dr. Brownrigg, and the Rev. Mr. Parish treating of 'the stilling of waves by means of oil.'"

30 *St. James's Chronicle,* March 14, 1775, "A Lover of Order" blamed "Dr. F. and false friends in England for much of the present troubles in America." See also *Scot's Magazine,* March, 1775, 116.

clever one. Obviously, patriotic Britons could not hold him in high esteem so long as Pennsylvanians were singing:

> Come join hand in hand, all ye true loyal souls,
> 'Tis LIBERTY calls, let's fill up our bowls,
> To Wedderburn and North now confusion we'll drink
> Their dastardly souls we will cause them to shrink;
> Then join hand in hand here's a full flowing bowl,
> 'Tis FRANKLIN and LIBERTY enlighten the soul.[31]

The British press assumed that Franklin sailed for the Colonies to take up a position of leadership in the American cause. Many Englishmen seized every opportunity to disparage him. "He was said," wrote one contributor to the *Public Advertiser*, "to be planning to put himself at the head of the rebels and to try whether he cannot do more Mischief with the Sword than with the Pen."[32] By the spring of 1776 the abuse reached its climax, for he was by then definitely considered a rebel. The *Morning Post*, defining a "patriot" as one who endeavored to "take the Treasury Bench by storm," deduced that Franklin, with the other "worthies" of his ilk, was supporting the colonial cause for financial gain. If this were so, suggested one correspondent, England should cater to his cunning duplicity. If Walpole could corrupt a nation, surely Franklin could corrupt a few colonies. "Bid him a price," the author concluded, "and he will soon put the United Congress into discord and confusion."[33]

Few articles complimentary to Franklin appeared in the press during the latter half of 1776. War had come, and his accomplishments in the field of learning could not compensate for his distasteful political allegiances. By autumn he was being abused in a fashion reminiscent of the treatment John Hancock and Samuel Adams had received twelve months earlier. One correspondent to the Tory *General Evening Post*, upon learning that Franklin had left for France shortly after his arrival in America, reported that the "old sinner" fled from his friends in Congress because "his own wonderful rods" could not protect him from the storm that was going to burst upon their "frantic and rebellious heads."[34] The *Morning Post* assumed that he had sailed from America "on

31 "A Song," taken from the *Pennsylvania Ledger* and quoted by *Scot's Magazine*, July, 1775, 39.
32 *Public Advertiser*, December 13, 1775.
33 *Morning Post*, March 27, 1776.
34 *General Evening Post*, December 21, 1776.

pretence of negotiating with the French." Its final issue for 1776 gave the "true reason" for his departure:

> Had Franklin's true reasons for sailing away
> > To his long ear'd, deluded companions been known
> It is odds they'd have forced the old traitor to stay,
> > Or at least, that he not departed alone!

> Like the devil in Milton, sole cause of their ruin!
> > He quits PANDEMONIUM for ease and for pleasure;
> Saves his own wily pate from the storm that is brewing,
> > And leaves his poor gulls to be damn'd at their leisure![35]

In January, 1776, *Common Sense* was anonymously published in Philadelphia; three months later it was reprinted in London. There was much speculation as to the authorship of this "inflammatory treatise," and one uncertain reviewer, conceding that it was designed to promote the absolute independence of the Colonies, did not believe it was penned by either Franklin or Samuel Adams. Yet he would not venture a guess as to its authorship.[36]

Franklin's connection with the American cause seemed so intimate by this time that most London editors ascribed *Common Sense* to him. The author's statement of his "disconnection with any party" would not exclude him, for a man already a traitor could easily be a liar. But Franklin's many friends noted that the "abusive stile and illiberality of sentiment" than ran throughout the pamphlet was "inconsistent with the good sense and spirit of the writings of the great philosopher."[37] The *Morning Post* reported that the King, having been called among other things the "Royal Brute," took such offense at this pamphlet that he commissioned Samuel Johnson to answer "Dr. Franklin's Common Sense."[38]

It was not surprising that John Almon, the radical publisher of London's *Evening Post*, was responsible for the English edition of *Common Sense*. Almon had previously published John Dickin-

---

[35] *Morning Post*, December 30, 1776. Bate's attacks upon Franklin never ceased. On August 22, 1780, a poem, "On Benjamin Franklin," appeared in the *Morning Post*, telling the Philadelphian of "the plentitude, magnitude, and terpitude" of his crimes.

[36] *London Magazine*, August, 1776, 437.

[37] *Morning Chronicle*, June 5, 1776.

[38] *Morning Post*, June 12, 13, 1776.

son's *Letters From A Farmer In Pennsylvania* and other pro-American propaganda tracts upon commission from Benjamin Franklin. However, he realized that the anonymous author of *Common Sense* went beyond the bounds of what London printers considered journalistic propriety, so he did not preserve all the passages of the original manuscript from Philadelphia.[39] He omitted the bitter attacks upon the monarchy and left the spaces blank, a device that permitted the reader to use his imagination or encouraged him to secure a copy of the unexpurgated French edition in order to discover what had been excluded. Most Londoners knew exactly what sections of the original work had been deleted, and they managed to secure and read them, despite the fact that no printer dared publish them. William Woodfall, who published long excerpts from *Common Sense*, explained the ellipses: if he published the whole work, he believed, he might justly be accused "of printing more foul mouth'd abuse against our gracious Sovereign than ever yet issued from the press of this country."[40] Criticism and indecency were quite different matters, and *Common Sense* was judged indecent by most editors whether or not they were friendly to the general ideas propounded. "The violence of party was still not expected to carry an author beyond bounds," concluded Woodfall's *Morning Chronicle*.[41] The press of both political viewpoints maintained a degree of propriety when direct attacks upon the King were concerned. George III was the symbol of all that made Great Britain great, and to slander him was to slander all Englishmen.

Thomas Paine was unknown on both sides of the Atlantic, and this anonymity helped the popularity of his pamphlet in Britain. Instead of its being hailed as the work of a disgruntled traveler, *Common Sense* was viewed as the production of some leading figure on the American political scene. Looking upon this cogent treatise as a representative pronouncement of the American rebels, the *Morning Post* inferred: "Hancock, Adams, and Franklin are the men . . . and common sense abounds among them."[42]

The *Morning Post* reported that no less than 46,000 copies of

[39] Almon's *Evening Post* printed long extracts (with deletions) from *Common Sense* on May 28 and 30, 1776. The *Morning Post* published almost the same passages on June 13.

[40] *Morning Chronicle*, June 5, 1776.

[41] *Morning Chronicle*, June 5, 1776; *Morning Post*, June 13.

[42] *Morning Post*, June 12, 1776. The *General Evening Post*, April 6, 1776, surmised that *Common Sense* was written "by one of the leading MEMBERS of the CONTINENTAL CONGRESS."

Common Sense were printed and circulated in America, and the results had been "attended with a greater effect than any other public performance of the kind that ever appeared in any country, and gave the decisive spirit for independency."[43] The paper furnished no statistics on the number of copies distributed in England (Almon did not divulge this information either), but it expressed the opinion that all segments of British society were affected by this work.[44]

The language of the pamphlet was so abusive, yet eloquent, that the work could not be expected to receive fair treatment at the hands of those it criticized. Both its style and content—especially the stress upon the desirability of American independence—inspired a host of overwhelmingly hostile retorts. One writer to the *General Evening Post,* attributing *Common Sense* to Samuel Adams, assumed that its arguments were a consequence that naturally flowed from the principles of Franklin's English friend Dr. Richard Price "and other advocates for America." As a result of this clamor for a separate and independent state on the other side of the Atlantic, "a speedy and vigorous opposition to the present unnatural rebellion" would be necessary, he concluded.[45] The *Morning Post* believed that only one of the observations of this "celebrated pamphlet" was worthy of the least attention: the idea that premiums be paid to shipbuilders who construct warships in the national interest. The plan seemed so reasonable to this newspaper that it recommended that Britain adopt it in some measure, "not despising it on account of the quarter it comes from."[46] The *St. James's Chronicle,* however, printed an extract of a letter from Jamaica, dated June 29, 1776, which asserted that *Common Sense's* recommendations about naval premiums were not borne out by the facts.[47]

An unrivaled best seller in both America (over 120,000 copies were sold in three months) and France, *Common Sense* also exerted a powerful influence in England. In America Paine's words reflected the feelings of a substantial segment of the population; in both France and England they alerted the doubting public to

---

[43] *Morning Post,* August 19, 1776.
[44] *Morning Post,* August 19, 1776. The *Morning Post* reported that "the Queen once found the Prince of Wales reading Dr. Franklin's pamphlet *Common Sense."*
[45] *General Evening Post,* April 6, June 1, 1776.
[46] *Morning Post,* June 8, 1776.
[47] *St. James's Chronicle,* August 27, 1776.

the immediacy of America's desire for independence and to the probability of war unless reconciliation was swift.

While, in 1774, Thomas Paine traveled across the Atlantic to become an American and, the following year, Benjamin Franklin sailed for his homeland, most of the transatlantic traffic during the next decade would be Americans sailing in the other direction. Hundreds of colonists, many of them, like Governor Thomas Hutchinson and Joseph Galloway, representing the former wealth and political talent of their communities, fled to England early in the war to find safety and to plead for compensation for the property they had lost at the hands of the rebels. Settling down in Kensington, the loyalists regularly petitioned for pensions, proffered military and political advice in innumerable pamphlets, and in general lived unhappily as exiles.

No sooner had the loyalists arrived in London in appreciable numbers than they were attacked by the Opposition press for not only failing to bring the colonial dispute to a fair and equitable settlement, but also for lacking the courage to stand on their own ground and help subdue by force of arms the rebellion that they had helped the country to blunder into.[48] Despite wide publicity given the terrible suffering being inflicted upon the King's supporters in America,[49] the Opposition press insisted that much of their plight was of their own manufacture. "His Majesty's worst enemies could not have conducted his business, either here or in America, in a manner more shameful and ruinous than they have done," exclaimed a critic in the *Gentleman's Magazine,* while the more partisan *Public Ledger* presently called the loyalists "a herd of parasites who were instrumental in bringing on the fatal conflict in North America."[50] The Opposition would come to resent strongly the pensions paid by the Treasury to the American refugees who, it believed, were "growing fat upon the vitals of this country, after plunging it into the most unnatural war that ever disgraced mankind."[51] Why, exactly, the loyalists were to blame for the Revolution, the Opposition rarely spelled out in detail.

Knowing that most of England's channels of public opinion

[48] *Gazetteer,* "OPTIMUS," July 20, 1775; *Morning Chronicle,* January 6, 1776.
[49] *General Evening Post,* May 4, 1776; *Morning Post,* June 17; *St. James's Chronicle,* December 30; *Lloyd's Evening Post,* January 21, 1780; *Morning Post,* March 28, 1781.
[50] *Gentleman's Magazine,* June, 1777, 312; *Public Ledger,* December 13, 1777; *Courant,* February 19, 1780.
[51] *Courant,* November 2, 1781.

were decidedly hostile to them, the American loyalists constantly dipped their own quills in order to defend the ministerial policies they believed served the best interests of King, country, and themselves. Notwithstanding repeated attempts to present their case in a strong and sympathetic light, the Opposition press and even segments of the loyal press were convinced that the proper place for the King's American friends was America.

CHAPTER III

The First Failures
of Reconciliation

IN FEBRUARY, 1775, Lord North tried to reach a peaceable settlement with the Americans. Parliament, by his proposal,
would lay only regulatory taxes on any Atlantic province that
would consent to tax itself to provide funds for its defense and
for its civil and judicial administration. North calculated that his
plan, if accepted by any of the Colonies, could well breach American unity. This divisive factor was the argument he used to convince the King that conciliation, based upon the proposal of self-
imposed taxes, would be of extreme value even if most of the
Colonies should reject it.

As soon as the press learned that North's "judicious motion"
had the royal assent, some pro-Ministry publications immediately
expected success. Stressing the opportunity for the provinces to
return safely and honorably to their old allegiance,[1] they filled
their columns with laudatory comments about the Prime Minister.
One writer even believed this proposal of an olive branch the
wisest step North had taken throughout his whole administration.[2]
But most loyal contributors to the press were horrified at what
they felt was the Ministry's attempt to compromise the dignity of
the Crown for an ephemeral treaty with "banditti." Realizing

1 *General Evening Post*, February 26, May 10, 1775.
2 *Morning Post*, March 2, 1775.

50

that the most they could hope for even under these undignified conditions was a favorable reply from one or two provinces, they were certain this conciliatory gesture would prove an embarrassing failure. True, the King had given the royal assent, but only because he was led to believe that New York probably would accept and thus split the rebel forces. Still, to send emissaries "with the fullest powers of Bribery, and a carte Blanche" to America and then to lay the dignity of Parliament "at the Feet of seven-and-twenty Assemblymen in New York . . . for the single favour of ceasing to oppose," was more than many loyal Englishmen could bear.[3] One pronounced the ministerial offer too "futile and feeble" to be considered a valid attempt at settlement.[4] *Lloyd's Evening Post* added its warning against extinguishing the "indignant flame of British honour" by making even the smallest concessions to the rebellious colonists.[5] "A True Briton," writing in the *Gazetteer*, likewise cautioned his countrymen against sacrificing the prerogatives of a state to a group of rebellious Americans. An Englishman who was willing to make any other terms than that the colonists "must lay down their arms, humbly beg the royal pardon, and submit themselves as in duty bound, to the laws and ordinances of the British legislature, should answer it with his head on Tower Hill," he declared.[6]

Unfortunately for the North ministry, its offer of reconciliation reached New York a few days after the province learned of the actions at Lexington and Concord. London discovered that no American colony could give the proposals serious consideration after both British and American blood had been shed. Had the proposal arrived a week earlier, North may well have won New York with the liberal "tax yourself" idea that both Grenville and Townshend had called unthinkable a few years earlier.

The Opposition press in England was not surprised at the failure of the colonists to act favorably upon a motion that did not stipulate clearly the percentage or the amount of money the American assemblies were expected to raise for their military, administrative, and judicial expenses. A correspondent to the *Morning Chronicle* attacked the North proposal for being "absolutely indecisive," and he affirmed that this motion did not afford

3 *St. James's Chronicle*, March 9, 1775.
4 *St. James's Chronicle*, March 9, 1775.
5 *Lloyd's Evening Post*, April 3, 1775. See also March 24.
6 *Gazetteer*, August 29, 1775. Cf. answer by "Moderation," August 30.

the Americans any certain ground whereupon to stand.[7] Making the same point, but in more abusive terms, Almon's *Evening Post* called the North proposal an "EQUIVOCAL, SUBTLE, DASTARDLY, TEMPORIZING, ENSNARING MOTION, aimed at stopping, if possible, the clamor of the day, without a retrospect to the whole of the evil."[8] What the "whole of the evil" was, the paper did not state.

Most of the loyal journals also expected the Americans to reject the Ministry's proposal. They made political capital of the Colonies' refusal to cease opposition to Crown and Country. "Well! What think our Readers of American Grievances now?" exclaimed *Lloyd's Evening Post.* After so "wickedly" spurning Mother England's olive branch, "could the Americans still possibly have one Advocate amongst a Rational people?" it asked. Declaring that Britain had treated the rebels with unparalleled lenity, it concluded with the statement, "It was now necessary that the British supremacy should shine forth in its full lustre."[9] The *General Evening Post* agreed that Britain, which "with the indulgence and patience of a parent, soothed, flattered, and even courted them to a reconciliation . . . [holding] out the olive-branch when she ought, perhaps, to have stretched forth the rod of correction," should now restore "the just authority of this kingdom."[10] The loyal press's solutions to the questions surrounding the war in America reflected the popular belief that, regardless of the justice of the Colonies' cause, once the Americans took up the sword, Britain was duty bound to crush the opposition and then, as a forgiving mother, to deal justly with her refractory children. In September, 1775, Rockingham wrote Burke that the Ministry's "violent measures towards America are freely adopted and countenanced by a majority of individuals of all ranks, professions, or occupations, in the country." These words were echoed by Lord John Cavendish, the Duke of Manchester, Sir George Savile, and by all of Britain's Tory press, most of her moderate press, and occasionally even by an Opposition journal.[11]

---

[7] *Morning Chronicle,* March 21, 1775.

[8] *Evening Post,* February 28, March 2, 25, 1775.

[9] *Lloyd's Evening Post,* July 26, December 13, 1775. See also March 29, 1776, article stating that the Ministry was ready to redress any "real grievances of which the Colonies have just reason to complain."

[10] *General Evening Post,* January 4, 1776.

[11] J. Steven Watson, *The Reign of George III,* 203; John Heneage Jesse, *Memoirs of the Life and Reign of King George III,* III, 433-34; Simon Maccoby, *English Radicalism, 1762–1785,* 228. See also *Morning Chronicle,* September 14, 1775; *Middlesex Journal,* September 21; *Chester Chronicle,* June 5.

Notwithstanding these references to the necessity for a military decision in America, the hope for a reconciliation remained one of the major themes of the press, despite the fact that most Englishmen expected any peace overtures to be as fruitless as the earlier attempts to avoid war. The *Gazetteer* believed reconciliation necessary, not so much for the political arguments involved, but because England's tremendous economic losses—created by the cessation of American trade—outweighed a "punctillo of honour." Further, this newspaper now expected "French and Spanish treachery." Logically, it concluded, it was both uneconomic and impolitic for the Government to sacrifice so considerable a profit for the "bare nothing" that English troops were fighting for in America.[12] In spite of its devout wish that the "virtuous and wise" of all parties should unite in effecting a plan satisfactory to all concerned,[13] the *Gazetteer,* along with most of its contemporaries, could offer few solutions to the problems that confronted Britain and her colonies. It was indeed easier to criticize Parliament, the Ministry, or the Americans than to produce a solution agreeable to both sides in a civil war.

Just as the press correctly assumed that the Americans would reject Lord North's conciliation measure, so it realized how impolitic it would be for the Ministry to give serious consideration to an American peace proposal. The Colonies' "Olive Branch Petition," proffered in July, 1775, had to be rejected by the North Government, for it was made by the same session of the Continental Congress that had turned down the North proposal. In fact, the Ministry gave such scant consideration to the American petition that "A Briton," writing in the *Morning Chronicle,* wondered how an accommodation should take place, "when the petitions and prayers of the Americans, with that of the citizens of London, are rejected and treated with scorn?"[14]

While most newspapers and magazines recommended that the Ministry continue its attempts to negotiate with the colonists,[15] they were forced to report that the conditions surrounding the regularly publicized rumors of peace invariably proved either un-

[12] *Gazetteer,* July 12, 1775. See also Robert L. Haig, *The Gazetteer, 1735-1797,* 139.

[13] *Gazetteer,* July 27, 1775.

[14] *Morning Chronicle,* October 13, 1775. See also October 6, letter by "CANDIDUS" wishing for, but not expecting an accommodation to take place, because "no terms whatever are held out to the Americans by our despotic masters."

[15] *Gentleman's Magazine,* October, 1775; *Gazetteer,* May 23, 1776.

workable or completely fraudulent. Most of the panaceas suggested in 1775 were based upon the assumption that Anglo-American relations had commenced deteriorating in 1763, when the French sword (believed to have hovered so menacingly over the heads of the Protestant English colonials) was permanently removed. The period before 1763 was regarded as the halcyon era of Empire relations. What, then, was to preclude King, Parliament, and American subjects from turning back the clock and re-entering the tranquil era? Could not George III regain "SEVEN MILLIONS *of hearts,*" asked one enthusiastic correspondent, simply by ordering the Colonies back into the same state they enjoyed the morning his grandfather died? In two months, the time necessary to get the message across the Atlantic, he predicted, peace would be restored.[16] The *Evening Post* also commented favorably upon the plan to go back to 1763. Although not so optimistic as the previous writer, it believed that "in the present miserable prospect of things," removing all of the post-1763 legislation from the books and thereby removing all American grievances could be the first step in restoring the dignity of Britain and bringing peace to America.[17] But a return to the days before the Seven Years' War was impossible unless, of course, Britain returned Canada to the French—in which case the remedy would be worse than the disease. The press occasionally printed suggestions that Canada be returned to the French for just such a purpose, but no publication ever considered this solution seriously. The dream of restoring imperial relationships to their pre-1763 status never materialized, for the conditions that had prevailed a dozen years before would, most Englishmen hoped, never return.

Meanwhile, in late 1775, the Opposition forces in Parliament once again made efforts to negotiate a settlement with the Americans. Needless to say, the good wishes of both the Whig and the independent newspapers went with them. The *Morning Chronicle,* referring to an impending speech by Edmund Burke for reconciliation with America, expressed the hope that the theme would be "the olive instead of the sword," and it begged both sides to "listen to something practicable, ere the means of deliberation may be torn from them for ever."[18] However popular might be Burke's idea that Parliament should be permitted to

16 *General Evening Post,* October 7, 1775.
17 *Evening Post,* December 12, 1775.
18 *Morning Chronicle,* November 8, 1775.

lay only commerce-regulating taxes upon the Americans[19] and that even these collected monies be remitted to the Colonies, it was clear that the North ministry was in no position to accept or to support any conciliatory proposals suggested by the eloquent spokesman for the Opposition. In spite of the *Gazetteer's* claim that only men blindly and strongly devoted to a ministry with no plan of its own could oppose it,[20] this newspaper acknowledged that the measure would not pass. The *Morning Chronicle*, reporting that some ministers supported Burke's bill, pointed out that, in order to clear Parliament, a peace proposal would have to originate with the Ministry, as the North forces could easily defeat any Opposition measure in either House.

Burke's address to the Commons in November was as fruitless as were his remarks in March, 1775. On that earlier occasion, though for over three hours "the attention of the House was rivetted to him," his brilliant plea for conciliation with the Colonies "afforded the most exquisite entertainment, but had no other effect."[21] Likewise, Lord Chatham's plan to legalize the American Congress, to receive a delegation of its representatives, and to allow the Congress a vote on all revenue measures affecting the Colonies (in return for which the Americans would vote a revenue to the Crown), did not impress Parliament. Though the *Middlesex Journal* believed that the adoption of the Chatham plan would demonstrate how easy was the road to peace and reconciliation, few expected a Tory Parliament to follow the lead suggested by a Chathamite newspaper that, among other misdeeds, had supported John Wilkes in the Middlesex County elections.[22]

With all of the Opposition's conciliatory measures doomed to defeat in Parliament and North's one major peace proposal rejected by the colonists, the desire for an end to the difficulties by negotiation continued to pervade the newspapers. If only the colonials would come begging forgiveness, then Mother England, with a magnanimous heart, could peaceably settle the struggle upon the Ministry's terms and all would be well; Parliament and Crown would have their dignity restored, the Ministry could

[19] *Morning Chronicle*, November 10, 1775.

[20] *Gazetteer*, November 10, 1775.

[21] *Gentleman's Magazine*, March 22, 1775, 201. See also 305: "Mr. Burke may fail to convince, but he never fails to charm."

[22] *Middlesex Journal*, December 30, 1776. See also *Lloyd's Evening Post*, July 17, 1775.

place some sorely needed laurels upon its own brow, and the Opposition would lose the issue. A year before it became a Ministry newspaper Bate's *Morning Post* expected the Americans at any moment to take the initiative in making peace. It had earlier maintained that the Colonies could not survive without Britain's commerce.[23] It now reported that economic affairs in the Colonies were so seriously disrupted that almost all the men of property wished for a prompt reconciliation even if it meant giving up some of their cherished pretensions.[24]

But the *Morning Post* was to learn that this was merely wishful reporting. The Americans were not backing down; the war in which "every humane heart, and disinterested being, must unite in wishing a speedy reconciliation upon honourable terms to both nations"[25] continued, with no sign of peace visible to either politician or newspaperman. In an unusually direct editorial, the *Gazetteer* accused a divided Ministry of persevering in the American war "with all enthusiastic madness" when a swift reconciliation appeared to be "the only means of rescuing from impending ruin the safety or prosperity of this kingdom."[26]

The final hope for a peaceful end to hostilities centered about the "one last effort" the King was to make. After appointing the Howe brothers as peace commissioners on May 3, 1776, George III sent them to America with an olive branch in one hand and a sword in the other. The Howes' instructions were clear: They were not to negotiate with any colony until all extralegal congresses had been dissolved by the Americans. If the "deluded malcontents" treated with contempt this final offer of peace, the Howes were to employ such powers as "cannot fail to open the Americans' eyes."[27] Despite these inflexible terms and even before the first meeting with the Americans on Staten Island in September, the *Gazetteer* and the *Morning Chronicle* hopefully

---

23 *Morning Post*, April 22, 1775.
24 *Morning Post*, July 2, 1776. See also September 2: "From the best information, it is asserted, that the majority of Americans anxiously wish for a reconciliation, and look upon the disposition of some of their leaders, who talk of resigning their property, burning their towns, and flying to the deserts, as little short of madness." See also *St. James's Chronicle*, May 25, 1776: "It is reported that the Americans, touched with a sense of the Havock which must attend the Prosecution of the present war with England . . . have sent over a proposal to the Ministry to put an End to the present bloody and unnatural war."
25 *Gazetteer*, July 4, 1776.
26 *Gazetteer*, July 16, 1776.
27 *Morning Post*, May 9, 1776.

reported that a peace plan had already been transmitted to London by the British commissioners.[28]

Before learning that the Americans' refusal to revoke the Declaration of Independence (as a necessary preliminary) had produced polite disagreement, much of the British press had predicted the failure of the conference. *Gentleman's Magazine* announced, "The sword is drawn, and the slaughter of the people is begun."[29] Notwithstanding the dream that, somehow, someone would bring this unpopular blood bath to an end honorable to all parties, the press reconciled itself to the military difficulties ahead. The loyal newspapers, incensed by the intransigence of the Americans, attacked the colonists, who they believed were intoxicated with their own power and were involving America in that ruin "which all good men hope will fall only on some of the basest of those individuals."[30] Only the extreme "republican" position continued to call for an immediate cessation of hostilities, even if it meant a complete military withdrawal from America. "If ministry are not above news-paper advice," affirmed the *Packet*, "they should dispatch orders for Lord Howe, with the army to evacuate America, and to sail immediately . . . to England."[31] The *Packet* soon was to discover that as far as the Opposition press was concerned, the North Government remained above newspaper advice, unless, of course, the advice was planted by a Ministry writer.

England by late 1776 was not thinking of withdrawing from America or of commencing serious negotiations with the rebels. The army, and not a set of peace commissioners, was expected to bring the Americans to their senses before Britain's traditional enemies could lend them support and further complicate an already serious situation.

28 *Gazetteer,* August 6, 1776; *Morning Chronicle,* September 6.
29 *Gentleman's Magazine,* September, 1776, 476.
30 *General Evening Post,* November 12, 1776.
31 *Packet,* October 28, 1776.

CHAPTER IV

The Press Establishes
War Guilt

Now, good men of the law! pray who is in fault,
The one who begins, or resists the assault?[1]

G RANTING THAT BOTH SIDES were to blame for the misunderstanding, bias, and downright ignorance that enabled mother country and Colonies to commence the War of American Independence, Britain's Opposition press insisted that the greater guilt belonged to the unpopular ministry that controlled its own government. The *Evening Post, Public Ledger,* and *Middlesex Journal,* three of London's leading radical newspapers, at first led the assault upon the North ministry. By 1776 they were joined by the more moderate and independent *Gazetteer, St. James's Chronicle,* and *Morning Chronicle.* Even the loyal publications occasionally criticized the Ministry, as did almost every other important publication.

Lord North was one of the most frequently assailed men of his era. He had been severely criticized since the spring of 1774, when he was instrumental in pushing the Coercive Acts through

[1] *Evening Post,* August 12, 1775.

Parliament, but the denunciation of his "obstinate, cruel, and unjust perseverance against the Americans"[2] reached its climax a year later when his effort to bring peace to the Colonies failed. His personal popularity within Parliament rarely was reflected in the columns of the London press.

Though Opposition editors realized how much the imperial relationship had deteriorated by early 1775, they refused to concede that war was the only means to bring about a rapprochement. Consequently, any allusions by the Ministry to a military action met with spirited criticism from the Opposition newspapers. Almon's *Evening Post* was the most radical in its denunciation of the Ministry. Labeling the American war "unnatural, unconstitutional, unnecessary, unjust, dangerous, hazardous, and unprofitable," it charged the "cowardly and treacherous" ministers with drenching themselves with the blood of their countrymen by passing cruel and inhuman laws aimed at starving and murdering them.[3] The *St. James's Chronicle* agreed, as it rated the North ministry the most "obstinately cruel and diabolically wicked" ever to inhabit the earth.[4] It published a stream of censure directed against Lord North for beginning the war in America, and it reiterated the charge that he was the "arch Rebel against whom all our Vengeance should be directed."[5] Further, the outbreak of hostilities did not surprise Henry Baldwin, publisher of the *St. James's Chronicle*, for this newspaper had been quoting both Lord Chatham and Lord Camden to the effect that war would be the inevitable consequence of the Ministry's actions. Even before the news of Lexington, this newspaper warned its readers about "the things most to be feared in a popular government":

A Foolish, obstinate and unrelenting King, an abandoned Ministry, a profligate House of Peers, a venal House of Commons, . . . Soldiers without courage, an exhausted Treasury, . . . Heavy taxes, . . . sound ships breaking up, and rotten ones building to defend our coasts.[6]

---

2 *Morning Chronicle,* March 7, 1775.

3 *Evening Post,* April 11, May 15, June 15, 1775. See also June 20, 22, 27, March 18, 23, 1775.

4 *St. James's Chronicle,* June 2, 1775. See also March 10.

5 *St. James's Chronicle,* May 31, June 5, 1775. The *St. James's Chronicle,* however, opened its columns to Tory letter writers. See April 14, letter from a "south Briton," condemning the "mock-patriots of London" and stressing that "he would not hesitate to wield the Sword against the American Rebels." See also August 25 letter attacking the "Minority Patriots."

6 *St. James's Chronicle,* April 15, 1775.

The *Middlesex Journal* also asserted that North's attitude toward the Americans would bring "eternal dishonour" to the Ministry. "If the undaunted Chatham had been at the steerage," it believed, "rebellion would have been crushed *in embryo*, and prevented from arriving at formidable maturity."[7] While endeavoring to replace the North ministry with a Chathamite coalition and at the same time stressing that the Court was terrified at the thought of Chatham's "by force of public misfortunes coming into power,"[8] it held out little hope for the success of its efforts. On October 14, after noticing the fragmenting of the Opposition in Parliament, the *Middlesex Journal* ruefully predicted another session in which the minority was to be split into small factions instead of forming a closely knit union. It had never expected governmental stability from "so heterogeneous a body as the King's ministry," but it admitted that the minority was as diverse and faction-torn as was the majority party in Parliament.

By the close of 1775 the ranks of the Opposition press were swelled with the addition of other heretofore impartial newspapers. The *Gazetteer*, previously used by "Poor Old England" and "A Boston Saint," two of the most notorious anti-American letter writers of the day,[9] surprised many with its editorial change. Previously, this newspaper had published numerous letters blaming the Chatham faction for causing the war in America. One contributor alleged that the Chathamites were using the American issue to further their own ambitions and interests,[10] while another traced all of the "unhappy disturbances in America" to Chatham and his followers.[11]

The reasons for the *Gazetteer's* conversion from lukewarm Tory to intransigent Whig in late 1775 were many: It feared the

7 *Middlesex Journal*, August 5, September 19, 1775.

8 *Middlesex Journal*, August 8, 17, 1775, May 16, 1776.

9 On March 14, 1775, "Poor Old England" had written the *Gazetteer* that "ignorance, ingratitude and presumption" were the principal qualities of the Americans. See also March 15 for his defense of "virtual representation." "A Boston Saint," June 5, warned the "crew of hirelings" writing for America in the British press that they "ought to have been in custody long ago," and that he "should not be surprised to hear of their being lodged in Newgate." On July 1, he charged that the Americans started the war by firing the first shots at Lexington and Concord. See also June 8, July 14, 1775.

10 *Gazetteer*, September 15, 1775.

11 *Gazetteer*, September 2, 1775. See also September 4, for "PALINURUS," and September 6, for "DECIUS'S" defense of the North ministry.

great loss to Britain's commerce; it abhorred the introduction of Hanoverian mercenaries into a purely British struggle;[12] it became convinced that the Ministry (dominated by the King's "Favourites"), in order to sustain its program in America, was resorting to bribery and corruption to guarantee itself parliamentary majorities; and, perhaps most important of all, it feared the consequences of an all-out war in America. Asserting that all the colonial legislation had been passed in a hasty manner, without due consideration of consequences, the *Gazetteer*, in a rare direct editorial, stated that so long as England was ruled by the King's favorite, rather than by a qualified ruler, she would experience distraction in her councils and distrust among the people.[13]

Less than two weeks later this newspaper announced that because of increased sales it would go to press at an earlier hour.[14] Its new political position apparently enlarged its circulation in London's heavily Opposition precincts. By mid-1776 the *Gazetteer*, now in complete agreement with other radical journals in London, declared that the most effectual way to distress the Americans was to send them Britain's present Administration.[15]

In 1776 William "Memory" Woodfall's *Morning Chronicle* joined the *Gazetteer* in attacking the North ministry for its prosecution of the war in America. Before taking this stand, the *Morning Chronicle* had been impartial in political matters, but as the middle ground became more difficult to maintain, Woodfall's newspaper drifted closer to the Opposition. Previously, it had praised Chatham, Camden, and Burke, but it had also opened its columns to "Poor Old England," "PACIFICUS," "TRUTH," and other outstanding defenders of the Ministry.[16] While opposing the Government, the *Morning Chronicle* nevertheless came out decidedly against American independence.[17]

Woodfall not only regretted the "unexpected misfortunes" that had attended Britain's plans for subduing America, but he also feared new parliamentary legislation that would place a luxury tax on newspapers. He believed that the new halfpenny excise

12 *Gazetteer,* December 7, 1775.
13 *Gazetteer,* November 30, 1775.
14 *Gazetteer,* December 18, 1775.
15 *Gazetteer,* June 19, 1776. See also *Morning Chronicle,* June 18, 1776.
16 *Morning Chronicle,* July 1, 1775, "Poor Old England." For the letters of "PACIFICUS" and "TRUTH," see November 21 and July 29, 1775.
17 *Morning Chronicle,* September 6, 1776.

which the Ministry contemplated placing on the press would prove itself such a burden upon "an already oppressed public" that it could jeopardize an Englishman's liberty and property. He was convinced that the North ministry, aware that most newspapers were opposed to it, was attempting to muzzle the press by driving its price out of the reach of as many readers as possible.[18]

As did the *Middlesex Journal*, which supported the Chatham-Camden faction in Parliament, the *Morning Chronicle* realized that the Opposition did not have the power to defeat the North ministry. Although it praised the "warmth and great abilities" of the minority leadership, it knew that it was hammering in vain at the all-powerful Ministry of George III.[19] "VERITAS," a regular contributor to the *Morning Chronicle*, wrote in a public letter addressed to Edmund Burke, "It is a rule with some men, to oppose everything that comes from you." He was not surprised "that men who hate virtue should detest those who profess it."[20]

While favoring a Rockingham coalition, William Woodfall's *Morning Chronicle* rarely reflected as extreme a political position as did his other newspaper, the *Packet*. The *Packet's* appeal was to a lower level of reading audience. Its tales, rumors, and violently anti-Ministry position were rarely emulated by its sister publication. If, however, the *Morning Chronicle* valued a story that appeared in the *Packet*, it copied the story verbatim, clearly stating the source of the information, which was usually a speculative rumor. For example, the tale that the Ministry had offered Canada to France "on condition she assists England to subdue the Southern part of America," appeared first in the *Packet*, with an editorial comment that "this is the conciliatory plan of the great and good Ministers of wretched, hapless England." This article, without the comment, was copied by the *Morning Chronicle*.[21] In criticizing the Ministry, Woodfall's two newspapers took different approaches: the *Morning Chronicle* the moderate "high road"; the *Packet*, the violent "low road."[22]

18 *Morning Chronicle*, January 9, May 4, 1776.
19 *Morning Chronicle*, February 21, 1776.
20 *Morning Chronicle*, May 10, 1776.
21 *Morning Chronicle*, January 11, 1776.
22 The *Morning Chronicle*, however, opened its columns to Tory sentiments. Unlike the *Packet*, it never blinded itself to the fact that there was justice in many ministerial, or anti-American arguments. See June 26, 1776, for a virulent attack upon the shortcomings of the Opposition. By the time France entered the war in mid-1778, the *Morning Chronicle* could be counted upon to present the news in a manner sympathetic to the Ministry. Woodfall in 1776 sold the *Packet*, which he had purchased three years before, to a group of London radicals.

Most English publications, Whig or independent, attacked the Ministry on four specific counts: First, Lord North was believed to be a weak, vacillating Prime Minister; second, many thought he was only a front for a more nefarious group of advisers (the "Double Cabinet"), who were either deceiving or being deceived; third, the men in this "Double Cabinet," who were running the Government with George III and Lord North, were believed to be of decidedly inferior caliber; and last and perhaps most important, the Ministry, by endeavoring to corrupt Parliament was destroying England's cherished constitutional balance between the King and Parliament.

None of these counts was directly related to the war in America. The Wilkes and Almon factions of the radical press had been making these charges for the past decade, at least, but they expected the war in America to provide them with the ammunition necessary to bring down the North ministry. The ministers, of course, were well aware of the Opposition's tactics. As early as May 30, 1775, Germain wrote in disgust to his friend General Irwin that the American version of the battles at Lexington and Concord had been sped to Britain on a ship in ballast, whereas General Gage's report, obviously sent on a slower ship laden with goods, hadn't as yet arrived. On the previous night Almon's *Evening Post* had brought out an extraordinary issue, carrying the American account of the battles. Germain, North, and, presumably, the King learned of these significant clashes in distant Massachusetts by buying the *Evening Post* for threepence. Germain concluded, accurately, that "the many joyful faces" of the Opposition evinced expectations "that rebellion will be the means of changing the Ministry."[23]

The *Middlesex Journal* regularly printed letters and poems and, occasionally, editorials stressing the political shortcomings of the Prime Minister. "CONSISTENT," a frequent contributor to this newspaper, attacked North for being so inconsistent, and, after comparing him to a weathercock in a whirlwind, the writer switched his metaphor and implored North to quit the helm, "and hide below decks, from all human sight, or the ship will be forever lost by thy bungling steerage."[24] The *Middlesex Journal* demanded a program of firmness and decision. It insisted that the Government stop doing things by halves and either come to a treaty

[23] HMC, Stopford-Sackville MSS, I, May 30, 1775.
[24] *Middlesex Journal*, March 2, 1775.

with the Americans or conquer them. This Chathamite newspaper repeatedly derided "this doing and undoing, this shifting policy, this turning and doubling, this going backwards and forwards, furious today, lenitive tomorrow, and consistent never."[25] It continued to stress this theme throughout the next two years.[26] The *St. James's Chronicle*, likewise criticizing the weaknesses of the Government, noted that the Prime Minister was at all times ambiguous and evasive.[27] In July, 1775, a contributor to the *Gazetteer* told North not to trifle and recommended that, if he meant to reduce the Americans to obedience by the sword, he should "be not niggardly either in the military or naval force."[28] By the end of that year the *Gazetteer* was convinced, however, that resolution could not come from the pusillanimous Prime Minister. On December 5 this newspaper charged that Lord North changed opinions more often than he changed his clothes. Before being converted to the ministerial side, Henry Bate's *Morning Post* also attacked the Administration for the inconsistent course it steered in American affairs. In May, 1776, it announced that, since news of General Howe's evacuation from Boston arrived, the plan for prosecuting the war in the Colonies had been changed three times by three consecutive Cabinet councils.[29] Alluding to the Minister's recent fall on a slippery palace floor, it reported:

> In spite of all N**TH's Courtly pains,
>   Poor *England* will take harm!
> For weakly must he hold the reins,
>   Who hath—*a broken arm!*[30]

These weaknesses and vacillations of the Prime Minister were

25 *Middlesex Journal*, March 14, 1775.

26 *Middlesex Journal*, August 19, September 21, 1775. See also *St. James's Chronicle*, June 20, 1775; *Chester Chronicle*, June 19, July 18, December 11; *Courant*, March 18, 1782.

27 *St. James's Chronicle*, April 18, 1775.

28 *Gazetteer*, July 13, 1775. See also *Augustus Henry, Third Duke of Grafton, Autobiography and Political Correspondence*, William R. Anson, ed., 303: " . . . while the affairs of the Americans were directed by wonderful ability, wisdom and fortitude, our Ministry were only acting on the spur of the occasion, without plan and without system."

29 *Morning Post*, May 16, 1776.

30 *Morning Post*, October 4, 1776. Lord North's frequent physical indispositions were the butt of much political laughter in the newspapers. On January 4, 1776, almost all of the newspapers carried the story that he had been forced to miss work for a few days because of a severe inflammation of the eyes. On January 5, the *Morning Post* assumed that the inflammation was caused by North's reading the reports from Canada that Quebec had fallen to the Americans.

symptoms of a more serious situation, many editors suspected. North, despite his occasional cleverness in debate, his talent for financial administration, and the respect given him even by political foes, was believed to be only a feeble puppet, repeating in Parliament the phrases fed him by a group of all-powerful advisers who worked behind the scenes at St. James's and who wielded the greatest influence with the King. The *Morning Post,* in discussing North's powers, declared that he and "the ruling junto" did not have a shadow of authority at Court or in Parliament, independent of the royal smile.[31] The *Middlesex Journal* was more specific. It announced that the King received the opinions of Mansfield, Earl Gower, Charles Jenkinson, Richard Rigby, and Sir Gilbert Elliot "in private," and the opinions of this small group appeared in the royal dictates as the word of the King and his First Minister. Harping at these men for forming what Burke liked to call "a double cabinet," it blamed "this set of underworkers behind the curtain" for most of the intransigent measures that were taken against the Americans.[32] One writer to the *Morning Chronicle,* imploring his sovereign to rise above petty political faction, warned that kings who showed themselves partial to a party "had the service only of the worst part of their people, and these reigns were commonly anxious and unquiet."[33] Burke's allegations of "secret advisers" and an "inner cabinet" were frequently paraphrased in the Opposition press, which clearly was taking its cues from the anti-Government leadership in Parliament. Burke's expressed belief that Lord Mansfield was "sitting in silence behind the curtain . . . guiding the political machine" was widely echoed throughout the period of the war.[34]

By 1776 most English publications represented Charles Jenkinson, a Treasury subminister without family or fortune, as the

[31] "Crito," writing in the *Morning Post,* March 3, 1775, stated that "North's power is fixed beyond all the endeavours of party to remove him," because the King had given him his complete support.

[32] *Middlesex Journal,* March 14, July 4, 6, 13, 1775. See also July 26, for a statement claiming that Lord Chief Justice Mansfield and Lord North were in favor of a suspension of arms in America and were opposed by Charles Jenkinson; and January 6, 1776, for a statement that North favored acknowledging the Congress, "but others more powerful, think differently."

[33] *Morning Chronicle,* June 21, 1775.

[34] "Toby," in the May 23, 1775, *Evening Post,* asserted that Lord Mansfield was both the law and the government. See also George Herbert Guttridge, *English Whiggism and the American Revolution,* 104; John Nichols, *Recollections and Reflections during the Reign of George III,* 385. Nichols, a former Opposition M.P., was certain George III had a "double cabinet."

power behind the throne of England. The *Middlesex Journal* expressed a certainty that Jenkinson, who formerly had been the political secretary of Lord Bute, would succeed North if and when he resigned.[35] The *Morning Post* repeated the "fact that Mr. Jenkinson is to be minister whenever Lord North goes out; he might have been so some time ago, but he declines it as long as he can find a man that will submit to be his deputy."[36]

While North should not have been considered anybody's deputy but the King's, the press was correct when it reported that Jenkinson was the man most frequently recommended to succeed North if and when George III should allow his First Minister to resign. It was North who recommended that the King appoint Jenkinson as Secretary at War in late November, 1778.[37] Further, the following February North wrote the King that Jenkinson was "without exception, by much the fittest person in England to have the direction of the finances of this country."[38] While the press could not be expected to be privy to the contents of the letters between the King and his chief minister, it did not doubt that Jenkinson was a power in the councils of the Ministry. Opposition editors widely distrusted him not only because he had been a part of the unpopular Bute Administration, but, still more important, because in the first three years of the war he appeared to be in a policy-making situation although he held no major position of responsibility.

Though Jenkinson was thought by many to be the leader of the "Kings Party" (Horace Walpole described him as "sole confidant of the King," while Edmund Burke labeled him "the real minister"), Lord Sandwich, First Lord of the Admiralty, and Lord George Germain, Secretary of State for the American Department, were the men in the Government who, next to North, were most severely criticized. Jenkinson's work was usually done out of the public view, but Sandwich and Germain were tilling a field more readily watched by Opposition papers and politicians.

35 *Middlesex Journal*, January 18, 1776. See also *Morning Chronicle* and *Gazetteer*, January 22, for identical articles speculating about North's resignation.

36 "XY," in a letter to the *Middlesex Journal*, May 7, 1776, listed the "chain of unimportant, poor, and unconnected beings that govern this country." Jenkinson's name headed the list, followed by those of Sir Gilbert Elliot, Richard Rigby, Lords Barrington, Weymouth, Sandwich, Suffolk and Germain. Lord North was listed last. See also April 11.

37 Fortescue, *Correspondence of King George III*, IV, 24 November 1778, North to King, and 26 November 1778, King to North, authorizing the appointment.

38 *Correspondence of King George III*, IV, February 1, 1779, North to King.

Sandwich's tormentors in the press accused him of indolence and—still worse—criminal negligence for the way the navy was being permitted to deteriorate. The prolonged holidays and high living standards of "Jemmy Twitcher" caused serious rumblings of discontent and editorial demands for his removal long before irregularities in the navy were exposed. The *Morning Chronicle*, referring to Sandwich's remark that the colonists were "pusillanimous," commented that "at play his lordship may be competent to speculative calculation, but at *political hazard* we find him a mere pidgeon,"[39] while the *Packet* assured its public that "all official business sat so easy on Jemmy Twitcher that he has been these two days on a party of trout-tickling."[40] The *Morning Post*, just prior to its conversion to the ministerial party, reported that Sandwich had been "relaxing in all the stile of rural indulgence" during the preceding fortnight—a time when the Admiralty required the fullest exertion of his abilities to meet the critical situation in America.[41] Earlier, the *Middlesex Journal* had demanded the removal of the negligent First Lord.[42]

As violently as Lord Sandwich was disliked by the press, Lord George Germain was even more unpopular. Here was the individual who was derisively named "The Minden Hero" for his failure to deliver a crucial victory in the Battle of Minden during the Seven Years' War. A military court-martial had forbidden him service in any capacity at any time with His Majesty's forces, yet, because of the King's friendship, he was now in full command of the military operation in America. The press believed "Lord Minden" was a "very great favourite with George III,"[43] and Germain was, consequently, heartily disliked by Englishmen long before his mistakes in America made his presence in the Government a very heavy liability. So long as the King could command the requisite votes in Parliament he could remain oblivious of public opinion, but his support of one of the most unpopular men in the Empire was a tactical error that eventually would haunt him.

Until its conversion late in 1776, the *Morning Post* was one of Germain's severest critics. Declaring that it was well informed

39 *Morning Chronicle*, October 2, 1775. See also *Morning Post*, same date.
40 *Packet*, April 5, 1776.
41 *Morning Post*, May 17, 1776.
42 *Middlesex Journal*, January 25, 1776.
43 *Middlesex Journal*, January 25, 1776.

of the fact that Germain had undertaken on his own responsibility "the whole of the American bloody business" and had pledged himself to be singly and totally answerable for the next campaign in America, it noted that, if the campaign failed, "he only is to have the blame."[44] The *Gazetteer* frequently pleaded for his removal,[45] and by June, 1776, the *Morning Post* was hopefully reporting that the Secretary had fallen into royal disfavor and would presently be replaced.[46] But this, too, represented wishful thinking. The *Morning Post,* which never had expected much from Germain and the "pompous promises of his party," commented, "how wretched is the present alternative." The Whig *St. James's Chronicle* surmised ironically that upon the success of their measures in America

> Lord North staked his—*Popularity.*
> Lord G. G. his—*Honor and Reputation as a Soldier.*
> And Lord Sandwich his—*Virtue and Morality.*

"What a heavy loss will these Gentlemen sustain should the ensuing campaign prove unsuccessful!" it concluded.[47]

Perhaps because his skin had become so thickened in the decade after Minden, Germain appeared impervious to criticism. As Secretary for the American Department, he was in a position to dispense Secret Service monies and to set up paragraphs and articles favorable to himself and his policies, but he appeared as uninterested in winning over the public as was his sovereign. Convinced he was fighting the good fight, the Secretary apparently pocketed any Secret Service funds that came his way. He rarely lifted his pen or his purse to counter the attacks being leveled against himself by the Opposition and, later on, by the loyal press, which owed allegiance either to Lord North or to Lord Sandwich.[48] Aside from an occasional pamphlet by Israel Mau-

---

[44] *Morning Post,* January 24, 1776.

[45] *Gazetteer,* January 17, 1776.

[46] *Morning Post,* June 5, 13, 1776.

[47] *St. James's Chronicle,* March 28, 1776.

[48] Aside from occasional requests to include certain material in the *London Gazette,* the correspondences of both Germain and Knox yield no evidence that Germain wished to be defended in the press. Further, the Opposition rarely accused him of endeavoring to corrupt the press—charges it regularly leveled against both North and Sandwich, especially after it became known that some anonymous friends of the latter were supporting the *Morning Herald* in 1780.

duit or Joseph Galloway, very little comment pleasing to Germain could be found in any English publications.[49]

Incessant reports of quarrels within the Ministry did little to persuade readers that their Government was stable. On March 30, 1776, the *Evening Post,* stating that North and Germain were quarreling and shifting the blame for "each blunder" in America, declared:

> When two such lads of mettle,
> Cannot their business settle
> Good people, where's the wonder,
> If England's rent asunder.

Two months later, this newspaper asserted that the friction between the Bedford faction (of which Sandwich formerly had been a leader) and Germain was such that the Secretary's resignation was momentarily expected.[50] A correspondent to the *St. James's Chronicle* remarked that it was "no Wonder the present Ministry are so successful at home and abroad, when we consider what wonderful Harmony reigns among the Ministers, and those they employ." After cataloguing the "natural Coalitions" that existed between North and the Bedford party and the other factions that were splitting the Ministry, he concluded: "While men are thus paired, their joint Endeavours must continue to produce similar Effects with the past."[51]

Despite these complaints about the ineptitude and the quarrelsome character of the "King's Friends," many newspapers continued to assert that George III was not directly responsible for England's poor political and military showing in America. The King was looked upon as a sincere but naive leader whose endeavors to bring the difficulties in the Colonies to a swift and equitable conclusion were doomed to failure because of the unwise advice that his ministers were giving him. He was to be pitied, not condemned, for England's misfortunes.[52] Ignorant of the actions of his friends, who were oblivious of a public opinion

---

[49] See Israel Mauduit, *Remarks Upon General Howe's Account of His Proceedings on Long Island,* 7: "Lord George Germaine . . . gave a vigour to our councils unknown to them before"; and *Morning Herald,* January 15, 1781, for a summation of the relationship between Germain and Joseph Galloway.

[50] *Evening Post,* May 22, 1776.

[51] *St. James's Chronicle,* August 29, 1776. See also *Gazetteer,* December 1, 1777, for a later report that North and Germain were at odds.

[52] *St. James's Chronicle,* June 18, 1775.

that condemned them, George was being duped.[53] The results of this deception were disaster in America and lack of confidence in the sovereign and his ministers at home. One gentleman in a coffeehouse, reported the *St. James's Chronicle,* upon learning of General Howe's evacuation of Boston, was certain that this depressing information would open the King's eyes to the realities of the war in America. But "honest Hibernian" retorted that George would never open his eyes until they were shut forever.[54] The *Evening Post,* in a column dedicated to the King, stressed that his ministers could not distinguish truth from falsehood and advised him that the difficulties in America were due to the wrong measures instituted by the men around him. It lamented that even the piety of George III could not influence the men who surrounded him, and it concluded by predicting:

> . . . the plot is laid to make
> Their King a royal Slave . . .[55]

Not all editors believed that George was being led astray. Some maintained that the King was his own chief minister and that upon his shoulders must be placed the responsibility for England's distressed state of affairs.[56] If the "royal smile" made and unmade royal advisers, then the sovereign would be held responsible for the policies of his ministers.

Perhaps the press's major reason for a lack of confidence in its King and Government was its belief that the Ministry, in trying to carry its program through Parliament, was corrupting the legislature more completely than had Walpole. Burlesquing Parliament's sale of itself to the Government, the *Evening Post* published "a Song by the Tory Ministry, to the tune of 'a begging we will go'":

> Tis money makes the Members vote,
>   And sanctify our ways:
> It makes the Patriot turn his coat,
>   And money we must raise
>   And a taxing we will go, will go, etc.

[53] *St. James's Chronicle,* July 12, 1775. See also September 23: " . . . our good King, like most other kind Masters, shews too much Readiness to credit and protect bad servants."

[54] *St. James's Chronicle,* May 9, 1776.

[55] *Evening Post,* June 8, 1775, November 12, 1776. See also March 23, 1775, for an appeal to "GEORGE AND CHARLOTTE!" and April 18 and September 25.

[56] *Morning Post,* March 3, 1775.

> But second thoughts are ever best,
>   And lest our force should fail,
> What fraud can do, we'll make a test,
>   And see what bribes avail.
>   And a taxing, etc.
>
>   . . .
>
> Each colony we will propose,
>   Shall raise an ample sum;
> Which well applied, under the nose
>   May bribe them—as at home.
>   And a taxing, etc.[57]

The *St. James's Chronicle,* also mocking the "'tis money makes the Kingdom go 'round" policies of Government, printed a "Political Dictionary and Catechism," which included the following questions and answers:

Q.—What is the Royal Prerogative?
A.—As much as it can get.
Q.—Wherein lies the privilege of Parliament?
A.—In the people's pockets. . . .
Q.—How does a modern Member of Parliament represent
    his constituents?
A.—By doing as they did—selling himself.[58]

Both the *Morning Post* and the *Gazetteer* stressed the point that by 1775 Parliament was no longer the true representative of the British people. Whether it had ever been so, they did not resolve. But they were so incensed at the present state of Parliament that they went so far as to suggest a course of civil disobedience to its legislation. One contributor, claiming that Parliament had forfeited its constitutional omnipotence by selling itself to the Ministry, concluded that when the legislature "degenerates into tyranny" the people have a right to resist it.[59] The *Gazetteer* also warned that the acts of Parliament were in jeopardy of losing their validity. "When a minister procures a corrupt majority in the Senate, and passes such laws as he thinks will please his master, and gratify his own private views, what are the people to expect under such circumstances?" it asked.[60]

[57] *Evening Post,* March 4, 1775.
[58] *St. James's Chronicle,* March 15, 1775.
[59] *Morning Post,* July 12, 28, 1775.
[60] *Gazetteer,* November 30, 1775.

Instances of the Administration's granting of a sinecure, pension, or contract to a key member of Parliament (by "bribery" the press usually did not mean direct cash handouts) were frequently cited, and with morality on their side the Opposition newspapers made the most of each opportunity. Having printed a letter (ostensibly by a Tory) advising the Ministry to "give Edmund [Burke] and his friend the Colonel [Barré] a snug sinecure, and we shall no more hear the flowing subtile harangues of the one, or the passionate declamations of the other, on the topic of national liberty,"[61] the *Gazetteer* soon published an answer that asserted that the two champions of the Opposition could not be bought and were not in politics for profit.[62] Enough other members of the Commons could be purchased, however. "Sir — D — was in full career to join the present opposition," reported the *Morning Post* before its conversion, "when by a fatal stumble over an Irish peerage" and into a contract for horses, "he was struck with such a mortal stroke of the gout, as benumbed his pride, and checked his patriotic ardour."[63]

Not only was the taxpayers' money being used to finance legislative bribes, but the royal and ministerial favorites were also mulcting the Treasury of additional thousands that went directly into their own pockets. The press charged that the man who profited most from the war in America was Richard Rigby, who previously had managed the Irish Commons when the Duke of Bedford was Ireland's Lord Lieutenant. Now a member of the "Double Cabinet," a "King's Favourite," and holder of the most lucrative position, Paymaster of the Royal Forces, "Mr. Rigby feels the sweets of the American war if nobody else does," reported both the *Gazetteer* and the *Morning Post* in June, 1776.[64] The following month the *Middlesex Journal* stated that Rigby would receive £26,000 that year, and it expressed no surprise on learning that he refused to quit the paymastership for any other government position.[65] Rigby frequently was identified, along

61 *Gazetteer,* August 2, 1776.

62 *Gazetteer,* August 5, 1776.

63 *Morning Post,* February 1, 1776. See also August 9, for a complaint that the government paid 4s. per gallon of rum to "a Scotch favourite," when rum was selling for 2s. per gallon on the open market. "One should think," lamented the *Morning Post,* "the calamity was sufficiently great, and the burthen sufficiently heavy to support this unnatural civil war, with the greatest economy, without doubling the expence to supply the avarice and rapacity of ministerial tools."

64 *Morning Post,* June 25, 1776; *Gazetteer,* June 13.

65 *Middlesex Journal,* July 27, 1776.

with North, Sandwich, Germain, Mansfield, and Jenkinson, as being one of the key men "behind the scenes running the government."[66] The press prophesied that all of the above-mentioned lieutenants of the Minister would build up large personal fortunes. It neglected to note that Lord North was going heavily into debt at this time.

The *Morning Post* informed its readers that they could never expect a full accounting of exactly where their tax money went. "By a new way just adopted in the public accounts," it reported in September, 1776, "Lord North will have it in his power to deceive both Parliament and the world." It charged that North's new method was contrived "in so entangled a manner" that even an attentive and knowledgeable audit would still be unable to unravel it. "The web of deceit is at present manufacturing," it warned.[67]

Money, which in Robert Walpole's time made the Empire go round, was now, many believed, making the Empire go down.

[66] *Middlesex Journal,* August 29, September 5, 1776.
[67] *Morning Post,* September 5, 1776.

CHAPTER V

Independence and the War
Britain Might Lose

W HILE FILLED with impassioned pleas for reconciliation, most
newspapers and magazines reflected the belief that the
instransigence of both the Ministry and the Congress made a
continuation of war inevitable. To read that over thirty thousand
troops were setting sail in June and July of 1775 for New York
made even the strongest dreamers of peace reconsider.[1] In May,
a writer in the *Morning Post* pleaded for the strengthening of
naval forces, in view of the impending war.[2] By September the
Morning Post had concluded that both sides had totally lost sight
of peace and that the issue would be decided "by dint of arms
and a compleat victory."[3] *Gentleman's Magazine* added that, if
the obstinate colonists refused the terms offered them by the
Administration, the Government "would employ the whole national force."[4] Most readers now assumed the inevitability of
employing force, and their correspondence to the editors naturally

[1] Almon's *Evening Post,* December 14, 1775, questioned the good faith of the
Ministry, when it noted that additional troops were being sent to America at the
same time commissioners were being considered to compromise the differences
with the Colonies.

[2] *Morning Post,* May 31, 1775.

[3] *Morning Post,* September 22, 1775; *Gentleman's Magazine,* September, 445,
446.

[4] *Gentleman's Magazine,* December, 1775, 597.

contained advice on military strategy. One suggested that the Americans be awed into submission by heavy bombardment upon their coasts; another recommended that they be swiftly brought to their senses with "one vigorous attack on the New England provinces."[5] A contributor to *Lloyd's Evening Post* summed up the Ministry's position when he exclaimed that the rebels had started this war, and Britain, never backward in taking up the cudgel, certainly would finish it.[6]

The Declaration of Independence, introduced into this atmosphere, surprised few Englishmen. *Common Sense*, along with numerous articles and pamphlets about the political and military difficulties to be expected from America, had adequately prepared Britain for news of a formal break. By May, 1776, all of London was speculating upon the possibility of such a declaration.[7] When it finally arrived in mid-August, most newspapers published the document verbatim. All agreed that it was "couched in the strongest terms," and even William Woodfall's *Morning Chronicle* now also assumed that the dispute with the Colonies would have to be solved upon the field of honor.[8]

As expected, the Tory newspapers were emphatic in their denunciation of the Declaration, printing scores of articles attacking the folly of the American position. After such an open avowal of republican principles, maintained the *Morning Post* two months before its editor was placed on the royal payroll, "every European power must now abandon them to the punishment due to their villainy and folly."[9] On August 20, it printed a reply to the Declaration of the "DISUNITED STATES in AMERICA," chastising the "pride, hypocricy and dishonesty," which, "in the course of human events," led "a subordinate community to shake off the duty and allegiance which in honour and in necessity they owe." The *General Evening Post* returned to one of its earlier themes when it

---

[5] *General Evening Post*, October 23, 1775; "Crito," in the *Morning Post*, December 19. For a retort favorable to the Americans, see "Humanitus," *St. James's Chronicle*, December 26.

[6] *Lloyd's Evening Post*, March 11, 1776.

[7] The *General Evening Post*, May 18, 1776, reported seven of the provinces in favor of independence and five opposed. Cf. "VERITAS," in the Opposition *Evening Post*, who declared that "the question of independence has NOT been agitated in the Congress." The *Morning Post*, July 1, reported that the Congress was in such discord that it could not come to any resolution about independence.

[8] *Morning Chronicle*, August 14, 1776. This newspaper printed the verbatim text of the Declaration on August 17. The *St. James's Chronicle* and the *General Evening Post* printed it on August 15, 1776.

[9] *Morning Post*, August 19, 1776.

asserted that America's proponents of independence were in a state of absolute poverty, with war and independence their only hope of either fortune or consideration.[10] Maintaining that the Declaration had driven most of the dispassionate members from the councils of the Congress, it repeated the *Morning Post*'s opinion that the Americans' hope of forming an alliance with some powerful European nation was an "absurdity."[11] The Ministry's official denunciation of the American Declaration appeared in October with the anonymous publication of James Macpherson's *The Rights of Great Britain asserted against the Claims of America*. In this eighty-page pamphlet Macpherson defended the supremacy of the British legislature, its right to tax the Colonies, virtual representation, and the Quebec Act. He then attacked, paragraph by paragraph, the "pretended arguments justifying rebellion." Macpherson asserted that the "folly" and "ignorance" of the Declaration did not reflect American opinion. He stated his belief that men of property were, from interest, enemies of confusion and that these men had been terrified into silence by "misled rabble." He expressed doubt concerning the economic resources of the colonists and France's ability to aid them. His conclusions were clear: Great Britain had no choice but to crush the rebellion by force, for "to permit the Colonies to gain by one rebellion, is to sow the seeds of another."

The Opposition press, which had heretofore recognized much justice in the claims of America, was not embarrassed by the Declaration. While the *Morning Post* asserted the minority could not support independence in England without risking an immediate impeachment for high treason,[12] many newspapers and members of Parliament continued to support the Americans. None who put forward a belief that independence would be a benefit to both England and America were prosecuted.

The Opposition also knew that the overwhelming sentiment of the British public supported the Ministry in its attempt to crush the rebellious Americans. When, on August 25, 1775, Lord Sandwich wrote to Admiral Graves that "the nation (except some factious and interested opponents) are in a manner unanimous in

---

10 *General Evening Post,* September 3, 1776; *Morning Post,* September 4. See also *Gentleman's Magazine,* December, 1776, 573, stressing the "rage for independence chiefly prevailed among the multitude. The men of property were for adhering to the old constitution."

11 *General Evening Post,* August 10, 1776; *Morning Post,* August 12.

12 *Morning Post,* October 1, 1776.

their resolution to crush the unnatural rebellion that has broken out in America by force of arms, which to our great concern we now find the only expedient left," he was making a statement that in the next year could have been made by any one of a score of influential Englishmen of any political persuasion. The Duke of Grafton, long an anchor of opposition, corroborated Sandwich's words when he wondered, "Who could have imagined that the ministry could have become so popular by forcing this country into a destructive war and advancing the power of the Crown to a state of despotism?" And on January 15, 1777, Sir George Savile wrote to a Marquis of Rockingham so disconsolate that he usually attended Parliament only for the transaction of private business, "We are not only patriots *out of place,* but patriots out of *the opinion of the public.*" Savile estimated that the British military successes in New York, which followed on the heels of the Declaration of Independence, "had converted ninety nine in one hundred." The London press, in reflecting the radical, frequently pro-American viewpoint, clearly was running contrary to the popular tide. The Opposition editors agreed with Charles James Fox, Dr. Richard Price, David Hartley, and a handful of London radicals that the Americans in 1776 were fighting for the same Whig principles that Englishmen had fought for successfully in 1688.[13] For the next six years John Almon's *Evening Post,* Mary Say's *Gazetteer,* William Parker's *General Advertiser,* Henry Baldwin's *St. James's Chronicle,* and the several editors of the *Courant, Packet,* and *Public Ledger* saw to it that their readers looked upon the American cause as the cause of late-seventeenth-century English Whiggism. Rockingham, Shelburne, and Burke had all but given up hope of a change in Ministry until some tragedy should befall the British forces and make Englishmen change their minds about the prosecution of the war in America. Meanwhile, the Opposition press kept stressing the impossibility of winning a war in which both the physical and spiritual values of the conflict were arrayed against the mother country.

If their proclamation was to become effective, the Americans would be compelled to support their pens with their swords. The Opposition press was certain that the rebels could gain independence on the field of battle. As early as the spring of 1775 the Chathamite *Middlesex Journal* foresaw an American military

---

[13] George Thomas, Earl of Albemarle, *Memoirs of the Marquis of Rockingham and His Contemporaries,* II, 297, Fox to Rockingham.

victory and independence, and it stressed the "absurdity and madness" of fighting a war of such magnitude at such a distance.[14] "MISOPSEUDUS," in the *Morning Chronicle*, maintained it had long appeared certain that sooner or later the Americans were going to form themselves into one or more distinct empires, totally divorced from European dependence.[15] On April 12, 1776, both the *Morning Chronicle* and the *Morning Post* quoted an article that had appeared in the *St. James's Chronicle* the previous day, reporting that a British war council had received a communication from their General Staff in America, arguing against the prosecution of the war because of "total impracticability of carrying it into execution with any prospect of success." While this report probably was a figment of some Londoner's imagination, it was given wide credence; it was the kind of paragraph that the Opposition liked to read in its newspapers. "GRACCHUS AMERICANUS," in two and a half columns in the *Public Ledger*, mournfully stated that Britain would be obliged either to yield or to wage perpetual war.[16] The violently Opposition *Packet* declared that "the odds are that North America is forever lost to England,"[17] while the *St. James's Chronicle* and the *Evening Post* agreed, the latter commencing an alphabet for children with "A Stands for America —now for ever gone."[18]

In late 1775 and early 1776 the *Morning Post* printed many letters stressing the madness of prosecuting the war against a "united, active, able, and resolute" foe who would yield ground only by inches and at the same fatal expense to Britain as she paid for Bunker Hill.[19] By July, 1776, however, Bate indicated that "if the Congress had in America twice the force both by sea and by land which they have at present, there would be little chance even then of their succeeding."[20] The loyal *General Evening Post*, in the belief that the war was necessary and that the King's forces probably would win, also derided those who rec-

14 *Middlesex Journal*, April 15, June 13, 1775. See also *Chester Chronicle*, July 18, 1776.

15 *Morning Chronicle*, August 7, 1775. See also "North Briton," in the *Morning Post*, June 28.

16 *Public Ledger*, August 16, 1775.

17 *Packet*, January 26, April 5, 1776.

18 *St. James's Chronicle*, May 23, 1776; *Evening Post*, September 7.

19 *Morning Post*, December 5, 1775, January 9, 1776.

20 *Morning Post*, July 13, 1776.

ommended that Britain surrender at the commencement of the war for fear she should be defeated in the end.[21]

While adequately preparing its readers for the struggle with America, the Opposition press emphasized the possibility that Britain might lose the struggle to its determined colonists. The reasons for this widespread negative outlook were not difficult to discover: Englishmen had tremendously overestimated the strength of the colonists while deprecating their own military prowess. Most publications expressed fear of the Americans because of their reputedly overwhelming numerical superiority in the field. "There is no doubt," stressed the *Middlesex Journal* in July, 1775, "of the Americans having about 70,000 men well armed, with arms for 30,000 more."[22] At the same time, a *Morning Post* contributor reported that the New England militia alone had a force of 80,000 well-trained, well-equipped men who "can and will fight."[23] Less than a year later, the *Middlesex Journal* revised its initially high estimate upwards to 165,000 men enrolled and armed, while the *Morning Post* assured its readers that the Ministry believed the colonists could assemble 130,000 men "very well armed" and keep them supplied in the field for upward of two months.[24] Even if the rebels had the 100,000 men that many estimated, *Lloyd's Evening Post* questioned that an army of this number could be adequately provisioned by the colonists.[25]

The *General Evening Post* was one of the few British publications to challenge seriously the reputed numbers and war-making potential of the Colonies' military. Noting America's want of ammunition and its aversion to the paper money issued by the Congress, it predicted the rapid dissolution of the rebel army.[26] This loyal newspaper also correctly maintained that the overwhelming numbers that were said to be supporting the rebels' cause were to be considered rather as "curious efforts of invention than as a matter deserving credit." Deriding a letter

[21] *General Evening Post*, November 12, 1776.

[22] *Middlesex Journal*, July 11, 1775.

[23] *Morning Post*, June 5, 1775. See also *Morning Chronicle*, October 24, for a letter from "A TRUE BRITON," who was all but amazed at the accuracy of the American riflemen.

[24] *Morning Chronicle*, March 4, 1776. The *Middlesex Journal*, March 19, concluded, "We ought to consider well before we engage in a contest with a people so well prepared, and who are animated with the keenest spirit to oppose us; especially when all we get by arms may so much easier be acquired by negotiation."

[25] *Lloyd's Evening Post*, July 14, 1775.

[26] *General Evening Post*, March 9, 1776.

written by Robert Merrop stating that the American army had over 50,000 men, the *General Evening Post* advised the public to "disbelieve the whole narration."[27] It was almost alone, however, in asserting that the Americans were not numerous and well equipped. Englishmen read in the other London journals that the colonials had between 50,000 and 100,000 men under arms.

It should be noted that almost all figures quoted in the press relative to the Americans' war potential were imaginary. At this time even the American military commanders were not certain of the numbers of men and supplies they could put into the field. Washington probably never had more than 25,000 men in his army at the same time during the entire war. Perhaps the Opposition press in London, unable to convince the Ministry that negotiations for peace must be successful, attempted to stampede it into gestures toward peace with fantastic figures about America's men and supplies. They might thus force the Government into making a compromise rather than risking a war at such a distance against so great a number. Further, when war threatens, military men usually claim that they have neither enough men nor equipment to bring the war to a swift and successful conclusion. Thus did General Thomas Gage write Lord Barrington, his superior in London, late in 1774: "If you think ten thousand men sufficient, send twenty, if one million is thought enough, give two; you will save both blood and treasure in the end."[28]

The King and his ministers, however, were never taken in by these inflated figures or by panicky appeals from their commanders in America. In November, 1777, just two weeks before the news of the defeat at Saratoga arrived in London, George III wrote to Lord North that he believed Washington never had as many as 10,000 regular troops in the field. Including militia, he estimated the total number at, perhaps, an additional few thousand. Information supplied by an American deserter and numbers gathered by Lord Jeffrey Amherst agreed upon this figure.[29] Yet, if the Ministry published its estimates of Washington's strength, it ran the risk of being entirely disbelieved and of being accused of trying to lull the nation into a false sense of security. On the other hand and still worse, it would incur criticism for

[27] *General Evening Post,* August 9, 1775.

[28] Gage Correspondence (Clements), II, 658-59. See also John Richard Alden, *General Gage in America,* 219.

[29] Fortescue, *Correspondence of King George III,* III, King to North, November 17, 1777.

levying additional taxes in order to raise more troops to crush a rebellion that the Opposition would claim could be overcome easily with the numbers of troops already in America. So, Englishmen continued to be impressed with the imagined figures that passed for America's fighting potential. In this respect the Opposition press can be credited for helping to dampen the initial enthusiasm that most Englishmen felt at the outset of the struggle in America.

Comparing its own fighting potential with the inflated estimates of American strength, the press concluded that neither in numbers nor morale was the British army prepared to take the field against the colonists. The sagging spirit of England's military service was evidenced by a plethora of articles reporting the difficulties of raising and keeping men in the army and navy. Recruiting was proceeding so slowly in Britain, the *Morning Post* reported, that there were between two thousand and three thousand men wanting to complete the quota of the army in North America.[30] The *St. James's Chronicle* added weight to the discouraging picture when it publicized the rumor that General Gage was resigning because, among other complaints, not enough reinforcements were being sent him.[31] The *Middlesex Journal*, while acknowledging that the army could not raise men, bewailed the fact that the King's Guards had to be sent to America.[32] It also regretted the hiring of "Hanoverians" and other Germans to be used in America. The English officers ordered to the Colonies were so dissatisfied with their assignment, it angrily reported, that the Government was forced to employ foreigners. It insisted that, if this were a genuine English war, the hiring of mercenaries would not have been necessary.[33] The *Morning Post* made the same point, regretting that the war was to be waged by a nation so exhausted of men that it was obliged to hire foreigners.[34]

The press was further disturbed by recurring rumors that Russian troops would be used if enough Germans could not be

---

[30] *Morning Post*, May 15, 1776. See *Evening Post*, April 22, 1780, for a reiteration of the lament that the British military never seemed to have enough men.

[31] *St. James's Chronicle*, March 18, 1775.

[32] *Middlesex Journal*, February 1, 1776. Cf. *General Evening Post*, March 14, praising the "brave stout fellows" of the Guards for volunteering to go to America.

[33] *Middlesex Journal*, November 9, 1775.

[34] *Morning Post*, December 5, 1775. See also *Packet*, January 6, March 17, December 31, 1777; *St. James's Chronicle*, February 27, 1777.

hired to fill the ranks in America.[35] Negotiations between Sir
Robert Gunning and the Empress of Russia, Catherine II, for a
loan of 20,000 Russian troops to be sent to Canada had so raised
the hopes of the British Ministry that in December, 1776, editors
confidently predicted that Russian troops presently would de-
part for America.[36] But Catherine eventually refused London's
request, and Anglo-Russian rapport, which was taken for granted
in 1776, began to wane. When the question of neutral rights on
the high seas arose a few years later, relations between the two
countries had cooled perceptibly. Russia eventually joined the
League of Armed Neutrality, which was formed to protect neutral shipping from British depredations. Needless to say, Russian
troops were never sent to America.

The British Navy, as had the army, found it almost impossible
to recruit personnel. Sailors were reluctant to go to America,
especially when merchant ships paid better wages, offered better
living conditions, and held fewer dangers to life and limb.[37]
The navy resorted to force in order to fill ranks heavily depleted
by death and desertion. Press gangs were widely used, and newspapers constantly reported "a hot press on the Thames yesterday." Most journals were severe in their condemnation of this
inhumane but ancient method of recruitment, but some condoned it as a necessary evil.[38] None doubted that the navy was
short of able-bodied seamen.

Added to the difficulties of raising men for the services was the
task of maintaining morale among the officers and men already
procured. The enlisted men appeared "spiritless and averse to
the service," recorded one provincial newspaper.[39] When person-

---

35 *Evening Post*, November 21, 27, 1775.

36 For the British-Russian troop negotiations, see Isabel de Madariaga, *Britain,
Russia, and the Armed Neutrality of 1780*, 9-10. See also *St. James's Chronicle*,
December 7, 1776.

37 *St. James's Chronicle*, March 15, June 6, 1775. *Gentleman's Magazine*, September, 1781, 401-2, quoted a Navy Office report, dated 23 January, which claimed
that from 1776 to 1780 the navy had lost 1,243 men killed and 18,545 dead; 42,069
had deserted during this period. The army had lost an additional 10,022 dead
and 3,701 deserted, it added.

38 *Morning Post*, October 30, 1776; *General Evening Post*, November 5. Recognizing the unpopularity of impressment, the *Morning Post*, January 7, 1777, affirmed that the King reluctantly supported such a measure only after Lord Sandwich had convinced him that it was the "quickest, readiest, surest, and cheapest"
way to raise a navy. The *St. James's Chronicle*, May 26, 1778, reported that whenever sailors with "Protections" (press exemptions) were pressed, "Coals rose, and
Stocks fell."

39 *Chester Chronicle*, September 11, 1775.

nel at the great army staging center at Cork, Ireland, learned that they were presently to embark for America, so many officers applied for permission to sell their commissions that all applications were summarily refused.[40] The press reported that great numbers of officers in England were endeavoring to resign and, still worse, that the commanders in America were applying for permission to be relieved.[41] On April 13, 1776, the *St. James's Chronicle* declared that "no less than nine general officers of superior rank refused the command of the troops in America, before General Howe accepted it." It did not name the men, but it was generally known that leaders as important as Admiral Augustus Keppel and the Earl of Effingham, among others, had refused to serve in the Colonies.[42] One disgusted correspondent wondered how so many "cowardly Poltroons" could have gained such important positions in the forces. "If this be a specimen of our valiant commanders the Americans have nothing to fear from our military Gentry," he concluded.[43]

Desertions were numerous, and regimental commanders frequently utilized newspapers to advertise descriptions of deserters and to offer rewards for apprehending the runaways.[44] Some soldiers, the *Gazetteer* declared, were choosing to die in debtors prison rather than go abroad "and imbrue their hands in the blood of their fellow-subjects." But Englishmen knew there were few of this type.[45] The *St. James's Chronicle* struck an accurate chord when it printed extracts of a letter from Boston reporting that disease more commonly than the sword was making America the grave of Britons.[46]

The public read also that the Ministry was negligent in bring-

[40] *St. James's Chronicle*, May 8, 1775; *Evening Post*, September 2.

[41] *Evening Post*, September 19, 1775; *Morning Post*, November 8; *St. James's Chronicle*, September 14.

[42] Thomas, *Memoirs of the Marquis of Rockingham*, II, 275.

[43] *St. James's Chronicle*, May 29, 1775. See also December 7, 1775, and March 5, 1776. The *Evening Post*, March 30, 1775, suggested that the "aversion of the soldiers to be the instruments of oppression against their fellow subjects" explained the poor state of military morale. See also the *St. James's Chronicle*, March 11, May 2, 1775.

[44] *Chronicle*, November 28, 1776. See also *Lloyd's Evening Post*, December 31, 1779; *Edinburgh Evening Courant*, April 7, October 10, 1781. On December 26, 1781, this Scottish newspaper listed the names and descriptions of 43 seamen "deserted from HM's Tender Adventure, at the Isle of Arran on 20 December."

[45] *Gazetteer*, March 4, 1776. Cf. *Morning Chronicle*, March 6, which answered that there were only two soldiers in debtors prison, one of whom had been there for two years past.

[46] *St. James's Chronicle*, April 25, 1775.

ing more men under arms. Throughout 1775 and 1776 the *Morning Post* charged that the Government maintained a force in America too small in number to render any decisive military results.[47] "CRITO," in the *Morning Post*, blamed Lord North for "raising not a single company," when England either should have sued for peace or raised 40,000 men.[48] Further, this daily asked whether England could support a war that demanded over twenty thousand men, all the resources of the Royal Navy, and economic sacrifices at home "and be at the same time in any condition to look France and Spain in the face."[49] On June 20, 1776, it announced that shortly there would be 52,000 men in America "or the War Office is a liar." This number, it estimated, was the minimum necessary to subdue the rebellion. Rarely could the War Office count upon half that number of effective troops in America.

The press did much to convince Britain that the war against the Colonies would be long, bloody, and—worst of all—fruitless. Noting the thousand casualties at Bunker Hill, a spot "which will hardly furnish graves for the slain," the *Public Ledger* expressed fear of the consequences if all America had to be obtained at so costly a price; a general war would kill tens of thousands of British soldiers.[50] This pessimistic view was widely echoed. Commenting that many peers turned pale on hearing William Penn's account of how well the Americans were provisioned for a "long and tedious war," the *Morning Post* wryly noted, "The whole assembly became Quakers."[51]

In other days men may have believed that a war, properly conceived and executed, could work wonders for a nation's economy, but the Opposition press was convinced that America in 1775 was for Britain neither the proper place nor the proper time for hostilities. While some contributors maintained that the Treasury, impoverished by the previous long and costly war with France, could swiftly be refilled by a heavy taxation upon "Amer-

---

47 *Morning Post*, November 1, 1775: "They sent 5,000 men to do what 10,000 could have executed, and 5,000 more who when they arrived were no more than so many witnesses to the folly of the men who sent them. Now they adopt the measure of doing the work by means of foreign troops. If they sent 30,000 men, the scheme might probably have a decisive effect."

48 *Morning Post*, August 5, 1775.

49 *Morning Post*, January 22, 1776.

50 *Public Ledger*, July 31, 1775.

51 *Morning Post*, November 13, 1775.

ican superabundance,"[52] most knew that increased trade, not taxes, "once more would replenish our sacks."[53] As both American trade and taxation came to a halt in 1775, English commercial and manufacturing elements were forced to weigh their economic futures. On May 2, an important provincial newspaper confessed that Britain's entire scheme of nonexportation to America had failed because the colonists were receiving their produce from the Dutch, who, in turn, were purchasing much of it in England. It seemed that America would survive, and the wily Dutchmen would pocket much of the profits.[54]

In order to calm fears that England would suffer more than the Colonies in a total economic rupture, the loyal press assured its readers throughout the summer of 1775 that the stock exchange would not be affected by events in America because the British economy, despite the colonists' nonimportation agreements, "was never in so flourishing a condition."[55] What made it flourish was not explained. Further, some correspondents maintained that America's prosperity was so dependent upon the British economy to feed back wealth to its "dutiful children,"[56] that the Colonies could, if necessary, be economically strangled by the mother country.

Despite these opinions, the majority of British newspapers reflected the fears of London merchants that the economy and the nation could not afford to carry the burden of a war against one of England's best customers. Because most of the provincial press parroted the London publications, English journals appeared to be overwhelmingly of the opinion that some merchants (like those in Manchester who supported the Ministry with their petitions) were blind to their own interests and that the state of British manufacture and trade could be accurately measured by the regular and ever-increasing lists of bankrupts in the *London Gazette*. With these conditions, there is little wonder that credit was difficult to secure; and taxes were climbing as swiftly as the national debt.

All political, economic, and military arguments considered, most newspapers agreed that Britain could not afford the war in America. She may have had political right on her side, but

---

[52] *Chronicle*, March 21, 1775, "A Manufacturer."
[53] *St. James's Chronicle*, April 18, 1775, "Poet's Corner."
[54] *Chester Chronicle*, May 2, 1775.
[55] *General Evening Post*, June 30, July 24, August 22, 1775.
[56] *St. James's Chronicle*, July 26, 1775.

enforcing right is not always expedient, especially if it is costly—
in this instance, an estimated ten millions in sterling, perhaps as
much as a hundred thousand lives, and the complete destruction of the lucrative American trade.[57] While one columnist in
the *Morning Post* labeled the Americans "Ungrateful monsters!"
and "detested homicides," a second, in the next column, admitted
that the public finances could not stand a war with France and
Spain, which, he predicted, would be the result of the struggle
in America.[58] Englishmen wanted victory in America, but they
feared that their Government could not afford to purchase it.[59]
Amateur mathematicians were able to add conclusive proof that
Britain did not have the funds necessary to continue the struggle.
The *Courant,* which assumed that the increasing national debt
would decrease the value of stocks on the Exchange, predicted
that in five additional years of war the debt would skyrocket another thirty-five million pounds sterling. It feared that a sum
this immense could bring on national bankruptcy.[60]

Added to these acknowledged financial weaknesses were the
woeful reports that the lucrative West Indian trade was in
jeopardy. No more were American flour, corn, fish, and rice reaching the islands in sufficient quantity, and the scarce commodities
that did arrive sold for incredibly inflated prices. Then, too, the
fear that the Indies presently would be overrun by Americans,
Frenchmen, or Spaniards caused many of the leading families in
the islands to put their plantations up for sale, despite depressed
prices.[61]

By the spring of 1776, the destruction of the American trade,
coupled with fear for the safety of the Indies, was clearly reflected upon the London Exchange. The sagging prices of stocks
led the *Gazetteer* to affirm that next to the "corporal sufferance"
of the soldiers in America, British investors as a group suffered
most because of the war.[62] Since the market fluctuated as a re-

57 *St. James's Chronicle,* September 1, 1775.

58 *Morning Post,* September 18, 1775, "Scourge" and "Crito."

59 *Evening Post,* January 4, February 10, July 11, 1776. See also *Chester Chronicle,* April 4.

60 *Williamson's Liverpool Advertiser,* July 10, 1778, copied the same article,
but added: "According to this account we are safe for five years." See also *General
Advertiser,* December 26, 1778.

61 *St. James's Chronicle,* September 27, December 21, 1775, May 23, 1776; *Evening Post,* November 7, 1775.

62 *Gazetteer,* May 25, 1776. See also *Kentish Gazette,* March 7, 1781, and *Packet,*
November 29, 1782, for evidence that rumors of an American peace had a tonic
effect upon London's sagging stock exchange.

sult of the news from the Colonies, most of the great battle reports that circulated in London were manufactured in London in order to facilitate the settling, not of the war between brothers, but of the battle "between the BULLS and the BEARS," as one newspaper put it.[63] Added to the discomforts caused by "the present deplorable state of the stocks,"[64] Englishmen read that not only were prices of provisions becoming dearer,[65] but that their Ministry was concocting new methods of raising money. One correspondent reported that the Government's planned nationalization of the turnpike system and of the public charities would mean the ruin of the already inadequate road and relief structures.[66] Another writer, commenting upon current fashions in women's hair dressing, proposed the idea that, as almost every article that could be thought of was already taxed, the addition of a tax upon ladies' heads, assessed by the altitude of the headdress, was in order. "Such a tax," he concluded, "would raise money sufficient to humble France, without distressing the industrious and middle rank of life."[67]

Only the Tory *General Evening Post* did not envision any financial or military difficulties in crushing the rebellion. Again taking issue with the majority of papers, it saw "such an universal ardour prevailing among our forces for the service (notwithstanding the interested representation of some inflammatory prints)" that it expected the fighting in America to end sometime in late 1776. Never stressing the difficulties of budget or supply, the *General Evening Post,* under a sponsorship that was certain that what it wanted to happen in America actually would happen, was almost alone in its expressions of optimism.[68] But most Englishmen, reading about the depressed state of their nation's economy and of the small numbers and poor condition of their military forces in comparison to the American army, had little choice but to entertain the repugnant belief that perhaps the Colonies would humble the mother country in the field and make their Declaration of Independence a reality.

[63] *Morning Chronicle,* August 12, 1776.
[64] *Evening Post,* October 26, 1776.
[65] *Public Ledger,* May 22, 1776.
[66] *Evening Post,* November 12, 1776.
[67] *Morning Chronicle,* June 11, 1778. See also September 4, 1776, and *Middlesex Journal,* March 14, 1776.
[68] *General Evening Post,* February 29, 1776. Cf. *St. James's Chronicle,* September 14, 1775, and *Evening Post,* November 28, 1775.

CHAPTER VI

The War and Its Commanders

WHEN NEWS of the first armed clashes in New England reached London in the summer of 1775, the public read that the Americans were ably commanded by General Israel Putnam, whose earlier services under Lord Jeffrey Amherst the press widely praised.[1] The Tory *Lloyd's Evening Post*, sensing that "Old Put" was being made into a hero, ringingly denounced the "bravados and exploits of one Putnam, whom they have dubbed a general." *Lloyd's* concluded that England would not be excelled in military ability by such "canaille."[2] But Putnam, it was soon learned, was to play a subordinate role in the Colonies' military scheme. Able as he reputedly was, he was passed over by the Congress when it selected a military chief. The man chosen to be the commander-in-chief of the American military forces was unknown to most British readers before the summer of 1775. The appointment of George Washington and the story—partly fact, partly fiction—of his swift and sudden rise to power were, however, soon well publicized.

Although a rebel leader could hardly be expected to be clasped to the bosoms of Englishmen, the first impressions of Washington to be given in the press were most favorable. *Scot's Magazine* pictured him as a man of sense and integrity, polite, in the prime

---

1 *Morning Post, St. James's Chronicle,* June 9, 1775; *General Evening Post,* June 9, July 7; *Evening Post,* June 8, August 3.

2 *Lloyd's Evening Post,* July 31, 1775.

of life, with much dignity and modesty in manners.[3] Stressing his "unimpeachable" character, *Gentleman's Magazine* assured its readers that Washington was a firm believer in constitutional processes and not a would-be military usurper, such as were Oliver Cromwell and William of Orange. It noted that the Virginian had promised to resign his sacred trust as soon as the hostilities ended.[4]

Washington's military movements, commencing with the fortification of Dorchester Heights and his ensuing occupation of Boston, forced upon Englishmen the realization that perhaps here was a man of true military stature. His encircling Boston with captured cannons made untenable General Howe's further occupation of that city. *Gentleman's Magazine* surmised that the colonists' seizing of Ticonderoga and of Crown Point, which heretofore were thought the actions of "a few private desperadoes," were in fact preconcerted measures aimed at capturing some badly needed artillery for the siege of Boston.[5]

Despite intense disappointment at the loss of New England's most important city, many English newspapers commended Howe on his effective evacuation.[6] Editors understood why Howe, short of supplies and surrounded by a hostile countryside, chose to sail for Halifax. But when a Colonial army could force the withdrawal of thousands of redcoats, indeed the world was well on its way to being turned upside down. The Opposition press, more to embarrass the Government than to condemn Sir William, who was a Whig, made capital over this turn of events.[7] Not knowing that Howe had been authorized by the Ministry to abandon Boston if he deemed it necessary, the *Evening Post* criticized him directly for his inability to hold the city and recommended, as a title for a "circulating library," *The Deserter*, by General Howe.[8]

Though many journals respected Washington's talents if not his politics, Robert Dodsley's *Annual Register*, conceding that neither side had a monopoly of right or wrong, was effusive in its praise of the American commander.[9] Reporting that the victorious Washington marched into Boston "with drums beating,

---

[3] *Scot's Magazine,* August, 1775, 562.
[4] *Gentleman's Magazine,* August, 1775, 405.
[5] *Gentleman's Magazine,* August, 1775, 397.
[6] *General Evening Post,* May 4, 1776; *Morning Chronicle,* May 17.
[7] *Middlesex Journal,* May 4, 1776.
[8] *Evening Post,* June 20, 1776.
[9] *Annual Register,* 1775, 141.

colours flying, and in all triumph of victory" and was received by the townsfolk as a deliverer,[10] the paper left no doubt that the Bostonians thought highly of their new Commander-in-chief. Dodsley invariably found something in Washington to admire. When the Virginian was suffering defeat on Long Island in August of 1776, the *Annual Register* stressed that the arduous retreat was undertaken and executed with great ability. So, too, did it acknowledge that in the course of his evacuation from New York, Washington fully performed the part of "no mean Commander."[11]

Britain, unfortunately, had no military hero of her own to compare with Washington. General Gage inspired little confidence in official and public circles because he favored a policy of serious mediation with the rebels and, failing that, the crushing of the uprising with a force far vaster than was thought necessary by his superiors in London. His recommendation that Parliament temporarily suspend the Coercive Acts, while getting ready for battle should mediation fail, prompted George III to label it "the most absurd that can be suggested."[12] Further, Gage was believed to have allowed the rebellion at Boston to get out of hand by stressing caution and verbal eloquence rather than military action:

> And yet, great Guard of
> *Boston* Town,
> Before your Prince can thank
> ye,
> You'll knock a Thousand old
> Words down,
> But not a single Yanky![13]

His American wife made his position still more vulnerable. In September, 1775, when Mrs. Gage's return to London was rumored, the *St. James's Chronicle* bitingly reported that it was really the General returning, disguised as his wife. The newspaper assured its readers that Mrs. Gage, left behind to command in America, would prove a much more formidable enemy to the rebels than would her husband.[14]

---

10 *Annual Register*, 1776, 50.

11 *Annual Register*, 1776, 173. Cf. *General Evening Post*, October 8, 1776; *Lloyd's Evening Post*, October 11, 14; *Morning Post*, October 17.

12 Fortescue, *Correspondence of King George III*, III, 154.

13 *St. James's Chronicle*, September 21, 1775.

14 *St. James's Chronicle*, September 23, July 27, 1775.

Gage's unpopularity in the Opposition press is difficult to understand. He favored conciliation, as did the London editors, and with them he believed it was impossible to subdue the rebellion with his insufficient arms and men. His critics probably intended to embarrass the Ministry rather than to expose his defects as a military leader. While never again given an important command, Gage did not consider embracing the Opposition, as would some other former comrades in arms. By early 1776 he was back in London; his name slipped quietly from the list of British commanders being discussed in the press, and editors looked elsewhere for the military hero who could again bring Britain glory from the New World.

No British military figure in America received repeated accolades from the press in 1776, but occasional letters or paragraphs in praise of a particular commander did frequently appear.[15] William Woodfall's *Morning Chronicle* expressed the hope that the rebels so respected the Howes that the brothers were assured of military success.[16] The capture of Long Island further convinced Woodfall that Sir William Howe was an able commander who tempered courage with humanity.[17] The *St. James's Chronicle* remained unconvinced. After a study of the action at New York, it concluded that Howe's maneuvers would bring him no credit.[18] Englishmen could not forget the tragedy at Bunker Hill under Howe's command, yet he was the closest they had to a military hero. If his tactics in the battle for New York were dilatory, the British press took little notice.

The news of Sir Guy Carleton's unexpectedly successful defense of Quebec in the closing hours of 1775 was not, surprisingly, viewed in London as a great British victory. The press had been certain that Quebec could not be held. In early January, 1776, John Almon's *Evening Post* reported that the Ministry had given up all hope of holding the city.[19] The following week Almon even published the story of its capitulation "on the same conditions that Montreal had done to General Montgomery."[20] He surmised that the Quebec Act of 1774, which he believed the Canadians

---

[15] *Chronicle,* November 28, 1776: "See how in this heroic line,/ Brave Percy and Cornwallis shine. . . . "

[16] *Morning Chronicle,* May 18, 1776. See also May 1.

[17] *Morning Chronicle,* October 21, 1776.

[18] *St. James's Chronicle,* September 23, 1775. See also July 27.

[19] *Evening Post,* January 2, 1776.

[20] *Evening Post,* January 9, 1776.

"abhorred and detested," was the reason Canada joined with the Americans. "The Canadians express the greatest satisfaction and joy, at this change of masters," he announced. Quebec's fall was considered so certain that Almon may well have been excused for his premature announcement. By January, 1776, almost all London publications had prepared their readers for this news and for the consequent surrender of all Canada.[21]

The initial description of the gallant defense of the Canadian capital by its badly outnumbered garrison elicited few stirring accounts in the newspapers. Carleton was not at first pictured as a brave defender before whom the hated rebels fled. Few believed the early reports that trickled into London in late February, and those few who rejoiced in the victory were reminded that defensive victories rarely won wars. The *Morning Post* affirmed that the saving of Quebec was but a "trifling temporary success,"[22] and Englishmen read that the Americans would be back presently with more men than before.[23] At best, Carleton's success was a reprieve. A correspondent in the *St. James's Chronicle*, mentioning "the great joy which appears in every Face at Court," pointed out to those who were joyous that the war was still far from over.[24]

Detailed accounts of the victory at Quebec were received in London in March. The hero of this battle, according to the British press, was the fallen American commander, General Richard Montgomery, and he received a eulogy as great as that of any soldier killed during the war. Perhaps the English in victory could afford to be magnanimous; perhaps this eulogy was another impassioned plea for peace; perhaps the press expressed a general regret that someone of such fine British stock had been forced to lay down his life in battle against King and Country; or perhaps the press, hungering for a hero, chose to lionize this young Irishman rather than the cold, formal Carleton, who would probably lose Quebec anyway on the next American attack.[25] The encomiums of Montgomery in the Opposition press were of such a touching nature (Almon bordered the March 12 edition of the *Evening Post* in black) that Lord North rose in Parliament to "censure the

21 *Morning Chronicle,* January 17, 1776; *Morning Post,* January 29.
22 *Morning Post,* February 26, 1776.
23 *Morning Chronicle,* June 27, 1776.
24 *St. James's Chronicle,* February 22, 1776.
25 *Morning Chronicle,* June 8, 1776. See also *Morning Post,* October 23, denying that Carleton had been replaced in Canada.

unqualified Liberality of the Praises bestowed on General *Montgomery* by the gentlemen in opposition, because they were bestowed upon a rebel"; still, North acknowledged the validity of the praises that Burke, Barré, Fox, and even General Burgoyne lavished upon Montgomery. Admitting that the American was "brave, able, humane, and generous," the Prime Minister declared that a verse of the *Tragedy of Cato* might apply to Montgomery: "Curse on his Virtues, they've undone his country!"[26]

Almost all London publications reflected the praise given Montgomery in Parliament by the minority. The *Evening Post* commented that North would never be able to persuade Englishmen that Montgomery was a rebel. Indeed, it charged, he was a man who chose to die with virtue and honor "rather than live like the corrupt Prime Minister."[27] The less emotional *Morning Post* quoted a simple poem for its eulogy:

> Tears shed for me, methinks the hero spake!
> For me they're vain! Weep for my country's sake![28]

Scot's Magazine even compared Montgomery to General Wolfe:

> In Abram's plains they lie interr'd
> the virt'ous and the brave:
> Among the rest no more preferr'd
> than bold Montgomery's grave.[29]

There were, however, some absences from the chorus of praise for the fallen American hero. The loyal *General Evening Post* admitted that he would be remembered as a good soldier if not as a good subject, and it editorialized that, since Canada was the key to the northern continent, the whole force of the kingdom would have been exerted to recover it. Thus, even if Montgomery had been successful, his victory would have been only temporary. The *General Evening Post* also was one of the few publications to praise the commander and defenders of Canada while deprecating the efforts of both the vanquished Americans and their commanders.[30] By June the *Morning Post* came to agree

---

[26] *Evening Post*, March 16, 1776.

[27] *Evening Post*, March 12, 19, 1776. See also *Annual Register*, January, 1776, 15.

[28] *Morning Post*, March 26, 1776.

[29] *Scot's Magazine*, May, 1776, 267.

[30] *General Evening Post*, March 9, 1776: "If Ireland has been unfortunate in producing a Rebel General, she has made ample amends by giving birth to his conqueror. The gallant Carleton . . . [is] distinguished for every accomplishment which can do credit to his character, either as an officer or as a man."

that Canada must be held at all costs and that Montgomery was killed in an absurd attempt to gain what the British lion would never yield. Five months earlier it had stated that the Americans' attempt to take Canada could not fail, but now a correspondent derided both Montgomery's ghost and "one immortal ARNOLD," who it claimed, were well assisted by three hogsheads of Irish whisky as they "beat their brains out for madness against the only impregnable part of the walls of Quebec."[31] The *Morning Post* later added a poem, "The Siege of Quebec":

> Montgomery fell among the dead,
> Arnold and Campbell—wiser—fled!
> Gen'rals surpass their troops in cunning,
> And there fore should excel in running.[32]

The last soldier to fire the imagination of the Empire had long since been buried under the Plains of Abraham. Since a new hero had failed to emerge, Wolfe, dead for over a decade, was still eulogized. Until a replacement could be found, a few publications spent their energies in condemning Washington. *Town and Country* magazine, for example, never known to avoid rumor of a good scandal, utilized a story written by "an Officer at New York" who discussed at length Washington's "saintliness and heroism." It related in much detail how a Mrs. Gibbons, a royalist lady of "beauty and good sense," made a patriotic virtue of necessity and, while compelled to live with Washington in New York, regularly rifled his pockets, had his secret messages copied, and thus acquainted Howe with all of the American's intended operations.[33] Intimating that the retreating Virginian was a "bloodthirsty ravager," this magazine accused him also of ordering New York City put to the torch before it was abandoned.[34] And at almost the same time that *Scot's Magazine* was reporting that Washington was universally beloved in America,[35] the *Morning Post* was asserting that his malconduct had caused the Congress to reduce

---

[31] *Morning Post*, June 28, 1776. See also *Lloyd's Evening Post*, July 10.

[32] *Morning Post*, September 4, 1776. See also *Morning Chronicle*, June 18.

[33] *Town and Country*, Supplement, 1776, 678. This letter concluded that Washington eventually learned of these raids upon his pockets "and hung everyone connected"; but on the following page we learn that Mrs. Gibbons managed to stay behind when Washington was forced to evacuate New York, and "at the price of so great a sacrifice," she helped save her country.

[34] *Town and Country*, Supplement, 1776, 679.

[35] *Scot's Magazine*, August, 1776, 426.

him to the ranks.[36] This type of manufactured-at-home reporting, so often found in the London press, stressed Washington's folly or, still worse, his death, demotion, or desertion.[37] In endeavoring to provide lively reading material, these journals did their audience the extreme disservice of obscuring the fact that the rebels were competently led.

When Washington's attack upon Trenton took Major Rall and his Hessian forces completely by surprise, it forced the North ministry into recognizing that the American war could be long and costly; it did not surprise London's Opposition press. Having always respected Washington's talents and having objected to the use of German troops in a purely domestic quarrel, the Opposition invariably expected little from the Hessians. Thus, it was disappointed but not shocked over the events at Trenton on Christmas Eve, 1776, and over the fate of Colonel Baum and his forces at Bennington ten months later. In short, the Opposition believed that if Britain could not win the war using her own sons, she would not win the war. Apparently, a supreme effort was necessary to outfox and outfight the wily Virginian, who seemed to gain strength from adversity and confidence from his occasional victories.

Literate Englishmen were forced to recognize, underneath the ink of some slander and much rumor, that George Washington was both a gentleman and a formidable soldier. The *Annual Register*'s affirmation that the "American Fabius" had by his military tactics in New Jersey earned great respect both in Europe and America was frequently echoed in Britain.[38] By 1777 most remarks aimed at discrediting Washington were forgotten as the press turned to the greener pastures of victorious battle reports. Howe's successes, however modest, made better copy than did

---

[36] *Morning Post*, June 4, 1776.

[37] Among the other rumors prevalent in 1775 and 1776 were reports of Howe's death (*Middlesex Journal*, September 30, 1775); reports that the English or Hessian forces slaughtered 1,500 Americans captured on Long Island (*Evening Post*, October 17, 1776); and a claim that General Clinton's troops were "scalping, slaying, roasting, and eating alive the victims that fall into their hands" (*General Advertiser*, December 28, 1776). The *Morning Post*, January 19, 1776, heard that the pro-American and republican-oriented Mrs. Catherine Macauley of London was soon to embark for Philadelphia "to take command of a large corps of American amazons, who are to be called the *Hancock* volunteers."

[38] *Annual Register*, January, 1777, 20. The *Gazetteer*, May 29, 1776, reported that Washington demonstrated his humanity and politeness, "not the usual characteristics of a rebel," by returning a captured medicine chest the evacuated British had left behind at Boston.

rumors about the American Commander, which, when disproved, discredited the publication that carried them.

Added to the respect for Washington as a soldier in the field, by early 1777 the feeling gained ground on both sides of the Atlantic that the rebels' Commander was becoming the American cause incarnate; he had replaced Hancock as the symbol of Colonial freedom, and his subsequent treatment in the British press revolved not only about his personal or military traits but also about the cause that he had come so completely to symbolize.

If English editors could admire George Washington, they could not respect Charles Lee, one of his highest ranking officers. A retired British colonel on half pay who lived on a large Virginia plantation and advertised himself as more American than the Americans, Lee had an impressive military record, achieved while serving with distinction in Portugal and Poland as well as with Braddock in America.[39] He had lost two fingers in 1758 at Ticonderoga, and he was an intimate friend of the Indians, having married the daughter of a Seneca chief. Above all men, it was believed, Lee was the one who could whip an undisciplined army into shape. Since he was an Englishman, the press never forgave his conversion to the American cause. Considered more as an opportunist than as a traitor, he was more pitied than despised. Looking upon him as an eccentric who could not, by his nature, play a leading role in the Colonies' military or political scheme, the *Morning Chronicle* predicted that, should his caprice meet with any coolness from the Congress, Lee would defect immediately to the King's side.[40]

It was believed that Lee was not an abettor of insurrection, but that, motivated primarily by personal gain, he could be expected to surrender his allegiance to the American cause as soon as the tide of battle turned against him and his allies. Assuring its readers that he was a late joiner in the American crusade, *Gentleman's Magazine* discounted his role as a leader of the uprising and concluded that the Americans were armed, disciplined, and "determined to fight for their liberty long before they heard of General Lee."[41]

39 *Morning Chronicle,* September 5, 1775, praised Lee's "glorious conduct" in Portugal. See also September 7, for the text of "Speech of the brave General Lee."
40 *Morning Chronicle,* June 22, 1776.
41 *Gentleman's Magazine,* June, 1775, 295.

Learning of these attacks upon his character and motives, Lee took it upon himself to defend his stand with some lengthy letters, which he dispatched to London's leading newspapers. His remarks upon the problems of war, peace, and imperial relationships evoked both praise and sharp comment from many editors and readers. Not often is a newspaper afforded the opportunity to print a series of debates with an enemy general. Lee's correspondence rarely appeared verbatim; instead, his main points were usually summarized and then discussed. In reviewing the essence of one of his letters the *Morning Post* commented that it abounded with infidelity rather than with political information.[42] For the benefit of its still unenlightened readers, it added a summation of the past record of "that gadfly" and stressed that his rambling nature had carried him into the Polish, Russian, and Portuguese service before he joined the American cause. According to the *Morning Post*, Lee was more likely to be in the service of "the Grand Seignor" two years hence than in that of the Congress.[43]

Lee's nature was quarrelsome and overbearing; newspapers pictured him disputing with his officers of both inferior and superior rank.[44] His difficulties with Washington, in particular, were treated in headlines in London. Though not exactly clear on the details of the Washington-Lee feud, the press surmised correctly that the relationship between these two men was strained. The *Evening Post* quoted detailed accounts from Boston to confirm its earlier reports of "disagreement grown into a quarrel between Washington and Lee" and to stress the consequent weakening of the rebel army's morale.[45]

When an erroneous report from Governor Tryon to Germain reached London that Lee had been captured by royal troops in Virginia, many British editors looked upon this occurrence as a blessing in disguise for the Americans. The slovenly, dog-loving eccentric was even accused of betraying his forces into the hands of the enemy.[46] Only the *Annual Register* mourned Lee's loss to the Americans. While praising his military proficiency and stressing the need for his talent among the "raw American forces," this journal gave little hope that his great skill and knowledge

---

[42] *Morning Post*, February 22, 1776.
[43] *Morning Post*, September 4, October 25, 1776.
[44] *Gazetteer*, May 15, 1776.
[45] *Evening Post*, December 14, 1775.
[46] *St. James's Chronicle*, June 1, 1776; *Morning Post*, June 4.

could soon be replaced by the inexperienced and undisciplined Americans.[47]

Some demands were heard in London and in America for Lee's neck. The Tory *General Evening Post*, in a poem by "Q," made one of them:

> Ambition's dupe, a lawless Faction's *tool*,
> Must live a *madman*, and must die a *fool*.
> Here read thy *character*, thy peril, *Lee*;
> A traitor's name, a traitor's destiny.[48]

With Washington, he was castigated for taking the field against the "British Constitution." His reputed military ability, unimpeachable background in the Royal Army, and popular correspondence with the press, however, precluded complete condemnation by most editors or politicians. In the general sentiment, a few months in a dungeon would probably make this turncoat see the light.

The discussion of Lee's capture was all but silenced when London learned that not only had Lee not been taken prisoner, but he was still very much in command of rebel forces and operating successfully against the British. But Lee soon validated the earlier discussions by falling into British hands in December, 1776. This time newspapermen were more wary. On February 14, 1777 the *Public Advertiser* refused to credit the story. When Howe's letter to the Ministry corroborated it, all of the earlier arguments were aired again. On February 18 the *Public Advertiser* announced that Lee would be brought to trial in England. This, indeed, was the Ministry's plan, but before it could be executed, both Congress and General Washington moved to negotiate for his exchange.[49] Fortunately for Lee, an American effort to capture General Richard Prescott (who had once before been captured and exchanged) was successful in July, 1777. The lengthy negotiations for the Lee-Prescott exchange (it was thought that Howe was in no hurry to trade the talented Lee for a British general whose chief talent seemed to be in getting captured) were finally consummated in April, 1778.

As the quarrel between Britain and her Colonies went on, Brit-

---

[47] *Annual Register*, January, 1777, 7.

[48] *General Evening Post*, March 30, 1776.

[49] The *Evening Post*, April 19, 1777, protested that, instead of bringing Lee to England to hang him, the British were using him in an attempt to reopen negotiations with the Americans.

ish publications, with but a few Tory exceptions, came to recognize the military prowess of the colonists. Believing that the rebels had adequate men, material, and more than adequate leadership in the persons of Washington, Lee, Arnold, and scores of other lesser officers both French and American, the press predicted a long and fierce war. Certainly, the press was not to blame if the King and his ministers were slow in heeding the warnings that it repeatedly offered.

CHAPTER VII

Military Disaster

I N EARLY 1777 the Ministry of George III viewed the military situation in America with more than its earlier optimism. Canada was safe; British forces in New York City were getting as much local cooperation as could be hoped for an occupying army; and Washington's ragged forces, after a disheartening retreat across the Jerseys, appeared in an almost hopeless situation, despite their victory at Trenton. Britain's loyal press, reflecting the expectations of the Government, optimistically reported that the spring campaign would be the final one.[1] The war could not last much longer, for had not the helpless American Congress sunk so low in power and prestige that it could muster only seven members to attend a meeting?[2] Could the rebel army, wanting in almost every necessity and with a widespread disposition to mutiny and desertion, be expected to remain in the field?[3] Even the Opposition *Packet,* after noting that the rebels had been forced to abandon Fort Washington, "not through cowardice, but the want of ammunition,"[4] admitted that they were falling back on all fronts. The royal troops, said the *Chronicle,* were showing

---

[1] *Morning Post,* January 17, May 1, 1777. Cf. *St. James's Chronicle,* January 30, for a protest against the "next spring we will win the war in America" attitude of the Ministry. The *Chronicle,* March 18, also warned its readers against the unfounded optimism that pervaded the loyal press every spring.

[2] *Morning Post,* January 11, 18, 1777.

[3] *Chronicle,* May 1, 1777.

[4] *Packet,* January 10, 1777.

great humanity to the "deluded people" falling into their hands. "These poor wretches," it concluded, were now forsaken by a "barbarous" Congress that had beguiled and then abandoned them by not providing money, subsistence, or clothing.[5]

In the spring Englishmen again read that the American Commander had died of illness and that the rebellion would not long survive him.[6] With victory in sight, the *Morning Post* in a magnanimous editorial gave Washington a notable obituary. Acknowledging that the Virginian had served with distinction during the Seven Years' War, it praised him for being a humane, brave, and skillful officer who had done more toward keeping the "provincial banditti" under arms than "all the hypocritical invocations of the whole Republican Congress put together."[7] No sooner, however, had the *Morning Post* discovered that Washington was very much alive than it declared that he had made himself dictator of America.[8]

Surely, a group of heretofore loyal subjects, now half-starved, ill-equipped, and led by a tyrant, could presently be expected to come to their senses. In this expectation, the *Morning Post* was already making its victory settlement, announcing that Franklin, Adams, and Hancock, "the three great incendiaries," were "*destined to the cord*." The other members of the Congress were to be banished from the Empire.[9] Many Opposition and independent newspapers also were preparing their readers for the news of Philadelphia's capture and the collapse of the rebellion. "All Philadelphia is in the utmost consternation," reported the *Chronicle*, as it described the city's inhabitants fleeing with their families and effects as swiftly as possible.[10] Quoting a letter from New York dated 14 February, the *St. James's Chronicle* stated that trade, commerce, and all mechanical occupations in the American capital had stopped. "The poor Wretches who have returned to Philadelphia from the Rebel Army are in a calamitous Situation,

5 *Chronicle*, January 4, 1777.

6 *Morning Post*, May 1, 1777. See also May 7; *St. James's Chronicle*, April 29; *Chronicle*, May 1; *Packet*, April 28. On June 30, however, the *Packet* claimed that Washington had been taken prisoner by the British. The *General Evening Post* reported the same rumor on December 18.

7 *Morning Post*, May 1, 1777.

8 *Morning Post*, May 19, 1777, refuted Colonel Barré's statement of the previous day in the Commons that Washington was not dictator of America. It insisted that "all authentic accounts confirmed the fact repeatedly."

9 *Morning Post*, February 3, 1777. See also January 13.

10 *Chronicle*, January 4, 1777.

under the Oppression of many Diseases, and Want of common Necessaries," it concluded.[11] Still, the *Packet* cautioned that hostilities could be prolonged, even if the Americans were weakening, because the Ministry had so bungled the supply line across the Atlantic that even in victory the redcoats were suffering from the "absolute want" of all military necessities. Further, it maintained that if Howe needed to force all of Washington's entrenchments, "everyone must see the probable consequences."[12]

Despite the optimism of the previous months, London became more nervous in the summer of 1777 as the reports from across the Atlantic became less frequent. Widespread speculation suggested that this lack of news was intended to conceal a new military defeat. Even the pro-Government *Morning Post* protested that the public had been "in the dark" on the actions of General Howe for almost a year. Although it charged the censors with having no appreciation of public opinion, it soon quoted George III as saying, "How cruel is this! No news!"[13]

In the midst of this ignorance and anticipation, the *Morning Post,* in June, suddenly commenced publication of a series of articles demanding the recall of the Howe brothers. When the most popular Ministry organ stressed that the Howes "let the grass grow under their feet, which unfortunately has been too much the case during the course of the last two summers,"[14] it was clear that the Government was tiring of the dilatoriness of its commanders in America. By July the *Morning Post* was telling its readers that the Howes should certainly be recalled if some major stroke was not effected by them before the end of the current campaign.[15] Informed Englishmen assumed, however, that the lack of news from Howe—at least recently—was due to his having sailed for Philadelphia.[16] Howe's overly long and complex voyage prior to his attack of Pennsylvania (his fleet required from 23 July to 25 August to make the ninety-mile trip from New York to Head of Elk) now drew ridicule from the press of his own party. On October 30 Almon's *Evening Post* criticized him for being "17 days beating about Chesapeak Bay, before he could

11 *St. James's Chronicle,* March 22, 1777. See also April 29, reporting that the American army in the Philadelphia region was suffering from "epidemical and Camp Distemper . . . and want of almost every Necessary."

12 *Packet,* July 18, 1777.

13 *Morning Post,* October 8, 11, 1777.

14 *Morning Post,* June 16, 1777. See also June 11.

15 *Morning Post,* July 12, 1777.

16 Wilkes Papers (Clements), III, September 18, 1777.

effect the landing of a single soldier, during which time he lost about 200 men by sickness." On October 4 the *Morning Post*, despairing of a swift British victory, quoted a humorous correspondent, who reported that the Howes' reluctance to fight was a result of their conversion to Quakerism.

Small wonder that when the news of Philadelphia's capture finally reached London in late 1777 it was looked upon as a stale, long-overdue item. A few weeks before it arrived, the *Packet*, which had long expressed a conviction that the war in America could not be won anyway, warned that Howe, far removed from his supplies, would have to force the issue against Washington who, "with all the prudence of a Fabius," would probably make the price of his defeat "such a slaughter of the British troops" that "humanity will have sufficient cause to mourn."[17] News of the fall of the rebel capital did little to convince Englishmen of the imminence of the fall of the rebel cause and nothing to convince them that the Howes should be allowed to keep their commands much longer. On January 8, 1778, the *St. James's Chronicle* reported that General Howe had expressed a desire to be recalled. Alluding to the fact that the Ministry newspapers had been heaping "the most rancorous abuse upon the Howes," it intimated that the brothers hoped to return shortly to seek vindication for their actions in the American campaign.

Unlike Howe, John Burgoyne in 1777 enjoyed the complete confidence of his King and the Ministry. Popular with his troops because he refused to train men as one trained "spaniels by the stick," Burgoyne had to his credit twenty years of honorable service, having most recently fought with distinction on the Continent during the Seven Years' War. After serving in America under both Gage and Howe, he returned to London in the winter of 1776, where, the press reported, he was most popular with the royal family.[18] In fact, it was rumored, the frequently discussed plan to isolate New England by moving an army down from Lake Champlain to the upper Hudson was conceived by Burgoyne and approved by George III and Germain. The public at first had no idea that part of Burgoyne's master plan called for a strong force

[17] *Packet*, October 29, 1777. The *Evening Post*, December 2, reprinted the entire *London Gazette Extraordinary* covering Howe's capture of Philadelphia.

[18] *Chronicle*, January 9, 1777. See also March 20, and *Packet* and *Morning Chronicle*, March 17.

under Howe to move up the Hudson and join with him at Albany. When he sailed for North America in the spring of 1777 Burgoyne carried with him the hopes of his sovereign and nation.

In the autumn the attention of the British press focused upon Burgoyne's army as it plodded slowly through unfamiliar and difficult terrain with an abnormally long supply train.[19] The letters, orders, and reports from Canada were given priority by all editors. No sooner had word reached Britain that Burgoyne was on his way south from Canada than the Opposition press began warning its readers of the possibility of his defeat. On September 30, 1777, "JANUS," writing in the radical *Evening Post* proved himself almost clairvoyant with his report that the colonists under Arnold were at Saratoga, waiting for Burgoyne. On October 7 the *Evening Post* accurately reported that Howe was in the Chesapeake area, thus freeing the northern colonies from any apprehensions about having their army caught between Burgoyne and Howe and allowing them to send their entire force north against Burgoyne. On October 25 this newspaper reported there had been no news whatever from Burgoyne since the announcement of his successful investment of Ticonderoga. (First reports of this victory carried the news that 5,000 Americans had fallen with the fort, but when they soon were disproved, the victory was not thought crucial.) Further, the glad tidings sent by an "Officer in America" and carried in *Adams's Weekly Courant* on October 28, announcing that Burgoyne had killed five hundred Green Mountain boys and captured Albany, were ignored by the metropolitan press. So, too, was a letter from Paris, quoted by the *Gazetteer* on November 1, reporting that the "rash and impolitic" Burgoyne was killed in action, because on October 29 numerous reports of the battle at Bennington reached London. On October 30 the *General Evening Post,* propounding rumors of the battle, asserted that, while the Americans fought with more obstinacy and valor than they had demonstrated during the entire conflict, the stiff British resistance (it maintained the redcoat foraging party was outnumbered 3,000 or 4,000 to 500) forced the rebels to retreat, leaving behind 600 dead and 900 prisoners.

Almon's *Evening Post* of the same date agreed that the Americans had fought as well as any European veteran troops could

---

[19] *Gentleman's Magazine,* October, 1777, 472-74, published a detailed account of the rivers, creeks, and woods that "inevitably retard the Progress of a Northern Army through the uninhabited Countries of America."

have fought, but it interpreted the battle's outcome differently. In three articles it quoted letters from Quebec, all stressing the fact of Burgoyne's defeat at Bennington and the consequent necessity for him to return to Canada, his mission unfulfilled. The *Evening Post* reported that Burgoyne now was encamped about three miles north of Saratoga. A more specific article in the same issue quoted at length a Mr. Cumming, an agent victualer just returned from Quebec, who brought the complete picture of what happened to the foraging party that was attacked at Bennington. None of the reports carried in the *Evening Post* mentioned Colonel John Stark as the American hero of the engagement; one article identified General Thomas Conway as the most conspicuous American officer, although Conway was not involved in the battle.

Choosing to completely disbelieve a narrative propounded by the Opposition, the *Morning Post* informed its readers on November 1 that the accounts from Bennington were contradictory and therefore not to be credited. On November 3, however, the *London Gazette* published the official version of the Battle of Bennington. It was copied by all of the publications in the metropolis, and it proved the *Evening Post*'s earlier reports to be substantially accurate. The one exception was the detail that in truth it was a Hessian rather than a British detachment that was so badly mauled by the colonists. As was the case at Trenton almost a year before, so too at Bennington would Englishmen believe that the fault for their defeat was to be found in the utilization of German rather than British troops for an important military operation.[20]

Its patriotism whetted by this victory and fired by Burgoyne's alleged boast that he would turn his Indians loose against the Americans (this was untrue), the *Evening Post* again warned its readers that the worst in America was yet to come.[21] Further, on November 22 it quoted from a letter, purportedly written by Burgoyne, that stated he would never have attempted so great a march with such a small force had he not received the strongest assurances before leaving England that he would be assisted by a large body of troops from New York. The *Evening Post* reported that the Government, cognizant of its failure to reinforce the Canadian expedition as promised and, consequently, fearing the worst, refused to make public this letter. The paper added that

[20] Pamphlet, *Considerations Upon the American Inquiry* (1779), quoting a Colonel Kingston who testified before the Commons and reportedly was quoting General Frazer, in command at Bennington.

[21] *Evening Post*, October 30, 1777.

the Ministry had ordered its "runners, writers, and assassins" not to attack Burgoyne as they had formerly attacked both Gage and Howe, because of the fear that the General could adequately answer all charges. Before news of Burgoyne's first contact with the enemy at Saratoga reached London, the Opposition decided that, should he fail, the Ministry would be to blame.

Still, the press wanted to know why Burgoyne, like Howe, was so slow in reporting his progress. The usually mild and impartial *Gentleman's Magazine* charged that he had belatedly dispatched news of the battle at Freeman's Farm three weeks after it had been fought. It commented that there was "hardly an instance upon record, since military men could write, of a General's withholding intelligence from his Sovereign of an event so important for such a length of time."[22] On November 10 the *Packet* tried to account for the silence of Britain's commanders in America. "The most natural inference that can be drawn is big with disappointment, and affords the most gloomy prospect," it concluded. By late November most London newspapers were admitting that Burgoyne was far from his base of supply, that the countryside swarmed with enemy troops, and that, indeed, "Gentleman Johnny" was in a difficult position. The Opposition press regularly quoted Chatham and other members of the parliamentary minority when they predicted defeat for the British forces in northern New York. Expressing what Sir John Fortescue called "that heedless malignity of faction which would cheerfully wreck an Empire to pull down a Ministry,"[23] the Opposition made it clear that a major defeat in the New World would force Englishmen of all political persuasions to rethink many of their patriotic, but illogical, ideas about the American rebellion. On November 20 Charles Jenkinson, whom the Opposition considered adamant in his insistence that the war be prosecuted at all costs, admitted that Britain was in a "wretched state with respect to politics." The voting of supplies without awareness of the military situation in America or what the next step should be depressed even this firm ministerialist, who added a touch of surprise to the fact that, despite these conditions, the public was still as zealous as Parliament in its support of the war.[24] The Opposition expected that additional news from America presently would force Englishmen

---

22 *Gentleman's Magazine*, November, 1777, 549.
23 Sir John Fortescue, *A History of the British Army*, III, 244.
24 BM Add. MSS 38306-9, and no. 78, dated 20 November 1777.

to abandon much more than a few particles of their zeal. Still, no publication of any political persuasion would have forecast that the entire British army in northern New York was to surrender en masse. In fact, *Adams's Weekly Courant* refused to credit the news of Saratoga two weeks after it was officially announced.[25]

The initial reports of the disaster that befell Burgoyne were picked up by the press on December 1. On that date the *Morning Post* warned its readers that, if there was any truth to the rumor that Burgoyne's forces had been decimated by illness, "there is certainly ground for disagreeable apprehensions" about his forthcoming battle with the Americans. But it mentioned no battle. On the following day the *General Evening Post* carried the full and authoritative account of Burgoyne's defeat at Saratoga. Using glowing descriptions of the "small but gallant handful whose numbers hourly diminished in the unequal contest" to soften the blow of defeat, it praised Burgoyne's "brave and skilful" endeavors to extricate himself from a difficult situation. Once he realized that the superior valor of his troops was not enough to hold back the overwhelming numerical superiority of the rebel army, Burgoyne, though inflicting heavier losses than he was receiving, was anxious to spare lives "which must otherwise be thrown away to no purpose." He resolved to propose such terms of "honourable surrender" as the rebels would think it imprudent to reject. The one consolation this loyal newspaper offered its readers was the information—inaccurate—that the able American general Benedict Arnold was killed in action. The *Morning Post* also praised British heroism while stressing the statement that Burgoyne was outnumbered by 32,000 men. It, too, completely exonerated the General, who, it informed its readers, sustained two wounds before he was forced to capitulate.[26] It asked "the feeling Briton" to make every reasonable allowance for the perils of Burgoyne's situation and not to calumniate this "brave, and enterprising officer, merely because he has been unfortunate."[27] To the *Morning Post*, the sole blame for the "ill success of the Canada expedition" lay with General Howe, whose orders, it asserted, were directly contrary to entering Pennsylvania.[28] It maintained that, had Burgoyne

[25] *Adams's Weekly Courant*, December 16, 1777.

[26] *Morning Post*, December 4, 1777. This article also reported Arnold's death. The *Morning Chronicle*, December 6, also agreed the Americans had "upwards of 30,000 rebels."

[27] *Morning Post*, December 6, 1777.

[28] *Morning Post*, December 6, 1777.

been reinforced, he would not have been defeated—and Howe had not reinforced him. This loyal newspaper apparently had no idea that Germain was cognizant of Howe's operations in Philadelphia.

Britain was stunned by the news of Saratoga. The Duke of Grafton, a member of the Opposition in Parliament, adequately summed up popular feeling when he reported that "the amazement of the whole nation was equalled only by the consternation they felt."[29] Even the historian Edward Gibbon, good Tory M.P. that he was, threatened revolt. Refusing to consent to "the prosecution of a war from whence no reasonable man entertains any hope of success," he concluded it was better to be humbled than ruined.[30] Gibbon told Horace Walpole he was convinced that all but twenty men in the House were ready to vote for peace. Walpole recorded that he "did not think it very decent in so sensible a man to support the war and make such a confession."[31] David Hartley, friend of Benjamin Franklin and a minority M.P., did not share Gibbon's difficulties of conscience. In his *Letters on the American War*, published in the autumn of 1778, he concluded with the now more widely held but still not very popular belief that America definitely was lost. Hartley, incidentally, was defeated in his bid for re-election to Parliament in 1780.[32]

The Opposition press, in an attempt to take advantage of an aroused public opinion, renewed its attacks upon the Ministry's war strategy. Its argument was clear: The battle at Saratoga was not lost in America, but, as for all other losses, the blame was to be found in London.[33] Further, it contended that it would be "national suicide" for England to continue the American war.[34]

[29] *Augustus Henry, Third Duke of Grafton, Autobiography and Political Correspondence,* William R. Anson, ed., 296.

[30] *Letters of Edward Gibbon,* J. E. Norton, ed., II, 169-71.

[31] *Walpole's Journal,* II, 166, dated 2 November 1777.

[32] George Herbert Guttridge, *David Hartley, M.P.,* 291.

[33] Although the *Evening Post,* December 23, 1777, criticized Howe for not giving succor to Burgoyne's besieged army, it reserved its most critical remarks for the Government, which, it claimed, had no plans founded in political or military wisdom. See also May 21, 1778, for another article blaming the Ministry for the plan that led to the defeat at Saratoga. This article also warned that "Ministerial Runners" were busy at work "whispering away" Burgoyne's reputation.

[34] *Gazetteer,* December 25, 1777; *Packet,* January 12, 1778. See also *Annual Register,* 1777, 176, for this magazine's opinion that the difficulties of distance and terrain that played so great a part in Burgoyne's defeat could not be overcome by Britain in the future.

When Charles Fox, on January 27, 1778, moved in the Commons for an inquiry into the reasons for Burgoyne's defeat, both he and his supporters were attacked by Colonel Henry Luttrell for expending their incomes in having their "inflammatory" anti-Ministry speeches published in the newspapers.[35] As a matter of fact, Fox and his Opposition colleagues rarely had to pay for their words to be inserted into a London newspaper. Rather, these men were quoted at length because they were saying, perhaps more eloquently, what the press had been saying all along: The war in America could not be won. After Saratoga, this opinion was held by no means exclusively by the Opposition or even by loyal but wavering members of the Government like Edward Gibbon. On January 18 John Robinson wrote that in a Cabinet council called to consider a new plan of action for the war in America, Sir Jeffrey Amherst stated his belief that it was not possible to subdue the rebellion without an additional force of 30,000 men. Amherst also urged that future operations in America be chiefly naval.[36]

The Opposition press at first joined with the Ministry publications in exonerating Burgoyne. It placed the blame for the loss of over five thousand regulars and Hessians (the Indians had long since fled) squarely upon Lord George Germain for not ordering the necessary reinforcements sent to Burgoyne. The *Evening Post* even predicted that Howe now would be caught between the armies of Washington to the south and of Gates to the north "and all will be over."[37] The *Packet*, which had cleared Burgoyne with the first report of his capitulation, also pointed out that Howe was now on the defensive. It advised that his army should be either recalled or heavily reinforced.[38] About two weeks later this newspaper predicted that Howe's fate would parallel that of Burgoyne.[39] (Copies of the *Packet* could have worked wonders for Washington at Valley Forge.)

Private letters, purporting to come from "informed sources" in America, soon flooded the press with the "true reasons" for Burgoyne's surrender. One maintained that the British army was

---

[35] *Parliamentary History of England*, T. E. Hansard, ed., XIX (1778), 644-47.

[36] HMC, Abergavenny MSS, 10th Report, Appendix, Part VI, 19, January 18, 1778.

[37] *Evening Post*, December 4, 1777. See also *General Evening Post*, March 10, 1778, for a report that Washington, with 27,000 men, was preparing to attack Howe at Philadelphia.

[38] *Packet*, December 5, 1777.

[39] *Packet*, December 17, 1777.

three days without any provisions whatever; another stressed that General Clinton, hurrying north from New York City, was within a day's march of Burgoyne when the latter asked for terms;[40] but almost all correspondents had no doubt that the greatest empire of its time was now on the defensive in America. None suggested that the colonists' triumph at Saratoga was a fortuitous stroke effected by a handful of banditti.

In a direct editorial the *Public Ledger,* which had opposed the American war since its inception, castigated the Ministry for previously representing the Americans as cowards whom two regiments of British troops could easily subdue. The King, too, it asserted, in opening the past three sessions of Parliament with a promise of conquest "the next campaign," proved himself "a very lying prophet." In utter disgust, it summed up the American war: "Fifty thousand veteran troops, have not, in three years, been able to obtain secure possession of fifty miles of ground in America!"[41]

In spite of the misfortunes at Saratoga, Burgoyne emerged from the pages of the press with a reputation more enviable than the one held by the more often victorious—and more often maligned—Sir William Howe.[42] Few guessed at this time that the military career of the universally vindicated Burgoyne was at an end,[43] for even the *Morning Post* declared that Burgoyne must stand acquitted in having done "more than could naturally be expected from him in his unfortunate situation." If Burgoyne lost the battle, it contended, he managed at least to win the peace by rescuing his troops from the indignity of becoming prisoners of war, which General Gates "had the arrogance to demand, but

---

40 *Chester Chronicle,* December 12, 1777. Even the commercial *Daily Advertiser,* December 18, reprinted from the December 15 *London Gazette* Burgoyne's full letter of explanation to Germain.

41 *Public Ledger,* December 12, 1777. See also *Evening Post,* December 23, commenting that the "cowards and poltroons" (as the loyal press had called the colonists) in America had "disgraced our British generals more than any foreign enemy yet has done in the annals of our history."

42 *St. James's Chronicle,* January 8, 1778.

43 *St. James's Chronicle,* December 18, 1777, quoted reports that the King was satisfied with Burgoyne's conduct in America. The *Morning Chronicle,* December 20, stressed that Burgoyne was universally vindicated. Quoting Cato, it told Burgoyne: " 'Tis not in mortals to command success, but you've done more, you have deserved it.' " See also *Gazetteer,* same date: "Whole armies have often been obliged to lay down their arms . . . yet the officers who commanded were all acknowledged to have done their duty, and were never censured," and the *Chronicle,* June 27, 1778, quoting a letter that stated that Burgoyne's soldiers in Quebec still spoke well of him.

not the courage to enforce."[44] Thus did the *Morning Post*, with its sister Tory journals, find itself in the uncomfortable position of praising British courage, leadership, and magnanimity while explaining that these qualities were defeated primarily because of the Americans' overwhelming numerical superiority, a superiority the Ministry publications had regularly and vehemently denied the Americans had ever possessed.

One correspondent to the *Morning Chronicle*, mocking the arguments over whether Burgoyne, Howe, or Germain was to blame for Saratoga, ventured the opinion that the entire fault should fall upon General Arnold and General Gates. He then recommended that these two men be taken into custody and "ordered to attend at the Bar of the House for contempt."[45] The point was well made. Aside from the London radical press, few English publications had considered the possibility that their armies were being outfought and outgeneraled as well.[46] Surely the Americans were exaggerating when they told the story of Saratoga in heroic epic style,[47] but it was obvious that their soldierly skills caused some of Britain's military difficulties on the other side of the Atlantic. Nonetheless, the Tory press refused to face this fact as it continued to shift the blame for defeat. The *General Evening Post* suggested that the Americans' victory was the result of their use of buckshot in their muskets, thus inhumanely wounding a man in two or three places at a time.[48]

The *Morning Post* offered less novel explanations. On March 21, 1778, it maintained that Burgoyne's misfortune arose from the single circumstance of his having an unnecessarily complex supply train, sufficient for an army of 50,000 men, which slowed his march for well over a month, "full time enough on the whole for him to have pushed on to Albany, and with plenty of pro-

[44] Cf. *Evening Post*, December 13, 1777, praising the moderation shown Burgoyne by the Americans. See also *General Evening Post*, December 23, 1777, and *Adams's Weekly Courant*, January 20, 1778.

[45] *Morning Chronicle*, February 12, 1778.

[46] The *Evening Post*, August 12, 1778, reported that the British maneuvers in America were, at best, an imitation of Swift's ballad for children:

> Here we go up, up, up
> And here we go down, down, downy
> There we go *backwards* and *forwards*
> And here we go round, round, roundy.

[47] *Gentleman's Magazine*, February, 1778, 89-90.

[48] *General Evening Post*, December 23, 1777. See also *Morning Chronicle*, December 21, 1778, claiming that a great number of British troops died of their wounds because the Americans used poisoned bullets.

visions." Two months later the paper reverted to its earlier position, blaming Howe for the misfortunes that befell Burgoyne. Now it quoted Burgoyne's letters, which condemned Howe for not creating a diversion farther up the Hudson River with a force of almost 3,000 men that he "might well have spared." Had Sir William so used his resources, "the entire reduction of all the northern rebellious colonies would have ensued."[49] It appeared that Burgoyne did not know that Germain approved of Howe's foray to Philadelphia.

Burgoyne was his own best defender. Taking his seat in the Commons in May, 1778, he was impatient to begin an inquiry into the conduct of his command at Saratoga. One provincial editor thought this eagerness might be a mark of innocence,[50] but newspapers of all political persuasions agreed that an officer on parole (as Burgoyne was from the Americans) could not be tried.[51] Further, all of the key witnesses necessary for an effective inquiry were still in America.[52] Nonetheless, during the summer of 1778 Burgoyne was tried in the British press. The *Gazetteer* stated the case by maintaining that error or neglect remained either with the generals or with the ministers. Anticipating the Government's defense, it affirmed that if the minister who formulated the Canadian plan could not justify his advising the expedition, "his head should answer for his temerity."[53]

The *Morning Post* belatedly reversed its earlier treatment of Burgoyne and opened an attack upon his character and talents, coupled with a complete defense of the Ministry's policy. "Common Sense," one of its most constant contributors, after mourning "the wretched conduct of our military operations in America," declared himself surfeited with the explanations of speechmakers, letter writers, proclamations, and "rhapsodies of pompous bombast"; he expressed his wish that "one of our generals" had paid as much attention to another weapon as he did to the goose quill.[54] The following week the *Morning Post* charged that factious elements were extolling the merits of Burgoyne "in order to excite the public compassion in his favour, and thus rouse the indignation of the people against the ministry."

49 *Morning Post*, May 20, 1778.
50 *Adams's Weekly Courant*, May 26, 1778.
51 *Gazetteer, Morning Post*, June 1, 1778. See also *Morning Post*, July 1.
52 *St. James's Chronicle*, May 28, 1778.
53 *Gazetteer*, June 9, 1778.
54 *Morning Post*, June 24, 1778.

Earlier, Howe had become enmeshed in politics when the Opposition rallied to his defense; now Burgoyne was embraced by the Opposition press because he, too, was at odds with the Ministry. The *Morning Post* denied that "that gallant officer" was to be made into a scapegoat. Englishmen, it asserted, should not be so uncharitable as to ascribe the worst motives to the actions of ministers.[55] Some months later, it is interesting to note, this loyal print was using the term *Burgoyn'd* as a synonym for *trapped* or *surrendered*.[56] Notwithstanding the Tories' defense of the Ministry and the Opposition's defense of both Howe and Burgoyne, the *Morning Chronicle* blamed both generals "for making a wretched hand of it." It expressed hope for better success at sea in the coming struggle with France that, it predicted, would be the direct result of the American victory at Saratoga.[57]

The Opposition press defended Burgoyne with the same arguments it had employed in its defense of Howe: The conquest of America was an impossibility, regardless of who was in command, and the "unthinking and ignorant" were making the Colonies a burial ground for British military reputations by expecting mortals in officers' uniforms to effect the impossible.[58] Further, the Government was to blame for endeavoring to make these unthinking and ignorant plans a reality. By the summer of 1778 politics and military disaster had made such strange bedfellows that General Burgoyne found himself voting in Parliament alongside his adversary General William Howe.

While the loyal press condemned these two men for the defeats in America and the Opposition newspapers blamed the Ministry, the few impartial publications hedged their stances by suggesting that there was blame enough to spread to both politicians and soldiers. This latter statement probably was closest to the truth.

Burgoyne's capitulation had a pronounced effect upon the already low state of morale among the British military stationed in

---

[55] *Morning Post*, July 1, 1778.
[56] *Morning Post*, March 8, 1779.
[57] *Morning Chronicle*, August 15, 1778.
[58] *Gazetteer*, November 24, 1778.

England.[59] One newspaper reported that "great chopping and changing" prevailed among the officers in the Guards, "some few being willing to go to America, others wanting more to stay at home."[60] Most, it seemed, wanted to stay at home. The Royal Navy and the merchant marine also were having difficulties. The scarcity of seamen was so dire that ten thousand or twelve thousand foreigners would eventually have to be taken into British pay in order to man the warships then in commission, moaned the *Gazetteer*.[61] The paper explained why so few volunteered for the army, since, it reported, weakness and disease were the lot of the unfortunate troops stationed in America.[62] In the first week of May, 1778, the *London Gazette* printed an offer of a free pardon to all the deserters of the different divisions of the Royal Marines who would surrender themselves before the end of June. Picked up and printed by other London newspapers,[63] this announcement was construed as an official confession of the low state of morale in one of the toughest branches of the service. Not only had "the flower of our army been thrown away in a wicked and mad war in America," cried the *Evening Post*, but the few remaining regiments were mouldering away from famine and disease. It asserted that the only way to spare this needless effusion of blood was an immediate cancellation of the "ignorant, inhuman, and villainous measures of the present Ministers," which had not only lost an army, but had lost an empire and had thrown "the trade and strength of thirteen flourishing colonies into the hands of the old and natural enemies of this country."[64]

Aware of the tremendous losses and hardships that the future promised, most independent and all loyal publications nevertheless favored a continuation of the war in America. British pride had been shaken; still worse, the ancient enemy France was expected presently to show her hand.[65] Granting the horror

59 Months before news of Saratoga arrived in London, the Opposition press announced that there were not enough troops in America or enough reserves supporting them in Britain. See *Packet*, January 6, March 31, June 20, 1777. See also *St. James's Chronicle*, March 20.

60 *St. James's Chronicle*, December 25, 1777.

61 *Gazetteer*, January 26, 1778.

62 *Gazetteer*, April 27, 1778.

63 *Morning Chronicle*, May 6, 1778.

64 *Evening Post*, July 28, 1778.

65 Even before Saratoga there were warnings that the war had to be a long one, because if Howe and Burgoyne did too well the French would have "thrown off the mask." See *Chronicle*, June 5, 1777.

and devastation that followed in war's train, the *London Magazine* asserted that it was sometimes necessary in order to secure a permanent enjoyment of peace. It maintained that the sword, once drawn, could not be sheathed "till either obedience to that power is restored upon its ancient footing or till political necessity obliges the parent state to leave her former colonies to their own assumed independency."[66] To some observers it appeared that the victory at Saratoga would eventually cause the Americans more harm than good because it had shaken British complacency.[67]

By the end of 1777 the American war was again enmeshed in the web of British domestic politics. It was not just a coincidence that all the Ministry newspapers favored a continuation of the war while most of the Opposition press demanded a cessation of hostilities. Saratoga had given the Opposition a golden chance to reiterate the point of view that eventually would bring it political victory: The war in America could not be won. On December 16, the *Evening Post* again attacked the "absurdity, folly, and wickedness" of the Ministry's resolution to continue the war. Where would they get the money? it asked. Only the Jacobites and the Scots—the two groups most distrusted in London's radical precincts—did not see the "madness and mischief" of supporting the American war. In concluding that England was undone if the struggle were not given up,[68] the *Evening Post* took issue with William Woodfall's *Morning Chronicle*, which was closer to popular opinion when it said that the public would demonstrate a want of both spirit and sense if it gave up the struggle. It approved of the Ministry's desire to conduct the fight "in a new manner, and with a greater spirit than ever."[69]

Bate's *Morning Post* voiced Lord Sandwich's sentiments when, in a series of articles and paragraphs that dominated its columns during the final week of 1777, it demanded renewed effort to win the American war. It reported that the country gentlemen be-

---

[66] *London Magazine,* November, 1778, 514-15. See also *Morning Post,* January 6, and *General Evening Post,* January 13, for statements favoring a continuation of the American war.

[67] J. H. Jesse, *George Selwyn and His Contemporaries,* III, 248, quoting A. M. Storer, who was soon to be appointed a member of the Carlisle Peace Commission.

[68] *Evening Post,* December 16, 1777. See also December 20, blaming the King for resolving to continue the war.

[69] *Morning Chronicle,* December 13, 1777. See also *General Evening Post,* December 6, and *Adams's Weekly Courant,* December 16.

lieved their honor so at stake that they were determined at all costs to crush the rebellion. The only hope of the Congress "and their republican abettors on this side of the Atlantic," it continued, "lay in England being soon sick of the expence." The *Morning Post* happily predicted that the republicans were likely to be "miserably disappointed."[70] Further, it would be foolish to think of treating with the colonists, "flushed as they are with the trifling advantage they have gained over Burgoyne." A treaty conducive to the welfare of both parties could be written, it assured its readers, only after the "next campaign," when it was expected the rebels would receive a sound drubbing "so as to restore them to their senses."[71] In its closing issue for the year, this loyal newspaper advised the "transatlantic insurgents" to view the vigorous military preparations being made in England "at the *voluntary expence* of the people at large."[72] No other publication, however, noted any great voluntary expenditures by the English public. It seemed that Englishmen wanted to win the American war quickly, but few wanted to fight or to pay the heavy taxes necessary to make victory a reality.

The press was aware that despite their success at Saratoga the Americans were facing serious troubles. Throughout 1778 the newspapers stressed the discipline, money, and supply problems of Washington and his forces. The *Morning Chronicle,* in a typical article, declared that so little discipline was observed in the rebel army "that their chiefs were not only disobeyed, but frequently insulted with opprobrious language."[73] Quoting American accounts, the *Morning Post* added that the rebels were in want of military stores, clothes, and accouterments. It reported also that vast numbers of desertions had reduced Washington's army to less than 9,000 effective men, a number by no means able to stand before the British forces already in America.[74] Other reports, stressing the lack of medical supplies in the Colonies,

---

70 *Morning Post,* December 24, 1777.

71 *Morning Post,* December 29, 1777.

72 *Morning Post,* December 31, 1777.

73 *Morning Chronicle,* January 16, 1778; *Gazetteer* and *Morning Post,* May 5. See also *General Evening Post,* December 24, 26, stating that "America was in a spirit of mutiny."

74 *Morning Post,* February 12, 1778. See also January 21, for a report that General Israel Putnam was behaving "in a very mutinous manner."

demonstrated that the Americans, despite their one great victory, were still in serious straits.[75] In addition, dissension in the rebel high command was highlighted in the loyal press.[76] The *Morning Post* asserted that not only was Washington jealous of Gates's recent triumph, but also the American Commander and the Continental Congress were in such complete disagreement that "a revolution was hourly expected among the rebel chieftains."[77] It soon predicted that the next news from America would contain an announcement from Washington declaring himself "Protector" of the United States.[78] If and when the American revolution-within-a-revolution took place, Washington could count upon the editorial support of the *Morning Post*, which agreed, with what it called "the warmest partizans" of the American cause, that the Congress should be viewed in the most contemptible light. Although loyal Americans "could scarcely suppress the public ridicule of the mock dignity" of the Congress, this loyal British print admitted that a favorable estimation of Washington still obtained in the Colonies. It stressed, however, that the American Commander's recent lack of victories had of late "considerably diminished his public consequence."[79] In short, Washington's situation was "exceedingly uncomfortable."

Britain was fed not only subsequent reports of his resignation[80] but also stories claiming that Washington's large retinue of foreign officers was "retiring in disgust." Lafayette, one loyal newspaper stated, was the only French officer who chose to remain in the American service, doing so only because the Congress had promised him a large allotment of land.[81] The *General Evening Post* alleged that the officers remaining in the rebel army

[75] *General Evening Post*, April 21, 1778.

[76] *Morning Post*, March 3, 1778.

[77] *Morning Post*, January 8, 1778, letter II of "Aristides," which was continued from January 6. For a report of Gates's unhappiness at serving under Washington, see *Morning Chronicle*, November 17, in which Gates alleged that Washington "had not even skill enough to lead a band of fishermen in their attack on a whale."

[78] *Morning Post*, March 9, 1778.

[79] *Morning Post*, July 1, 1778. See also July 4, for an article stressing the friction that allegedly existed between Washington and the Congress. The *Morning Chronicle*, July 16, sided with the American Commander because it considered the Congress "a junto of tyrants."

[80] *Morning Chronicle*, April 30, 1778.

[81] *General Evening Post*, July 23, 1778.

were busy cutting one another down in duels of honor.[82] In this fashion did the press convince its readers that despite their victory at Saratoga the Americans "groaned under such a Load of complicated Calamities as is scarce credible."[83] *Adams's Weekly Courant* reported that the colonists were experiencing not only distress and poverty, but, still worse, "every Evil deducible from lawless Tyranny."[84] The *Morning Chronicle* also indicated that America was in a far from enviable position as it reported that the devastation of the land affected all classes of the American economy.[85] Small wonder then that the rebel army, which "it has often been asserted was composed of the dregs of the people," was in such a rebellious mood, said the *Morning Post.*[86]

After publicizing the wretched state of the Colonies, many editors expected that a serious renewal of hostilities had an excellent chance of success. Most, however, were now so cautious that they dared not predict victory "in the next campaign." They contented themselves with making suggestions of a military nature that, they hoped, would prove more fruitful than the plans carried out in the past. Even the Ministry *General Evening Post* recommended that, if another campaign were decided upon (and it admitted the possibility that it might not be), it should be an attack upon New England "where an army will always have a plentiful country to forage in."[87]

But the "next campaign" began in the South, and it was so successful that even the Opposition antiwar newspapers confessed that in Georgia, for the first time since the beginning of the war, British forces had acted both "offensively and successfully."[88] In the northern colonies, too, editors saw victory to be imminent. As early as the spring of 1778, when the wound of Saratoga was still fresh, newspapers had predicted that the new Brit-

---

82 *General Evening Post,* August 25, 1778, alleging that General Thomas Conway, "a French officer in the service," was killed by a general identified only as Cadwallader of Philadelphia. The "Conway Cabal" was not known of in Britain at this time. For other reports of American unrest, see November 14, and the *Morning Chronicle,* November 17.

83 *Adams's Weekly Courant,* August 4, 1778.

84 *Adams's Weekly Courant,* August 4, 1778.

85 *Morning Chronicle,* January 5, 1779. For a later declaration of the same point, see the *Courant,* December 23.

86 *Morning Post,* December 26, 1778. This issue accurately reported that the "Conway Cabal" had been exposed and that this minor threat to Washington's command had been easily disposed of.

87 *General Evening Post,* February 7, 1778.

88 *Packet,* February 8, 1778.

ish commander in America, Sir Henry Clinton, his army in high spirits, would soon make Englishmen forget the defeats of the past by conquering Gates and his dissipated forces.[89]

For the loyal press Clinton was to be the man of the hour in America. The Opposition *Packet* reminded its readers that scarcely six months earlier "the intrepid Burgoyne was a perfect meteor," then "fame and panegyric" spread to Howe, and now Clinton was hailed as the new hero![90] This plea for caution was of no avail. The *Morning Chronicle* stated that, considering Sir Henry's circumstances and situation, his evacuation in June of Philadelphia and his retreat across the Jerseys to New York "must be acknowledged a great piece of generalship." Conceding that no immediate advantage accrued to the British forces because of this withdrawal, it nevertheless announced that Sir Henry had performed more in ten days "than three years campaign by a former commander could accomplish."[91] It would be a mistake to interpret Clinton's withdrawal as a defeat, suggested the *Morning Post*. Not only did this "brilliant maneuver" do him "immortal honour," but, more important, from it one could draw "the most happy presage of future victories."[92] However, the Opposition *Evening Post*, scoffing at the tortuous logic of Bate's *Morning Post*, predicted glumly that Clinton's fate would be the same as that of Howe and Burgoyne. "Sir Henry Clinton is to do wonders," it warned, "at the financial expense of all Englishmen"; the inevitable new loan might again prove only to provide "the whale another tub."[93]

Many editors continued to think that America could be crushed at minimal expense. A naval blockade, as General Amherst had recommended, seemed the best way to starve the commerce of the Colonies and bring them to their knees without risking another Saratoga. Rumors that the war was to be pursued along these lines persisted. Newspapers were "positively asserting" that the Government had resolved to win the war by destroying every seaport town of consequence in America and to recall its troops, some of whom were to reinforce the West Indies.[94] The

[89] *General Evening Post*, April 16, 1778.

[90] *Packet*, July 3, 1778.

[91] *Morning Chronicle*, August 26, 1778.

[92] *Morning Post*, August 27, 1778. See also October 14, for an article praising Clinton's capture of Rhode Island.

[93] *Evening Post*, August 29, 1778.

[94] *Gazetteer*, June 5, *Chronicle*, June 13, 1777.

Morning Post did not approve of this line of action. By successfully blockading America, it prophesied, the British would be imposing a blessing upon a people in possession of a country "in itself so capable of producing everything so desirable in life."[95] It maintained also that to support a fleet in the Atlantic was almost impossible. If America were to be crushed, the job would necessarily be accomplished on land, and General Clinton, it was hoped, would carry the day against the rapidly weakening colonists.

Soon, however, discussions of the accomplishments of Clinton and his army lost importance. Interest now was centered upon Britain's final attempt to make peace with the colonists before commencing serious hostilities against "Perfidious Gaul." The French had showed their hand after Saratoga, and Englishmen of all political persuasions now hoped for a quick end to the American war so that Britain's total might could be used to support this new struggle against an old foe.

95 *Morning Post*, December 17, 1777.

CHAPTER VIII

Another Failure
at Reconciliation

*Amidst the hoarse thunder of war, the still voice of Reason
cannot be heard. Reconciliation, indeed, seems to be the
wish of all parties; but where is the party that points to the
fair road that leads to accomplish it?*[1]

B Y 1777 most London editors conceded that the war with
America was unpopular; "enough of war," "enough of
slaughter," and "negotiation and conciliation" were the phrases
most prevalent in the press that year.[2] As soon as the news of the
defeat at Saratoga was announced, the Opposition press clamored
again for an immediate end to the "carnage." The *General Advertiser* complained that the war had already cost over thirty
million pounds and about thirty thousand men, and it reminded
its readers that "at the end of every campaign we are worse off
than we were at the beginning."[3] Even *Gentleman's Magazine,*

1 *Gentleman's Magazine,* Preface, 1777.

2 *Gentleman's Magazine,* January, 1777, 38; June, 286. See also *St. James's
Chronicle,* January 4, reporting successful talks of conciliation, and the *Packet,*
April 23, May 5, July 23, 1777.

3 *General Advertiser,* December 5, 1777. See also *Packet,* December 31, and
Gazetteer, November 22, reporting the "desires of a great number of reasonable
men for reconciliation."

121

one of London's less partial publications, recommended that those who favored the prolongation of the war read the gory verse "Desolation of America," which it reviewed in February, 1778.[4]

For most editors the moment to end the American war had come; France had finally showed her hostile intentions. Could Britain swiftly furnish a counterproposal to induce the Colonies to return to their former allegiance? The Opposition press had its doubts. The *Gazetteer* expressed the wish that peace measures had been taken sooner, for it assumed that any overtures made in early 1778 would be too late.[5] In the light of the results of Saratoga, an accommodation with the rebels was imperative; the paper was of the opinion that "the finest troops in the world" could not win in America.[6] The colonists had done so well in the field that the war could no longer be expected to bring about the desired results. Peace rumors and demands were the order of the day. Had France not allied with the Americans, British public opinion probably would have brought pressure on the Government to consider a new series of negotiations with the Congress.[7]

While few Englishmen at first acknowledged that the colonists should be treated as equals, many grudgingly admitted that if three years of warfare could not humble them, perhaps England needed to reconcile herself to an independent America.[8] So long as Britons read that the Colonies could put about 100,000 men

---

[4] *Gentleman's Magazine,* February, 1778, 83-85. See also "Ode for the New Year," January, 39, for the reconciliation theme in a semiofficial document: "Forgive at once, and be forgiven/ and Discord is no more." Cf. *Chronicle,* January 1, 1777: "It is curious to observe how all ranks of ministerial dependents are obliged to alter their note relative to America. This time two years ago the Laureat in his New Year's Ode, laughs at the American contest and exultingly exclaims, 'Can Britain fail! the thoughts were vain!/she rules the empress of the main.' But this year his flights of poetry are lowered; and, borrowing a little piety from the Court, he appeals to God Almighty alone to settle quarrels by saying, 'Tis *he alone* can reunite/The foes who once were friends.' " See also January 8, 22, 1778.

[5] *Gazetteer,* January 9, 1778; *Chronicle,* January 8.

[6] *Gazetteer,* January 10, 1778.

[7] The *Morning Post,* January 31, February 6, 1778, reported that Franklin was informed by the Congress that its disposition was changed from war to peace and that a reconciliation with Britain soon would be negotiated.

[8] *Packet,* January 3, 4, 1777; *Adams's Weekly Courant,* April 7, 1778; *Chronicle,* April 28, 1778.

in the field, they could safely assume that, barring an unforeseen miracle, America was lost to the Empire.[9]

Englishmen were anxious to have their government talk peace with the Colonies, but few were able to agree upon what should be discussed at a peace conference. All believed that an accord with America, built upon terms that could bind the warring parties together, was highly desirable.[10] Exactly what terms of accommodation could bring the Americans to cast aside an impending French alliance was a moot question. At the same time the *Chronicle* declared that only the ailing Chatham could save the day by coming up with a proper solution,[11] the loyal *General Evening Post* assured its readers that Lord North would soon produce a conciliatory bill "so well calculated to answer the desired end of finishing the war with America, that it is imagined it will meet with little or no opposition in either House of Parliament."[12]

On February 18, 1778, Britain read that North's proposal included a repeal of the Tea and Coercive Acts, a promise that Parliament would impose no more revenue taxes upon the Colonies, and provision for the establishment of a peace commission to deal with the Congress, and—if necessary—to recommend that Parliament suspend all legislation concerning America that had been passed since 1763. Most of the readers of this news believed that the Prime Minister, having no taste himself for this war, had at last suggested fair and honorable terms of reconciliation. True, North hoped the Americans would lay down their arms, but the press expressed fear they would refuse to do so.[13] Nonetheless, so liberal a proposition could not be scoffed at. The *Gazetteer*, commenting on the tardiness of the offer, stressed that it would have been accepted with joy had it been submitted years earlier.[14] It was widely predicted that North, who admittedly was offering

---

[9] On December 13, 1777, the *Morning Post*, discussing the probable strength of a free America, doubted that an independent United States could ever become a commercial or a maritime state. See also March 9, 1778, and *Evening Post*, November 6, 1777. The *Morning Chronicle*, January 16, 1778, speculated that American independence would make Ireland much more important to Britain's economy and would give the Irish a chance to export something besides people to England.

[10] *Chronicle*, January 31, 1778.

[11] *Chronicle*, February 10, 1778.

[12] *General Evening Post*, February 12, 1778; *Gazetteer*, February 16; *Chester Chronicle*, February 20. See also *Morning Chronicle*, *Morning Post*, February 16, for variations on the same article.

[13] *Packet*, February 13, 1778.

[14] *Gazetteer*, February 19, 1778.

these magnanimous terms to forestall a Franco-American alliance, would find his magnanimity canceled by his tardiness.[15] Though it was hoped that his propositions could end the war if they were transmitted to the Congress promptly,[16] the King's commissioners spent an additional month preparing to embark for America.[17]

On March 25, 1778, two weeks after George III had given the new conciliatory measure his assent, North wrote the King that England's condition was so deplorable that "it is totally unequal to a war with Spain, France, and America." This pessimistic report concluded with the statement that "peace with America, and a change in the Ministry are the only steps which can save the country."[18] The Prime Minister's words might have been written by John Almon, William Parker, or by any of a number of London propagandists for the Opposition. The King lost no time in realizing the seriousness of the situation. The following day he wrote North that, while he detested Benjamin Franklin, he thought it so desirable to end the American war "to be enabled with redoubled ardour to avenge the faithless and insolent conduct of France," that he recommended keeping open "the channel of intercourse with that insidious man."[19]

North threw his not inconsiderable weight behind the negotiations by encouraging the publication of one of the most startling pamphlets of the entire era. Israel Mauduit, whom North in his letter to the King on March 25 had called "one of the most zealous friends of Great Britain in her disputes with America," brought out an anonymous broadside entitled *A Hand bill advocating American Independence, inspired by the English Ministry. . . .* At a time when Chatham, Rockingham, and Shelburne were not yet prepared to support a demand for American independence, North encouraged the publication of this broadside recommending it. Perhaps the Prime Minister, disgusted with the rebellion as he genuinely was, wanted to end the American business once and for all; perhaps he had hoped that an aroused public opinion would insist that the arguments of Mauduit went too far and that

15 *Morning Chronicle, Morning Post,* February 18, 1778.

16 *Morning Post,* February 23, 1778. See also *Morning Chronicle,* May 20, article predicting that the commissioners would beat the French Toulon squadron to America, thus averting a Franco-American alliance.

17 North's conciliatory measure was introduced on February 17 and enacted by royal assent on March 11. The newly appointed commissioners met on March 13, but they did not embark for America until April 16.

18 Fortescue, *Correspondence of King George III,* IV, 25 March 1778.

19 Fortescue, *Correspondence of King George III,* IV, 26 March 1778.

America should be won over by liberal terms rather than lost by complete independence. In any event, Mauduit voiced the arguments that had become all to familiar to even occasional readers of London's Opposition press. He was certain that with French support America could not be defeated. Further, once independence was recognized, the main quarrel with France would disappear. Britain would again command her full share of the American market, and the free trade that Adam Smith wrote about in 1776 would, of course, bring some of the thirteen colonies back into England's political and economic vortex. Mauduit feared that a long war would certainly Gallicize America. Thus, if Britain had to fight France, she should make her peace with America first. Fighting both enemies at once was an invitation to certain defeat.

At almost the same time, there appeared the anonymous "Letter to the English Nation, on the Present War with America . . . From which the absolute Impossibility of Reducing the Colonies will sufficiently appear, and the Folly of continuing the contest demonstrated." Sir George Savile wrote the preface to this obviously Opposition-oriented pamphlet, whose author was identified only as "an Officer returned from that [American] service." After praising Savile and attacking the idea of virtual representation in America, "the Officer" delivered the same arguments as had been advanced by Mauduit.

While it appeared that—on the surface at least—Britain was almost unanimous in its desire for peace with America before embarking upon a French campaign,[20] the Ministry *Morning Post* expressed a doubt that anything hopeful could come of these negotiations. It believed that the Congress' "designing leaders" would turn a deaf ear to the pleas of America's "starving inhabitants" and would continue the war despite the desire of most Americans to be reunited with Britain.[21] Thus, the *Morning Post* assumed, the proposed olive branch would be coupled with a sword; if the Americans did not accept the offer, Britain would

[20] See also Alexander Dalrymple's pamphlet, *Considerations on the Present State of Affairs Between England and America,* for another example of the desire for peace, motivated by the belief that it was impossible to secure a military victory over the colonists.

[21] *Morning Post,* February 18, 23, 1778. See also Wedderburn Papers (Clements) Vol. I, Sec. X, 1-9, demonstrating that even the adamant Attorney General was by 1778 in favor of a peace treaty with America.

be compelled to utilize her total national strength in order to compel obedience from the provincials.[22]

Much of the Opposition press also maintained that the attempts at reconciliation would fail, but for reasons quite different than those used by the *Morning Post*. One newspaper suggested the "*High, Mighty*, and *Independent* States of America" would probably demand an indemnification for the expenses incurred by the war,[23] while another judged North's proposals ridiculous because the "good natured" British, defeated in war, were now making an offer of peace.[24] The *Westminster Journal* accurately noted that the much-talked-of treaty between France and the United States was consummated on February 6, 1778. Negotiation, heretofore fruitless, was now even more difficult.

It was also believed that George III was quite cool to any offer of reconciliation,[25] especially if the offer was tantamount to an admission that the Americans had "darkened the orb of Britain's eclipsed sun of glory."[26] However, when the Earl of Carlisle, chief of the newly appointed peace commissioners,[27] finally set sail in mid-April with the approval of a reluctant sovereign, English hopes soared. Before this departure, Britons had been reading that some of their most prominent political figures were re-evaluating their earlier intransigent stand toward America.[28] The catastrophe at Saratoga had done more than any argument in Parliament or in the press to make the landed gentry wonder if the struggle was worth the investment.

[22] *Morning Post*, February 24, March 3, 1778.

[23] *Gazetteer*, February 24, 1778.

[24] *Westminster Journal*, February 21, 1778. One correspondent in the *Gazetteer*, March 21, wrote that North's conciliation bill reminded him of the old saying: "If the mountain will not come to Mahomet, Mahomet must go to the mountain." Thus was it necessary for North to go to the Americans.

[25] *Morning Chronicle*, March 14, 1778.

[26] *Packet*, March 9, 1778.

[27] *Morning Post*, June 20, 1777, reported that the ambitious Earl was disappointed at not having been made Ambassador to Spain. Two months before news of Saratoga, Carlisle, who considered himself "very ministerial," admitted having his fears about the outcome of the American war. J. H. Jesse, *George Selwyn and His Contemporaries*, III, 215.

[28] *Gentleman's Magazine*, March, 1778, 127, reviewed most favorably William Pulteney's *Thoughts on the Present State of Affairs With America and the Means of Conciliation*. The author, a great landholder in Scotland, an heir by marriage to the Earl of Bath, an M.P. from Shrewsbury, and a brother of Governor Johnstone, who was also a member of the Carlisle Commission, wrote: "We are now cured of the dream of an early conquest, and we awake to the disadvantage of continuing at such a distance for any length of time, a war of so much expence. . . ."

Despite prior pessimism (the *Evening Post* just two weeks earlier had warned that the struggle could be concluded only if England abdicated its American rights),[29] most newspapers stated hopefully that the colonists would now meet King and Country half way and settle all outstanding differences once and for all. No sooner had Carlisle sailed than the *Gazetteer* assumed there would be no military actions of consequence until the outcome of the conciliatory offers were known; battles would make negotiations more difficult, and, if at all possible, they were to be avoided. On April 7 it alleged that rumors of peace began to gain credit, and the following day it reported a cessation of hostilities. By April 21 it noted that London merchants were storing up goods to ship to America. These statements, based more firmly upon the hopes of an editor and his readers than on reliable information from the other side of the ocean, were repeated regularly in most publications.[30] While the *Morning Post* completely shifted its earlier position (Bate never regarded consistency as a virtue) and now foretold "a full and mutual accommodation,"[31] many Opposition papers reiterated their position that independence was the only possible ground upon which the Americans would negotiate.[32] Mauduit's pamphlet notwithstanding, the commissioners were not empowered to discuss independence. Even the fact that the colonists were busily creating a permanent framework for a separate and independent nation received little publicity in the press. Englishmen did not concern themselves with the work of a rebel government that, they hoped, would not last much longer anyway. Consequently, a document so important as the Articles of Confederation and Perpetual Union received scant notice from most London publications.[33]

By June the optimism had faded. On June 15 the *Packet* reported that the Americans would not even treat with the commissioners; two weeks later it declared that talks, even if gotten under way, would fail because the Americans would certainly raise the unacceptable standard of independence as a *conditio*

29 *Evening Post,* February 11, 1778.

30 *Chronicle,* April 7, 20, 1778; *Morning Post,* April 10; *General Evening Post,* April 9, 21. All reported that Franklin had left Paris for America to confer with the Congress and to prepare himself to meet with the British commissioners.

31 *Morning Post,* April 11, 1778.

32 *Chronicle,* April 16, 1778; *Evening Post,* April 30.

33 The *Gazetteer,* March 10, 1778, printed without comment the text of the Articles. It had copied the document from the Connecticut *Courant.*

sine qua non for peace.[34] Every morsel of information relative to the Carlisle mission was avidly read,[35] but there were so many conflicting reports it was impossible to find the truth.[36] At any rate, the dreams of a negotiated peace were to be smashed upon the rock of independence, and with every passing day the Americans became a little more secure in their triumph.[37]

When word arrived that the Congress was willing to negotiate only for a withdrawal of British forces from America and for the recognition of independence, the press finally gave up all hope of attaining a *status quo ante bellum*. It admitted that further talks would be fruitless. The war that few Englishmen wanted was to continue indefinitely, and the *Morning Post's* assertion that the belligerents "will amicably shake hands before the first of January next,"[38] was generally construed as only a faint graveyard whistle. On September 16, 1778, the *Packet* again confessed that America was lost;[39] the loyal *Adams's Weekly Courant* made the same admission a week later.[40]

The blame for the failure of this final peace offer clearly lay with the Americans, most editors agreed.[41] After publishing the full text of the Carlisle correspondences, *Gentleman's Magazine* rebuked the members of the Congress, "jealous, perhaps, of their own existence," for subverting the peace efforts rather than seriously pondering if the terms offered them met with the wishes of their constituents.[42] The *Morning Chronicle* also castigated the

34 *Packet,* June 15, 1778.

35 The *General Advertiser,* August 11, 1778, published all of the reported correspondences between the Congress and the Commissioners; this edition sold out so fast that the material was reprinted on August 12 and 13. See also *Morning Post* for these dates and the *Evening Post,* August 8.

36 The *Morning Post,* June 16, 1778, stated that recent letters from America intimated the colonists would accept the proffered olive branch, but on July 8 and 30 it stressed the "redoubled vigour" with which England would pursue the war if the commissioners' report was unfavorable. On August 11, it asserted that the Congress had not yet answered Carlisle. See also *General Evening Post,* July 18, claiming that Clinton's unmolested march from Philadelphia to New York left little doubt that negotiations were seriously contemplated by the Americans. Cf. *General Advertiser,* June 24, and *St. James's Chronicle,* June 27, which reported that the Americans were procrastinating because "if they can but delay the Dispute a year or two longer, England must of Necessity give up."

37 *Evening Post,* July 28, 1778; *Morning Chronicle,* August 15.

38 *Morning Post,* September 2, 1778. See also July 25, October 6.

39 *Morning Post,* November 18, December 23, 1778, for statements that "America is irrecoverable."

40 *Adams's Weekly Courant,* September 22, 1778.

41 *Gentleman's Magazine,* September, 1778, 413-14. See also *London Magazine,* August, 365-67.

42 *Gentleman's Magazine,* October, 1778, 489.

colonists,[43] but along with many other publications it continued to express the belief that the Americans would be free because they had won their battle for independence.[44]

The press realized that, if Britain could not defeat the rebels after all the efforts of the past three years, she surely could not do it while concentrating upon a war with France. Gradually it came to acknowledge the need for a complete abandonment of hostilities in America. Suggesting that Britain should have sued for peace with the colonists before becoming involved in a European war with France, "ARATUS," the *Evening Post's* most widely publicized contributor, believed the Americans had so changed their leadership as the war progressed that the moderates who had been in control months before now were replaced by intransigent radicals who insisted upon a continuation of war. Seeing that America, which could not be defeated, insisted upon continuing the struggle, this writer concluded that Britain had no choice but to turn her arms against the French and "leave America cool," for, if left to themselves, the colonists would always prefer trading with England.[45] Two days later, the *Evening Post* pointedly asserted that George III "ought to be convinced of the impossibility of success in further carrying on the American war." It then recommended that the sovereign make a virtue of necessity and withdraw his forces from America in order to defend his dominions from attack by the French.[46]

This "peace with America—war with France" theme, which was to permeate the press in late 1778 and early 1779, was not new; it was suggested by the *St. James's Chronicle* as soon as Lord North introduced his measures of conciliation to Parliament. As early as February, 1778, this newspaper demanded a war with France, on the grounds that it had aided the Colonies with whom

---

[43] *Morning Chronicle*, October 8, 1778. On October 17, this newspaper printed copies of the official papers between the Congress and the Carlisle Commissioners. Its source was the August 29 edition of the New York *Royal Gazette*.

[44] *Morning Chronicle*, May 12, 1778; *St. James's Chronicle*, October 17; *General Advertiser*, November 28, 30, December 31. See also *Public Ledger*, November 24: "Let the present parliament sit only until America be conquered, and the sovereign will, during his life, be spared the trouble of his issuing his fiat for a dissolution." See also *Evening Post*, December 22, 1778, and *Packet*, January 18, November 10, 1779. Cf. *Packet*, December 27, 1779.

[45] *Evening Post*, December 22, 1778. See also November 20, December 14, 1779, January 4, 1780. Cf. *Morning Post*, April 5, 1779.

[46] *Evening Post*, December 24, 1778. See also January 28, 1779: "The abandonment of the war in America though privately resolved in the cabinet, will not be declared to the public for some time."

Britain was now hoping to make peace.[47] An American settlement notwithstanding, France had to be punished, and the *Gazetteer*, in bold print, demanded:

WAR WITH FRANCE

AND

PEACE WITH AMERICA.[48]

While *Gentleman's Magazine* explained that the "haughty tone" assumed by the Americans toward the Carlisle Commission was undoubtedly owing to the flattering declarations of the French King "which gave new investiture to their sovereignty,"[49] the *General Advertiser* saw good cause for American haughtiness: Had not Lord Amherst, considered the greatest soldier in all Britain, informed the Cabinet, "THE PRESENT DESTRUCTIVE WAR WITH AMERICA SHOULD BE IMMEDIATELY ABANDONED"?[50] The *Morning Post* also admitted that matters were going so badly that the Commons had already given notice of sponsoring no less than five different public hearings on the official conduct of the Administration.[51]

It was clear that public opinion toward the American Revolution, as reflected in the British press, had drifted so far that, one year after Saratoga, sentiments that would have been construed as almost treasonous after the battles at Lexington and Concord were now believed to be intelligent readjustments. When the *Gazetteer* called for Englishmen to reconsider their ideas about North America on the basis of losing the twelve rebellious colonies (it considered Georgia loyal), it was not attacked as had been the articles and pamphlets of Josiah Tucker, Richard Price, and the others who had considered almost the same ideas in 1775. When, in early 1779, it voiced optimism because of the belief that Canada, the Floridas, Georgia, and Nova Scotia, once peopled and cultivated, could more than compensate Britain for its present

47 *St. James's Chronicle,* February 17, 1778.

48 *Gazetteer,* March 19, 1778. See also *General Evening Post,* October 3, 1778, and *Morning Chronicle,* March 1, 1779: "Be England to herself but true/ To France defiance hurl'd,/ Give peace, America, with you,/ And war with all the World."

49 *Gentleman's Magazine,* Supplement, 1778, 629-38.

50 *General Advertiser,* January 29, 1779. This newspaper gave no citation for its quotation of Amherst. While the language is obviously Parker's, the advice indeed was Amherst's. It took a full year for his words to get from the Cabinet Council to the press. See HMC, Abergavenny MSS, January 18, 1778.

51 *Morning Post,* February 19, 1779.

loss,[52] there were no cries of "Treason!" The war had gone so badly for the mother country (though the strength of the Colonies was also seriously depleted at this time), that the Englishman's concept of tolerance toward America broadened with each day. The hopes that, somehow, mediation and conciliation could bring the Americans, happily and of their own volition, back into the Empire, never quite faded, however, from the columns of the press.[53]

[52] *Gazetteer,* April 9, 1779.
[53] *Gazetteer,* July 30, August 17, 1779.

CHAPTER IX

Perfidious Gaul

I T WAS COMMON KNOWLEDGE THAT, since the beginning of England's difficulties in America, the French had been observing the problems of their cross-Channel neighbors with more than passing interest. Englishmen assumed that France was only awaiting a propitious moment to enter the war on the side of the Colonies. They also believed that, in the event of such an enlarged war, Spain would join with its Bourbon cousins in an attempt to destroy the British Empire.

While acknowledging France's wish for a British defeat, many editors had believed, in the first months of the American Revolution, that the French were in no position to aid the rebels with men, money, or armaments.[1] Still, the overwhelming majority of publications conceded that, if the uprisings in the Colonies were not quickly crushed, they could easily flare up into a general European conflict that would pit England against a Bourbon coalition. Anticipating this, the *Morning Post*, as early as April 13, 1776, reported "betts of three to one" that either France or Spain would declare war upon Britain before May of the following year. A few weeks later it affirmed that the Bourbons were "meditating some stroke, which may prove fatal to the honour and interest of the British Empire."[2] The press was also warning its readers that the French had heavily reinforced their bases in both the

[1] *Middlesex Journal*, May 6, 1775. See also *Evening Post*, April 26, 1776; *Morning Post*, March 27, August 9, September 20, October 28.

[2] *Morning Post*, May 2, 1776.

East and West Indies "with probable object for its employment, but what must be hostile to us."[3]

In spite of France's repeated professions of peace and friendship at St. James's, it was apparent to the press that "Perfidious Gaul" would support the rebels.[4] Even the Paris press ("that heavily licensed and bribed tool of their ministry") was publishing "audacious and groundless libels against the English in order to incense the French nation against us." Should it succeed, concluded the *Morning Post*, a war would be inevitable.[5] Nonetheless, the paper did not predict a sudden rupture with France, for it held that public opinion was absolutely necessary for the prosecution of a successful war and that the French public "seemed to enter very little into the matter."[6] In stressing that it would be national suicide for Louis XVI to lead France into a war without first obtaining the support of *his* subjects, the *Morning Post* simply assumed that the majority of Englishmen supported George III. (It branded the majority of the London press "a mere factious element.") Even if it were true that French public opinion would not support another war so soon after their latest defeat, this loyal newspaper cautioned its Ministry to keep a sharp lookout across the Channel because of the large-scale operations at French dockyards and troop encampments.[7]

At first the Opposition press, in the fear that Britain could not win the war in America, strove to avoid the additional and perhaps fatal burden of a European conflict. The *St. James's Chronicle* admitted, however, that a war could not be prevented indefinitely; France would make the first hostile move as soon as the Americans were in danger of being crushed. She would then give the colonists assistance enough to "do them no good, and to do Great Britain much harm."[8] By throwing just enough oil on the fire to keep it burning, France could destroy her traditional foe at no real cost. Further, if the struggle should take a turn favorable to the Americans (and the *St. James's Chronicle* did not deny this possibility), Louis, with a swift declaration of war, could help

---

3 *General Evening Post,* May 2; *Morning Chronicle,* May 3, 1776.

4 *Morning Post,* May 14, 22, July 2, 17, 22, 1776.

5 *Morning Post,* July 8, 1776.

6 *Morning Post,* July 8, 1776.

7 *Morning Post,* July 15, 1776. On July 29, the *Morning Post,* after publishing the contents of an alleged treaty between America, France, and Spain, mocked the colonists for promising to return both Canada and Nova Scotia to France without first possessing them.

8 *St. James's Chronicle,* October 12, 1776. See also *Chronicle,* June 5, 1777.

dictate the peace terms. Win or lose, then, England should gird herself for the eventual action from Versailles that would force her into war.[9]

The *Gazetteer*, prior to the proclamation of American independence, confidently reported that both France and Spain had offered to recognize America's freedom and to send upward of 20,000 men to defend it "in consideration of an absolutely free trade," in case Congress' demands were not met by Parliament.[10] This paper concluded that the American Declaration was issued only after a correspondence between the Congress and "our natural enemies," who had assured the colonists of every assistance."[11] On July 4, 1776, the *Morning Chronicle* reported the "absolute fact" that a powerful French fleet was ordered to America to augment the colonists' navy. In addition, this newspaper was certain that the French were not only helping England's enemies in North America,[12] but they were also making extraordinary warlike preparations at home. Accordingly, the paper quoted the rules laid down by Grotius in his *Law of War and Peace*, which inferred that England was within her moral rights of self-defense to declare immediate war against "a neighboring prince making war preparations without convincing his neighbor that these preparations will not be used against him."[13]

Certainly in 1776 the press accurately reflected English public opinion toward France. All publications stressed the need for naval preparedness and expressed hopes that the mighty Channel and West Indian squadrons could deter an attack.[14] At the same time caution was recommended against the false security encouraged by the honeyed tones issuing from Versailles.[15] It was conceded generally that Britain did not have the strength to commence hostilities immediately. The newspapers speculated, therefore, about the exact time, place, and issues that would precipitate the eventual French (or force the English) declara-

---

9 The *St. James's Chronicle*, December 24, 1776, reported "on good authority" that France had agreed to assist the Americans "to the utmost of their power."

10 *Gazetteer*, July 1, 1776. The *Evening Post*, October 17, more realistically stated that a restitution of Canada to France was the latter's price for entering the war. Spain's recompense was to be the island of Jamaica. On October 22, this paper commented that, if this was true, a French war was inevitable. See also *Chronicle*, February 24, 1778.

11 *Gazetteer*, August 13, 1776.

12 *Morning Chronicle*, October 4, 1776.

13 *Morning Chronicle*, October 26, 1776.

14 *Evening Post*, August 22, 1776; *St. James's Chronicle*, December 24.

15 *Morning Chronicle*, October 30, 1776.

tion of war. Even the *Morning Post,* which supposedly was reflecting the Government's optimism about France's friendly overtures, confessed that the Ministry also was fearful of war.[16] The
Americans, it was believed, had received assurances of support
from the Bourbons.

If and when the European war did break out, the *Morning Post*
predicted that the "old arch-rebel" Benjamin Franklin would be
at the bottom of it. Believing that the wily Doctor was in Paris
because he was safer there, "against the approaching day when
the Republican Congress must be called to a severe account, for
the calamities they have wantonly drawn upon both countries,"[17]
it nonetheless alleged that Franklin had found listeners when he
offered Florida to Spain and Canada to France in return for military and economic aid.[18] By March 13 it affirmed that the sci-
entist-turned-diplomat had met with such success in Paris that
he was off to Vienna in search of additional allies.[19] The *St. James's
Chronicle* also reported Franklin's mission to France to be so
successful that the latter had agreed to help America in every
way short of war, "which means an eventual war."[20] But while
the Opposition *Public Ledger* construed French military preparations and pronouncements for America as a harbinger of impending war,[21] the *Morning Post* was reporting that Franklin
and Silas Deane were being ostracized in both Paris and at Versailles.[22] The French, who for reasons unspecified by the paper
no longer were apprehensive of a war, were slackening considerably their naval preparations.[23] Two weeks later, however, it
confessed that the accounts "[which] the heads of parties at
present give of the state of France, are so perfectly contradictory,
that no truth can be gained from them."[24] Notwithstanding this
confession of confusion, the *Morning Post* soon announced with

[16] *Morning Post,* January 3, 4, 7, 1777.

[17] *Morning Post,* January 31, 1777.

[18] *Morning Post,* March 7, 8, 1777. Franklin never made this offer.

[19] *Morning Post,* April 7, 1777.

[20] *St. James's Chronicle,* March 1, 1777. Cf. article, June 2, stating that the
Court of France had refused Franklin's request.

[21] *Public Ledger,* April 7, 1777.

[22] *Morning Post,* April 18, 1777. On June 4 it admitted that even Lord Stormont's "extraordinary allowance for secret service" did not get all of the information on Franklin and Deane in Paris and Versailles.

[23] *Morning Post,* April 30, 1777.

[24] *Morning Post,* June 16, 1777. See also August 5, September 4, 6, October 3,
and especially December 24, 1777, when the *Morning Post,* in two separate articles,
reported that there would—and would not—be a French war.

finality that the Court of France had refused Franklin "more from sound policy than friendship to Great Britain."[25]

By mid-1777 the press was busy preparing its readers for the coming conflict with France. The *Packet* stressed that the "high spirits, spruce countenances and current language" of French officers was an unerring prognostic of an approaching war.[26] The "treacherous and insidious behaviour" of the French, Spanish, and Dutch had so irritated George III, declared the *St. James's Chronicle,* that the King favored an immediate declaration against all these powers, but his council dissuaded him from any such measures as improper and hazardous "at the present juncture."[27]

To the strongly Opposition *Evening Post,* the reasons for the impending war were clear: The Ministry was attempting to trick the nation by diverting its attention from ministerial misconduct at home and abroad.[28] In this position, however, the *Evening Post* stood alone. Closer to the truth was the *Daily Advertiser's* explanation of why England "would not long enjoy the Sweets of Peace." It maintained that the American military successes pointedly demonstrated that England could not remain indifferent to neighbors who cooperated in her misfortunes.[29] The American victory at Saratoga had convinced the French that the propitious moment had come, and, entrenched and armed from the East and West Indies to India and to its Channel ports, France was ready for war.[30]

As early as January, 1778, the British press regularly reported the contents of an alleged Franco-American treaty,[31] and a revised series of betting odds on the probable date that hostilities would commence reappeared in the newspapers.[32] Not only were the French now openly aiding the Americans—and handsomely profit-

---

[25] *Morning Post,* June 23, 1777. On June 27, this paper asserted that the finances of France and Spain were in such a "tattered state" that they could not afford to continue arming themselves at this rate for much longer.

[26] *Packet,* July 7, 1777. See also *Morning Post,* July 18, "Paris Correspondent," and *Morning Post* and *Gazetteer,* January 5, for the assertion that France wanted a war with Britain.

[27] *St. James's Chronicle,* July 22, 1777. This rumor was false.

[28] *Evening Post,* December 6, 1777.

[29] *Daily Advertiser,* January 7, 1778.

[30] *St. James's Chronicle,* December 25, 1777; February 19, March 21, 1778. See also *Westminster Journal,* February 14, 21, 1778; *Morning Chronicle,* March 17; *Morning Post,* January 4.

[31] *St. James's Chronicle,* February 3, 1778; *Morning Post,* January 7.

[32] *Gazetteer,* January 2, 1778; *Morning Post,* February 13, 14.

ing thereby[33]—but it was believed that Paris agents, "creatures of Sartine and Beaumarchais," were also undermining the British economy by speculating, rumoring, and "plundering" the London stock exchange.[34] Before the authentic Franco-American treaty arrived in London in March, the entire press agreed it would be only a matter of time before "this insulted nation may wreak a just revenge on our insidious Gallic neighbours"[35]—this, despite the *Morning Post*'s claim of assurances from Lord Stormont, Britain's Ambassador to Versailles, that France was inclined not to break with Britain.[36] Stormont, however, never believed that France would stay out of the war, and on March 16, the day before London learned of the treaty, even the *Morning Post* retracted its earlier claims when it warned that war was expected within twenty-four hours.[37] The strongly Opposition *Packet* conceded that a French treaty with the Americans would be looked upon as an invitation to war.[38] It then used this opportunity to attack the Ministry for having been so lulled into a false sense of security that it believed France's "deluding assurances of friendship" and sent its troops and ships to America, thus leaving the British Isles exposed to an invasion.[39]

Little doubt was expressed in the press that a French war would be as popular as the American war was unpopular. When George III ordered a special performance of Handel's *Judas Maccabaeus* to be performed at the Drury Lane, the *Morning Post* reviewed the oratorio both as a musical performance and as a patriotic gesture. Affirming that the parts that breathed a martial spirit were greeted with much applause, it reported that the audience was "filled with a true spirit of indignation and resentment against our natural, and insidious enemy, and as Judas is described, 'like a lion's whelp roaring for its prey.' "[40] The *Evening Post* was soon

33 *Gazetteer*, January 5, 1778, essay on Beaumarchais's relationship to the American Congress. See also *Morning Post*, August 27, 1777.

34 *St. James's Chronicle*, January 8, 1778. The *General Evening Post*, January 3, reported that talk of a French war being unavoidable drove the stock market down 2 per cent. See also *Morning Post*, March 16.

35 *Morning Post*, February 28, March 26, 1778; *Packet*, March 18, April 1.

36 *Morning Post*, March 12, 1778. See also *Chronicle*, March 7.

37 On March 18, this paper reported that the King had sent his message on the French treaty to Parliament, and "war is expected to be declared tomorrow."

38 *Packet*, March 13, 1778.

39 *Packet*, March 13, 1778. See also June 1 and *General Advertiser*, July 3, for demands that England undertake some "bold stroke of daring" to overcome France's advantage in the coming battles.

40 *Morning Post*, March 21, 1778.

to agree. By April 30 it, too, was referring to France as "our insidious neighbour." The *St. James's Chronicle* commented that at long last Britain's fighting spirit was roused.[41] William Woodfall's *Morning Chronicle,* assuming that Stormont's sudden recall from Paris was tantamount to an eventual declaration of war, affirmed that Britain could have no question of the justice of its cause.[42]

Still, the Americans constituted an enigma. Englishmen could understand why the Colonies would desire a military alliance with the French, but they found it difficult to believe that the Americans, who, after all, were only dissatisfied Englishmen, could be duped into a commitment of amity and commerce with an utterly befuddled monarch who was completely dominated by an overbearing queen and her unscrupulous faction.[43] The *Morning Post* argued that only a small minority of the colonists could possibly favor such an alliance.[44] Summing up the bewilderment of the press at this "strange bedfellow" agreement, the *General Evening Post* queried:

> Say, *Yankees,* don't you feel compunction,
> At your unnatural, rash conjunction?
> Can love for you in him take root,
> Whose Catholic, and absolute?
> I'll tell these croakers how he'll treat 'em;
> *Frenchmen,* like *storks,* love *frogs*—to eat 'em.[45]

As the Congress had decided to tie its political, economic, and military fortunes to Versailles, all segments of the press agreed that now the war in America could be won by defeating the French in Europe. The *Morning Post* surmised that a few successful expeditions against France would leave the Colonies friendless and penniless, thus forcing them soon to capitulate to the formidable British force already in America.[46] Even the Opposition *Packet* was in rare agreement with the *Morning Post* when it

41 *St. James's Chronicle,* May 7, 1778.

42 *Morning Chronicle,* March 17, 21, 1778.

43 *General Evening Post,* April 14, 1778.

44 *Morning Post,* March 14, 1778.

45 *General Evening Post,* August 11, 1778. See also *Morning Chronicle,* January 30, 1779, for a discussion of the compatibility of an alliance between Puritan and Roman Catholic habits, politics, and religion.

46 *Morning Post,* August 12, 1778. See also April 6, 1779; "This summer the fate of America will most probably be determined in the seas of Europe." The *Morning Herald* voiced the same thought on February 7, 1781.

argued that France could be neutralized and America consequently beaten by the capture of the French West Indies.[47] It
suggested that the troops for this expedition should come from
those already in America.

The press of all political factions concurred in the belief that
the first blows of the new French war would come at sea, and
rumor and speculation in the spring of 1778 centered chiefly upon
the whereabouts of the enemy's Brest and Toulon fleets and the
action being taken by the Royal Navy to counter these movements.[48]

While Englishmen wondered whether the first battle would
come before or after a formal declaration of war, their Government adhered to a strange silence concerning any declaration of
hostile intent toward the French. The *Morning Post*, supporting
the Ministry, affirmed that an immediate pronouncement of war
was forced to be postponed in order to avert the multimillion-
pound profit that would be pocketed by French gamblers on the
London Exchange. A few more days of forebearance would avoid
this loss, it advised, while giving no further illuminating information.[49] The same argument appeared in the Opposition *St. James's
Chronicle*, which said that "almost a million" would be turned
over to enemy speculators by means of policies purchased through
agents, if war was declared before April 1.[50] On April 7 the *Morning Post* probably came closer to the truth in its report that the
delay was due to the Ministry's awaiting dispatches from America
commenting upon Britain's latest olive branch and statements
from Madrid as to its intentions on the American continent.
The *Packet* had its own explanation for the delay. It reported
that the declaration of war awaited the arrival of the Quebec fleet, which would be endangered on the high seas were
hostilities prematurely declared.[51] The most radical view was
taken by the *General Advertiser*, which maintained that the Ministry "like cowards, are endeavouring to avoid a war with France."
Declaring that the intrepid Chatham would have instantly waged
war upon the Bourbons, it added that the Ministry "in the true

---

47 *Packet*, November 30, 1778.

48 *St. James's Chronicle*, March 5, 1778; *Morning Post*, March 7, April 4; *Evening Post*, April 30, June 6; *Gazetteer, Morning Chronicle, Morning Post*, May 22.

49 *Morning Post*, March 21, 1778.

50 *St. James's Chronicle*, March 17, 1778. On March 31, it reported that a declaration of war was postponed until news from America arrived. This news it
expected in mid-April.

51 *Packet*, February 4, 1778.

dastardly stile, crouch and submit to every insult," and that nothing else could be expected from such a "desperate, despicable, and mercenary faction."[52] Despite these heated accusations, serious war preparations continued, and the *Evening Post* noted that General Craig, by command of the King, had augmented the war effort by ordering army and militia officers to abstain from drinking claret and all other French wines.[53]

By mid-1778 Britons were reading that their forces were ready for contact with the enemy. When news arrived in June that Admiral Augustus Keppel (the Opposition-oriented officer who gladly returned to the colors now that France, rather than America, was the foe) and his Channel fleet had drawn first blood even before war had been formally declared, the press—reflecting both parliamentary and popular opinion—showed both relief and joy. The *Evening Post* expressed happiness that a good omen had appeared at the start of the war, and it hoped that the Ministry was now "perfectly cured of its hitherto pusillanimous behavior."[54] Although the much-publicized "Ode for His Majesty's Birth-Day" implored Britannia to recall that "for freedom's reign she had burst the Norman's feudal chain,"[55] no declaration of war was yet forthcoming. In fact, the *Gazetteer* picked up a rumor, "strongly reported in the city," that the Ministry intended to return the two ships captured from the French by Keppel, in order to prevent war.[56] All knew, however, that by July Keppel again was prowling the sea in search of the French fleet, despite Stormont's return to Versailles.[57]

Conflicting expect-war, expect-peace, expect-war reports pervaded the press all during the summer of 1778.[58] An indecisive battle off Ushant, followed by charges and recriminations by

---

[52] *General Advertiser*, June 24, 1778. Cf. July 1, article stating that the war with France was inevitable: "From the moment that Count D'Estaing sailed from Toulon it was war; and any ministry, but the present, would have been prepared for it."

[53] *Evening Post*, June 6, 1778.

[54] *Evening Post*, June 25, 1778. See also accounts in the *Chronicle*, same date, reporting, "The British flag as usual, came off triumphant."

[55] *Gentleman's Magazine*, June, 1778, 278, "Poetical Essay."

[56] *Gazetteer*, July 1, 1778; *General Advertiser*, August 14.

[57] The *Chronicle*, July 26, 1778, claimed that Stormont was protesting in vain, but, on September 4, it stated that he succeeded in having the French agree they would not allow American privateers to dispose of their booty in French ports.

[58] The *Morning Post*, July 16, 1778, reported that all "ranks and parties" agreed that a peaceful accommodation between Britain and France would soon take place. But on July 20, it asserted that all who wished their country well exulted at the news of a war.

Keppel and his second in command, the Tory Admiral Hugh Palliser, resulted in two courts-martial—one for each admiral. Keppel was vindicated before he resigned his commission (the Opposition press was certain that this was a political persecution that had nothing to do with Keppel's naval talents). As soon as the trials ended, stories of sea skirmishes, most of them false,[59] again filled the press. With so little action taking place, Opposition editors surmised that this was to be a "peaceful war," with much braggadocio and little actual combat. The *Packet* stated that both the sovereigns of England and France wished the war carried on "in the most *pacific* manner—without any *fighting* at all."[60] The *Morning Post* advertised the far-fetched theory that the war was slow in coming because the martial spirit was so roused in England that the people of France, aware of the disaster that would ensue from an active war, were of late extremely averse to hostilities.[61] Of course the French Court and a few Parisian merchants stood to profit by a war, though "le Grand Monarque," it was now said, was in favor of peace. Bate reported that, unfortunately, Louis XVI was dominated by Marie Antoinette and her war-party favorites.[62] The *Morning Chronicle* added that the French populace "though they dare not speak out as we do in England" was said to be execrating the day that Franklin tempted their King to fight America's battles "and exhaust the little remaining strength and treasure he could boast."[63] Earlier, both the *Morning Chronicle* and the *Gazetteer* had noted that the French and English navies were avoiding each other, pending peace negotiations.[64] Few believed these rumors; most felt it was the French who had hesitated at the critical moment, "ashamed to yield and yet afraid to fight." Small wonder then that the *Morning Chronicle*, after reporting rumors of impending war for almost six months, cheerfully concluded that the future was promising: The fleets of D'Estaing and D'Orvilliers had accomplished nothing of late, General Clinton had showed an active spirit in America, and British privateers were proving themselves "wonderfully successful."

[59] *Morning Post*, July 30, 1778; *Gazetteer*, July 31; *Morning Chronicle, General Evening Post, General Advertiser*, August 1.
[60] *Packet*, August 7, 1778.
[61] *Morning Post*, September 23, 1778.
[62] *Morning Post*, October 10, 1778.
[63] *Morning Chronicle*, November 14, 1778.
[64] *Morning Chronicle*, October 5, 9, 1778; *Gazetteer*, October 7.

In the closing weeks of 1778, when the long-awaited formal announcements of hostilities finally were made, they brought no great change in British press policy. Englishmen had expected a war with France for years, and little further conditioning of public opinion was necessary. While William Whitehead's "Ode" hailed the new year because

> Britannia from her rocky height,
> Points to the Gallic coast and lifts her spear,[65]

most Englishmen expected that a swift and successful operation against France would take place in Channel waters. Discussions of the coming naval war so dominated English publications in the spring and summer of 1779[66] that *Gentleman's Magazine* in May omitted temporarily its regular section of "American News."

Talk of an impending struggle with Spain also helped dislodge America's position of priority in the press. A Spanish war could be expected to receive exceptional treatment because it kindled memories of 1588, that glorious year in British history. In fact, no sooner had the difficulties between Britain and her colonies arisen than correspondents—some with names as descriptive as "HATE SPAIN"—warned the nation that Madrid was arming for revenge of the humiliation that dated back almost two centuries.[67] It was surmised by the public that there was little love lost between the courts at London and at Madrid, and the English assumed that Spain's intent could always be considered unfriendly. Further, because the press judged Spain a second-rate power, fear of her rarely concerned editors as much as it did ministers.[68]

The English knew that Spain wished France well, but they were not certain how much Madrid actually would help Versailles. Some British newspapers thought it was politically expedient for Spain to remain neutral.[69] It was believed that Spain, trembling for her southern settlements in America, also wished a plague upon the Congressional house.[70] In addition, she was fearful that her

65 *London Magazine*, January, 1779, 40; *Gentleman's Magazine*, January, 37.
66 *Morning Post*, April 6, 1779; *Morning Chronicle*, July 29, August 9, *et passim*.
67 *Morning Chronicle*, May 12, 1775; *Morning Post*, May 24, 30.
68 The *Morning Post*, July 17, 1777, suggested that the Royal Navy transport 60,000 Moors into Granada "to keep the Spaniards busy."
69 *Evening Post*, July 9, 1778, speculated that Spain's "peaceable disposition" was explained by her huge merchant fleet still being on the high seas and in danger of being intercepted by the Royal Navy. See also *Chronicle*, October 8, 1778; *Morning Post*, June 7, 1779; *Gazetteer*, June 8; *Morning Chronicle*, June 9.
70 *St. James's Chronicle*, April 16, 1778.

merchantmen might become easy prey for the British navy. "There is nothing to be got by beating beggars," exclaimed the *Morning Post*, referring to the French merchant fleet, but prospects of a battle with Spain raised the hopes of British seamen "touching the hard dollars."[71] This newspaper frequently assured its readers that Spain had no intention of joining the French or Americans.[72] Knowledgeable Englishmen believed that the *Morning Post*'s insistence on Spain's friendly intentions toward England was dictated by Bate's being on the Spanish payroll.[73] Bate obviously did not think his loyalties were divided; he felt little compunction, evidently, about accepting money from both George III and Charles III, since he was trying to bring their policies into peaceful harmony. Only three months before the outbreak of hostilities with Spain, the *Morning Post* noted that all apprehensions of a war were over for the ensuing year because Madrid had made no provisions for a war in its yearly budget![74] Nevertheless, almost all other publications agreed that the French and Spanish fleets would presently be joined.[75] One loyal publication warned that this combined force would number nearly seventy-five sail of the line,[76] but an Opposition newspaper reminded its readers that during the Seven Years' War huge numbers did not dash the British spirit and the Union Jack had eventually brought these combined fleets "almost on their knees."[77]

By April, 1779, reports of a war with Spain became so frequent that even the *Morning Post* echoed the conjectures made in other London publications.[78] On June 18, when the declaration of war finally was made, the *Morning Post* joined an almost unanimous press in asserting that it was an event "that has been long and universally looked for." Spain, most editors expected, was about to give France the same vain support that had made her the

71 *Morning Post*, July 13, 1778.

72 *Morning Post*, September 21, November 12, 1778, March 6, 1779. See also March 24, 1778, for the rumor that Madrid would mediate the differences between Britain and France.

73 HMC, Stopford-Sackville MSS, I, June 8, 1779, William Wardlaw to Germain.

74 *Morning Post*, March 20, 1779.

75 *General Advertiser*, August 20, October 20, 1778; *Chronicle*, August 29, December 1; *Gazetteer*, September 21, 24, 30, October 12, 1778, January 12, 25, 1779.

76 *General Evening Post*, September 17, 1778.

77 *Gazetteer*, July 2, 1778.

78 *Gazetteer*, March 31, May 12, 1779. The *Morning Chronicle*, April 3, was certain Spain would join France in the fight against Britain. See also April 6; *Morning Post*, April 27, June 7.

laughing stock of all Europe at the close of the Seven Years' War.[79]

If Englishmen smiled when they read that "the *Spanish* Ambassador took *French* leave of the *British* Court,"[80] they were also sobered by the difficult task ahead. England's last traces of lethargy had been shaken. The *Morning Chronicle* prophesied that Spain's insolence would soon be corrected by a determined Britain.[81] Woodfall was certain that "whilst we remain steady we shall prove much more than a match for the drones of Spain, and the scribblers of France."[82] Meanwhile, the *Universal Magazine* was popularizing a new song in which "The Jolly Soldier" reminded the forgetful Bourbons of the "drubbings and dressings they formerly had" and concluded:

> Havannah we'll put in our pockets again,
> And blow both the Bourbons quite out of the main.[83]

England's morale was not appreciably heightened by reports in the *Morning Post* that South Carolina, in order to reap a huge profit by fitting out privateers to sail against Spanish merchantmen returning from South America, presently would come over to the British.[84] No other newspaper predicted a rupture between the colonies as a result of Spain's entry into the war. Rather, all agreed that a settlement with America was now a secondary concern that would necessarily await the outcome of the European war. The *Gazetteer* reminded those who suggested a separate American peace before Britain launched the battle against the Bourbons that the colonists were treaty-bound to make no peace without France and, still more important, that England should consider no terms until "she had brought France to her own terms."[85]

News from America had so slipped into the background by September, 1779, that the *General Evening Post* reminded its

---

[79] *Morning Chronicle, Morning Post*, June 18, 1779. *Gentleman's Magazine*, August, 417-18, looked upon the war with Spain "not without astonishment," asserting that the Spanish King had tried unsuccessfully to avoid it.

[80] *Gazetteer*, June 21, 1779.

[81] *Morning Chronicle*, June 22, 1779.

[82] *Morning Chronicle*, July 8, 1779.

[83] *Universal Magazine*, July, 1779, 39. See also *Gentleman's Magazine*, July, 357, for a favorable review of the Reverend William Tasker's "Ode to the Warlike Genius of Great Britain," which interpreted the war as a struggle between freedom and tyranny, with Britain championing the cause of freedom.

[84] *Morning Post*, July 2, 1779.

[85] *Gazetteer*, July 16, 1779.

countrymen that "we seem to have lost sight of America, the origins and cause of the misfortunes of this country."[86] News of the Bourbons' naval preparations, rumors of peace negotiations, and general patriotic enunciations dominated the press during the second half of 1779,[87] as Englishmen came to assume that they had lost to France the race for America. The United States, buttressed by her new ally, would maintain its independence, while Britain found itself faced by the dilemma of being too proud to back down from its posture of war in America and of being too weak to negate the Declaration of Independence on the field of battle. In addition, its well-armed Gallic neighbor was in an excellent position to take advantage of this uncomfortable situation by bringing the war that had commenced three thousand miles away not only to England's waters, but to her shores as well.

[86] *General Evening Post,* September 18, 1779.

[87] *Chronicle,* October 19, 1779; *General Evening Post,* August 12, September 7; *Universal Magazine,* Supplement, "Ode for the New Year." See also *General Advertiser,* October 12, 20, December 31, 1779.

CHAPTER X

The Sagging Home Front

I N CASE ANY ENGLISHMEN entertained thoughts of discontinuing the war in America in order to fight the French and Spanish, the loyal *Morning Post* reminded its readers that abandoning America would mean abandoning the West Indies and the New-foundland fisheries as well.[1] This newspaper's earlier calcula-tions that an act of attainder against the defeated rebels would more than compensate for the sacrifices necessary to continue the Atlantic struggle,[2] brought little comfort to its readers, who knew that the already heavy burden of the war held the prospect of becoming much heavier before it would lighten.[3]

The chief consolation offered Englishmen by their press was a detailed study of the chaos of the American economy, coupled with the obvious conclusion that the Colonies were suffering

[1] *Morning Post*, June 24, 1777. See also *St. James's Chronicle*, June 10, report-ing that the West Indies were doing so poorly that many there feared a slave uprising.

[2] *Morning Post*, January 11, February 6, October 11, 1777.

[3] *Morning Post*, July 9, 1777, admitting that English credit was very poor on the Dutch market. On July 22, it commented that "so great are the arrears and unfunded debts, that the government would have to borrow an additional eight million pounds next year." On October 30, it admitted the value of landed prop-erty was falling, and money, even at 5 per cent interest (the usual prewar rate was 4 per cent) was difficult to find. The *Morning Chronicle*, April 10, 1776, asserted that the countryside in particular was feeling the "ill-effects of the Ameri-can war," while the *St. James's Chronicle*, May 4, 1776, complained that specie was being drained off to America to pay the troops. Cf. the loyal *General Evening Post*, same date, challenging the paragraphs that stressed the decay and distress of the economy. See also *St. James's Chronicle*, September 15, 1778.

more heavily than the mother country. Before the battle at Saratoga the acute situation in America was widely publicized. Reporting that the "vile continental currency" was worthless and not even passable in Philadelphia when the Americans still held their capital city, the *Chronicle* maintained that those lucky few who held gold, silver, and copper were hoarding these coins and avoiding all dealings with the continental currency, "a cart load of which they know in a little time would not purchase a single dollar."[4] Further, provisions and necessities of all kinds were scarce, even if one had the hard money to purchase them. But the *Morning Post,* while asserting that America's commerce and lucrative fisheries had been almost ruined by the war, conceded that the farmers were busily paying off their debts with paper money and selling their produce to the British for specie. Indeed, some farmers (despite the insignificance of America's farm exports) were in better financial condition in 1777 that they had ever been.[5] Even with the addition of a handful of successful privateers to the number of prospering husbandmen, none of this prosperity, the press stated, was spilling over into the coffers of the rebel army. While granting that its earlier reports of "naked Americans" was absurd, the *Morning Post* quoted from what it identified as Washington's order book, allegedly captured at New York, to demonstrate the wretched state of supply of the colonial army.[6]

The crucial question by 1778, then, seemed not to be which side would cover itself with glory upon the field of battle, but rather, which of the struggling combatants could outlast its weary and impoverished antagonist. On September 24 the Opposition *St. James's Chronicle* reflected a hope common in England in its report that the weak Congress could not possibly finance the war for another year and that, consequently, Britain could expect to win the struggle by default. News of the distressed state of American affairs could not, however, relieve the concern most Britons felt over their diminishing trade, the threat of rising taxes and debts, the downward trend of the stock market, and, still worse, the new war with the Bourbons.[7]

---

[4] *Chronicle,* January 4, March 1, 1777. The *Morning Post,* January 3, reported America was "perfectly deluged" with paper money.

[5] *Morning Post,* January 8, 1777. See also June 24, stating that America's farm exports, which once were over £1,300,000 per year, were now nil.

[6] *Morning Post,* January 3, 7, February 5, 1777.

[7] *Westminster Journal,* January 3, 1778.

London stock prices kept tumbling. "Stocks fell again on Wednesday upwards of two per cent," was the terse comment of the Opposition *Westminster Journal*, as it noted that public credit likewise was declining rapidly.[8] The *Reading Mercury* reported in early 1778 that talk of a French war "continues so strong that stocks fell yesterday pretty much. Within the last three weeks only, they have fallen almost five per cent."[9] When rumor of a French invasion of the Malabar Coast alarmed London, the tumbling East India Company securities pulled all the prices on the Exchange down 4 per cent, according to *Adams's Weekly Courant*.[10]

The Ministry newspapers reflected a substantially different condition. The *Morning Post* boasted that London merchants were pleased over the rupture with France because it would afford a chance to destroy the marine traffic "of our neighbouring perfidious enemies and their new paltry allies."[11] On April 1, 1778, it reported that France and Holland, although on the brink of war with England, had such confidence in the British economy that they were investing heavily in London stocks! Foreigners, it concluded, whether friends or enemies, had "a much better opinion of our public credit than some mock-patriots could wish."

The *Morning Post* was almost alone with its fantasies. By mid-1778 Britain's economic condition was such that almost every magazine and newspaper recognized and admitted the existence of many obvious ills. Prices of commodities rose so high that the *Westminster Journal* expressed fear that inflation was driving the English working class into the military services.[12] The *Packet*, on June 8, 1778, reported, with irony, that many ruined merchants were preparing to emigrate to America in order to recoup their fortunes.[13]

---

8 *Westminster Journal*, January 10, 1778. See also *General Evening* Post, January 3: "A war with France was yesterday talked of as unavoidable. Stocks fell two per cent. . . ." See also *Morning Chronicle*, January 7.

9 *Reading Mercury*, January 5, 1778; *Morning Post*, January 7.

10 *Adams's Weekly Courant*, February 17, 1778. On April 7, the *General Evening Post* reported that talks of conciliation with the Congress drove the stock prices up 2½ per cent in one day.

11 *Morning Post*, May 23, 1778. See also *Packet*, January 16.

12 *Westminster Journal*, January 10, 1778. Cf. *Public Ledger*, February 3, 1776, for an article stating that many Americans, ruined by the war, were forced to enter the continental army for sheer survival.

13 *Packet*, January 26, 1778; *St. James's Chronicle*, July 30.

Bitter over shortages of both civilian and military commodities, the rising costs of those things that were still obtainable, and the increasing tax and expenditure rates, most papers confessed that these heavy sacrifices were accomplishing nothing militarily or politically. In fact, the picture seemed gloomier in late 1778 than it had in the earlier part of the year, when the first flush of patriotism carried the press to statements of guarded optimism. The *General Advertiser,* which had conceded that America was lost, announced that the ministers privately were confessing that the West Indies also were gone.[14] Some newspapers worried about the loss of the East Indies, while others feared it would be only a matter of time before the Irish followed the Americans' example.[15] The *Evening Post* classically demonstrated the Opposition's concern with the turn of events. In reporting the results of the second battle at Stony Point, in which the British suffered almost 700 casualties in losing a fortified position to bayonet-wielding Colonials, it concluded, "After having lost the best part of four regiments, the British had gained no object, but lost time. This mode of carrying on a war, at *three thousand miles distance,* must in the end ruin the richest and most populous country in the world."[16]

But even as Englishmen brooded over the ruin of their trade,[17] painfully learned how to cultivate and cure tobacco at home,[18] and read that the reduced revenue caused by the loss of so much commerce and territory "as well as the best blood of the nation"[19] would result in still more taxes, they realized that the worst had not yet befallen them. For by early 1778 Britain was girding itself for a tragedy she had not dreamed possible one year before—a French invasion.

The Ministry *Morning Post* reflected the widely held belief that, as soon as France and Spain should complete their war plans, they would send another great armada against Ireland, where, of course, the invaders would be welcomed as liberators by their

[14] *General Advertiser,* December 29, 1778. See also *St. James's Chronicle,* January 2, 1779, predicting that the West Indies would be lost to the French.
[15] *Packet,* January 22, 1779; *Gazetteer,* May 7.
[16] *Evening Post,* October 7, 1779.
[17] *General Advertiser,* October 8, 1779.
[18] *Universal Magazine,* October, 1779, 199.
[19] *Packet,* November 24, 1779.

Roman Catholic brethren. The path of action for England was clear: Prepare to defend the Empire against invasion, and start treating the Catholics in Ireland better![20]

As early as the spring of 1777 Britain had known her coasts to be vulnerable to attack.[21] American privateers, freely patrolling the Irish Channel, were wreaking such havoc upon the linen fleets sailing from Ireland to England that the Royal Navy was forced to supply frigates for domestic convoy duty. Ireland was not the only target for England's enemies. The *Chronicle* wrote that dwellers on Jersey and Guernsey were horrified to see the Americans cruising between them, in search of provision-laden merchantmen.[22] Even the shipping lanes from London to Plymouth, the *St. James's Chronicle* acknowledged, were no longer to be considered safe.[23] The addition of French and probably Spanish ships to the American fleet that was already harassing the coasts led many to expect an invasion in the spring of 1778. The *Morning Post* attempted to quiet these fears by noting that the Royal Navy was never "in such a flourishing condition as it is at present."[24] But the *Gazetteer* betrayed doubts. After reporting that Ireland was preparing to withstand attack, it protested that Scotland was the only part of the Kingdom fully prepared and defended, because the King had unwisely given the great naval commands to Scotsmen.[25]

While Britons worried about the rumored invasion of their homeland, their press introduced them to an American sea captain who was to strike more fear into their hearts than probably any other foreigner had done in centuries. John Paul Jones was to become such a legend that his name could evoke a shudder in almost any corner of the Empire. Reports of his whereabouts, coupled with tales of his intrepid maneuvers, were always well publicized. One of Jones's feats—a daring raid upon England's Irish Sea port of Whitehaven in late April, 1778—caught the imagination of almost all Britain. Even the *Morning Post* ruefully paid admiration to the thirty men from the privateer *Ranger* who had rowed to the shore with muffled oars, burned one vessel, and spiked most of the guns in both of the town's

20 *Morning Post*, February 17, 22, March 14, 25, 1777.
21 *St. James's Chronicle*, May 20, July 17, 1777. See also *Packet*, June 27.
22 *Chronicle*, July 3, 1777.
23 *St. James's Chronicle*, August 14, 1777.
24 *Morning Post*, March 19, June 17, 1778.
25 *Gazetteer*, March 24, April 24, 1778.

harbor batteries.[26] These accomplishments were not considered a fortuitous American victory. They were viewed as part of a well-conceived and well-executed program, and all England suffered apprehensions about Jones's next strike. Even Whitehaven was not secure.[27] The *Morning Post,* worriedly reporting panic on the coast of Ireland, demanded a fleet of frigates to defend the waters around the Channel Islands and the Irish Sea.[28]

Jones next attacked St. Mary's, the island estate of Lord Selkirk, who, ironically, was one of the few Scottish peers who were not anti-American in sentiment.[29] Jones had intended to kidnap Selkirk and exchange his prisoner for an unnamed American held by the British. Though this daring maneuver failed only because the Earl was not on the island at the time of the raid, it succeeded in so panicking Britons who lived along the exposed coast that it was probably worth its cost a hundredfold. The *Morning Chronicle* reported the northwest coast of England and Scotland to be so fear-stricken "that a general intimidation discovers itself on every appearance of a sail."[30] Jones knew well how to create an aura of flamboyance about himself. The *Gazetteer* noted that he had repurchased at public auction in Paris the silver tableware taken from the dining room of Lady Selkirk, and the gallant Jones was reported to be forthwith returning it to the lady[31]—though not in person, most Scotsmen hoped. When he returned to Bordeaux or Brest to refit his tiny fleet, the worried press speculated about the place of his next attack. There was general agreement that it would be Ireland, which, despite some reinforcements, was still the worst-defended sector of the British Isles.[32]

Jones's demonstration that the British coast was vulnerable augmented the widespread belief in the spring of 1778 that a French invasion was imminent. The *Morning Post* interpreted the

[26] *Morning Post,* April 28, 1778.

[27] The *Gazetteer,* May 18, 1778, reported that a door-to-door campaign at Whitehaven collected over £1,000 for the purpose of refortifying its harbor. See also *Morning Chronicle,* May 5.

[28] *Morning Post,* April 29, 1778.

[29] *Morning Post,* May 5, 1778.

[30] *Morning Chronicle,* May 8, 1778.

[31] *Gazetteer,* June 22, 1778.

[32] *St. James's Chronicle,* August 27, 1778. Ireland never was adequately fortified. See Henry Grattan, Jr., *Memoirs of the Life and Times of Henry Grattan,* I, 326-27, 344-45: "So complete an abdication on the part of a Government is rarely to be found in the history of any nation," wrote Buckingham, Ireland's Lord Lieutenant, on May 16 and 17, 1778.

appointment of the Duc de Broglie as France's supreme army commander to be a bad omen, for it noted that the French officer (whom it identified as "Broglio"), during his recent prolonged sojourn in England, always sat down to a meal with the most detailed maps of Sussex, Essex, and Kent lying on the table before him.[33] Public concern over the increasing number of French troops that were reportedly gathering on the coast of Normandy also was reflected in the Ministry's pronouncements.[34] The Government's admission of the possibility of an attack prompted the Opposition *General Advertiser* to declare that this "nonsense talk of invasion" was inspired by the Ministry "only as an excuse for their wanting so much money."[35] Still, the *Morning Post* maintained that the French could not plan an immediate attack because their Brest fleet was not yet completely manned;[36] it would take place as soon as the Bourbons could train sailors in invasion tactics. In the meantime, if the Toulon fleet, which had been seen sailing through the Straits, was really headed for North America or the West Indies, the British Isles were temporarily safe, reported the *Gazetteer*.[37]

According to Almon's *Evening Post*, if the expected invasion did not materialize, Providence, rather than "the unbearable conduct of the ministry," was to be thanked. "If the French had invaded us any time these three months, they would have found not above 9,000 troops to resist them, with a militia which wanted almost every thing."[38] But Bate's *Morning Post* confidently assured its readers that England, "thanks to the attention of our ministry," was so ready to defend her shores that she could either deter an attack completely or "make the enemy wish they had never thought of so mad an enterprize."[39]

When news arrived that the French fleet had set sail from Brest in late June, 1778, the jittery press again began speculating on invasion sites. The most likely locations were the Cork or Belfast areas of Ireland,[40] the northeast coast of Scotland,[41] or

33 *Morning Post,* May 5, 1778.

34 *Evening Post,* May 19, 1778; *Gazetteer,* May 22, June 1; *General Advertiser,* May 29, 30.

35 *General Advertiser,* June 11, 1778.

36 *Morning Post,* June 13, 1778. Se also *Gazetteer,* June 8.

37 *Gazetteer,* June 8, 15, 1778.

38 *Evening Post,* June 16, 1778.

39 *Morning Post,* June 22, 1778.

40 *Chronicle,* June 25, 1778; *Williamson's Liverpool Advertiser,* July 17.

41 *Evening Post,* August 20, September 3, 1778.

the Thames Valley![42] Englishmen now read that the days of speculation and rumor were over; the Battle for Britain was about to begin.[43] The Royal Navy's Channel squadrons were England's only hope.[44] In the event of their failure, there was nothing to prevent French transports from landing their men.[45] The *Morning Chronicle* warned that the invasion would be preceded by a series of diversionary attacks against the Scottish and Irish coasts, while the main body of enemy troops—estimated at between 20,000 and 50,000 men—would invade the Sussex coast and be in immediate striking distance of London.[46]

When the expected attack was not launched, the *Morning Post* assured its public that any French invasion plans were laid aside for the season,[47] and the *Morning Chronicle* thereupon published a poem congratulating Britons for again demonstrating that great spirit which had always "conquer'd and chastiz'd her foe."[48]

After the winter's respite, spring brought new rumors that the Spaniards were to sail against Ireland[49] and that Jersey and Guernsey were again being scanned "with an evil eye" by the French.[50] To these familiar fears was added the new alarm that a thrust against the Thames Valley was merely a feint to throw Britain off guard while the French invaded the West Indies.[51] The *Morning Chronicle*, delving into England's heroic past, besought its countrymen to emulate the example of their ancient forefathers, who postponed their intestine feuds and went united to war against the Roman invaders under Julius Caesar.[52] Breathing fire at the thought of a French investment of London, this newspaper challenged the foe to come, "If they dare!"[53] But on the following day, the *Gazetteer* meekly announced that only a militia of volunteers was ready to defend against "the Great Spanish Armada."[54]

[42] *Gazetteer,* July 17, 1778.
[43] *Evening Post,* July 28, 1778. See also *Packet,* July 22.
[44] *Chronicle,* June 25, September 3, 1778; *St. James's Chronicle,* September 18.
[45] *Gazetteer,* August 11, 1778; *Morning Chronicle,* September 4.
[46] *Morning Chronicle,* September 8, 1778.
[47] *Morning Post,* September 29, 1778.
[48] *Morning Chronicle,* November 9, 1778.
[49] *Middlesex Journal,* February 20, 1779.
[50] *Gazetteer,* May 7, 1779.
[51] *Morning Post,* May 22, 24, 1779.
[52] *Morning Chronicle,* June 26, 1779.
[53] *Morning Chronicle,* July 16, 1779. See also July 26, August 7.
[54] *Gazetteer,* July 17, 1779.

Summer saw no abatement of the press's fears, because Englishmen were aware that summer was the "invasion season." While the *Gazetteer* and *Morning Chronicle* proudly printed the three-column list of names of persons who contributed funds "to promote recruiting and the better defence and security of the county of Middlesex, and the city and liberty of Westminster, in case of an INVASION, or imminent danger thereof,"[55] the Ministry newspapers avoided all references to the patriotic motions of this strongly anti-Ministry section of London.

The *Morning Post* tried to buoy up the sagging spirits of its readers by assuring them that the French, too, were worried about an invasion—a British one![56] Coming but one week after Londoners had trembled at the accurate reports that a French fleet had been sighted off Plymouth, this optimism was viewed as a patent absurdity. The *General Evening Post*, another loyal journal, stated with certainty that, if and when the great battle did occur, France would do the invading and Britain the defending.[57]

All speculation notwithstanding, when reports of disease and discord among the French and Spanish fleets made it evident that an attack was not forthcoming in the second summer, the feeling gained ground that, perhaps, the enemy lacked the necessary leadership, men, or equipment to launch a successful invasion. This view was reinforced when a series of privately published pamphlets to this effect were widely circulated.[58] By September, 1779, it was agreed that an invasion was no longer to be feared. Although the privateering feats of John Paul Jones were still given much publicity (the Earl of Carlisle wrote that "Jones flings us all into consternation and terror, and will hinder Lady Carlisle's sea bathing"),[59] it was now recognized that his

[55] *Gazetteer*, August 19; *Morning Chronicle*, August 20, 1779.

[56] *Morning Post*, August 14, 21, 1779.

[57] *General Evening Post*, August 10, 28, 31, October 2, November 23, 1779. See also *Evening Post*, August 21 and 24, for an account of the appearance of the French and Spanish fleets off Plymouth. While disease and discord upon the Bourbon ships precluded an invasion of England, the sighting of the enemy off England's shores was enough to unify, at least temporarily, British opinion. See also *London Magazine*, August, 379.

[58] See Dean Tucker of Gloucester's "Reflections on the present Terrors of Invasion," *Universal Magazine*, August, 1779, 91-95. On August 31 the *Evening Post* gave two full columns to "A Bristol Whig's" analysis of Dean Tucker's argument that England could not be successfully attacked. The "Whig" had his doubts.

[59] J. H. Jesse, *George Selwyn and His Contemporaries*, IV, 255. See also *General Evening Post*, September 28, 1779.

raids—no matter how successful—were nuisance raids only. One Opposition newspaper continued to protest that he was "burning more property in one day, than the British fleet in America can in three months,"[60] while another feared that the savage conduct of the British army in New England would be revenged by Jones in a series of raids during which Scottish towns would be burned to the ground.[61] But Jones could no longer terrify the English. His whereabouts evoked lively interest from the press all during the latter part of 1779,[62] but by Christmas, Londoners, in an atmosphere of increasing confidence, sang the latest ditty from the hit musical, "Plymouth in an Uproar":

> Let French and Spaniards vainly boast
> No danger shall annoy our coast,
> While we've a British navy. . . .[63]

At last England's shores were believed safe from attack by the Bourbons.[64] True, there was a slight chance that Ireland, still the weakest link in Britain's defense, might be attacked, but this, too, was becoming only a remote possibility. Britons might have been frightened in the spring of 1778 by "A Vice Admiral's" fears that, after losing the West Indian, African, Newfoundland, American, and Mediterranean trade, their merchants now would face the possible loss of their domestic trade because of Jones's activities, but by the autumn of 1779, this fear had faded.[65] So long as the tiny fleet of John Paul Jones, not a vast armada from France and Spain, threatened her shores, the Vice Admiral's forebodings could be washed down in toasts to the Royal Navy. The winter of 1779-1780 brought to Englishmen a sense of security they had lacked for two years. The worst, it was hoped, was over. Some of Britain's fears had been products of her own imagination; there would be no invasion; and perhaps the coming spring would find England carrying the campaign into the enemy's waters for a change—if, of course, there was to be a next campaign.

[60] *Packet,* October 1, 1779.

[61] *General Advertiser,* October 11, November 18, 1779.

[62] *Packet,* October 13, 1779; *Evening Post,* November 13. See also *Packet,* March 1, 1780, for an incorrect report of Jones's whereabouts.

[63] *Chronicle,* October 1, 1779. See also *Gentleman's Magazine,* October, 513, "Poem."

[64] *Chronicle,* November 18, 1779.

[65] *Courant,* November 26, 1779.

CHAPTER XI

The False Dawns and Dusks of 1780

I N EARLY 1780 the loyal press, which had, for five years, been assuring its readers that victory was imminent, confidently reported that the rebel cause was now so desperate that Congressional deputies were already in contact with Lord North "for the purpose of reconciliation on any terms."[1] Recent defeats in the South were dealing the final crushing blows to America's morale,[2] and victory, the loyal editors wrote, was at last in the offing. The plight of the colonists was such that the canny American Indians, always shrewd about committing themselves, had with renewed enthusiasm recently decided to aid the British.[3] Most moderate and Opposition publications did not concur in these sanguine predictions. The *Westminster Magazine* found no apparent reason for optimism as it concluded that the "long lingering and consumptive war" with the Colonies bade fair to last

[1] *Lloyd's Evening Post,* January 14, April 10, 1780. The *Morning Chronicle,* January 19, reported that "John Adams and his secretary Francis Deane" had arrived in Paris to receive a British peace proposal, but they had no authority to offer any terms.

[2] *Lloyd's Evening Post,* January 21, 1780. See also February 16, and *Chronicle,* May 2.

[3] *Lloyd's Evening Post,* January 26, 1780. A correspondent to the *General Advertiser,* February 12, protesting the shipment of razors to the beardless American Indians, surmised that the Ministry sent them for use on American throats.

longer than the Trojan War or Israel's peregrination through the wilderness. With all England worrying about attacks by the French and Spanish, the war in America seemed to have been forgotten. This Opposition magazine was of the opinion that the conflict with the Colonies might last the biblical forty years or more.[4]

Much of this optimism and pessimism rested upon an editor's political prejudices rather than upon solid information. By early 1780 the dearth of news from America was such that *Gentleman's Magazine* again abandoned its monthly "American Section."[5] This lack of information, however, did not stop the editors' speculations. The *Gazetteer*, for example, reminding its readers that, in the past, official silence was often a portent of defeat, nonetheless affirmed that no new disaster had befallen the British army. Evidence for this statement lay in the fact that the foreign newspapers did not carry any fresh battle reports from the New World.[6] Official and foreign press silence was due not only to lack of news from America, but also to the preoccupation with the new Bourbon war.

As the conflict in the Colonies admittedly was a serious obstacle in the path of Britain's attempt to crush France, sentiment for a negotiated peace with America again became prevalent. A few journals refused to concede the feasibility of negotiation,[7] but most reflected great satisfaction at the prospect of an end to hostilities,[8] especially if the colonists could be forced by military events to sue for a settlement.

The trickle of reports that "loyalists abounded all over the colonies" and that the rebellion was in "its last gasp"[9] was soon replaced by the familiar, but reassuring, flood of declarations that at long last the ensuing campaign would bring the rebellion to an end. The battle for Charleston, it was thought, was to be this Armageddon. The fall of the South's queen city would bring instant victory to the redcoats. Should the price in men and material be exceedingly dear,[10] the engagement would yet prove to be a bargain in the long run. Victory for Sir Henry Clinton's forces

4 *Westminster Magazine,* January, 1780, 49.

5 *Gentleman's Magazine,* 1780, Introduction.

6 *Gazetteer,* April 12, 1780. See also April 1, and *Morning Chronicle,* April 22.

7 *Courant,* March 17, 1780; *Evening Post,* April 29. Cf. *Morning Post,* April 8; *Chronicle,* letter, April 29.

8 *General Advertiser,* March 21, 1780.

9 *Chronicle,* April 29, 1780.

10 *Gazetteer,* May 1, 1780.

was so certain (and so desired) that the *Chronicle* announced the capture of the city six weeks prematurely, going so far as to lay a great deal of the credit upon the shoulders of the harassed loyalists, who, it reported, proved much more numerous than even the most sanguine Tories had expected.[11] The *Morning Post* refused to give this report credence, but it did predict that peace would soon follow the fall of Charleston.[12] It noted that London's "republicans" were most fearful because they, too, were convinced that all their hopes for the success of the American cause would go down with Charleston. The following week it announced that the flower of the rebel army was in the city, and should it be forced to surrender, "we may consider the war there at an end."[13] With Washington's army in sad plight, and with Charleston reputedly forcing the French to realize the error of their alliance (Lord Stormont recently had written the King that "nothing can be more unpopular than the American Cause now is at Paris"),[14] it was an interesting question as to whether the American army, the French navy, or the Continental Congress would capitulate first. Further, Virginia also was "momentarily expected" to surrender.[15] Small wonder then, that Englishmen saluted "the dawn of returning peace, which seems to illuminate the political horizon."[16]

Not all editors anticipated an immediate end to hostilities. The Opposition could not see how one victory, however glorious, could bring an end to the war in thirteen different colonies. Surely one triumph was "no more in the scale of the conquest of America, than a drop of water is in the bucket,"[17] but some editors were convinced that a few more victories in rapid succession would force the Colonies to conciliation.[18] One Opposition publication glumly surmised that, despite the optimistic turn of events, the British public would still be the great loser, because the incentive that the capture of Charleston would give the

[11] *Chronicle,* May 2, 1780.

[12] *Morning Post,* May 3, 1780.

[13] *Morning Post,* May 15, 1780.

[14] Fortescue, *Correspondence of King George III,* IV, December 21, 1779, Stormont to King.

[15] *Town and Country,* June, 1780, 330; July, 385. See also *Lloyd's Evening Post,* July 19; *Morning Chronicle,* July 25.

[16] *Gazetteer,* July 8, 1780; *Lloyd's Evening Post,* July 21; *Morning Chronicle,* July 26, 28.

[17] *Courant,* October 23, December 18, 1780. See also *Evening Post,* September 23: "A few temporary conquests decide nothing ultimately."

[18] *Lloyd's Evening Post,* May 15, 1780; *Gazetteer,* May 19.

Cntnid 156 — 159

Xerox: reactions of Brit

Prow to capture of Charleston

Ministry to press on to the ultimate victory would have to be supported by the public with additional taxes.[19]

The forebodings of the Opposition were indeed closer to the truth than were the premature celebrations by the loyal press. "The Old Fox" Washington was still far from being snared.[20] Presently, the *Morning Chronicle* admitted that the prospects for the conquest of America still seemed equivocal,[21] for so long as news was spread in Washington's camp that French troops were daily arriving in America, the rebel army could be expected to remain intact.[22] On September 29, 1780, Sir Grey Cooper, a secretary of the Treasury who sat from Saltash, summed up the disappointment of both the Government and its loyal press when he wrote to William Knox that he "feared the golden dreams we had after the taking of Charlestown are all over."[23] The *Gazetteer* substantiated Cooper's fear with the report that the recently returned British general officers admitted but very small hope of subjecting the northern colonies. These officers attributed their pessimistic view to the difficulties involved in defeating Washington, whose "wary conduct as a Commander in Chief" they much respected.[24]

Since America's newly reinforced army was increasing to formidable proportions,[25] hope of peace through British victory soon gave way to discussions about how to negotiate successfully with the Americans.[26] Talk of conciliation appeared to be benefiting the London stock exchange,[27] but Englishmen were uncertain as to the conditions that could bring about peace. Many were horrified at the thought of being forced to deal with the colonists upon terms of equal sovereignty, while others, not concerned with maneuverings or negotiations, insisted that the economies of Britain and North America remain interdependent so England could again enjoy American commerce.[28] Many

---

19 *Evening Post,* June 15, 24, 1780; *Courant,* June 19.

20 *Evening Post,* August 1, 1780.

21 *Morning Chronicle,* September 13, 1780. Cf. *Lloyd's Evening Post,* October 6, 9.

22 *Morning Chronicle,* September 27, 1780. See also *Lloyd's Evening Post,* June 30, July 26, October 23, December 1, 11.

23 HMC, Knox Papers, September 29, 1780, Cooper to Knox.

24 *Gazetteer,* October 18, 1780. See also *Town and Country,* October, 561.

25 *Morning Chronicle,* November 13, 1780.

26 *Morning Chronicle,* September 29, 1780.

27 *Gazetteer,* October 23, 1780.

28 *General Advertiser,* February 1, 1780. See also *Gentleman's Magazine,* January, 1780, 36.

publications continued to reflect the belief that American independence, both political and economic, was "as fixed as Fate," and one of them even printed a favorable comparison of this new nation to the infant Hercules, for it predicted that, with the years, America too would grow to fantastic strength through nurturing itself in its own wilderness.[29] It thus behooved Britain to recognize and take advantage of the great commercial possibilities that would certainly arise, once North America was emancipated from its provincial state.[30] The idea that America would be not only free but strong as well was adequately planted by the Opposition press in 1780.[31]

On June 2, 1780, London was torn by a series of riots that perhaps were the worst in all her history. Fired by Lord George Gordon's anti-Catholic Protestant Association, the mob vented its fury upon prisons, banks, homes of ministers and judges, and any other likely (and profitable) targets it could discover. On June 6 Lord Sandwich narrowly escaped being murdered, despite his heavy guard. Lord North's house was attacked by the rioters, but saved by the military, while the homes of Justice Mansfield and Justice Hyde were completely destroyed.[32] After a week of riot and pillage, the Royal Army restored London to a near normal state.

The press's search for the reasons behind this harrowing week led it down many alleys, most of them blind. The *Gazetteer* asserted that the passage of the Quebec Act a half dozen years before had not only alienated the Americans, but now its effects had returned to the homeland to incite thousands of feeling Britons.[33] The *Courant*, while deploring "the outrages committed by a tumultuous populace," also avowed that the causes of the riots were to be found in the unpopular conduct of the Administration.[34] On June 9, the day Gordon was sent to the Tower, a handbill circulated anonymously through the city, stating that the tumults were begun and implemented by French money. It

29 *Gentleman's Magazine,* January, 1781, 31-32, "A Translation."

30 *Gentleman's Magazine,* January, 1781, 31-32.

31 *Evening Post,* October 26, 1780.

32 *Lloyd's Evening Post,* January 8, 1781; *Town and Country,* June, 1780, 330. For the contemporary coverage of the riot trials, see *Gentleman's Magazine,* "Historical Chronicle," for July, 1780.

33 *Gazetteer,* June 5, 1780.

34 *Courant,* June 9, 1780.

was reprinted and widely discussed in the press.[35] On June 14 the *Morning Chronicle* furnished additional publicity for the handbill's statement by maintaining that the rioting was financed by Versailles and "carried on by French and American spies of inferior station."[36] The *Gazetteer*, in support of the theory that money and Frenchmen were behind the disturbances, offered a reward of £100 to anyone able to furnish evidence concerning the financial backers of the riots.[37] One correspondent to the *Chronicle* placed all of the blame upon those "patriotic" Englishmen whose pro-American "inflammatory speeches and seditious insinuations" he saw as the source of all the recent troubles.[38] The Opposition *Evening Post*, however, after berating the Ministry for being slow to crush the riots and quick to hang the rioters, reminded its countrymen that the weighty problems of the European and American wars slept while Englishmen busily discussed domestic defense, holiday camps, Lord George Gordon, and the coming hangings, etc., which "form almost the whole of public conversation."[39]

It was not until late summer that the press placed the Gordon outbreaks in their proper perspective: They were neither plotted nor financed by the French or Americans. Triggered by Gordon and a handful of zealous bigots, the lawlessness that paralyzed London in early June was perpetrated by the blind and ignorant fury of mob drunkenness and seconded by the professional interest of thieves and housebreakers.[40] The flames of the riot kindled by a "mischievous madman," as Gibbon called Gordon, "admonished all thinking men of the danger of an appeal to the people."[41] If a choice had to be made between the actions of Lord North and the anarchy of the mob, the memory of the first week in June would frighten many critics of the Government, at least temporarily, to retreat into the camp of the Ministry[42] and would render still easier the task of re-electing a House of Commons favorable to the North Government.

Lord North had enough loyal supporters tied to him either through fear of the mob, Treasury boroughs, war contracts, places,

35 *Morning Chronicle,* June 10, 1780; *Gazetteer,* June 12.
36 *Morning Chronicle,* June 14, 1780.
37 *Gazetteer,* June 23, 1780.
38 "R.S.," August 10, 1780.
39 *Evening Post,* July 4, 13, 1780.
40 *Gentleman's Magazine,* August, 1780, 269.
41 D. M. Low, *Edward Gibbon,* 286.
42 J. Steven Watson, *The Reign of George III,* 235, 239.

and pensions to assure his Ministry of an easy victory in the parliamentary elections to be held in the autumn of 1780. Aware of these political facts, the Opposition press concentrated its electioneering efforts on those few areas where it believed the genuine choice of the freeholders was being subverted by Ministry funds. On September 19 Almon's *Evening Post* warned the electors of Surrey that "the hirelings of administration have been labouring with insidious application," utilizing "all the dirty means that power and artifice can accomplish" in order to help defeat Sir Joseph Mawbey and Admiral Augustus Keppel. Almon was certain that the independent freeholders of Surrey would demonstrate at the polls renewed confidence in their two Opposition representatives.

One of the few surprises provided by editors before the election came when Henry Sampson Woodfall's *Public Advertiser* supported the Earl of Lincoln rather than Charles James Fox in his bid for a seat from Westminster.[43] Almon's *Courant*, however, attacked Lincoln's campaign against Fox and Sir George Bridges Rodney as "immoral"; the paper prophesied that Lincoln would go down to defeat before "the honest, uninfluenced electors of Westminster."[44] While Lincoln and the other candidates who tried to unseat Fox, Mawbey, and Keppel may have gone down to defeat, and while a few new influential members of the Opposition, such as the playwright Richard Brinsley Sheridan, may have entered Parliament for the first time in 1780, the Opposition knew that this new Parliament could not be expected to change the Ministry's plan concerning America. More was required than convincing speeches from Edmund Burke (who had just lost his seat from Bristol, and now sat from London) or from Charles Fox to force a change in the views of a new Parliament, which, in fact, looked very much like the old one.[45]

If the British Government seriously desired to negotiate peace

[43] *Public Advertiser*, September 19, 21, 1780.

[44] *Courant*, September 22, 25, 1780. The election provided an excellent source of revenue for the London press. The *Public Advertiser*, September 28, advised its readers that it would accept advertisements of "moderate length" at 3s. 6d. each. All during late September most London publications carried about a full page of election advertisements, which was about one half of all the advertising space carried.

[45] From April 29 to July 8, 1779, the *Evening Post* published serially "A Freeholder's" "Short History of the Representatives in Parliament." Cf. *Public Advertiser*, October 24, 1780, listing the membership of the new House of Commons.

with America in the midst of its election campaign, it was afforded a perfect opportunity when Henry Laurens, one of the most prominent and influential rebels, was taken prisoner on the high seas by a British man-of-war. At first the Ministry did not know whether to receive this wealthy South Carolina merchant and former power in the Continental Congress as captive or to pack him off to Newgate as a common traitor. The newspapers, however, assured their readers that the Ministry would not let so propitious an opportunity for opening peace negotiations go for nought. "It seems as if Providence caused his captivity for some such purpose," wrote the *Gazetteer*.[46] The prisoner presently was sent to the Tower, pending a decision on how to treat with him and the American Revolution. Eventually, he was interrogated at great length, but his insistence that independence was a condition for peace led the ministers to realize that negotiations would be fruitless at this time. Laurens was not used as an opening wedge for peace, because the Ministry remained convinced that it would be able to subdue the Americans and their French allies and eventually dictate the terms of peace to the Colonies. Expressing this belief, the loyal press condemned Laurens for his unintelligent, intransigent stand.[47] On the other hand, the Opposition defended the prisoner and condemned the cruel treatment the American, who was ailing, allegedly received at the hands of the Ministry.[48] Quartered in the Tower, Henry Laurens spent the remainder of the war as a political-military prisoner, nursing his gout and probably receiving no small satisfaction from reading in the Ministry's new and most trusted journal that "such is the distraction of the times, that while one party sentence him to the scaffold, the other would vote him into Parliament."[49]

By November, just when Englishmen had all but reconciled themselves to the impossibility of a negotiated peace with America, the news of Benedict Arnold's desertion rekindled hope. Arnold, now praised by the loyal press for his brilliant exploits at

[46] *Gazetteer,* October 5, 1780. See also October 4.

[47] *Lloyd's Evening Post,* October 6, November 29, 1780. The *Morning Chronicle,* October 9, related that Laurens was marked by "a certain weakness of character," which explained his fondness for pomp and show. See also *Public Advertiser,* October 7, for a two-column article by "PUBLIUS" attacking both Laurens and the American cause.

[48] *Courant,* November 1, 1781.

[49] *Morning Herald,* November 2, 1780.

Quebec, Saratoga, The Lakes, and many other places, by his defection from the American cause furnished new and unequivocal
evidence of America's ruinous situation. His announced confidence in the swift success of the King's forces[50] had certainly influenced his decision to abandon the cause of his countrymen.
Thus, his desertion was saluted as a sure sign America was preparing to return to its former allegiance, for it was assumed
that many of his officers and enlisted men would follow him and
rejoin the Royal standard.[51] The *Morning Post* affirmed that the
rebellion was now a "mere rope of sand," kept together by the utmost efforts of France and Spain.[52] Henry Bate's newly created
Morning Herald asserted that the "coffee-house orators" who had
insisted Arnold was America's martial pillar were now silent.
Bate was certain that Washington, who "can only act in avoiding to fight," could not—alone—furnish enough leadership for the
Americans to continue in rebellion. In addition, the *Morning
Herald* noted that the French already were considered obnoxious by most colonists, specie was not to be had in the Colonies,
disaffection was the hallmark of the rebel army, and the poor
were everywhere. As Britain remained willing to forgive the
penitent, there was "every prospect of a peace being brought
about by a general revolt," it hopefully concluded.[53]

If these conditions really obtained in America, the loyal press
was certain that Arnold's treason was not to be considered an
isolated instance, but rather the first in a long series of desertions from the American officer corps. On December 1 *Lloyd's
Evening Post* reported that a General Morris, "a firm supporter of
independence," abandoned the rebel cause as soon as he discovered that the Congress intended to make America "an abject
appendage to the Crown of France." Three days later, along with
most other London publications, it declared that General John
Sullivan also had deserted.[54] Reports that General Greene and
General Parsons, "next to Arnold the best officers in the American

[50] *Morning Post,* November 15, 1780. See also November 14; *Lloyd's Evening
Post,* November 13, December 1; *British Mercury,* November 16.
[51] *Morning Herald,* November 15, 1780.
[52] *Morning Post,* November 16, 1780.
[53] *Morning Herald,* November 20, 1780.
[54] *Evening Post, Morning Chronicle, Morning Herald, British Mercury,* December 4, 1780. *Lloyd's Evening Post* continued reporting the spread of American
"desertion fever" throughout the first half of 1781. On January 26, it reported
that Ethan Allen and his troops came over to the British, and on June 27 it
repeated the oft-circulated rumor that Washington had resigned his commission.

army," were about to follow suit appeared in the *Gazetteer* on December 5, while some days later the Ministry announced that Charles Lee was coming over to the British army and Horatio Gates was likely to follow his example.[55] How, then, could victory be far off, if it was so "evident that all the rebel general officers are on the eve of throwing up their commissions?"[56]

As the new year dawned, prospects of peace again were held out to Englishmen as the press reported that the ubiquitous Congressional commissioners were arriving in England with terms of accommodation.[57] *Lloyd's Evening Post,* in its initial edition for 1781, reflected this note of optimism when it stated that Americans were now willing to negotiate under the terms of the Carlisle Peace Commission. In addition, it predicted that, once Virginia was conquered, the Colonies would lose their prime export article of tobacco, "and the neck of the rebellion will be broke." The *Morning Herald* also saw the war so close to its end that it reported members of the Cabinet already were contending "for the honour of subjugating America."[58] The *Morning Post,* paraphrasing remarks it had been making for almost five years, stated confidently that the Congress was powerless and that the Americans were plagued by "an army without a general, an alliance without friendship, and a currency without value—politics without principle, councils without unanimity, obstinacy without hope, and conduct without wisdom."[59] It concluded that no one could entertain a doubt that the rebellion was in its last gasp.[60] The loyal press added that the King had expressed a desire for peace to be restored with America, as this "depredatory war, of all others, is the most repugnant to his Majesty's principles."[61] The Poet Laureate's "Ode for His Majesty's Birth Day" for 1781

[55] *Gazetteer,* December 16, 1780.

[56] *Morning Herald,* December 4, 1780. See also *Town and Country,* February, 1781, 107, for an account of the rank-and-file desertions in Washington's army.

[57] *British Mercury,* December 1, 1780; *Chronicle,* December 7; *Morning Herald,* December 11.

[58] *Morning Herald,* January 3, 1781.

[59] *Morning Post,* March 19, 1781. See also *Morning Herald,* April 5; *Lloyd's Evening Post,* May 26.

[60] *Morning Post,* March 31, 1781. On May 29 it claimed that Washington himself had instituted peace negotiations. This article was copied by the *Edinburgh Evening Post,* June 2. The *Morning Herald,* July 4, 1781, celebrated the fifth birthday of American independence by asserting that the rebellion was in its "last gasp." See also July 17; *Edinburgh Evening Courant,* May 12; *Lloyd's Evening Courant,* July 18.

[61] *Morning Herald,* June 27, 1781. This newspaper assumed that "peace" meant a victorious settlement, rather than a compromise.

benevolently reflected the hope that the rebels soon would return to the "protecting shield of the Monarch."[62] Believing the King in a magnanimous mood (George III was always willing to open peace negotiations on his own terms) and the colonial war effort collapsing of its own weight (one newspaper even quoted Shakespeare to depict the horrible state of the American army),[63] the loyal press reflected certainty that good news was close at hand.

Not all Englishmen allowed Arnold's defection to blind them to the realities of the American scene. The Opposition understood that, unless Britain made the initial overtures, peace would not come, regardless of how fervently it was desired. Why, suddenly, should the Americans be expected to surrender? The *Evening Post*, stressing the fact that not one man had come over with Arnold, saw no immediate advantage to be derived from his apostasy.[64] In fact, Arnold, who at best was considered but a poor substitute for the lost André, should have realized that his treason would strengthen the American cause by making the colonists more cautious and alert and by rekindling their "dormant fires" of patriotism.[65] Further, the Opposition press joined with the overwhelming number of other British publications that condemned the entire affair.[66] The turncoat's unhappy future in England could have been predicted after a cursory study of the contemporary press. Granting that he was a brave man and a gallant officer, the *Westminster Magazine*, in a representative editorial, predicted that the time was not far distant when Arnold, in whatever degree he "may be caressed at present," would soon feel the stings of contempt and ignominy "which the remembrance of his treachery can produce."[67] The *Morning Post*, berating Arnold for attempting to surrender his troops rather than going silently into retirement to protest the policies of his countrymen, found "it is not possible too much to reprobate or despise his conduct."[68] The loyal *British Mercury* described "that infamous traitor" as a person of "mean and low extraction," who, as the

---

[62] *Gentleman's Magazine*, June, 1781, 283.

[63] *Morning Herald*, July 26, 1781: " 'Big *Mars* seems bankrupt in their beggar'd host.' (*Henry V*)." See also July 28, 30.

[64] *Evening Post*, November 11, 14, 1780; *Courant*, November 15.

[65] *Evening Post*, November 18, 1780; *British Mercury*, November 28.

[66] *Gazetteer*, November 20, 1780, is typical of the anti-Arnold and anti-Administration tone of the Opposition.

[67] *Westminster Magazine*, Supplement, 1780, 667-90.

[68] *Morning Post*, November 25, 1780.

American Commandant in Philadelphia, "committed such acts of tyranny, oppression, and depredation" as to make himself so obnoxious to the populace that his removal was requested and granted.[69] The Tory *Lloyd's Evening Post* affirmed that Arnold, who was made a brigadier general in the British army, was most unpopular with his new forces,[70] while the *British Mercury* added that Royal officers dared not trust and refused to serve under "the revolting general," for fear he would betray his new command "as he had done that which he so lately disgraced."[71] The Opposition *Courant,* after condemning the entire affair, attacked the Ministry for attempting to accomplish by bribery and corruption what British arms had failed to gain. If the purchase of one general cost the Ministry an estimated £20,000 sterling (where it derived this figure it did not say), imagine the cost of corrupting the entire American army, to say nothing of the Congress and the great popular leaders of the several states![72]

The Arnold affair produced the first great British martyr of the war. Major John André,[73] considered by many "without exception, the most promising man of his class in the whole army,"[74] was quickly doomed by an American court-martial for his role as a spy. Unfortunately, the rules of military honor forbade Clinton from negotiating successfully for André's return (the Americans insisted upon receiving Arnold in exchange).[75] The stirring accounts of the young major's execution (his last moments allegedly were noted down by a servant attending him)[76] brought a feeling of pride and shame to most Englishmen. Just as the Arnold affair was expected to stir Americans to a renewed effort, so too did the demands to avenge André's death stir the English. General Clinton, the press reported, announced that the martyr's fate had created "such a rage for revenge" in his army that he was having the utmost difficulty restraining his troops.[77] The *British Mercury* declared that André's execution had roused the

---

[69] *British Mercury,* November 28, 1780.

[70] *Lloyd's Evening Post,* December 11, 1780.

[71] *British Mercury,* December 9, 1780.

[72] *Courant,* December 18, 1780.

[73] The *Morning Chronicle,* November 14, 1780, identified the Major as "St. Andree" and the *Morning Herald,* same date, listed him as "Major Sinclair." The following day it used the name St. Andree, but the next issue corrected the mistake.

[74] *Morning Chronicle,* November 14, 1780.

[75] *Gazetteer,* November 14, 1780.

[76] *British Mercury,* November 18, 1780.

[77] *Lloyd's Evening Post,* November 15, 1780; *Morning Chronicle,* November 16; *Gazetteer,* November 17.

Government from its passive lenity, "which had hitherto marked their proceedings against the abettors of the Americans on this side of the water."[78] The *Morning Herald*, with the rest of the press, preferred revenge to come at the expense of the rebels. Publishing its own version of André's epitaph, this newspaper implored its countrymen to strain every nerve, arm, and hand:

'Till the fell foes bewail their guilty deed,
And slaughter'd thousands round their victim bleed![79]

While condemning the harsh sentence imposed upon the young officer by Washington and his staff, most newspapers admitted that, according to the accepted rules of warfare, the sentence was proper.[80] Moreover, a serious military lesson might be learned from the André story: If Washington had the temerity to order Clinton's Adjutant to the gallows, the American cause was far from breathing its last. Washington, always a cautious man, would never have inflicted so severe a sentence had he the least reason to suspect that he, too, might presently find himself before a court-martial.[81] For this reason, serious doubts about the imminence of peace manifested themselves again in many publications. The *British Mercury* did not question Britain's ability to subdue America, "even should the war continue six years longer, which, however, every real patriot must hope will not be the case,"[82] but five years of war were enough for most of the other newspapers. The *Gazetteer*, calling America the "Grave of Englishmen," reported that by 1778 "not less than eighteen thousand brave fellows" had been placed in this grave, which, unfortunately, was still "gaping for some thousands more then languishing with wounds and sickness."[83] How many more men had been buried since that date, the *Gazetteer*, probably for lack of information, did not venture to guess.

It seemed, by early 1781, there had been so many false dawns in America that British editors should have become hardened to the realities of the struggle in the Colonies, but they continued

78 *British Mercury*, November 22, 1780.
79 *Morning Herald*, December 5, 1780. See also November 22; *Gentleman's Magazine*, April, 1781, 178, and May, 235-36, for Samuel Johnson's poetic assertion that Washington, in ordering the death of the young major, "showed his heart of Nero's colour dy'd."
80 *Gazetteer, British Mercury*, November 16; *Gentleman's Magazine*, Supplement, 1780, 610-16.
81 *Gazetteer*, November 20, 1780.
82 *British Mercury*, December 3, 1780.
83 *Gazetteer*, December 16, 1780.

hopeful. With the news that a broad segment of the American army—the Pennsylvania Line—was in revolt against the Congress in January, the loyal press immediately embraced this latest report of defection from Washington's ranks as another sure sign of impending victory. Utilizing extra large print and double spacing of lines, the *Morning Herald* quoted from Rivington's New York *Royal Gazette* that a force 2,200 strong, under General St. Clair, had spiked their cannons, destroyed their carriages, and completely abandoned their position at Morristown.[84]

The Opposition press again acted as a brake on the general enthusiasm, cautioning its countrymen about holding "the romantic prospect of conquering America," which could mislead them into continuing "that destructive war."[85] Even some Tory journals conceded that America was not yet bereft of resources. The wily Dutchmen would now lend them enough money to continue the war interminably, thus keeping their chief commercial competitors busy at very slight expense.[86] The thin veneer of optimism of some loyal newspapers was seen through by most of the press. So long as reports of military setbacks in America had to be rationalized as being "oftentimes productive of solid and permanent benefits" because they would force the British army to new heights of exertion and spirit,[87] the literate Tory could not peruse his morning paper with pleasure, especially when he soon read that none of the Pennsylvanians defected to the British (two of Clinton's emissaries were hanged by the rebels), and nothing came of a defection in New Jersey a few weeks later.

Few editors were as pessimistic as those of the Opposition *Courant*, which announced that the Americans were as "perfectly secure in their freedom and independence as this or any other country possibly can be."[88] Most realized that defeat of the Americans and their return to the mother country was but an impracticable dream. They now were willing to concede that some sort of semiautonomous status would have to be offered the Colonies if ever the war was to be ended.[89]

84 *Morning Herald, Lloyd's Evening Post,* February 9, 1781; *Morning Chronicle,* February 12. The King also received his first information about the mutiny from *Rivington's Gazette.* See *Correspondence of George III with Lord North,* W. Bodham Donne, ed., II, 358, letter 664, dated 8 February 1781.

85 *Courant,* March 29, 1781.

86 *Lloyd's Evening Post,* March 9, 1781.

87 *Morning Herald,* April 17, 1781.

88 *Courant,* April 20, 1781.

89 *Gentleman's Magazine,* July, 1781, 337.

Moreover, as Britons appeared less concerned with the paucity of news from America than with the whereabouts of the Brest fleet, the *Public Advertiser* cautioned them that even the slightest flagging of interest in the Colonies would be courting defeat, for "if nothing shall be done in America before the Rebels are strengthened by the intended reinforcements from France, nothing will be done from this Time for evermore!"[90] Yet, this newspaper admitted that even if Englishmen gave their undivided attention and resources to it, the war in America could not be won. Describing the conflict as inexpedient and impracticable,[91] the *Public Advertiser* derided the sentiments of the loyal press that Washington's army, "so long pining in want and despair," would be defeated in the "next campaign."

Long before the arrival of the news of Cornwallis' disaster at Yorktown, many Englishmen had reconciled themselves to the fact that the war in America could never be won.

[90] *Public Advertiser,* September 8, 1781.
[91] *Public Advertiser,* September 1, 1781.

CHAPTER XII

All the World an Enemy

ADDED to the seemingly endless procession of disappointments that appeared in the newspapers was the awareness that most of Europe, jealous of England's commercial superiority, hoped for her defeat. Along with the House of Bourbon, which all Britain assumed to be the primary enemy, the Dutch were considered a threat to the Empire. Although ostensibly England's friend and ally, the "Mynheers," crafty businessmen that they were, could be expected to make war at the first commercially propitious moment. Upon learning of America's plan to be independent, they commenced a lucrative—albeit "pernicious and illicit"—trade with the rebels. Reminding its readers that this was the same type of "extreme commercial avarice" that had earlier produced the Dutch "barbarity and ignominy at Amboyna," the *Morning Post* recommended that Englishmen continue to view the actions of Amsterdam "with a suspicious and watchful eye,"[1] while the *St. James's Chronicle* questioned the nature of an ally that professed friendship and at the same time supplied arms to the rebels.[2]

Despite the States General's frequently declared pacific disposition[3] and despite repeated assertions that the Amsterdam mer-

[1] *Morning Post*, October 9, 1776. See also August 3, and *Morning Chronicle*, March 30, for earlier accounts of Dutch commercial incursions into both the American colonies and the British West Indies.

[2] *St. James's Chronicle*, October 12, 1776.

[3] *General Evening Post*, March 24, 1778; *Morning Post*, March 26.

chants had such confidence in the British cause that they were investing tens of thousands sterling in London stocks,[4] it was understood that the Dutch, encouraged by the Bourbons, were being "spirited up against Great Britain."[5] Newspaper editors were not blind to Holland's increased military preparations, which all factions agreed were aimed at England.[6] Because of these circumstances, both the *Packet* and the *Gazetteer* advised the Dutch to remain strictly neutral so their commerce could continue to glean the best from two warring worlds, whereas an encounter with England would risk all their newly acquired carrying profits.[7]

Unfortunately, all suggestions of Dutch neutrality were in vain. By the first day of 1780 both the *General Advertiser* and the *Gazetteer* were warning that Anglo-Dutch naval hostilities would soon begin, and the strongly Opposition *General Advertiser* expressed fear of this struggle, not so much for its military as for its economic consequences. It was certain that the Dutch could be dealt with satisfactorily on the high seas, but another matter to be considered was that Amsterdam held between thirty and forty millions in British securities. Were these funds suddenly withdrawn from the economy, "a national bankruptcy would inevitably ensue."[8] The following day the *General Advertiser* added that a combined French and Dutch fleet could render England's supply lines from India quite precarious.[9]

By the spring of 1780 Britons were reading that Holland intended a war.[10] In any event, the press reported that Britain was ready to support its dignity against this "phlegmatic and artful people,"[11] and a stream of articles discussing the merits, military

4 *General Evening Post,* June 18, 1778; *Morning Chronicle,* June 22.

5 *Morning Post,* April 6, 1779. The *Chronicle,* October 19, claimed that a French ship flying British colors was pillaging both Dutch and Danish shipping.

6 *Packet,* April 22, November 20, 1778; *Morning Post,* July 6, 1779. See also June 2, and *Adams's Weekly Courant,* February 17, 1778, for reflections of the fear that a Bourbon-Dutch alliance "would render England very inconsiderable as a maritime Power."

7 *Packet,* September 23, 1778; *Gazetteer,* June 5, 1779.

8 *General Advertiser,* January 5, 1780.

9 *General Advertiser,* January 6, 1780. Cf. *Morning Post,* April 24, pointing out Holland's vulnerable position in Asia.

10 *Lloyd's Evening Post, Gazetteer,* April 24, 1780; *Morning Chronicle,* May 10. Cf. *Gazetteer,* May 9, 19.

11 *Town and Country,* April, 1780, 218.

and commercial, of the coming war[12] so conditioned the public for the struggle that when hostilities were officially announced in late December, Englishmen took the news as a matter of course. The declaration occasioned no immediate alarm on the stock exchange,[13] and one correspondent to the loyal *Lloyd's Evening Post* noted a "great alacrity and chearfullness in every countenance, the miserable Patriots alone excepted."[14] Well might the extreme "patriots" not have worn a cheerful countenance. The Ministry, not having business enough in a tripartite war, had chosen a quartetto, noted the *Evening Post.* Lord North, it exclaimed, "has now but the *French, Spaniards, Americans,* and *Dutch* to cope with—Whilst Old England pays the piper."[15]

Granting that at first their own manufacture and trade might suffer considerably, the English did not look with disfavor upon a war with the Dutch.[16] The idea that the Hollanders, who were "as distinguished for their cunning as their avarice,"[17] would now receive just punishment for their perfidy was a popular one in the press. Assuming that the greedy States General (at best but a "wretched oligarchy"),[18] not thinking it politic to let the French come in for the whole prize of North America,[19] was casting her lot with the Bourbons and with the Americans solely for booty, some newspapers predicted that this would be a brief encounter, lasting only long enough for the Dutch to realize they could gain nothing.[20] Others, of all political persuasions, however, feared the rapid increase of the forces that now faced Britain. The loyal *Morning Herald,* confessing that "the more daring part of the world" had deemed it impossible for England—unassisted and unallied—to continue much longer against such superior odds, was now in agreement with the violently Opposition *Courant.*[21]

[12] *Evening Post,* August 13, 1780; *Morning Chronicle,* August 16, December 26; *Morning Herald,* November 2, 24, December 1, 2. On December 21, this newspaper wrote that it expected England to "strip those miscreants of the greatest part of their East and West Indian possessions and commerce."

[13] *Lloyd's Evening Post,* December 25, 1780. Cf. *Morning Herald,* February 1.

[14] *Lloyd's Evening Post,* December 25, 1780.

[15] *Evening Post,* December 25, 1780.

[16] *Morning Herald,* January 6, 1781; *Morning Chronicle,* January 10.

[17] *Gazetteer,* December 23, 1780.

[18] *Kentish Gazette,* January 13, 1781.

[19] *Public Advertiser,* January 24, 1781.

[20] *Edinburgh Evening Courant,* February 24, March 7, 1781. See also *Morning Herald,* January 2.

[21] *Morning Herald,* February 1, 1781; *Courant,* March 5. Cf. *Morning Herald,* April 9, confidently reporting that England was "a match for the whole quadruple alliance."

Few editors doubted that Holland's declaration of war would help the Americans. It was known that increased loans to the rebels would be forthcoming from Amsterdam,[22] but it was believed that Dutch funds could not turn the tide of battle. The war would be fought in either Channel or West Indian waters, and the Royal Navy would eventually settle the score with Holland as well as with France and Spain.

When London learned that the Dutch West Indian outpost of St. Eustatius had fallen to the British in late March, 1781, the rejoicing was "extatic."[23] This tiny island entrepôt had supplied the Americans with military and commercial goods for the past five years, and, the *Morning Herald* asserted, "all the art and political cunning of the French" could not reconcile the Dutch to their great loss. Within two weeks Bate's new publication triumphantly concluded, "They pant for peace on any terms."[24] *Lloyd's Evening Post* echoed this sentiment, reporting that Dutchmen were now "at least ten to one against the war with England."[25] It seemed to Londoners that if Holland had a free press it would be as solidly opposed to a British war as the British press was opposed to an American war.

If there was any truth to the *Morning Chronicle's* boast in April, 1781, that more than three hundred Dutch vessels had already fallen into British hands without England's "having lost a single ship of any consequence,"[26] this perhaps explained why, during the ensuing summer, the Dutch avoided any serious naval engagements. Most publications assumed that Holland's commerce had already learned the might of the Royal Navy, and peace talks initiated by the States General could shortly be expected.[27] George III desired a separate peace with Holland,[28] thus giving some support to the speculation that the war might presently end. Nothing came of his desires, however, and while the *Public Ledger* declared itself "extremely happy" to inform its readers that negotiations were about to be successfully concluded, the

22 *Kentish Gazette,* March 7, 1781.

23 *Morning Herald,* March 29, 1781.

24 *Morning Herald,* April 21, 1781.

25 *Lloyd's Evening Post,* April 25, 1781.

26 *Morning Chronicle,* April 27, 1781.

27 *Public Advertiser,* August 16, October 20, 1781; *Morning Herald,* October 5, 18; *Edinburgh Evening Courant,* November 26.

28 HMC, Abergavenny MSS, August 29, 1781, King to North.

Chronicle more accurately reported that no peace with Holland was in sight.[29]

Late in January, 1782, dreams of a quick settlement were shattered by the news that the French and Dutch had recaptured St. Eustatius. "How we shall be able to make head against this additional enemy, now that they seem seriously to set their face to the war is a mystery, perhaps, not yet known at St. James's," noted the Opposition *Public Advertiser*.[30] The press actually had little difficulty analyzing this mystery: In one year of hostilities, British forces had failed to knock Holland out of the war, and the future appeared no more promising than the past.

With her forces fighting three major European powers upon three different continents, Britain sorely needed all the friendship she could find, but very little was offered her. A few years earlier, it was believed that Catherine of Russia was a trusted friend, and talk of a formal treaty of amity and commerce with St. Petersburg was one of the major themes of London's loyal press.[31] Russia was then expected to supply as many mercenaries as the British army requested. On June 12, 1777, the *Morning Post* declared that a proposal to send 20,000 Russian troops to America was overruled by St. James's because the Court considered additional troops unnecessary at the time. By August 27, it claimed 36,000 Russians would be sent to America as part of a new treaty with St. Petersburg. Further, the *St. James's Chronicle* added, this treaty stipulated that, in case of a formal declaration of hostilities between England and France, Russia would maintain a strong Baltic squadron for the protection of British trade.[32]

When the expected naval and military forces from Russia failed to materialize, most British editors were genuinely surprised. The *Packet,* demanding that the Administration explain the true reasons that prevented the shipment of the reputedly promised 20,000 Russians, continued to reflect the general belief that 35,000 men would soon be sent across the Atlantic from Germany and Russia.[33] At the end of the year, however, *Adams's Weekly Courant* carried the report that the Empress was not able to furnish

29 *Chronicle,* December 9, 1781.
30 *Public Advertiser,* December 31, 1781.
31 *Morning Post,* January 15, 30, 1777.
32 *St. James's Chronicle,* April 14, 1778.
33 *Packet,* April 23, 1777. See also January 2, 1778, for another report of 20,000 Russians being sent to America; five days later this newspaper revised the figure downward to 7,000 men.

troops, but would substitute cash. Even if true, this report failed to satisfy Adams, who declared that the British forces in America critically needed men, not money.[34]

By mid-1778 it appeared that not only were Russian troops not forthcoming, but there was a chance that they might even be used against Britain. Rumors of an impending Franco-Russian treaty filled the press. If consummated, this agreement would divest Britain of its last chance for a Continental alliance and would rob her of one of her last sources of naval supplies.[35] How, wondered the editors, could one of England's closest friends be considering so radical a reversal of policy as to enter into an agreement with France? Reflecting the Opposition viewpoint, the *Packet* answered that, in reality, Russia had never been England's friend. Rather, it asserted, propagandists in the pay of the Ministry had invented the entire story of Russian reinforcements in order to buoy up the spirits on the sagging home front.[36] Professions of Russian friendship persisted, however. The *Gazetteer*, which for almost a year had optimistically awaited news of an Anglo-Russian treaty,[37] in May, 1779, resurrected an old idea when it suggested that, if all other means of subduing America should fail, Britain could present New England to the Empress of Russia. Surely this gift would keep the Americans in obedience and at the same time satisfy the Empress of England's warm feeling for her.[38] The *Gazetteer's* editor apparently never considered that his suggested remedy might be worse than the disease. Such a suggestion, however, lends evidence to the belief that Russia, on the eve of her entrance into the League of Armed Neutrality, was considered by many as England's closest European ally.[39]

Only an occasional report in late March, 1780, helped cushion for the British public the blow of the agreement of Armed Neutrality. When copies of the agreement reached London, they were greeted with a mixture of general disbelief and ministerial silence.[40] Most newspapers waited for additional clarifying in-

[34] *Adams's Weekly Courant*, December 16, 1777.

[35] *Evening Post*, July 11, 1778; *General Advertiser*, July 15.

[36] *Packet*, July 27, September 18, 1778. See also *Morning Post*, March 27, 1779, pointing out Russia's reluctance to aid England and doubting Catherine's friendship.

[37] *Gazetteer*, September 16, 1778, January 14, 1779.

[38] *Gazetteer*, May 17, 1779.

[39] *Morning Chronicle*, January 11, 1780; *Lloyd's Evening Post*, January 26.

[40] *Lloyd's Evening Post*, April 10, 1780.

formation. They speculated about its seriousness, wondering perhaps if it was merely a bluff or even a treaty manufactured in London to suit some sinister purpose. By April 18, however, the loyal *Morning Post* editorially noted that all its golden dreams of an alliance with Russia were now completely dissipated. It did not speculate about Catherine's reasons for changing her mind. It confessed disappointment, nevertheless, that "various powers in Europe seemed determined to stand off and leave us to our fate."

"Various powers in Europe" appeared to mean practically *all* of Europe. As early as September 25, 1778, the *Morning Chronicle* prophesied that Prussia, Sweden, and Denmark would eventually come to the aid of the Bourbons. It hopefully reminded its readers that, at Cressy, Poitiers, and Agincourt, British forces—although outnumbered—had carried the day. A few weeks later it noted that Sweden was definitely in the enemy camp, being "the sworn ally of France."[41] In March, 1779, the *Morning Post* also admitted that Sweden and Denmark were in close alliance with France, and it presently added that Stockholm's costly naval preparations were being subsidized by the Bourbons.[42] Britain's seizure of Scandinavian shipping bound for hostile ports had finally returned to haunt her.[43] *Town and Country*, commenting about this new league, glumly concluded, "We must fight our own battles in every part of the world unassisted by any ally."[44] The *Gazetteer*, lamenting that "Poor credulous Britain" was duped into believing "ungrateful Russia was her friend," added that not only would this new northern confederation ruin Britain's commerce, but, more ignominious, it would subject her to insults from petty kingdoms like Sweden and Denmark.[45]

Perhaps the only way to emerge with any success from so perilous a position, suggested the *Gazetteer*, was to negotiate a peace with the Americans and, together with the newly allied Colonies, chastise these "perfidious friends and secret enemies." It listed an impressive score for Britain to settle with:

The barbarous and forgetful Russians; . . . the odious and black ingratitude of the unprincipled Maria Theresa; the shuffling and indecisive conduct of the roving Dane; the mercantile tricks and shameful chicanery of the wily Dutchman; the impudence of the pensioned

---

[41] *Morning Chronicle,* October 15, 1778.
[42] *Morning Post,* March 27, May 31, 1779; *Gazetteer,* July 7.
[43] *Gazetteer,* January 13, 1780.
[44] *Town and Country,* April, 1780, 218. Cf. *Morning Chronicle,* April 22.
[45] *Gazetteer,* August 15, 1780.

and faithless Swede; and the assumed importance and upstart arrogance of all the petty Italian states. . . .[46]

Only insignificant Portugal could be counted upon as a friend, it concluded. And John Almon, owner-editor of the *Evening Post* doubted even Portugal's friendship.[47]

The northern confederacy that now made almost all Europe a hostile camp was an invention of the Dutch States General, according to the *Gazetteer*, but the Tory *Morning Herald* labeled the alliance a product of French imagination.[48] Regardless of the source of the alliance, its success was beyond question, for England entered the year 1781 almost completely friendless and with an uncomfortable and ever-worsening shortage of naval stores.[49] Maria Theresa of Austria had banished all hope that perhaps she would be the answer to England's search for a Continental ally.[50] As the Opposition had predicted, Britain was now alone in a hostile world, reconciliation with America or a peace with the Bourbons being the obvious alternatives; and positive action on either course would have to await a change in the Ministry.[51]

Long after Catherine's inimical intent became clear, the North Government strove to appease Russian sentiment, hoping that St. Petersburg would reconsider and would renew the friendship St. James's so sorely desired. In April, 1781, Richard Oswald, a prominent merchant and a ministerial specialist in American affairs (he soon would be chosen to go to Paris to negotiate the peace with Franklin and the other American representatives), sent to Henry Dundas, Viscount Melville, his nineteen-page "Plan for an alliance with Russia, in order to carry on the American War." Oswald proposed that 5,000 or 6,000 Russian troops garrison New York so that the English force there could be withdrawn and sent to Nicaragua, to disrupt the Spanish

---

46 *Gazetteer*, July 10, 1780. See also *Morning Herald*, January 2, 1781: "That Portugal is our friend there cannot be a doubt."

47 John Almon, *The Remembrancer, 1775-1784*, 304-5, "Extract of a letter from Lisbon." See also *Morning Chronicle*, November 25, 1777, for an earlier fear that Portugal would join the Bourbon family compact.

48 *Morning Herald*, December 27, 1780.

49 *Kentish Gazette*, January 3, 1781.

50 The *Morning Chronicle*, February 22, 1781, reported there was no truth to the rumor of an English-Austrian alliance leveling a combined attack against The Netherlands. The *Morning Herald*, January 2, 1781, had given some credence to this rumor. See also *Gazetteer*, April 8, 1779, for an earlier affirmation that the Austrians favored the Americans, while their Emperor supposedly retorted, "I am by trade a Royalist," and hence opposed to the republican rebels.

51 *Public Advertiser*, March 10, 1781. See also August 12, 1780.

Empire in South America. He was not clear, however, about what, precisely, the Russians were to gain from this agreement.[52] Oswald's suggestion, was, of course, neglected. Nevertheless, it demonstrated that sources close to the Government believed as did the press: Sir James Harris, the British Minister at St. Petersburg, who was both a Whig and a close friend of Charles James Fox, had gained the friendship and respect of Catherine II. Further, British warships had scrupulously respected their orders not to interfere with Russian shipping, lest Catherine find additional fault with England. Surely Russia would reconsider.

To further appease Russian sentiment, in July the Court of King's Bench sentenced Joseph Cooper of the *Courant* to twelve months in prison, one hour in the pillory, and a fine of £100 for accusing Ivan Simolin, the Ambassador from Russia, of stockjobbing. Vincent Trehearn, printer of the ephemeral *Noon Gazette*, defended the charges in his paper and subsequently received eighteen months in prison and a fine of £100. James Barr, printer of the *Morning Herald*, received twelve months and was fined £100 for copying the libel, as did Mary Say, owner of the *Gazetteer*, who received six months and a £50 fine. In November, John Miller, Almon's printer for the *Courant* and *Evening Post*, was sent to prison for a year on the same charges. The publisher of the *Whitehall Evening Post* and the printer of the *Middlesex Journal* also were imprisoned for a year and fined £100. After apologizing for indiscreetly copying the offensive article, the printer of the *St. James's Chronicle* was fined but not imprisoned.[53] Worse slanders against the English King had gone unprosecuted, and it was understood that these harsh sentences were handed down more to mollify the sensitivities of the Ambassador from Russia than to enforce the much-neglected libel laws.

The loyal *Morning Herald*, its own printer imprisoned, joined with the Opposition in condemning the entire proceeding. It maintained that the convicted men were ignorant of the "accidental insertion" of the libel and that the anonymous author of the comment was the real culprit. Thus, the publishers were "surely objects of pity and compassion."[54] Because most newspaper contributions were clothed in anonymity, the courts could not

[52] Oswald Papers (Clements), April 12, 1781.

[53] *Morning Herald*, July 6, 1781; Lucyle Werkmeister, *The London Daily Press, 1772-1792*, 413.

[54] *Morning Herald*, July 6, 17, 1781.

accept so broad an interpretation, which might easily lead to complete irresponsibility. The editor or a publisher of a paper was held responsible for all that appeared in his publication, and this rarely applied rule had been applied with severity in this case. The incarceration of a half dozen newspaper publishers (all of whom save one opposed the Ministry), along with a show of British good conduct in northern waters, did nothing, it is interesting to note, to change Russia's attitude toward the agreement of Armed Neutrality.

Occasional reports that hinted at the commencement of negotiations with the Russians and their northern allies reflected only a pious wish on the part of some elements of the British press.[55] In addition, there was no doubt that Armed Neutrality was becoming increasingly destructive to the shipping interests of the Empire. The solid front of northern powers that had allied themselves to the House of Bourbon was reason enough for the gloom John Bull found in his newspapers in the autumn of 1781.

With almost all of Europe their enemy, Englishmen could take a little comfort in the belief that some of these enemies might be brought to such a weakened condition that, regardless of the war's outcome, they would have been heavily punished for their differences with England.[56] The nation that would probably suffer most severely in this war was Spain. Its mercantile classes, without any possibility of advantage accruing to them, were being crushed under the weight of taxes and restraints. Spanish commerce, enfeebled by the war with England almost at its outset, was in such straits that Madrid eventually would have to sue for peace "on any terms."[57] Spain's Treasury, believed an accurate barometer of her foreign policy, was "a pennyless pocket" that could not afford to continue the war even if Spanish hearts wanted to do so.[58] Added to these seemingly insuperable financial difficulties was the news that her Latin-American provinces had emulated the insurrection of their northern neighbors. The uprisings in Peru prompted the *Gazetteer* to offer thanks for the "interposition of that Providence who guides and disposes all human events

[55] *Courant*, October 1, 1781.

[56] The *Edinburgh Evening Courant*, August 13, 1781, comforted its readers by informing them that, should England lose, all of Europe would suffer, because this defeat would permanently upset the Continent's delicate balance of power.

[57] *Morning Chronicle*, January 13, 1780; *Gazetteer*, January 14; *Morning Post*, February 21; *Lloyd's Evening Post*, June 30.

[58] *Lloyd's Evening Post*, September 20, 1780; *Morning Chronicle*, September 21, 1780.

for good and wise purposes."[59] The Spaniards had abetted the North Americans in their rebellion, so surely they could not find fault with the South Americans. Further, Britain could now avenge herself by encouraging the new insurrectionists. The vision of a post-war climate in which many small, independent Latin-American republics would operate within a system of free trade and commerce was pleasing to English merchants and manufacturers.[60]

While the *Morning Post* prematurely congratulated its countrymen on the "commotions" in Spanish America, most English newspapers assumed that Madrid, mortified by its own colonial troubles, would not want to lose face by suing for a separate peace.[61] However seriously debilitated, Spain would remain in the war, hoping at least to salvage Gibraltar. She had besieged the fortress with so many men and ships[62] that Englishmen assumed their garrison would be forced to capitulate when its supplies were exhausted. An Englishman might be starved out by a Spaniard, but he could never be defeated by one on the field of honor! Of this all British publications were certain. When news arrived that the "pusillanimous and weak" Spaniards had failed to capture the fortress, despite their overwhelming numbers, the press joyously compared the Bourbons' attack to an adventure of Don Quixote. The *Morning Chronicle*, deriding the enemy's bungled military and naval efforts, reported that the failure had already cost Madrid "more than would have subdued a whole province."[63] The same story obtained in other corners of the globe —Spain had expended much and accomplished little. It was welcome news for Englishmen to read that the Iberian star had declined and that Britain, unaided and undaunted, happily deserved much of the credit.

France, too, could at best expect a Pyrrhic victory. Her alliance with Madrid was believed so heavily strained that some London editors expected her to take the initiative in suing for a separate

[59] *Gazetteer*, September 29, 1780. The *Morning Chronicle*, October 5, saw the uprisings in both North and South America as a part of a world-wide movement of "people who are held in slavish subjection" to emancipate themselves.

[60] *Lloyd's Evening Post*, October 30, 1780, "Xenophon." The *Hampshire Chronicle*, October 1, 1781, was pleased at the prospect of Britain's soon possessing "all of the advantages which our enemies have long availed themselves of in the North."

[61] *Evening Post*, October 17, 1780; *Gazetteer*, October 20.

[62] *Chronicle*, May 2, 1780.

[63] *Morning Chronicle*, July 31, 1781.

peace.[64] Further, the loyal press stressed the difficulties that had allegedly risen between the French and American troops in North America. "They most inveterately hate, and cordially despise each other," the *Morning Herald* affirmed.[65] So much "ill blood" had passed between General Rochambeau and General Washington, incorrectly asserted another loyal journal, that the French Commander had been recalled to Versailles.[66] In addition, although France's economy appeared to be more prosperous than that of Spain (it could hardly be worse), it was thought to be as poor as England's.[67]

Thus was England, though overwhelmingly outnumbered, able to withstand most of Europe. "This country owes its safety to its enemies," summed up the *Courant*, as it expressed thanks that the weakness of England's councils was counterbalanced by equally weak councils directing the operations of the Bourbons.[68] Just as Britain was losing the war in America, her European foes were losing their greatest opportunity to crush her. How much of the credit for the loss of this opportunity belonged to Englishmen and their government and how much of it belonged to their disorganized enemies, was not resolved by most publications.

64 *Gazetteer,* March 7, October 20, 1780; *Morning Post,* March 14; *Morning Chronicle,* September 26. See also *Morning Herald,* April 16, 1781; *Public Advertiser,* July 4, 1781.

65 *Morning Herald,* September 20, 1781.

66 *Lloyd's Evening Post,* June 29, 1781. See also December 31, 1778; December 4, 11, 1780; March 2, July 2, 1781. Cf. *Courant,* February 15, 1781: "Accounts received in France from New England say, that the French and American troops live together in the greatest harmony, and are in want of nothing."

67 *Lloyd's Evening Post,* August 24, 1781.

68 *Courant,* March 28, 1781.

CHAPTER XIII

Yorktown: Britain Reappraises Her American Policy

B Y MID-1781 Englishmen thought that at last their armies in America were well led. Although General Henry Clinton was considered a capable commander, his second, Earl Cornwallis, was singled out for most praise by British publications. The *Public Advertiser* noted that if Sir Henry was not so great a favorite with the public as he used to be, his eclipse resulted not from any diminution of his fame, but rather from the predominance of Lord Cornwallis, "by which Sir Harry is overlaid."[1] While Clinton's war in the vicinity of New York continued "in its usual dormant state," in the south Cornwallis "fights away and beats his Enemies, be they few or many," stated this Opposition newspaper, lamenting the fact that "so brave a man should be obliged to act in a subordinate station, when he shews himself so very worthy of the first."[2] Few other papers demanded, or even suggested, Cornwallis' promotion over Clinton. The press was reporting the greatest harmony between Britain's army commanders in America, and it was thought unwise to risk disturbing this happy situation.[3]

[1] *Public Advertiser,* June 7, 1781.
[2] *Public Advertiser,* June 19, 1781. See also *Morning Herald,* January 16, 1781, attacking Clinton's inaction. Cornwallis did hold a dormant commission that would have permitted him to succeed Clinton.
[3] *Lloyd's Evening Post,* October 20, 1780.

Unhappily, however, an occasional press report stressed that the same harmony could not be said to exist between Clinton and Britain's naval commanders. Clinton detested Admiral Marriot Arbuthnot,[4] with whom he shared the credit for the capture of Charleston and with whom he presently would refuse to serve. Perhaps this Clinton-naval rivalry (he had not gotten along well, either, with Sir Peter Parker, Arbuthnot's predecessor) helped convince the press that Cornwallis was far superior to his quarrelsome commander. Further, London read that, compared to Howe, Cornwallis was superb: He had marched his army in South Carolina one hundred twenty miles in less than four days, while Howe, under similar conditions in New York a few years earlier, could manage to move his men only eighteen miles in sixteen days.[5] The *Westminster Magazine* (which printed an engraved likeness of the Earl as part of a featured biographical account), while employing the standard encomiums of *bravery* and *integrity*, stressed that Cornwallis displayed all of the qualities necessary for intelligent and intrepid leadership.[6] The *Public Advertiser* quoted foreign sources to document its argument that Cornwallis' personal regiment was the best-trained infantry in the British service,[7] and this Opposition newspaper presently cited Shakespeare in its praise:

> The man commands
> Like a Full soldier.[8]

Unfortunately, the war in America had reached such proportions that it could not be won by an intrepid commander and his exceptional regiment.

At the same time the press was expressing admiration for Cornwallis, it was also warning of the approach of possible military disaster in his area. Seemingly alone and unable to make contact with other British units, the Earl could conceivably be trapped by General Greene, whose "unremitting courage and assiduity" appeared to be bringing about a situation that forced the *Courant* to compare Cornwallis' plight with that of Burgoyne three years earlier.[9] The *Gazetteer* also sensed His Lordship's difficult posi-

---

4 *Courant*, September 30, 1780.

5 *Chronicle*, October 19, 1780, "Aristides."

6 *Westminster Magazine*, January, 1781, 5-6. See also *Salisbury and Winchester Journal*, November 12.

7 *Public Advertiser*, May 15, 1781.

8 *Public Advertiser*, August 22, 1781.

9 *Courant*, April 5, 1781.

tion. Affirming that the plan to conquer America had collapsed, it declared that "a great, spirited, and gallant officer" was to be offered up as a scapegoat to expiate the "blunders, folly and madness" of a Ministry that continued to believe America could be unconditionally subdued.[10]

Cornwallis was indeed in serious trouble. He had marched north into Virginia hoping to crush all opposition, but he had at the same time exposed his army to possible defeat. If the French fleet blocked Chesapeake Bay and prevented the arrival of reinforcements from New York or from England, the garrison in Virginia could hold out only while its supplies lasted,[11] and this could not be for long. Aid from Clinton at New York clearly was not forthcoming. Washington's feint, before hurrying south, was so successful that some newspapers predicted the fatal battle would commence shortly in New York.[12] A few editors deduced that the Americans were marching south in order to retake Charleston,[13] but it soon became apparent that they were heading for Virginia[14]—and America's Armageddon would take place upon the peninsula between the York and the James rivers. The French navy had successfully bottled up the Chesapeake,[15] and Cornwallis found himself in the midst of such difficulties that it would not be reasonable for Englishmen "to expect from the bravest of men, what is beyond the power of mortal endowments."[16] The anxiety for Yorktown's safety, which the press mirrored weeks before news of the surrender arrived in London, and the Tory press's discussion of the political and military consequences that would follow "if the brave Cornwallis should be Burgoyn'd,"[17] clearly demonstrated that the British public was prepared for the worst.[18]

[10] *Gazetteer,* May 21, 1781.

[11] *Public Advertiser,* June 5, 1781; *Kentish Gazette,* September 5.

[12] *Courant,* September 14, 1781; *Kentish Gazette,* September 22.

[13] *St. James's Chronicle,* September 29, 1781.

[14] *Public Advertiser,* November 8, 1781.

[15] *St. James's Chronicle,* October 16, 1781; *Public Advertiser,* October 20, 24; *Gazetteer,* November 2.

[16] *Courant,* October 24, 1781.

[17] *Kentish Gazette,* October 24, 1781. The *Morning Herald,* October 27, asserted that the "Minden Hero" (Germain) was to blame, should Britain be defeated in America.

[18] *Public Advertiser,* October 24, 1781. Cf. *Edinburgh Evening Courant,* October 24, 27, stressing that the Yorktown forces were in a strong position and that the Ministry was confident of its safety. See also *St. James's Chronicle,* October 18, 20.

By autumn of 1781 there was no doubt that England was on the defensive in the Colonies.[19] Even the *Morning Herald* began to lose its customary optimism. On November 1 it asserted that the 2,300 French troops that, it estimated, had recently landed in the Chesapeake area were too negligible a force to turn the tide of battle; by November 5 it had raised its estimate to a slightly more respectable 2,900; three days later it admitted that "the present seems to be the most critical moment that has occurred during the course of the American war." It never mentioned that there was at least twice the number of French troops in Virginia as any of its earlier estimates had indicated. This loyal publication recognized that, if the French blockade was not immediately broken, Cornwallis would be compelled to capitulate.[20] It was imperative that the Royal Navy, or at least Clinton, who had erred in not impeding Washington's southward march through the Jerseys,[21] would have to hurry to Cornwallis' rescue, or all would be lost. The *Morning Herald* had finally come to the conclusion the other London publications had reached weeks before. Should reinforcements fail, the only hope the paper offered its readers was the slight one that perhaps the frosts, which were soon due in Virginia, would force the French to withdraw to winter quarters, thus affording England a chance to get Cornwallis off the peninsula, or, better still, to negotiate some sort of peace with the Americans before spring.[22]

Englishmen and Americans sensed that upon the Yorktown peninsula hung the fate of much more than the possession of a colony or the defeat of an army. Defeat, or even a draw, declared the *Public Advertiser*, would indicate that there was but little hope of ever reducing the Americans to obedience by force of arms. "We are already too exhausted to prolong the contest much longer," it noted.[23] It was believed, too, that if America should be surrendered to the rebels, Washington would then transfer

19 *Salisbury and Winchester Journal*, October 29, 1781; *Morning Chronicle*, November 18.

20 *Morning Herald*, November 8, 1781.

21 *Morning Herald*, November 10, 1781. But on November 15, it claimed Cornwallis' situation was not that desperate and that it was possible for Clinton to reinforce him without attempting to force his way up the Chesapeake. See also *Gazetteer*, same date, for the same article.

22 *Morning Herald*, November 13, 1781. See also *Lloyd's Evening Post*, November 12; *Derby Mercury*, November 15; *Edinburgh Evening Courant*, November 21.

23 *Public Advertiser*, November 23, 1781; *Courant*, November 5.

his armies to the West Indies to support his French allies.[24] Surely, if the American Commander could force the British to yield in North America, he could do so in the West Indies.[25] The same reasoning was applied also to England's Canadian outposts. If Clinton and a defeated Cornwallis left the Colonies, Canada and Nova Scotia would be at the mercy of the Americans.[26]

There was no hope of negotiating peace before the decisive battle was fought. The Ministry's opportunity to withdraw from America had long since passed. Perhaps, years before, Britain should have invaded South America rather than dissipate her strength against her own colonists.[27] Speculation as to what might have been seemed all that was left for the press. No honorable roads of retreat remained. Britain would make her stand and probably be defeated at Yorktown. The "crimson coloured curtain" would soon drop on the "dreadful TRAGEDY we have been acting in America,"[28] concluded the *Courant*.

On November 23, 1781, rumor of Cornwallis' surrender reached England. By November 26, when almost all publications carried copies of the articles of capitulation, it was painfully confirmed. Although earlier admitting the possibility of defeat, Englishmen now found the news almost impossible to accept.[29] By November 27 a general disgust with the entire American affair was reflected in almost every Opposition and neutral publication in Britain.

To aggravate matters further, Parliament was to reconvene on the day following the arrival of the news from Yorktown. Despite the "spirit of undaunted heroism" that the Tories expected their sovereign to display when he demanded a continuation of the war in his speech from the throne,[30] the loyal editors joined with the others in predicting that a change in ministers presently would take place, with the new Government committed to a program of peace with the Colonies and of war with the Bourbons. The political powers of George III had been so weakened by the disaster in America that even the *Morning Herald* ex-

---

[24] *Kentish Gazette,* November 3, 1781.

[25] *Hampshire Chronicle,* November 12, 1781.

[26] *Public Advertiser,* November 16, 1781.

[27] *Public Advertiser,* November 16, 1781.

[28] *Courant,* November 16, 1781.

[29] *Morning Herald,* November 26, 1781; *Morning Chronicle,* November 27.

[30] *Morning Herald,* November 26, 1781. See also *Kentish Gazette,* December 5, reporting that the King was resolved to pursue the American war "with redoubled vigour."

pressed doubt that Lord North and Lord Germain could remain in office much longer.[31]

The paper made no mention of the future of Lord Sandwich, the First Lord of the Admiralty. Considering that he was one of the sponsors of the *Morning Herald*, perhaps silence was its wisest course. While adding an occasional good word for Sandwich, Bate's new paper regularly demanded that Germain be replaced as Secretary for American Affairs.[32] The *Morning Post*, however, blamed Sandwich for the "complicated disasters" that befell Britain at Yorktown, and on December 21 it held out "a ray of hope" that at last Sandwich would be removed. The Opposition press, however, now in its strongest position since the outbreak of hostilities in America, decreed the removal of the entire Ministry as the first step toward peace negotiations with the colonists. How much influence the press's opinions would have inside the halls of Parliament was questionable, but it was believed, both in Parliament and the press, that the Ministry, already having trouble maintaining its majority in the Commons, presently would fall,[33] and the Opposition in both Parliament and the press would at last be vindicated.

Neither political faction blamed Cornwallis for his defeat. Even in surrender he had added "distinguished lustre to the name of Briton."[34] The *Gazetteer* even went so far as to clear Burgoyne of any blame at Saratoga, since "the surrender of the brave Lord Cornwallis is a sufficient evidence, that the greatest courage, similarly situated, must act alike."[35]

General Clinton received most of the blame for Yorktown, from all quarters of the press. He not only had allowed Washington to march past him through the Jerseys, but he had also refused to reinforce Cornwallis, and the latter was now justified in criticizing his superior officer. After excoriating Clinton, the *Kentish Gazette* commented that "never sure was a nation so ill served by its commanders."[36] Other editors were certain that Yorktown, like Saratoga four years before, was not lost on the field but,

31 *Morning Herald*, November 27, December 4, 1781; *Lloyd's Evening Post*, November 28.

32 *Morning Herald*, November 27, 30, December 6, 7, 8, 1781, January 8, 15, 17, 1782.

33 Lewis B. Namier, *Personalities and Powers*, 30, 76.

34 *Lloyd's Evening Post*, December 19, 1781.

35 *Gazetteer*, November 27, 1781; *Derby Mercury*, November 22.

36 *Kentish Gazette*, November 28, December 1, 1781; *Edinburgh Evening Courant*, December 12.

rather, in London's American office by a bungling minister,[37] while some placed the blame on the Royal Navy and mocked the old boast that "wherever a British soldier saw the sea he was safe." But the foremost reason for this latest defeat, the press was convinced, was that Sir Henry Clinton was outgeneraled by Washington. The American's thrust at New York so deluded him, reported the *Morning Herald*, that Sir Henry had the temerity to write the "gallant and unsupported" Cornwallis for a loan of 2,000 troops to help protect his army of 20,000 from the threatened attack of Washington and his 7,000 men![38]

Washington, the loyal press conceded, should receive a large share of the credit for the British defeat—but never so much as Sir Henry. The American Commander was thoroughly respected for his generalship in misleading Clinton and in forcing Cornwallis' surrender, and when news reached London that he had treated the captured Earl with all the honor and dignity due a gallant soldier, Washington was saluted for being a most admirable and considerate gentleman.[39]

Just as the battle at Saratoga had been refought in the press for three years, so now Englishmen would read and discuss why defeat had been inflicted upon their army's most competent commander. Scores of official and semiofficial inquiries were forthcoming,[40] and both Clinton and Cornwallis received a full hearing in the press. But the editors did not change their earlier position: Sir Henry was to blame. Although "Fabricus," one of the most prominent letter writers of the time, in a series of essays that appeared in both the *Chronicle* and the *Morning Chronicle*, attacked Cornwallis for keeping his army "inactive and idle in an unprepared and unfortified post, while a formidable force sufficient to overwhelm it was collecting,"[41] the Earl did not lack defenders. His popularity was such that, upon his return to Exeter, the citizens lionized him and carried him upon their shoulders.[42]

Englishmen wanted to forget Yorktown and the war in America.

[37] *Salisbury and Winchester Journal*, December 3, 1781.
[38] *Morning Herald*, December 4, 1781.
[39] *Lloyd's Evening Post*, December 28, 1781; *Morning Herald*, January 2, 1782. Cf. the *Edinburgh Evening Courant's* earlier fear, stated on December 3, 1781, that the Americans would execute Cornwallis' entire captured army.
[40] *Hampshire Chronicle*, December 31, 1781. *Morning Chronicle*, January 2, 1782.
[41] *Chronicle, Morning Chronicle*, January 22, 1782. Cf. *Chronicle*, March 19, 1781. See also *Packet*, January 4, 1782, for a defense of Clinton's position.
[42] *Morning Herald*, January 25, 1782. On March 9, it added that the majority of loyalists in America still admired Cornwallis.

By February 23, 1782, even "Fabricus" admitted that national apathy had reached such proportions that nobody seemed to care about the war in America any more. The wounds that time had begun to heal were reopened, nevertheless, with the publication in early 1783 of Sir Henry Clinton's famous *Narrative*. Clinton's claim that he disapproved of Cornwallis' taking possession of the ports of York and Gloucester while "undertaking operations in the Chesapeak, without having a naval superiority," was viewed by *Gentleman's Magazine* as an unsuccessful attempt by Sir Henry to defend his actions. Brushing aside the charges that most of England's misfortunes in America could be blamed upon the poor judgment of Cornwallis, it concluded that the impartial reader "will hardly think that Sir Henry Clinton has exculpated himself from directing the Earl to take post at York and Gloucester."[43] The same issue in which the *Narrative* was reviewed also presented Cornwallis' reply. It was quite clear where *Gentleman's Magazine* stood. It stated that the Earl had made as gallant a defense with the quill as he had with the sword in America, with but one material difference: Cornwallis "was there obliged to surrender an indefensible post to the far superior forces of his enemies, but in this entrenchment, we think, he has been able to repulse the warm attacks of his commander-in-chief." However, it stressed that it did not necessarily follow that Sir Henry was to blame for the defeat in America. Pointing out that the lack of naval cooperation given Cornwallis reminded it of a comment from Shakespeare's *Richard III*:

> —What do they in the North
> When they should serve their sovereign in the west?

Gentleman's Magazine added that the American loyalists, just as the Royal Navy, did not carry their fair share of the war burden. Of the varying reasons suggested for the defeat at Yorktown, it voiced the overwhelming sentiment of the British press when it concluded that the analysis by Cornwallis was much closer to the truth than the narrative of his former commander.[44] Further,

[43] *Gentleman's Magazine*, February, 1783, 147.

[44] *Gentleman's Magazine*, February, 1783, 155. For a detailed analysis of the Clinton-Cornwallis feud, see *The Campaign in Virginia, 1781: An Exact Reprint of Six Rare Pamphlets on the Clinton-Cornwallis Controversy* . . . , Benjamin F. Stevens, ed., and William B. Willcox, "The British Road to Yorktown: A Study in Divided Command," *American Historical Review*, 52 (October, 1946), 1-35.

returning French officers who had served at Yorktown likewise vindicated the Earl, reported the loyal *Morning Post*.[45]

It was a bitter irony of war that Cornwallis in defeat received better treatment at the hands of his compatriots than did Sir Guy Carleton, who, against overwhelming odds, saved Canada for the British Empire.[46]

Notwithstanding the vindication given the British Commander at Yorktown, the results of the surrender made it clear to Englishmen that the war in America was almost at its end. Although there were still as many British troops in the Colonies as were in the commands of Washington and Rochambeau, the English home front assumed it was necessary for the Ministry to abandon at least the land portion of the war. The shift of military as well as naval forces from an American to a French orientation "was the only means left for a renovation of our glory," affirmed the *St. James's Chronicle*.[47] Few wished to end the war with the Bourbons, for any peace drawn in late 1781 would of necessity have been an ignominious one. Upon the high seas, "our proper element," Englishmen could yet aspire to victory. "But from CONTINENTAL WARS, at *three thousand* miles distance, England prays, in one united voice, GOOD LORD *deliver us!*" exclaimed the *Gazetteer*.[48] The *Morning Herald*, speaking for people "high in ministerial circles," reiterated that the land portion of the American war certainly would be abandoned. "A naval system only" would be used against America, predicted the newspaper that reflected the Sandwich interest in the London press.[49]

By late 1781 Englishmen had become convinced, however reluctantly, that the position of the Opposition press for the past six years had been correct: The thirteen diverse American colonies could never be conquered; after expending a fortune in lives and money, England should revert to a limited naval war or completely abandon the struggle and accept the fact that the Colonies had made themselves a free and independent nation.

[45] *Morning Post*, July 8, 1783.
[46] *Public Advertiser*, February 22, 1782.
[47] *St. James's Chronicle*, November 29, 1781.
[48] *Gazetteer*, December 5, 1781.
[49] *Morning Herald*, December 4, 1781.

CHAPTER XIV

The End of the North Ministry and the Coming of Peace

WHEN IT WAS GENERALLY ACKNOWLEDGED, late in 1781, that the Americans would never return to their former status as colonists, Englishmen considered the terms of peace that would eventually have to be negotiated with the Congress. Surely the Americans had earned the right to a large share in their government, if not complete independence.[1] So long as the North ministry held sway in Parliament, however, the desired peace could not come to pass. While the American affair had totally failed in its hands, the Ministry's ability to carry all votes in Parliament —in spite of acknowledged division in its councils and lack of public confidence—was a strange political phenomenon, even to the Tories.[2] Unmindful of the "welfare and prosperity of Britain" and uncompromising in their desire to continue the American war, the ministers of George III were indeed out of step with the rest of the nation.[3]

The defeat at Yorktown gave rise to demands for changes in the Administration, especially in the American and Admiralty departments. Too widespread to be ignored, the demands gradually won many parliamentary fence-sitters over to the Opposi-

[1] *St. James's Chronicle,* November 6, 1781.
[2] *Lloyd's Evening Post,* December 14, 1781. See *Courant,* January 5, 1782.
[3] *Hampshire Chronicle,* December 3, 1781.

tion.[4] As the Ministry's majority lessened, Opposition editors proclaimed that each vote was a warning to the Ministry of its imminent downfall.[5] The inescapable fact that America was lost stripped the North Government of some of its most ardent country supporters. Most gentlemen conceded the impossibility of replacing the troops lost at Yorktown, even if Parliament had the desire to replace them. Soon it was common knowledge in the press that "the contest for independency" was ended.[6] Notwithstanding the *Morning Herald*'s recollection of the Gordon riots and its warning that freedom granted to America could give "the majesty of the British mob" some dangerous ideas that could well shake the British constitution,[7] most of the press agreed that there was little choice left. Cornwallis, long before his defeat, had repeatedly declared that the conquest of America was impracticable.[8] The Ministry had refused to believe him, and total defeat was the result. One Opposition newspaper concluded that the Americans deserved their liberty: "They have fought nobly for it, and have gained it. Long may they preserve it, unviolated by faction or ambition."[9]

By the beginning of 1782 the fall of the North ministry and the end of the war in America were understood to be a single issue. Britain could not have one without the other. Increasingly, petitions appeared at Court and in the press, imploring the King to dismiss those who advised the forceful reduction of "our brethren in America to obedience by force; a plan, which the fatal experiences of past losses has convinced us cannot be prosecuted."[10] The *Courant* reported that this growing pressure so divided the Administration that its meetings were "something similar to the confusion of tongues of the Tower of Babel." Certainly, George III no longer was consulting Sandwich or Germain upon any business of consequence.[11] One caustic critic of King and Ministry suggested that for the new year George and his advisers be presented with copies of *The History of Athens During The Peloponnesian War* and *The Dialogues of the Dead,*

[4] *Public Advertiser, Morning Herald,* December 15, 1781.
[5] *Gazetteer,* December 15, 1781.
[6] *Edinburgh Evening Courant,* December 10, 1781.
[7] *Morning Herald,* December 17, 1781.
[8] *Hampshire Chronicle,* December 17, 1781.
[9] *Courant,* December 26, 1781. Also quoted in *Noon Gazette,* same date.
[10] *Gentleman's Magazine,* December, 1781, 589.
[11] *Courant,* December 29, 1781.

studies that could remind Britain of the fate of Athens when it overextended its appetite for empire.[12]

On January 5, 1782, before Fox's inquiry into the conduct of the Board of Admiralty began, the *Morning Herald,* a newspaper founded by the Sandwich interests, confessed that two thirds of the public prints had already opened the "flood gates of abuse upon the Admiralty" so as to prejudice as much as possible those members of Parliament who were to decide the case. The Opposition's charges against Sandwich and his department were "groundless and sinister," it assured its readers, offering as proof the fact that the Earl, confident of exoneration, had personally called for a full and open inquiry, and "guilty men do not demand that light be shed upon their careers."[13]

Sandwich all but acknowledged the failure of the Administration's American plan, and he shifted the blame to Germain's department. Fox's motion succeeded in bringing the Sandwich-Germain feud into the open, and when the *Morning Herald* relentlessly attacked Germain because his promises to subjugate America proved to be "mere puffs," the Ministry's Tower of Babel was publicly exposed. Germain had no champion in the press. Aside from an occasional pamphlet penned by William Knox or Israel Mauduit, the Secretary did nothing to defend his department. The Secret Service funds that other ministers paid to Bate or Macpherson or to countless other penmen Germain considered perquisites of office, and the press therefore yielded up no defense of his policies in America. The King was probably the only man of importance in England to stand by his harassed minister, but the loyal press must have known that George III was quite prepared to abandon him if it could be done without demonstrating a change of policy. When pressure to remove Germain caused George III reluctantly to make him a viscount (the King believed the title, "Baronet," would have been sufficient), the *Morning Herald* reflected not only the opinion of Sandwich but the opinions of the vast majority of the members of the House of Lords when it exclaimed in a horrified tone that "[he] who has been haunted out of the Lower House like an *obnoxious Cur,*" had now

---

12 *Morning Chronicle,* January 1, 1782, "Misanthrope."
13 *Morning Herald,* January 5, 26, 28, 1782.

found asylum from his persecutions "in that *less scrupulous sanctuary—the Chamber of British Peers!*"[14]

With Germain gone from the American Department, some hope remained that perhaps something of the war in the Colonies could yet be salvaged. Carleton, the capable hero of Quebec, was spoken of as the next commander in America. Always uncomfortable while serving under Germain (he had disliked the American Secretary ever since Minden, and he had further aggravated Germain by his friendship with the Opposition-oriented Duke of Richmond; Germain had taken his revenge by passing over Carleton whenever a major command in America was in the offing), Carleton could now—with additional volunteers from the depressed manufacturing towns of England and the Highlands of Scotland—save the day.[15] However, it was generally agreed that it was far too late to salvage much on the field of battle.[16] Some sort of federal system—perhaps even a new national Parliament, to be comprised of elements from England, Ireland, and America —was offered as one solution.[17] The suggestion made by Benedict Arnold that a new commander in America and 16,000 fresh troops could still subjugate the colonists was dismissed without serious consideration by the press, for Arnold was suspect, and neither side wished to place firm confidence in him.[18]

Seven years of war had been enough. The reaction was so great that *Gentleman's Magazine* apologized to the pro-American and heretofore regularly maligned Josiah Tucker, Dean of Gloucester, with the declaration that, had the Dean's earlier advice that America be allowed to go in peace been followed, America indeed would have been independent, but "she would have been our ally and friend, and many thousands of lives and millions of money, would have been saved to both nations."[19]

14 *Morning Herald,* January 17, February 11, 12, 1782. See also *Packet,* January 21, for rumors of Germain's resignation. For the opposition in the House of Lords to the creation of the new Viscount Sackville, see Hansard, *Parliamentary History of England,* 1782, XXII, 1003-21.

15 *Chronicle,* February 19, 1782, "Fabricus." See also *Packet,* February 18, for a report that the Ministry was determined to continue the American war.

16 *Kentish Gazette, Packet,* January 26, 1782.

17 *St. James's Chronicle,* January 10, 1782. See also *Chronicle,* February 16, March 22, and *Chelmsford Chronicle,* February 15, March 22, for mention of other plans of accommodation with America.

18 *Kentish Gazette,* January 30, 1782; *Courant,* January 28. See also *Derby Mercury,* November 29, 1781; *Salisbury and Winchester Journal,* December 3.

19 *Gentleman's Magazine,* February, 1782, 82-83. See *Lloyd's Evening Post,* April 26, 1780, for an account of one of Tucker's earlier unpopular suggestions for a general pacification.

The slim majority of 22 votes that the Ministry mustered against Fox's motion to censure the Admiralty was greeted by the Opposition as a sign that the Government could not last much longer.[20] London newspapers stepped up their attacks upon the Ministry to help speed the day of its downfall. "A nation must be sunk to a wretched state indeed, which can place a blind confidence in men whose administration has lost America," asserted one paper, as another reminded its countrymen that the public interest rate had risen to 11 per cent, while the private one was a prohibitive 15 per cent.[21] As far as the press was concerned, it was obvious how poor times were and how badly a change in the Government was needed. The *Packet* noted that the persistence of the rumor that Carleton would indeed take the field with 15,000 fresh troops, thus forcing Englishmen into another new round of taxes, steadily brought heretofore loyal country gentlemen over to the Opposition.[22]

On February 25, 1782, the *Morning Chronicle* devoted three of its four pages to a verbatim account of the Commons' debates on the motion of General Henry Seymour Conway for the end of offensive war in America. The motion was defeated by 1 vote (193-194), but it was evident that it would be reintroduced—and carried—in a few days. Lord North, whom the loyal *Morning Herald* admitted would "find the patriotic irons too hot on the American question," would be forced into an immediate resignation, and both peace with America and a new Ministry appeared in the offing.[23] On February 27, when the Conway motion was reintroduced, the *Courant*, wishing it well, noted that the subjugation of America had long appeared impracticable and that the only reason for continuing the war would be to continue enriching "a herd of contractors and commisaries," and the "wicked and profligate ministry."

As the session of Parliament dragged on past midnight and into the early hours of February 28, many of London's newspapers postponed going to press. When at 1:30 A.M. Parliament voted, 234-215, to discontinue offensive military actions in America, the loyal journals published the news with a notable absence of com-

---

[20] *Packet*, February 8, 1782. The vote was 217-236. See *Morning Chronicle*, February 21, for fuller details, and *Town and Country*, February, 107, for editorial comment.

[21] *Kentish Gazette*, February 16, 1782.

[22] *Packet*, February 22, 1782.

[23] *Morning Herald*, February 26, 1782.

ment.[24] The Opposition, led by William Parker's *General Advertiser*, made capital, however, of the long-awaited event. Using type four times larger than normal, Parker's columns screamed, "PEACE WITH AMERICA!" In double-sized type, all capitalized, he joyfully related that the Commons had returned to its senses, ended the American war, "and set England upon her legs again." As a consequence he predicted the greatest illuminations and rejoicing that the metropolis ever remembered.[25]

Taking seriously Lord North's promise to deliver up the seals of office to the King if the voice of the people was against him, the *General Advertiser* predicted the First Minister's immediate resignation and the dissolution of his Ministry. It then reported how the multitudes that waited in the halls of Parliament "hailed and embraced as saviours of their country" those "noble and distinguished" leaders of the Opposition who, "by their steady perseverance and zeal, had overcome and broke into pieces the ruinous system of Ministers."[26] As its *coup de grâce* to the loyal press, it concluded its "victory issue" by remarking that the Ministry, as its last token of gratitude, had ordered suits of mourning for the editors of the *Morning Chronicle, Morning Herald,* and *Morning Post* "for their many *eminent* services in support of scandal, injustice, and oppression."

George III may well have wished to continue the struggle in America, but he was forced to see that both city merchant and country planter had had enough of war.[27] While most unhappy with Parliament's resolution of peace with America, he could (or would) do nothing to alter it. There would be peace, and the sovereign received little joy from reading that the next important motion to be introduced into the Commons would call for the resignation of his chosen lieutenants. The press judged this change to be the proper prelude to peace with America and victory in Europe, "which can only happen from unanimity at home, under an administration possessing the confidence of the public."[28]

While the *Courant* lashed out at the "filth and corruption" of the

24 *Morning Herald* and *Morning Chronicle,* February 28, 1782.

25 *General Advertiser,* February 28, 1782.

26 *General Advertiser,* February 28, 1782. See also *Westminster Magazine,* June, 1782, 297, and especially July, 241, for an attack upon the "meanness and disgrace" of the fallen Prime Minister and his Ministry.

27 *Courant,* March 15, 1782.

28 *Kentish Gazette,* March 9, 1782. See also *Packet,* March 1.

North ministry, the *Packet*, an equally staunch Opposition print, displayed greater concern over the apathy with which the populace submitted "to the accumulating misfortunes and heavy burthens which mal administration has brought upon this nation."[29] For the *Courant*, the moment of action was at last at hand. Reckoning an impressive list of grievances against the tottering Government, it insisted that the Ministry was to blame not only for involving Britain in the "complicated and disastrous war" that had cost her America, but also for the loss of the West Indian islands as well.[30] The time to remove it had long since arrived, and at last the requisite votes could be delivered.

Although George III and his supporters agreed to accept some changes in his Cabinet (the *Morning Chronicle* reported guardedly that "it may be adviseable to have a change of men and measures," while Henry Dundas was writing to John Robinson on the necessity of Sandwich swiftly following Germain out of the Cabinet),[31] the Opposition press maintained that only a completely new Administration, rather than a coalition dominated by the King, could regain the confidence of both nation and Parliament.[32] On March 6 the *Morning Post* reluctantly admitted that a total change of ministers was in the immediate offing.

When the vote of censure against the North ministry failed in the House of Commons on March 15 by only 9 votes, the large number of members daily coming over to the Opposition made it clear that, unless North resigned at once, the motion would be reintroduced and carried within a few days. Realizing the inevitability of censure, North handed over the seals on March 20. The joys of the Opposition knew no bounds.[33] Even the usually mild *Gazetteer* editorialized: "The news that we have *happily* got rid of a *servile minion* and an *headless Minister*, must give every real intelligent friend to his country the most heart-felt pleasure." Added to this was the *Gazetteer's* comforting opinion that Britain at last was to have an Administration both virtuous

---

[29] *Courant*, March 13, 1782; *Packet*, March 15.

[30] *Courant*, March 19, 1782.

[31] HMC, Abergavenny MSS, March 3, 1782, Dundas to Robinson. Dundas believed that a new coalition government should be based upon the principles of "an end to the American war, the best peace to be got, universal economy and a high-handed executive authority." See also *Morning Post*, March 11, predicting that Shelburne would replace Sandwich in the Admiralty office.

[32] *Morning Chronicle*, March 4, 1782; *Gazetteer*, March 20.

[33] *Morning Herald, Morning Chronicle*, March 21, 22, 1782. Cf. *General Advertiser, Courant*, same dates.

and able, led by two most reputable and experienced peers—Rockingham and Shelburne.[34]

With the fall of the North ministry, the *Morning Herald* took up its new position as London's semiofficial organ of dissent. On March 20 it condemned the "patriots" Fox, Burke, and Barré for craving the position of Prime Minister; on March 25 it eulogized North and his departed Ministry. But, uncomfortable in its new role, the *Morning Herald* rarely captured again the political verve it displayed when it so assiduously defended the actions of the North ministry in general and Lord Sandwich in particular.

Seldom in English history has a new Ministry been backed by so popular a mandate from all classes. The popularity of the new Government was nevertheless based upon wide dislike for the old rather than on genuine affection for the new. A provincial publication voiced a common thought when it expressed the hope that the new Ministry would be supported as unanimously as the old one was condemned.[35]

Just before the change was made, the *General Advertiser* asserted that the "great and weighty" problems awaiting the incoming Ministry dictated that this new Government be "the most powerful that ever was established in this country."[36] It then proceeded to make clear that Charles James Fox, "the darling, the delight of the people," was its candidate for Prime Minister. Dennis O'Bryen, Parker's new editor and Fox's new public relations man, had the *General Advertiser* grandly conclude that "it has long been universally allowed that Mr. Fox is by far the man of the greatest abilities this country has ever been blessed with."[37] Few other editors joined in this campaign for a First Minister. They all, however, were busily reporting the latest rumors concerning possible appointments.[38] Two days before North handed over the seals of office, the *Morning Post* came close to the mark when it predicted that North would be replaced by a Ministry that would include the Marquis of Rockingham as First Lord of the Treasury, Fox as Chancellor of the Exchequer,

---

34 *Gazetteer*, March 20, 21, 1782.
35 *Chelmsford Chronicle*, March 22, 1782.
36 *General Advertiser*, March 22, 1782. See also *Chronicle*, March 21.
37 *General Advertiser*, March 22, April 3, 1782.
38 *Morning Chronicle*, March 25, 1782, reported that the Bedford and Shelburne factions had the lead at this date.

Augustus Keppel as First Lord of the Admiralty, with important positions going to Richard Rigby (who had come over to the Opposition shortly after Yorktown), the Duke of Richmond, the Earl of Shelburne, Admiral Howe, and those three venerable hosts of parliamentary Opposition, Burke, Conway, and Barré. Only in the case of Rigby was the *Morning Post* woefully incorrect.

The move to set the new Government in motion soon followed, and the pace gave the press little additional time for speculation. On March 26, less than a week after North's resignation, the *Morning Herald* announced that Rockingham would become First Lord of the Treasury, and the official announcement of the accession of the Rockingham ministry was made the next day.

It took no time at all for the newspapers that formerly were in opposition to adjust to their new position as Ministry publications. The *Courant* made the first attack on the new minority press (which, indeed, now it was—in number, circulation, and political connection) when it commented upon the "very gloomy" appearance of the three Tory morning publications, the *Post*, *Herald*, and *Chronicle*.[39] The *Public Advertiser*, much more caustic in its treatment of the "degradation and disastrous Disgraces attending Lord North's Administration," used such epithets as "Miscreant," "the perverse ambition of dullness," and "the intellectual dregs of the people" to describe the outgoing Minister and his supporters. This newspaper evinced pleasure in reporting that the new Ministry was in all respects the reverse of the old, for the new combined property and talent rather than "unprinciple and a minister from the mob."[40] Parker may have admired Fox and the Americans, but he was no democrat.

The now loyal press stressed that the Rockingham Government would endeavor to put the British constitution back on its proper course by insisting that the King remain out of politics and "no longer labour under the imputation of being his own minister."[41] These were the conditions under which Rockingham had assented to the formation of a new Government, it declared. Further, all secret influence (what Burke referred to as the "Double Cabinet") was to be removed from the royal councils. Ministerial,

[39] *Courant,* March 26, April 6, 9, 10, 1782.
[40] *Public Advertiser,* March 28, 1782.
[41] *Chronicle,* March 28, 1782; *Gazetteer,* March 29.

not invisible, government once more was to prevail.[42] In addition, for a change, the incoming ministers were to be honest men, announced the *Chronicle*. When Burke and Barré, the new Paymaster of the Forces and Treasurer of the Navy, respectively, "very laudably" abridged their own emoluments of office, the *Chronicle* was quick to note that these actions were absolute portents of the honesty that could be expected from the Government.[43] "This country never saw before so many men of sound wisdom, political knowledge, and vigorous minds conducting her affairs," echoed the *Packet*. It later reported that the new Ministry consisted of "men of Herculean strength and ability."[44]

The Rockingham Government soon added to its large popular following. By reducing the civil list, attempting to placate Ireland, rejecting taxes upon soap and salt because they seemed harmful to the poor, and announcing that it would presently open peace negotiations with the Americans, the new Government convinced Englishmen that it was capable of swift and efficient action.[45] Most of England's editors wished these projects well.

Among the three major newspapers offering opposition to the Rockingham ministry, only William Woodfall's *Morning Chronicle* was to do it gracefully. Though believing Rockingham's policies were impractical, it conceded that the new Ministry had taken office with the good wishes and confidence of the people, and it concluded that "they merit and will have the prayers of all good men for their success."[46] The *Morning Herald*, however, could not accept its new role so well. Deducing that America would receive its independence and that Ireland, too, presently would achieve independence, it commented that peace would then be restored to "*Little* Britain," for it was of the opinion that the empire of Great Britain was gone forever.[47] It described the British constitution as standing crucified between the thieves of Jacobite principles on the right and republican principles on

[42] *Courant,* April 6, 1782.
[43] *Chronicle,* March 28, 1782.
[44] *Packet,* March 29, April 5, 12, 1782. See also *Town and Country,* March, 163.
[45] *Town and Country,* March, 1782, 163; April, 219; May, 274.
[46] *Morning Chronicle,* March 27, 1782. On May 6, it added that the new Ministry was so popular and was carrying out its program with such speed that it might "deeply wound the trunk and root" of the constitution while professing only to cut off the rotten branches. By June 8, the *Morning Herald* reported that "the popularity of the new ministry was like a feather." See also June 14, 18, 21, 24, for attacks upon the new Ministry.
[47] *Morning Herald,* April 1, 1782.

the left.[48] During the first week of April, each issue of the *Morning Post* virulently attacked the Rockingham ministry. By April 8 this newspaper was mockingly noting that radicals, such as John Wilkes and John Horne, were ministerialists.

In Wilkes's case, at least, the *Morning Post's* statement was half accurate. On April 2, 1782, Wilkes wrote to Rockingham to congratulate him on the formulation of his new Ministry. After wishing the First Minister every success, Wilkes asked to be appointed Receiver General of the Land Tax so that he could begin the reforms of the tax structure that he believed so necessary (he did not spell out precisely what reforms he had in mind).[49] Perhaps Rockingham did not live long enough to act upon this request, but more probably he did not consider the petitioner the man for the job. Wilkes and his radical colleagues in London had little in common with the more respectable elements of Whiggism from the country. The American war had, indeed, made strange bedfellows. Although it threw Wilkes into the arms of the Opposition leaders in Parliament, Rockingham was in no mood to embrace either Wilkes or the radical city press that supported him.

Despite Rockingham's coolness, the city press remained loyal to his Ministry. *Parker's General Advertiser* came to the defense of the new Government and its supporters by noting that the "wanton attacks on the new Ministry, in a profligate print," gave honor to the persons abused because of the source from which they emanated.[50] But while the *London Magazine* was saluting in verse "the blest change in the administration/ . . . Fox, Shelburne, and Burke claim our just veneration . . . ," it was also printing two full columns of bankrupts, listing over one hundred recent business failures.[51] A new Government was but the first of many steps necessary for the rebuilding and strengthening of Britain's precarious financial and political structure.

As the American war languished both in the field and on the seas, the *Courant* predicted that the Government would concentrate on the European struggle. Pending further political developments, the paper foresaw no fresh hostilities against the Ameri-

[48] *Morning Herald,* May 22, June 7, 1782.

[49] BM, Wilkes Correspondence, Add. MSS 30,872, Vol. 6, 190.

[50] *Parker's General Advertiser,* May 25, 1782. In May, Parker added his name to the title of the paper. See also June 28, for attacks by Parker upon the *Morning Herald* and the *Morning Post* "where almost every paragraph that appears is paid for by the infamous old Ministry."

[51] *London Magazine,* April, 1782, 168, 191-92.

cans.[52] The new policy was watchful waiting in America and watchful fighting in Europe. On May 13 *Parker's General Advertiser* and the *Morning Herald* reached a moment of rare agreement when they both supported the plan to prosecute vigorously the war against the French, Spanish, and Dutch.

It was hopefully reported that the Rockingham ministry sought to commence negotiations for a separate and "honourable peace" with Holland and the United States as a prelude to a decisive battle with the Bourbons. By April, 1782, London had discovered that the Dutch not only recognized American independence, but they refused to enter into any separate peace negotiations with the British.[53] With their independence now generally acknowledged,[54] the Americans could not be expected to sign alone. France would never allow her to do so, and the Congress was too deeply committed to Versailles to strike out on a separate path.[55] It was well understood in London that a final peace with America would have to be written as part of a general European treaty, which, it was hoped, would presently ensue.[56] While few wished an end to hostilities before France had been punished,[57] England's financial and military weaknesses dictated otherwise. In fact, wrote John, Earl of Stair, in the *Gentleman's Magazine*, given her present chaotic financial condition, no peace, short of absolute ruin, could be pronounced a bad one.[58]

If Amsterdam would not come to terms, it would have to be forced to the peace table by British arms. The news of a great victory over the Dutch in Ceylon encouraged a belief that Holland would now reconsider before losing more pearls from her sea of commerce.[59] But before Amsterdam or London could study the immediate results of this victory, reports of Rodney's stunning defeat of the French fleet under DeGrasse reached London. Al-

52 *Courant*, May 1, 1782.

53 *Courant*, April 19, May 1, 1782; *Packet*, April 12; *Morning Herald*, March 13.

54 The *Chronicle*, March 28, 1782, reported the abolition of the "secretary's Office for the American department." See also April 9, for an article asserting that Henry Laurens had informed the new ministry that independence was a prerequisite for peace with America.

55 *St. James's Chronicle*, February 28, April 16, 1782.

56 *Morning Herald*, March 5, 1782.

57 *Kentish Gazette*, April 6, 1782; *Chronicle*, April 16, 18.

58 *Gentleman's Magazine*, March, 1782, 128. English emotions, however, were not always in tune with English finances. The *Chelmsford Chronicle*, April 5, despite confessed shortages of men and money, called for a vigorous attack to be made upon the Bourbons by the now-united English people.

59 *General Advertiser*, May 17, 1782.

though this joyous news arrived two weeks after the announcement that Rodney was to be recalled by the Rockingham ministry, all Britain acclaimed the Admiral, who, embarrassingly
enough, had been appointed by North.[60] The *Morning Herald,*
as expected, gave all of the credit for this victory to the old
Administration, and it demanded that the new Ministry retract
the orders for Rodney's recall.[61] The Rockingham Government
was wise enough to join in the chorus of public praise for the
Admiral.

Spurred by Rodney's example, Englishmen now resolved at all
costs to drive home their advantage over the French. Papers as
diverse in opinion as *Parker's General Advertiser* and the *Morning
Post* condoned the "hottest press" on the River Thames in the
entire history of the war. On May 29 and 30 alone, over 1,300 men
were pressed into the navy.[62] Small wonder that the editor of
Town and Country, with copies of London's leading publications
in front of him, could announce that "a perfect unanimity visibly
prevails."[63] Parker's plea for "Peace with America, and war with
the rest of the Globe,"[64] reflected British opinion in the spring of
1782.

If America's future was to be settled in Europe, many editors
agreed that this future was secure, despite Rodney's victory. The
Dutch, to protect their large loans to the Congress, would, of
course, support the Americans' claims.[65] Even the Portuguese,
recognizing America's economic independence, had begun purchasing her flour and wheat.[66] Surely Britain could not stand
against both friend and foe; surely she would accept the inevitable. The *St. James's Chronicle* hopefully suggested that the
inevitable might be a federal system whereby the Colonies would
have their own legislature but would pay homage to the King.[67]
The *Kentish Gazette* more accurately captured the spirit of the
moment when it advertised for sale copies of the Declaration of

[60] *Packet,* May 24, 1782, *et passim.* See also *St. James's Chronicle,* June 22,
August 15.

[61] *Morning Herald,* May 21, 23, 24, 1782. Cf. *Parker's General Advertiser,* May
30, August 2.

[62] *Parker's General Advertiser,* May 30, 1782; *Morning Post,* May 31.

[63] *Town and Country,* June, 1782, 330.

[64] *Parker's General Advertiser,* May 30, 1782. Cf. *St. James's Chronicle,* July 20,
reporting that the French also were determined to pursue the war.

[65] *Morning Chronicle,* May 29, 1782.

[66] *St. James's Chronicle,* June 6, 1782.

[67] *St. James's Chronicle,* June 11, 1782.

Independence and the Articles of Confederation,[68] material that Britons had once scorned to read.

Richard Oswald was appointed by the Rockingham ministry to open negotiations with the Americans in Paris. His talks with Benjamin Franklin, the only Congressional commissioner then in the French capital, began in April. While formal conferences did not begin until Franklin's colleagues arrived in September, rumors of an impending cessation of Anglo-American hostilities were enough to drive up prices on London's nervous stock exchange.[69] In the early summer of 1782 hopes for a quick peace temporarily vanished with the death of Rockingham,[70] but it was soon made known that Lord Shelburne, the new First Minister, was realistic enough to concede that he would, however reluctantly, accept American independence.[71] Since the colonists were "in full and actual possession" of their freedom, it was futile for the new Ministry either to continue the war or to make plans for an agreement short of complete independence.[72]

During the brief period that Shelburne was First Minister the importance of the press as a vehicle for the control or perhaps even for the formulation of public opinion was duly noted. On November 26, 1782, Germain, now Viscount Sackville, took a good deal of pleasure in noting to his friend General Irwin that "we swarm with abusive pamphlets, and Lord Shelburne is the principal object of their invectives."[73] But Shelburne would not be so impervious to criticism as was the former American Secretary. Never popular with the public (he was frequently referred to as "the Jesuit"—not for religious reasons, but because he had a reputation for secret dealings and double dealings),[74] Shelburne took advantage of the Secret Service funds available to him to try to improve his public image. In slightly less than nine months he awarded almost £2,000 sterling to "various writers and editors of newspapers."[75] Much of this outlay apparently went to

[68] *Kentish Gazette,* July 20, 1782.

[69] *Gentleman's Magazine,* June, 1782, 305.

[70] *Packet,* July 5, 1782.

[71] *Packet,* July 12, 1782; *St. James's Chronicle,* November 26. **See also** *Gentleman's Magazine,* May, 1782, 420; June, 1783, 495.

[72] *Packet,* August 2, 9, 1782.

[73] HMC, Stopford-Sackville MSS, I, November 26, 1782.

[74] HMC, Knox Papers, January 16, 1783, Lord Hillsborough to Knox.

[75] Fortescue, *Correspondence of King George III,* VI, 342. See also Arthur Aspinall, *Politics and the Press,* 67.

Shelburne's old nemesis Henry Bate of the *Morning Herald,* who, by July, 1783, would have disentangled himself from the Sandwich interests and leased his newspaper to Shelburne and his supporters.[76]

As news from America became less frequent and less important throughout the summer of 1782,[77] English newspapers heavily publicized the Gibraltar garrison's magnificent defense against the Spaniards. General Eliott, "who lives like a private soldier and maintains his post," was compared most favorably to Burgoyne, who "needed a train of covered wagons to administer to the luxuries and pomp of his table."[78] For a pleasant change, good news appeared regularly in the press. Thanks to Rodney and Eliott, the closing chapters of the war were much happier than most Englishmen had hoped for. With two great successive defeats to daunt them, the Bourbons presently would be forced to sue for peace.[79]

Exactly when the American war would end now seemed to lie solely in Britain's hands. So long as she refused to recognize the *de facto* independence of the Colonies, sporadic warfare and fruitless negotiation would continue.[80] Editors recommended that British troops be immediately evacuated from America, before the colonists should reopen active conflict.[81] Most Englishmen had already lost interest in the American Revolution, and it would be almost impossible to rouse them to new military efforts against the Colonies. Even the negotiations that seemed to be dragging on interminably in Paris elicited little comment or curiosity. The *Packet* summed up this attitude when it noted that "the affairs of America are now scarcely attended to by the people of this country."[82] Why should Britons be concerned with Amer-

76 Lucyle Werkmeister, *The London Daily Press, 1772-1792,* 75. As early as November 30, 1781, the *Morning Herald's* attitude toward Shelburne was changing. This issue commended his "moderation" and reported that Shelburne was spoken of as Germain's replacement in the American Department.

77 *St. James's Chronicle,* August 6, 1782; *Packet,* August 23; *Kentish Gazette,* August 28.

78 *Public Advertiser,* August 20 [19?], 1782; *Kentish Gazette,* August 21; *Morning Herald,* October 8.

79 *Town and Country,* November, 1782, 611. See also September, 499; October, 555.

80 *Town and Country,* August, 1782, 443.

81 *Packet,* October 18, 1782; *Kentish Gazette,* October 23.

82 *Packet,* November 1, 1782.

ica, if "every idea of local affection and attachment" between the Colonies and the mother country was gone or transferred to France?[83] When the first news of England's acknowledgment of American independence reached London, it was greeted with indifference and little editorial comment.[84]

The preliminary articles of the general European peace were not popular when they arrived in London in late January, 1783. The *Packet,* for example, severely criticized the settlement, arguing that Britain had not only lost America, but she had also agreed to unnecessarily lenient terms for the Bourbons.[85] Most editors, however, agreed that the terms were acceptable. Peace without victory is rarely popular, and a nation impatient for an end to the war had to make concessions.[86] The *Morning Herald,* which on December 14, 1781, had labeled American independence "a mad idea" incapable of attainment, now came to the defense of the Paris agreements, including the one granting independence to the Colonies. The plight of Britain's economy ("We have not a shilling in our treasury") and of her armed forces (which "never were in a worse condition") made peace most desirable, Bate assured his readers on July 29, 1783. Even the *Packet* soon mellowed. By late summer and early autumn it, too, spoke of the blessings of peace as it warned that no good could come of peace-table wrangling.[87]

By early 1783, the press for the first time in almost a decade was paying primary attention to wholly domestic matters. The strange Fox-North coalition, which eventually brought down the Shelburne Government, and the ensuing political entanglements dominated English journalism for the remainder of the year.[88] In October, almost lost among scores of articles relative to do-

[83] *Packet,* December 27, 1782.

[84] *Kentish Gazette,* December 4, 1782.

[85] *Packet,* January 24, 31, February 3, 1783. See also *Journal and Correspondence of William, Lord Auckland,* William Eden, ed., I, 40, for a statement by Lord Loughborough showing his typically Tory dissatisfaction with the peace.

[86] *Middlesex Journal,* February 6, 1783.

[87] *Packet,* August 29, September 5, October 10, 1783.

[88] *Scot's Magazine,* February, 1783, 101; *Town and Country,* February, 107, March, 163; *Packet,* February 17, *et passim; Kentish Gazette,* May 10, *et passim; Morning Post,* July 15, *et passim.* For the Fox-Shelburne dispute, see HMC, Knox Papers, July 13, 1782, Sackville to Knox: "If I can believe newspapers, Mr. Fox and Lord Shelburne must settle their disputes in Hyde Park, for I never heard such language given by one gentleman to another, as Mr. Fox used in the last minutes of this Session."

mestic policies, a copy of the final treaty appeared in *Gentleman's Magazine*. The war was now officially over, and Englishmen could devote their full energies to the uncertain future.

CHAPTER XV

America's Future and Britain's

BEFORE THE CLOSE OF HOSTILITIES Englishmen had arrived at some definite ideas about America's future. Slavery to the Gallic yoke was to be the colonists' portion for friendship with Versailles.[1] The Tories especially stressed the fact that the House of Bourbon did not care for the idea of an independent America and was plotting to make the states either satellites or outright colonies.[2] Surely, affirmed the *Morning Post* as early as April, 1781, the French were not sending troops to Rhode Island merely to help the rebels capture New York; rather, their intent was to establish their own colors there.[3] In short, the Americans were the tools of the French; if it should ever seem to be their advantage to help subjugate America, the French would not hesitate to do so.[4]

The anti-North and more moderate elements of the press took a different position. The *St. James's Chronicle*, affirming that self-interest dictated a nation's foreign policy, predicted that the French would never seize an American colony and thus ruin their economic future with America.[5] French dreams in the New World were now commercial, not colonial, most papers agreed, and Versailles was proving this by wooing the Americans with

[1] *Town and Country,* July, 1781, 442; *Morning Herald,* December 14, 1781.
[2] *Lloyd's Evening Post,* January 14, 1780.
[3] *Morning Post,* April 11, 1781.
[4] *Morning Herald,* June 12, 1781.
[5] *St. James's Chronicle,* November 3, 1781; *Gentleman's Magazine,* March, 1782, 123.

remittance of their debts, with some judicious additions to her pension lists (both Washington and Robert Morris, along with the leading members of the Congress were on this roll, it was assumed),[6] and with a new fashion—larger fur hats—to encourage America's once-prosperous but now languishing fur trade.[7]

However naive the Americans had been, Englishmen believed that the Congress would soon realize it was only a pawn of the Bourbons. The new nation would find the French a more troublesome ally than the English ever had been, and it was expected that the Congress would one day beg its "old friend" to save it from the tyranny of its new master.[8] With a little patience, England could gain all that the fortunes of war had denied her. From late 1781 onward, the belief prevailed that soon an Anglo-American alliance would once more put the Gallic power in its proper place.[9] The *Morning Herald* predicted that the French and Americans would fall out in less than two years,[10] while the *Kentish Gazette* set the inevitable disaffection for earlier.[11] Regardless of party connection, most English publications agreed that America, from necessity, either "would call for the assistance of the mother country,"[12] or would remain neutral in any future struggle between Britain and France.[13] No publication predicted a long-term Franco-American alliance.

As they became more accustomed to the possibility of an independent nation across the Atlantic, Englishmen speculated frequently about the political and economic future of the new country. The *Westminster Magazine* published serially a rather accurate picture of each colony's geographic, social, and politi-

---

6 *Packet,* January 24, February 10, 1783. The *Kentish Gazette,* February 12, reported that Washington was drawing a marshal's pay, while Robert Morris, "the financier," had been granted a pension of a thousand livres a year. See also December 17, for a claim that "a liberal and judicious distribution of louis-d'ors among the congressional demagogues, has already had a considerable effect, in rendering the councils of the United States subservient to the intrigues of the French cabinet." See also HMC, Knox Papers, August 1, 1782, Sackville to Knox: "I am persuaded both Washington and the Congress are in the pay of France."

7 *Morning Post,* July 3, 1783.

8 *Morning Chronicle,* November 1, 1781.

9 *Edinburgh Evening Courant,* December 10, 1781.

10 *Morning Herald,* March 5, 1782.

11 *Kentish Gazette,* July 31, 1782. See also *Chronicle,* September 12, 14, December 10.

12 *Packet,* September 27, 1782.

13 *General Evening Post,* January 4, 11, 1783; *Kentish Gazette,* January 11.

cal structure.[14] Widespread publicity also was given to on-the-spot reports, such as Crevecoeur's *Letters from an American Farmer*.[15] Most favorable portraits of the American scene usually were featured, together with descriptions of the opportunities awaiting an emigrant who chose to settle in "the promised land, the land of the blessed."[16]

The belief that America was an idyllic haven for Europe's peoples gained wide credence during the closing months of the war. The *General Evening Post* stated the opinion that the French would have as much difficulty as Britain anticipated[17] in keeping their mechanics and manufacturers from emigrating to the land of opportunity. Further, it was said, most of the Hessian veterans were so happy with the parcels of land allotted to them by the Congress that they were sending to Germany for their families to join them.[18] "Not one man in five will return to Europe again," predicted the *Morning Post*.[19]

America's commercial potential was enormous, and many Englishmen feared that, if given economic independence, the Colonies would in a short time "vie with the most powerful nations in Europe." For this reason the *Chronicle* opposed the creation of an independent United States. Its worst forebodings soon were realized. In early June, 1782, it reported that the port of Philadelphia "never exhibited so splendid a show of commerce, ship-building and mercantile bustle."[20] Presently, *Gentleman's Magazine* declared that the most eminent banking houses in Amsterdam were so convinced of America's economic potential that they were ready to underwrite the Philadelphia Bank.[21]

While poets bemoaned France's ability to pluck those fruits that brave Albion once alone enjoyed,[22] journalists were aware of the ominous clouds that hung over the American economy. French treaties and Dutch guilders notwithstanding, *Gentleman's Magazine* reported, the American war debt of over forty-two

14 *Westminster Magazine*, August-December, 1780; January, April, 1781.

15 *Gentleman's Magazine*, November, December. Supplement, 1782; *Chronicle*, July 27, August 1, October 10. For an attack upon the "American Farmer's" "old woman's stories, calculated to excite wonder and astonishment," see *Gentleman's Magazine*, December, 1783, 1036.

16 *Gentleman's Magazine*, December, 1783.

17 *General Evening Post*, May 11, 1782.

18 *General Evening Post*, May 8, August 2, 1783.

19 *Morning Post*, June 30, 1783.

20 *Chronicle*, June 6, 8, 1782.

21 *Gentleman's Magazine*, August, 1783, 704.

22 *Scot's Magazine*, April, 1783, 175.

million dollars (with annual interest at over two and a half millions) was so staggering that the Congress' Superintendent of Finance (it never identified him by name) had resigned his office, dreading the embarrassment of being unable to meet it. "Such was the situation in America," it concluded, "when both the laurel and the olive-branch *providentially* came to their relief."[23]

For a time the Americans seemed intent upon their own destruction. The revolt of the Pennsylvania Line, back in January, 1781, convinced many Englishmen that, as soon as the United States no longer had a common enemy to unify her diverse elements, it would fall into chaos, with the military eventually establishing "the law of the sword."[24] A Caesar, Richard III, or Cromwell undoubtedly waited in the wings for his cue to enter the American scene.[25] The *Kentish Gazette* believed that the wisdom of a Solomon would be necessary to "curb the licentiousness of faction" rampant in America. Washington—no Solomon, but the Colonies' closest approximation—it assumed would rise swiftly to a place of power in the new government.[26] Privately, Lord Sackville was saying the same thing. He predicted that Washington would be called "to settle something like a government among these wild and absurd leaders of the different States."[27] Animosities in a fledgling government were to be expected, cautioned the *Packet,* as it advised England to aid the several states in the settlement of their problems. This paper was confident that the Fox-North Government would offer all possible aid to the former colonists.[28]

Added to speculation about America's weak condition were reports that London's leading Atlantic trading houses were receiving and refusing large orders from their former correspondents because the Americans had not remitted payment for prewar debts. The *Morning Post* presently affirmed that "the balance of trade must be greatly against the colonies for a very

23 *Gentleman's Magazine*, May, 1783, 436; *Scot's Magazine*, May, 267; quoted from *Pennsylvania Gazette*, no date. Cf. *Gentleman's Magazine*, June, 528.

24 *General Evening Post*, August 7, 1783.

25 *Packet*, August 18, 1783.

26 *Kentish Gazette*, May 24, 1783. See also *General Evening Post*, August 12.

27 HMC, Knox Papers, August 16, 1783, Sackville to Knox.

28 *Packet*, June 6, 1783.

considerable time to come."[29] *Scot's Magazine,* declaring that the American market was already glutted with European manufactures, added that America had neither money nor sufficient produce to send in return.[30] In Britain's eyes, America—though potentially wealthy—was in a state of near poverty.

The press expressed some serious doubts about the role Britain was to play in America's future. As early as September, 1781, the *Morning Herald* noted that, upon the conclusion of hostilities, Britain would not only need to overcome trade competition from America's new-found allies, but would also be forced to compete with an American domestic manufacture that, it believed, supplied more of its own needs than did that of any other foreign country.[31] About a year later, with most Englishmen already reconciled to the idea of an independent United States, the *St. James's Chronicle* reiterated Adam Smith's earlier contention that commercial connections between nations could bind them much tighter than could politics. Britain had now learned, it admitted, "that all Connexion which is not purely commercial is impracticable." In short, it was trade and not "political Scuffles" that had made Great Britain great.[32]

It was expected that the United States, knowing that only Britain could supply her with so many cheap and varied products, would soon reopen channels of trade between herself and Britain. The great advantages to be gained mutually from such trade, it was hoped, would take precedence over Congress' political debt to France. When, in February, 1783, the King favorably answered petitions requesting that trade with America immediately be reopened, he asserted that the two economies were soon again to be intertwined and that nothing on his part would be wanting to restore, without delay, the friendly intercourse "as ought to result from mutual interest and returning affection." This declaration greatly pleased George's business-minded subjects, and it was generally agreed that London presently would be a beehive of Atlantic-oriented commercial activity.[33]

[29] *Morning Post,* June 17, 26, 1783. Cf. *Gloucester Journal,* August 18, which wondered why, if America was in such a poor state, so many British ships kept sailing there with such valuable cargoes.

[30] *Scot's Magazine,* November, 1783, 590-94. This is part of a favorable review of John Lord Sheffield's *Observations of the Commerce of the American States.*

[31] *Morning Herald,* September 27, 1781.

[32] *St. James's Chronicle,* August 20, 1782. See also *Kentish Gazette,* August 9; *Packet,* September 19, 1783.

[33] *General Evening Post,* February 25, 1783; *Kentish Gazette,* February 26.

Many editors, the royal declaration notwithstanding, feared competition from America. Could not the former colonists build and sail ships much more cheaply than the British? If this were so, it would follow that they soon would become the carriers of Britain's profitable West Indian traffic, to the detriment of many powerful English and West Indian interests.[34] The *Kentish Gazette,* formerly a sympathizer with the American cause, answered these fears with a proposal that American trade be permanently kept out of the West Indies, for, once allowed in, their prodigious commerce would dictate that the Indies "must become naturally the appendage of America."[35] These fears were never realized, because Parliament, aware of the threat, prohibited American ships from West Indian ports.

The press did not abandon all hopes of a great British empire again rising in North America. All factions agreed that Canada was to become the nucleus of this new dominion. Its vastness was to be peopled not only by the fleeing loyalists,[36] but also by others "from the provinces now under the dominion of Congress."[37] Canada was envisaged as a refuge for discontented Americans, and it was assumed that there would be enough unhappy former Colonials to people it. The first step in making Canada great was the difficult one of cultivating the confidence and affection of her French population.[38] Even this task, the argument ran, would prove easier than might be expected. Although the Canadians had never been cordially reconciled to the English, it was believed that their aversion to the Americans was infinitely greater.[39]

This may have been true, but the dream of a new empire in Canada was not immediately realized. In the first place, disillusioned Tories reported to London that Nova Scotia "had nine months winter and only three months warm weather."[40] Few Carolinians or Georgians—or New Yorkers, for that matter— could be lured to the frozen northlands with promises of favorable land grants. Secondly, not only was England unable to find

---

34 *Kentish Gazette,* March 8, 1783.
35 *Kentish Gazette,* May 31, 1783.
36 *Gloucester Journal,* "Extract of a letter from London," January 13, 1783.
37 *Middlesex Journal,* February 4, 1783.
38 *Middlesex Journal,* February 6, 1783.
39 *Morning Post,* June 26, 1783.
40 *Gentleman's Magazine,* August, 1783, 704.

people willing to emigrate to Canada, she feared that her skilled classes would bypass the untried and cold North in favor of the more inviting atmosphere of the United States.

The threat of the depopulation of England was both real and feared by all segments of the press throughout 1783.[41] It was thought that shipbuilders and manufacturers especially, dreading the additional taxes that would be necessary to pay off England's war debts, would seek that "milder government" that America reportedly was offering. Both the Ministry and Parliament were urged to find ways to employ Britain's returning legions and to lighten the tax burdens of prospective employers lest both classes emigrate "and with them will go the Sinews of the Wealth and Power of England."[42] Both the Shelburne and the Fox-North governments shared the press's fears of the skilled classes' emigration to the former colonies. On April 19, 1783, a Secret Service payment of £52 10s. was made to John Swindell "as an additional reward for giving Intelligence of artificers who were Emigrating to North America who were in consequence stopped at Londonderry."[43] Although the *General Evening Post* supported the Government's sustained campaign to convince artisans that it would be madness to leave a nation whose market comprised nearly fifty million potential customers for one with only three million,[44] Englishmen continued to worry about keeping their skilled classes at home. Few suggested that a concerted effort be made to encourage emigration to Canada or to the West Indies.

It was to America, and not to the Empire, that most Britons looked for a return of commercial prosperity. In fact, so certain were British merchants of the swift passage of an American trade bill through Parliament that they bought heavily on credit and presently found themselves in peril of having to pay first installments to creditors before their goods had been granted permission to clear port for America.[45] When the official announcement of the reopening of trade was made in May, it was greeted with praises of economic deliverance. "It will give employment to

---

[41] *Packet,* July 25, 1783; *Kentish Gazette,* August 13. See also *Kentish Gazette,* March 8, for a report that France was encouraging the emigration of her silk weavers to America. On July 10, the *Morning Herald* noted that for £500 or £1,000 one could purchase in America a "magnificent" farm or orchard.

[42] *St. James's Chronicle,* November 7, 1782.

[43] Nepean Papers (Clements), Secret Service Payments, 1782-1791, April 19, 1783.

[44] *General Evening Post,* May 17, 20, 29, June 3, 1783.

[45] *Kentish Gazette,* March 29, April 9, 1783.

all, make money plentiful, and send it with a brisk circulation through the country," predicted the *Packet* in a statement reminiscent of the *Kentish Gazette's* promises of a month earlier.[46] Soon Englishmen were reading that all American ports were bustling with English commerce.[47] The "old friends" across the Atlantic were now shaking hands with their former partners in trade. Until the day America could produce its own industrial needs, this rapport surely would continue.[48]

By the time the Treaty of Paris was formally ratified, British commerce had revived to the point where economic optimism was reflected in her press for the first time in almost a decade. A restored American market was the reason for this optimism.[49]

As trade recovered and Englishmen forgot their wartime economic plight, they could not—or would not—forget the political difficulties that had plagued them for seven years past. With the fall of the North Government, the now pro-Ministry journals revived their campaign to reform Parliament so that never again could a ministry, with public opinion overwhelmingly against it (each editor assumed that his publication spoke for the majority), control Parliament. In May, 1782, both *Parker's General Advertiser* and the *Packet* commenced a sustained attack upon the rotten borough system. A bill for "regulating the representation of the country" was urged by the *Packet*, which stressed the point that political corruption over the past decade had reached a new high.[50] Any move "to make the people permanently free" could be expected to be slow in coming, for the weight of the rotten boroughs was such that it could crush any parliamentary effort to reform them.[51] The anti-Tory newspapers, fearful that their opposition would again gain control of the legislature, were almost unanimously in favor of some sort of parliamentary reform. Popular control of the legislature without the abolition of the rotten borough system they found impossible to conceive. Although another half century was to elapse before Parliament

46 *Packet*, May 16, 1783. Cf. *Kentish Gazette*, April 5.

47 *General Evening Post*, July 5, 19, 1783.

48 *Kentish Gazette*, September 6, 20, 1783.

49 *General Evening Post*, August 7, 1783.

50 *Packet*, May 3, 1782. See also *Courant*, April 10, for an earlier plea for parliamentary reform.

51 *Parker's General Advertiser*, May 14, 1782.

would bow to the pressure for self-reformation, the reform movement was well nourished by the London Opposition press during the era of the American Revolution.

With most Englishmen again demonstrating a degree of confidence in their government and its foreign policies, the only group of persons to receive almost no joy from their newspapers were the American loyalists, who clearly were out of step with the spirit of compromise that pervaded the British Isles in 1783. The interests of these refugees appeared incompatible with those of the English merchant and manufacturing classes. Because of Germain's sympathetic support, some of the more important Americans had been well compensated,[52] but the move to cut their pensions, partially as an economy measure and partially as punishment, received wide support—even from London's Tory press. Noting that in 1781 (the last year that records reportedly were available) the American refugees cost the Treasury over £68,000, the *Morning Herald* declared it "no wonder they are daily growing more numerous." It voiced the hope that Welbore Ellis, Germain's successor as Secretary for the American Department, would look well into the claims of the "transatlantic pensioners," because it suspected that these refugees possessed "in their own private fortunes, more than a genteel competency!"[53] The fall of the North ministry destroyed any immediate hopes that the loyalists may have entertained for just compensation.[54]

Although extremely unpopular, the loyalists were not completely friendless in the postwar period. The *Kentish Gazette*, an anti-Tory publication, approved of the section of the provisional peace treaty signed at Paris that called for the protection of their interests in America. Justice and gratitude dictated that fair compensation be made to ameliorate the sufferings of "those who have borne arms for us," it added.[55] But the loyalists on both sides of the Atlantic considered themselves abandoned by the treaty of peace. "A bare recommendation of Congress," it was agreed,

[52] *St. James's Chronicle,* November 15, 1781.
[53] *Morning Herald,* March 6, 1782; *Kentish Gazette,* October 30.
[54] *Chronicle,* November 2, 1782; *Kentish Gazette,* August 17, October 30.
[55] *Kentish Gazette,* February 1, 5, July 2, 1783. See also *London Magazine,* March, 114, for an attack upon both the King and Parliament for making peace and for granting America its independence "without securing *any restitution whatever* to the loyalists."

would not have sufficient effect to induce the several states to restore confiscated property,[56] and the news that the United States was not living up to this part of the treaty surprised few Englishmen and no loyalists.[57] The *Morning Post* warned that a Congressional proscription of the loyalists would have the same effect that the revocation of the Edict of Nantes had upon the French Huguenots: "Hundreds of thousands of useful subjects will flee," it predicted.[58]

With the war fever gone by mid-1783, Englishmen of all political persuasions seemed to mellow. Not many had ever laid eyes upon Joseph Galloway's moving pamphlet on behalf of the loyalists,[59] but most agreed that the American refugees who had suffered so long and so bitterly should at least be given some money and sympathy. Few suggested, however, that they be given either respect or honor.[60]

Once the Peace of Paris was signed, the British press concluded its searching post-mortem into the reasons for the loss of a war and the loss of an empire. The majority conclusion was the same as it had been almost a decade before: The war was begun through the bungling of George III's inept lieutenants on both sides of the Atlantic, and its loss was attributable to their leadership rather than to any defect in British valor. When, on January 26, 1776, Edward Gibbon wrote that he "much feared our Leaders have not a Genius which can act at the distance of 3,000 miles," he made a prophecy that the contemporary press and later historians would hold to be all too true.

[56] *Scot's Magazine*, May, 1783, 267.

[57] *Packet*, June 27, July 11, 1783.

[58] *Morning Post*, July 12, 1783.

[59] *The Case and Claim of the American Loyalists Impartially Stated and Considered*, published by G. Wilkie. The account books of London's leading publisher, William Strahan, indicate that Galloway personally paid for the printing and binding of his own tracts. See Strahan's Miscellaneous Papers, BM, Add. MSS 48890, number 10, for an account dated June 16, 1785, demonstrating that the tracts Galloway ordered published were still on hand and had not been sold.

[60] *Packet*, June 27, 1783; *General Evening Post*, July 5, August 2.

The Press and the Revolution

L ONDON WAS THE CENTER of British journalism during the era
of the American Revolution, producing over one third of the
nation's periodicals and almost all of her important ones. These
large metropolitan editions, usually well-financed joint-stock en-
terprises, frequently were both politically and economically independent. They were also blessed with a steadily rising circulation rate that was generated by the American war and the
ensuing European conflict. Only these publications could provide
swiftly the detailed news that all Britain demanded. Thus, the
country gentleman may have read his provincial paper for the
local business and social events, but he drew his information on
the weighty matters of war and of the state from the commercially
oriented London newspapers and magazines. For the interested
citizen to be forming his opinions on these bases did not augur
well for the ministry of George III.

While the *General Advertiser* supported the political interests
of Charles James Fox, the *Middlesex Journal* championed
Chatham's cause until his death in 1778, and the *Evening Post* was
identified with the more radical pro-Wilkes movement, most
other newspapers were in political opposition to the North Government because of the Ministry's policies concerning America,
which they believed to be misguided. The *Gazetteer, Public
Advertiser, St. James's Chronicle,* and innumerable other journals
were not appendages of any particular person or party. Rather,
they represented independently formed beliefs that the war

against America could not be brought to a successful end because the colonial cause was supported by overwhelming numbers of colonists who were well armed and well prepared to fight in their own back yards. Britain, with a navy and national wealth large enough to overcome these difficulties, failed to do so because of inept leadership. The press also believed the Government responsible for not bringing the hostilities swiftly to a negotiated end, once the sword was drawn. Editors were convinced that ministers unwise enough to blunder into a war with the Colonies that soon became a conflict against almost all of Europe could not safely lead Britain out of the wilderness that they alone had created. The defeats at Saratoga and Yorktown, painful as they were, had been anticipated by much of Britain's reading public.

Even by present standards the press was free. It quoted and reported the proceedings in Parliament; it employed notable (and anonymous) contributors both in and out of the Government; most important of all, it freely criticized the King, his ministers, and their policies. The influence of the press during this period (as during most other periods) cannot be accurately measured, yet it should not be underestimated. It is clear that the North ministry was unhappy with the fact that nearly all influential publications in Britain were decidedly hostile to it. While never publicly conceding that the London-oriented editors reflected accurately the whole of British public opinion, North and his ministers not only hired writers, but they also supported one newspaper and founded another in order to publicize their side of the political story. So long as George III controlled the requisite votes in Parliament (the Opposition was certain he was purchasing them), officially he could ignore the press and its hostile opinions; unofficially, he subscribed to the newspapers. So did every member of Parliament on both sides of the aisle as well as probably every important personage in the nation. Knowing this, the editors of Opposition and independent newspapers hoped that their arguments eventually would turn all literate Englishmen, and even the adamant King, against the unpopular Ministry.

While the history of this era as related in the press is laced with inaccuracies, even these inaccuracies afford clues to the desires of the editors. Rumors of a negotiated peace with the Americans recurred constantly between 1776 and 1782, and the reader is left with the impression that these represent wishful reporting.

Rumors of a war against the French, so prevalent in late 1777 and early 1778, also reflect a mixture of hope and expectation.

In conclusion, one must assume that the news sections of the newspapers shaped more views than did the editorials. The press functioned as the foremost vehicle for disseminating information rather than as the originator of public opinion. After learning of the Battle of Yorktown, the British public decided it had had enough of the American war. It reached this conclusion not so much because the editorials it read told it to do so (a majority of the press had been advising the abandonment of the war for over five years), but because the news of events in America forced it to do so. Of course, biased editors could, and did, color the news from America. But the battle reports were so disheartening to both the British taxpayer and the British soldier that the truth apparently emerged from the news, despite its various colorations. Even the most staunch supporters of the Government came reluctantly to admit that the opinions held by the Opposition had proved in the long run to be closer to the truth than those advertised in the pro-Ministry publications.

If, as Macaulay tells us, "the true history of a nation is to be found in its newspapers," then English history from 1775 to 1783 is the story of a free people desperately trying to salvage on the field of honor the laurels their leaders on both sides of the Atlantic were needlessly throwing away.

Appendix

SOME PERTINENT FACTS ABOUT THE LONDON PRESS

DURING THE ERA OF THE AMERICAN REVOLUTION

APPENDIX

SOME PERTINENT DATA ABOUT THE LONDON PRESS DURING THE ERA OF THE AMERICAN REVOLUTION*

NEWSPAPER	FOUNDED	PRINTER, PUBLISHER, OR EDITOR, 1775-1783	PUBLISHED	POLITICS	ESTIMATED CIRCULATION PER EDITION 1775	ESTIMATED CIRCULATION PER EDITION 1782
Daily Advertiser	1730	James Jenour (or Josiah Jenour)	Daily	None	3,500	3,500
Gazetteer and New Daily Advertiser	1735	1776-1779 editor unknown (J. H. Wynn?) 1780-1783 John Wall, editor Mary Say, owner during entire period	Daily	Anti-North Ministry	2,000	2,500
General Advertiser and Morning Intelligencer (changed to Parker's General Advertiser in 1782)	1766	1776-1781 William Parker, owner and editor 1781-1783 Dennis O'Bryen, editor	Daily	Anti-North	2,000	2,500
General Evening Post	1733	John Bew, publisher Charles Rathband, editor	Tri-weekly	Pro-North	2,000	2,000
Lloyd's Evening Post and British Chronicle	1757	1775-1778 W. Nicholl (or Nicholls) 1778-1783 John Rivington, publisher	Tri-weekly	Pro-North	2,000	2,000
(London) Chronicle	1757	J. Wilkie, publisher William Strahan, printer	Tri-weekly	Anti-North	2,500	2,500
(London) Courant and Westminster Chronicle	1779(?)	1779 Hugh Boyd 1779-1781 Joseph (or John) Cooper 1781-1782 John Fielding; T. Thirlwind 1783 John Stockdale	Daily	Anti-North	1,000	1,000
(London) Evening Post	1737	John Miller, printer John Almon, editor	Tri-weekly	Anti-North	2,000	2,500
London Gazette	1665	Official Government Publication	Semi-weekly	Official Government Publication	2,500	2,500
(London) Packet; or, New Lloyd's Evening Post	1770	1775-1776 William Woodfall, editor and printer 1776-1783 Control changed hands about six times; editors and owners unknown; probably Thomas	Tri-weekly	Anti-North	1,000	1,250

Publication	Founded	Personnel	Dates	Frequency	Politics	Circulation	
Middlesex Journal and Evening Advertiser	1769	William Griffin, editor; John Wheble, publisher; R. Ayre, printer		Tri-weekly	Anti-North	1,500	1,500
Morning Chronicle and London Advertiser	1770	William Woodfall		Daily	Anti-North (1775) Pro-North (1782)	2,500	3,000
Morning Herald and Daily Advertiser	1780	John Barr, publisher; Henry Bate, partial owner; editor; Alexander Chalmers, editor	1780; 1781-1783	Daily	Pro-North	3,500	3,500
Morning Post and Daily Advertiser	1772	Henry Bate; J. Jackman; C. F. Badini	1775-1780; 1780-1783; 1783	Daily	Pro-North	3,500	1,650
Public Advertiser	1734	Henry Sampson Woodfall		Daily	Anti-North	3,000	3,000
Public Ledger; or Daily Register of Commerce and Intelligence	1759	Henry Randall, editor; William Jackson, editor; Thomas Brewman, printer	1775-1776; 1776-1777; 1776-1780	Daily	Anti-North	1,000	Absorbed by General Advertiser, 1780
St. James's Chronicle; or British Evening Post	1761	Henry Baldwin		Tri-weekly	Anti-North	2,000	2,500
Westminster Journal; or New Weekly Miscellany	1763	Thomas Touchit (Pseud.); Simon Gentletouch (Pseud.)		Weekly	Anti-North	2,000	2,000
Whitehall Evening Post or London Intelligencer	1716	Thomas Wright; John Williams; Charles Corbett	1775-1778; 1778-1779; 1780-1783	Tri-weekly	Anti-North	2,000	2,000

*This chart excludes short-lived publications, such as the *Aurora*, which brought out 47 issues in 1781, and the *Noon Gazette*, which was quickly absorbed by the *Courant* in January, 1782, and of which there are only two issues extant. It also omits publications whose files have not come down to us in sufficient quantity to render accurate judgment of their politics and circulation; the *English Chronicle* and the seemingly pro-North *British Mercury* fall into this category. Among magazines, Edward Cave's *Gentleman's Magazine* sold over 10,000 copies per monthly issue. This was about twice the circulation of each of its nearest competitors, *London Magazine* and *Scot's Magazine*.

Bibliography

THE BURNEY COLLECTION in the British Museum contains comprehensive files of the London press for the period covered in this study. It also has scattered samplings of provincial newspapers. All of the following papers, except those marked with an asterisk, can be found there. R. S. Crane and F. B. Kaye, *A Census of British Newspapers and Periodicals, 1620-1800* (Chapel Hill, 1927), contains an invaluable list of British periodicals accessible in American libraries and also a list of those periodicals not available in the United States.

BRITISH PUBLICATIONS

LONDON NEWSPAPERS

Chronicle
Courant and Westminster Chronicle (changed in October, 1781, to *London Courant, Westminster Chronicle, and Daily Advertiser*)
Daily Advertiser
Evening Post
Gazetteer and New Daily Advertiser
General Advertiser and Morning Intelligencer (changed in May, 1782, to *Parker's General Advertiser*)
General Evening Post
Lloyd's Evening Post and British Chronicle

London Gazette
*Middlesex Journal and Evening Advertiser**
Morning Chronicle and London Advertiser
Morning Herald and Daily Advertiser
Morning Post and Daily Advertiser
Packet; or, New Lloyd's Evening Post
Public Advertiser
Public Ledger; or, Daily Register of Commerce and Intelligence
St. James's Chronicle, or British Evening Post
*Westminster Journal; or New Weekly Miscellany**
*Whitehall Evening Post or London Intelligencer**

LONDON MAGAZINES

Annual Register
Critical Review or Annals of Literature
Gentleman's Magazine
London Magazine
Monthly Review
Town and Country
Universal Magazine of Knowledge and Pleasure
Westminster Magazine

PROVINCIAL PUBLICATIONS

Adams's Weekly Courant
Bath Journal
Bristol Gazette
Chelmsford Chronicle
Chester Chronicle
Derby Mercury
Edinburgh Advertiser
Edinburgh Evening Courant
Gloucester Journal
Hampshire Chronicle
Hereford Journal
Kentish Gazette
Reading Mercury
Salisbury and Winchester Journal
Scot's Magazine
Williamson's Liverpool Advertiser
Yorkshire Post

MANUSCRIPT COLLECTIONS

BRITISH MUSEUM

Additional Manuscripts
Correspondence of John Almon, Add. MSS 20733

Liverpool Papers, Add. MSS 38470-71

Letterbook of the first Earl of Liverpool (Charles Jenkinson), Add. MSS 38306-9

Original Assignments of Manuscripts Between Authors and Publishers . . . , Add. MSS 38728-30

Accounts of the *Public Advertiser*, 1765-1771, Add. MSS 38169

Ledgers and Other Business Papers of William Strahan, Add. MSS 48800-48918

Wilkes Correspondence, Add. MSS 30872-95

Miscellaneous Letters of Henry Sampson Woodfall, Add. MSS 27780

Letters of William Woodfall, Add. MSS 21508, ff. 29, 31

Egerton Manuscripts

Minutes of the *Whitehall Evening Post*, 1795-1801, Egerton MSS 2236

CENTRAL LIBRARY, SHEFFIELD, ENGLAND

Burke Papers
Rockingham Papers
Wentworth Woodhouse Muniments (Fitzwilliam MSS)

WILLIAM L. CLEMENTS LIBRARY, ANN ARBOR, MICHIGAN

Croker Papers
Gage Correspondence
Germain Papers
Knox Papers (not calendared in HMC)
Lacaita—Shelburne MSS
Melville Papers
Nepean Papers
Oswald Papers
Sackville Supplementary MSS (not calendared in HMC)
Shelburne Papers
Sydney Papers
Wedderburn Papers
Wilkes Papers

REPORTS OF THE ROYAL COMMISSION ON HISTORICAL MANUSCRIPTS (HMC)

Abergavenny MSS. 10th Report, Appendix, Part VI, 1887.

Carlisle MSS. 15th Report, Appendix, Part VI, 1897.

Knox Papers. Report on Manuscripts in Various Collections, VI, 1909, 81-296

Rutland MSS. 14th Report, Appendix, Part I, Vol. I, 1888.

Stopford-Sackville MSS. 9th Report, Part III, 2 vols., I, 1904; II, 1910.

PAMPHLETS

Almon, John (pseud. "Independent Whig"), *A Letter to the Right Honourable Charles Jenkinson*. 1781.

———, *An Address to the Interior Cabinet*. 1782.

———, *Free Parliaments, or, a Vindication of the Parliamentary Constitution of England*. 1783.

Anon. *A Letter to the English Nation, on the Present War with America; with a Review of Our Military Operations in that Country*. 1777.

———, *Considerations Upon the American Inquiry*. 1779.

———, *Common-Place Arguments Against Administration with Obvious Answers*. 1780.

———, *Poetical Review*. 1780.

Dalrymple, Alexander, *Considerations on the Present State of Affairs Between England and America*. 1778.

Franklin, Benjamin [?], *Address to the Good People of Ireland, on behalf of America*. Dated Versailles, October 4, 1778.

Galloway, Joseph, *Letters to a Nobleman, on the Conduct of the War in the Middle Colonies*. 1779.

———, *Historical and Political Reflections on the Rise and Progress of the American Rebellion*. 1780.

———, *A Reply to the Observations of Lieutenant General Sir William Howe, on a pamphlet, entitled Letters to a Nobleman*. 1781.

———, *The Case and Claim of the American Loyalists Impartially Stated and Considered*. 1783.

Hartley, David, *Letters on the American War*. 1778.

Horne, John (Tooke), *The Trial of John Horne, Esq., for Libel*. 1777.

Howe, William, *Letters to a Nobleman*. 1780.

———, *The Narrative of Lieutenant General Sir William Howe*, 1780.

Knox, William, *The Claim of the Colonies to Exemption from Taxes imposed by Authority of Parliament, examined*. 1775.

Macpherson, James, *The Rights of Great Britain asserted against the Claims of America: Being an Answer to the Declaration of the General Congress*. 1776.

———, *A Short History of the Opposition During the Last Session*. 1779.

Mauduit, Israel, *Remarks Upon General Howe's Account of His Proceedings on Long Island. . . .* 1778.

———, *A Hand bill advocating American Independence, inspired by the English Ministry. . . .* 1778.

Price, Richard, *Origin, Progress and Establishment of National Society*. 1776.

———, *Observations on the Nature of Civil Liberty, the Principles of Government, and the Justice and Policy of the War with America*. 1776.

———, *Additional Observations on the Nature and Value of Civil Liberty, and the War with America; . . .* 1777.

——, *An Essay on the Population of England.* 1780.

——, *Observations on the Importance of the American Revolution, and the Means of Making It a Benefit to the World.* 1784.

Scott, John, *The Conduct of His Majesty's Late Ministers Considered.* . . . 1784.

Shebbeare, John, *An Essay on the Origin, Progress and Establishment of National Society.* 1776.

Tucker, Josiah, *A Series of Answers to Certain Popular Objections, Against Separating from the Rebellious Colonies, and Discarding Them Entirely.* . . . 1776.

——, *The Respective Pleas and Arguments of the Mother Country and of the Colonies Distinctly set forth; and the impossibility of a compromise of differences, or a mutual concession of rights, plainly demonstrated.* 1776.

——, *The true interest of Britain, set forth in regard to the colonies.* . . . 1776.

——, *Thoughts on the Present Posture of Public Affairs.* 1779. (Also published in *Public Advertiser,* July 24, 1779.)

——, *Dispassionate Thoughts on the American War.* 1780.

——, *The True Interests of Britain.* 1780.

——, *Cui bono?* or, *An inquiry, what benefits can arise either to the English or the Americans, the French, Spaniards or Dutch, from the greatest victories . . . in the present war?* 1781.

STUDIES OF THE BRITISH PRESS

Andrews, Alexander, *History of British Journalism.* London, 1859. 2 vols.

Aspinall, Arthur, *Politics and the Press.* London, 1949.

——, "Statistical Accounts of the London Newspapers in the Eighteenth Century." *English Historical Review,* 63 (1948), 201-32.

Cambridge Bibliography of English Literature, Vol. II. Cambridge, 1941.

Cambridge History of English Literature, Vols. X, XI. Cambridge, 1907, 1916.

Carlson, C. Lennart, *The First Magazine: A History of the Gentleman's Magazine.* Providence, Rhode Island, 1938.

Cochrane, J. A., *Dr. Johnson's Printer: The Life of William Strahan.* Cambridge, Massachusetts, 1964.

Collins, A. S., *Authorship in the Days of Johnson.* London, 1927.

——, "The Growth of the Reading Public During the Eighteenth Century." *Review of English Studies,* 2 (1926).

Couper, W. J., *The Edinburgh Periodical Press.* Stirling, 1908.

Crabbe, George, *The Newspapers.* London, 1785.

Craig, Mary Elizabeth, *The Scottish Periodical Press, 1750-1789.* Edinburgh, 1931.

Cranfield, G. A., *The Development of the Provincial Newspaper, 1700-1760*. Oxford, 1962.

Cushing, William, *Initials and Pseudonyms: A Dictionary of Literary Disguises*. New York, 1886.

Escott, T. H. S., *Masters of English Journalism*. London, 1911.

Ford, P. L., "Josiah Tucker and his Writings: An Eighteenth Century Pamphleteer on America." *Journal of Political Economy*, March, 1894.

Fox Bourne, Henry Richard, *English Newspapers*. London, 1887. 2 vols.

Franklin, Benjamin, *Benjamin Franklin's Letters to the Press, 1758-1775*, Verner W. Crane, ed. Chapel Hill, North Carolina, 1950.

Gibb, Mildred A., and Frank Beckwith, *The Yorkshire Post*. York, 1954.

Graham, W., *English Literary Periodicals*. New York, 1930.

Grant, James, *The Newspaper Press*. London, 1871. 3 vols.

Haig, Robert L., *The Gazetteer, 1735-1797*. Carbondale, Illinois, 1960.

Hanson, Laurence, *Government and the Press, 1695-1763*. London, 1936.

Hawke, Edward G., *A Brief History of the British Newspaper Press*. London, n.d.

Hindle, Wilfrid, *The Morning Post, 1772-1937*. London, 1937.

Hinkhouse, Fred Junkin, *Preliminaries of the American Revolution as Seen in the British Press, 1763-1775*. New York, 1926.

Hunt, Frederic Knight, *The Fourth Estate: A History of Newspapers and of the Liberty of the Press*. London, 1850. 2 vols.

Laprade, William T., "The Power of the English Press in the Eighteenth Century." *South Atlantic Quarterly*, 27 (1928).

MacDonagh, Michael, *The Reporters' Gallery*. London, 1913.

Marr, George Simpson, *The Periodical Essayist of the Eighteenth Century*. London, 1923.

Morison, Stanley, *The English Newspaper*. Cambridge, England, 1932.

———, *John Bell*. Cambridge, England, 1930.

Muddiman, Joseph G., *History of English Journalism to the Foundation of the Gazette*. London, 1908.

Nangle, Benjamin C., *Monthly Review*. Oxford, 1934.

Nichols, John B., *Literary Anecdotes of the Eighteenth Century*. London, 1782-1815. 9 vols.

———, *Illustrations of the Literary History of the Eighteenth Century*. London, 1817-1848. 8 vols.

Pebody, Charles, *English Journalism and the Men Who Have Made It*. London, 1887.

Plomer, H. R., G. H. Bushnell, E. R. McC. Dix, *A Dictionary of the Printers and Booksellers who were at Work in England, Scotland and Ireland from 1726 to 1775*. Oxford, 1930.

Porritt, Edward, "The Government and the Newspaper Press in England." *Political Science Quarterly*, 12 (1897).

Rea, Robert R., "Earl of Chatham and the London Press, 1775." *Journalism Quarterly*, 31 (1954).

——, *The English Press in Politics, 1760-1774.* Lincoln, Nebraska, 1963.

Rivington, Septimus, *The Publishing Family of Rivington.* London, 1919.

Salmon, Lucy Maynard, *The Newspaper and the Historian.* New York, 1923.

Siebert, Frederick Seaton, *Freedom of the Press in England, 1476-1776.* Urbana, Illinois, 1952.

Sinclair, G. A., "Periodical Literature of the Eighteenth Century." *Scottish Historical Review*, 2 (1905).

Smith, D. Nichol, "The Newspaper," in A. S. Turberville, ed., *Johnson's England*, Vol 2. Oxford, 1933.

Thomas, Peter D. G., "The Beginning of Parliamentary Reporting in Newspapers, 1768-1774." *English Historical Review*, 74 (1959), 623-36.

Timperly, C. H., *A Dictionary of Printers and Printing.* London, 1839.

Trusler, Rev. Dr., *London Advertiser and Guide*, 2d ed. London, 1790.

Wead, Eunice, "British Public Opinion of the Peace with America, 1782." *American Historical Review*, 34 (1929).

Weed, K. K., and R. P. Bond, *British Newspapers and Periodicals to 1800.* Chapel Hill, North Carolina, 1946.

Werkmeister, Lucyle, *The London Daily Press, 1772-1792.* Lincoln, Nebraska, 1963.

Williams, J. B., *A History of English Journalism.* London, 1908.

Yarborough, M. C., "John Horne Tooke: Champion of the American Colonists." *South Atlantic Quarterly*, 35 (1936).

MEMOIRS, CORRESPONDENCES, BIOGRAPHIES

Alden, John Richard, *General Charles Lee*, Baton Rouge, Louisiana, 1951.

——, *General Gage in America.* Baton Rouge, Louisiana, 1948.

Almon, John, *Anecdotes of the Life of William Pitt, Earl of Chatham.* Dublin, 1792. 2 vols.

——, *Biographical, Literary, and Political Anecdotes of Several of the Most Eminent Persons of the Present Age.* London, 1797. 3 vols.

——, *Memoirs of John Almon, Bookseller of Picadilly.* London, 1790.

——, *The Remembrancer, 1775-1784.* London, 1790. 17 vols.

Angelo, Henry, *Reminiscences.* London, 1904. 2 vols.

Belsham, William, *Memoirs of the Reign of George III.* London, 1795. 4 vols.

Boaden, James, *Memoirs of the Life of John Philip Kemble, Esq.* London, 1825. 2 vols.

Boswell, James, *Life of Johnson,* G. B. Hill, ed., rev. by L. F. Powell. Oxford, 1950. 6 vols.

Brown, Gerald S., *The American Secretary, The Colonial Policy of Lord George Germain, 1775-1778.* Ann Arbor, Michigan, 1963.

Burke, Edmund, *The Correspondence of Edmund Burke,* Thomas W. Copeland, ed. Vols. III, IV. Cambridge, Massachusetts, 1961-1963.

Burney, Fanny, *Diary of Fanny Burney,* A. R. Ellis, ed. London, 1889. 2 vols.

Campbell, John Lord, *The Lives of the Lord Chancellors.* London, 1845-1869. 8 vols.

Clinton, Henry, *The American Rebellion: Narrative of Campaigns, 1775-1782,* William B. Willcox, ed. New Haven, Connecticut, 1954.

Davies, Thomas, *Memoirs of the Life of David Garrick.* London, 1781. 2 vols.

Draper, John W., *William Mason.* New York, 1924.

Eden, William, *Journal and Correspondence of Lord Auckland* (William Eden). London, 1861. 4 vols.

Fitzmaurice, Lord Edmond, *Life of William, Earl of Shelburne.* London, 1876. 3 vols.

Fyvie, John, *Noble Dames and Notable Men of the Georgian Era.* London, 1910.

Garrick, David, *David Garrick's Private Correspondence,* James Boaden, ed. London, 1832. 2 vols.

———, *The Letters of David Garrick,* David M. Little and George M. Kahrl, eds. Cambridge, Massachusetts, 1963. 3 vols.

Correspondence of King George III, Sir John Fortescue, ed. London, 1928. 6 vols.

Correspondence of George III with Lord North, W. Bodham Donne, ed. London, 1867. 2 vols.

Gibbon, Edward, *Letters of Edward Gibbon,* J. E. Norton, ed. New York, 1956. 3 vols.

Grafton, *Augustus Henry, Third Duke of Grafton, Autobiography and Political Correspondence,* William R. Anson, ed. London, 1898.

Grattan, Henry, Jr., *Memoirs of the Life and Times of Henry Grattan.* London, 1839. 2 vols.

Guttridge, George H., *David Hartley, M.P.* Berkeley, California, 1926.

Hewins, W.A.S., ed., *The Whitefoord Papers.* Oxford, 1898.

Howell, T. B., *Complete Collection of State Trials.* London, 1816-1828. 34 vols.

Hutchinson, Thomas, *The Diary and Letters of His Excellency Thomas Hutchinson, Esq.,* Peter O. Hutchinson, compiler. London, 1883. 2 vols.

Jesse, John Heneage, *George Selwyn and His Contemporaries*. London, 1882. 4 vols.

———, *Memoirs of the Life and Reign of King George III*. London, 1901. 5 vols.

Johnson, Samuel, *The Letters of Samuel Johnson*, R. W. Chapman, ed. Oxford, 1952. 3 vols.

Journal of the House of Commons, 1774-1784, Vols. 35-39.

Journal of the House of Lords, 1770-1786, Vols. 33-37.

Keppel, Thomas, *Life of Augustus, Viscount Keppel*. London, 1842. 2 vols.

Kite, E. S., *Beaumarchais and the War of American Independence*. Boston, Massachusetts, 1918. 2 vols.

Low, D. M., *Edward Gibbon*. New York, 1937.

Marston, E., *Sketches of Some Booksellers of the Time of Dr. Samuel Johnson*. London, 1902.

Martelli, George, *Jemmy Twitcher*. London, 1962.

Nichols, John, *Recollections and Reflections during the Reign of George III*. London, 1822. 2 vols.

Norris, John, *Shelburne and Reform*. London, 1963.

Parliamentary History of England, T. C. Hansard, ed. Vols. XVIII-XXIII. London, 1813-1815.

Parliamentary Register; or Proceedings and Debates of the House of Commons, 1775-1783. London, 1775-1783.

Parliamentary Register; or Proceedings and Debates of the House of Lords, 1775-1783. London, 1775-1783.

Memoirs and Character of the Late Right Hon. Richard Rigby. London, 1788.

Roberts, William, ed., *Memorials of Christie's; A Record of Art Sales from 1766 to 1896*. London, 1897. 2 vols.

Russell, Lord John, *Memorials and Correspondence of Charles James Fox*. London, 1853. 4 vols.

Sandwich, *The Private Papers of John, Earl of Sandwich, 1771-1782*, G. R. Barnes and J. H. Owen, eds. London, 1932-1936. 3 vols.

Saunders, Bailey, *Life and Letters of James Macpherson*. New York, 1895.

Sichel, Walter, *Sheridan*. London, 1902. 2 vols.

Memoirs of James Stephen, Merle M. Bevington, ed. London, 1954.

Stephens, Alexander, *Memoirs of John Horne Tooke*. London, 1813. 2 vols.

Thomas, George, Earl of Albemarle, ed., *Memoirs of the Marquis of Rockingham and His Contemporaries*. London, 1852. 2 vols.

Tyerman, L., *Life and Times of John Wesley*. New York, 1872. 3 vols.

Walpole, Horace, *Horace Walpole's Memoirs of the Reign of King George III*, G. F. Russell Barker, ed. London, 1894. 4 vols.

——, *Horace Walpole's Journal of the Reign of George III, 1771-1783,* John Doran, ed. London, 1859. 2 vols.

——, *Letters of Horace Walpole,* Paget Toynbee, ed. Oxford, 1904. 16 vols.

Welsh, Charles, *A Bookseller of the Last Century: Being Some Account of the Life of John Newbery.* London, 1885.

Wilkes, John, *The Correspondence of the Late John Wilkes,* John Almon, ed. London, 1805. 5 vols.

WORKS CITED IN THE TEXT AND OTHER PERTINENT STUDIES OF THE PERIOD

Adams, Charles F., "Contemporary Opinion on the Howes." *Proceedings,* Massachusetts Historical Society, 44 (1911).

Ashton, T. S., *Economic Fluctuations in England, 1700-1800.* Oxford, 1959.

Brown, Gerald S., "The Anglo-French Naval Crisis of 1778: A Study of Conflict in the North Cabinet." *William and Mary Quarterly,* 3rd Series, 13 (1956).

Butterfield, Herbert G., *George III, Lord North and the People, 1779-1780.* London, 1949.

The Campaign in Virginia: An Exact Reprint of Six Rare Pamphlets on the Clinton-Cornwallis Controversy . . . , Benjamin F. Stevens, ed. London, 1888. 2 vols.

Clark, Dora Mae, *British Opinion and the American Revolution.* New Haven, Connecticut, 1930.

——, *The Rise of the British Treasury.* New Haven, Connecticut, 1960.

Christie, Ian R., *The End of the North Ministry, 1780-1782.* London, 1958.

Cone, Carl B., *Burke and the Nature of Politics.* Lexington, Kentucky, 1957.

Davidson, Philip, *Propaganda and the American Revolution.* Chapel Hill, North Carolina, 1941.

Einstein, Lewis D., *Divided Loyalties: Americans in England during the War of Independence.* London, 1933.

Encyclopedia of American History, Richard B. Morris, ed., New York, 1953.

Fortescue, John W., *A History of the British Army.* London, 1910-1930. 13 vols.

George, M. Dorothy, *English Political Caricature to 1792.* Oxford, 1959.

Gipson, Laurence Henry, *The British Empire Before the American Revolution.* Vols. 1-3. Caldwell, Idaho, 1936.

Greene, Donald J., *The Politics of Samuel Johnson.* New Haven, Connecticut, 1960.

Guttridge, George Herbert, *English Whiggism and the American Revolution*. Berkeley, California, 1942.

Lecky, W.E.H., *The American Revolution*. London, 1898.

Maccoby, Simon, *English Radicalism, 1762-1785*. London, 1955.

Madariaga, Isabel de, *Britain, Russia, and the Armed Neutrality of 1780*. New Haven, Connecticut, 1962.

Miller, John C., *Origins of the American Revolution*. Boston, Massachusetts, 1943.

Namier, Louis B., *Personalities and Powers*. London, 1955.

——, *The Structure of Politics at the Accession of George III*. London, 1929.

Olson, A. G., *The Radical Duke, Career and Correspondence of Charles Lennox, third Duke of Richmond*. Oxford, 1961.

Pares, Richard, *King George III and the Politicians*. Oxford, 1953.

Rae, W. F., *Wilkes, Sheridan, Fox, The Opposition Under George III*. London, 1874.

Ritcheson, C. R., *British Politics and the American Revolution*. Norman, Oklahoma, 1954.

Robbins, Caroline, *The Eighteenth Century Commonwealthman*. Cambridge, Massachusetts, 1959.

Schlesinger, Arthur M., Sr., *Prelude to Independence*. New York, 1958.

Spector, Margaret M., *The American Department of the British Government. 1768-1782*. New York, 1940.

Trevelyan, G. O., *George III and Charles Fox*. London, 1912. 2 vols.

Turberville, A. S., *English Men and Manners in the Eighteenth Century*. Oxford, 1926.

Ward, Christopher, *The War of the Revolution*. New York, 1952. 2 vols.

Watson, J. Steven, *The Reign of George III*. Oxford, 1960.

Willcox, William B., "The British Road to Yorktown: A Study in Divided Command." *American Historical Review*, 52 (October, 1946), 1-35.

Index

Adams, John, 40n19, 156n1

Adams, Samuel: and unrest in Colonies, 36, 37, 38, 40-41; and Whately Letters, 41-42; and *Common Sense*, 47; future hanging announced, 101

Adam's Weekly Courant: reports of Burgoyne at Albany, 104; on loss of America, 128; on decline in stock prices, 148

Almon, John: and *North Briton*, 13; and Ministry's use of pamphleteers, 15-16; London publisher of *Common Sense*, 45-46; and North proposal, 52; American cause related to Whiggism by, 77; and defense of Quebec, 91-92; praise of Montgomery, 92-93; report of battle at Bennington, 104-5; pessimism about war, 124; on invasion by France, 152; and North ministry, 162; opposition to Lincoln, 162; suspicious of Portugal, 178; as editor, 224

America: evacuation of, recommended, 206; as tool of French, 209; in British press, 210-11; trade with West Indies prohibited, 214; as source of British prosperity, 215-16

American commerce: ruined by war, 147; beneficial to England, 159-60

American Department: and selection of news to be published, 20; abolition of, reported, 203n54

American economy: subject of study in press, 146-47; as cause of end of war, 147; difficulties predicted, 211

Americans: as dissatisfied Englishmen, 138; as allies of England, 177

Amherst, Lord Jeffrey Amherst, Baron: estimate of American strength, 80; recommendations for carrying on war, 109; recommendation of naval blockade, 119; for abandonment of war, 130; mentioned, 88

André, Major John: loss regretted, 166, 167; execution of, 167

Annual Register: on Patrick Henry, 37; sympathetic to Colonies, 38; on Washington, 89-90, 95; on Lee's capture, 97-98

Anonymity of newspaper contributors, 179-80

Arbuthnot, Admiral Marriott, 184

Arnold, General Benedict: derided, 94; recognition as capable leader, 99; and Saratoga, 111; desertion by, 163-65; British opinions on, 166-68; mentioned, 195

Articles of Confederation: scant notice of, in British London press, 127; copies of, sold in England, 204-5

Aurora, 225

Austria: as ally of England, 178; as ally of America, 178n50

Ayre, R., 225

Badini, C. F., 225

Baldwin, Henry: publisher of *St. James's Chronicle*, 59; American cause related

237

feat by British, 203-4; aims in America discussed, 209-10; commerce with America, 209-10

Franco-American relationships, 209-10

Franco-American treaty: reported, 126, 129, 136-37

Franco-Russian treaty: rumored, 176

Franklin, Benjamin: influence on British press, 9; use of British press, 10, 20; pseudonyms, 10n35; and Whately Letters, 41-42; letters to British press, 20, 42-43, 42n25; in British press, 44-45; *Common Sense* attributed to him, 45; attacked by Bate, 45n35; future hanging announced, 101; on reconciliation, 122n7; detested by George III, 124; reported negotiating with France and Spain, 135; ostracized in Paris, 135; Secret Service information on, 135n22; and peace negotiations, 205

Freedom of press in England, 5, 220

Freeman's Farm: report of battle at, 106

French and American troops: relations of, 182, 182n66

French: vindication of Cornwallis by, 190-91

French fleet: sighted off Plymouth, 154n57

French forces: blockade of Chesapeake Bay by, 185; troops landed in Chesapeake area, 186

Gage, General Thomas: mentioned, 36, 37; request for men, 80; report of resignation, 81; and mediation with Colonies, 90; unpopular with Opposition press, 91

Galloway, Joseph: attacked by Walpole, 19; return to England, 48; pamphleteer for Germain, 68-69; and Germain, 69n49; pamphlet for loyalists, 218, 218n59

Garrick, David: and newspapers, 1; association with Bate, 24, 26; mentioned, 30

Gates, General Horatio: demand for prisoners, 110-11; victory at Saratoga, 111; and Washington, 117, 117n77; desertion reported, 165

Gazetteer: on reconciliation, 53; and Opposition, 60-61; on Parliament, 71; on corruption in Government, 73; on North, 73; American cause related to Whiggism by, 77; report of Burgoyne's

death, 104; on Saratoga, 108n34; on Royal Navy, 114; pessimistic about outcome of war, 122; and rumors of peace, 127; on loss of Colonies, 130-31; on French and Spanish aid to America, 134; on conditions for aid to America, 134n10; on Gordon riots, 160, 161; on desertions, 164-65; estimates of English dead, 168; on Dutch neutrality, 172; on Russia, 176; on Greene-Cornwallis engagement, 184-85; on Saratoga, 188; opposition to American war, 191; independent view of war, 219-20; mentioned, 224

General Advertiser: opposition to Bate, 26, 27; and *Public Ledger,* 34; American cause related to Whiggism, 77; on cost of war with France, 139; on invasion by France, 152; on Dutch neutrality, 172; support of Fox, 199, 219; mentioned, 224

General Evening Post: Tory paper, 23; on reconciliation, 52; on Declaration of Independence, 75-76; necessity of war, 78-79; on American strength, 79-80; on war's effects, 87; on Montgomery, 93; on Lee and Washington, 98; on Bennington, 104; on Saratoga, 107, 111; and strategy for war, 118; on North as conciliator, 123; on Colonies and France, 138; on stock prices related to conciliation, 148n10; on emigration to America, 211, 215; mentioned, 224

General Staff in America, 78

"Gentleman Johnny." *See* Burgoyne

Gentleman's Magazine: attitude toward Colonies, 74; on class attitudes toward independence, 76n10; on Lee, 96; on delay of Burgoyne's reports, 106; for end of war, 121-22, 203; rebuke to Congress, 128; "American section," 142, 157; on Clinton-Cornwallis feud, 190; peace treaty in, 208; on commerce with America, 211-12; mentioned, 225

Gentletouch, Simon (pseud.), 225

George III: attitude toward public opinion, viii; and newspapers, 7, 12; subscriber to *Public Advertiser,* 14; and rewards to Bate, 26; and Howe brothers, 56; and "double Cabinet," 65, 67; newspapers' views of, 69-70, 70n53; public's views of, 70; estimate of American strength, 80; and recon-

Newfoundland: fisheries at, to be lost in war, 146

News: as opinion shaper, 221

Newspapers: as investments, 1-2; readership of, 2, 14; circulation of, 2; as political instruments, 2; considered untrustworthy, 22; anonymity of contributors, 20, 179-80; anti-Ministry, 224-25; pro-Ministry, 224-25

Nicholl, W., 224

Nichols, W., 224

Noon Gazette: editor of, sentenced, 179; mentioned, 225

North, Lord Frederick, Earl of Guilford: attacked by "nonpartisan" press, 14n1; attack of Townshend by, 16; on Macpherson, 17; reward to Bate through, 25-26; charges against Bostonians by, 35; and reconciliation, 50-51; press reaction to, 50-53, 63-65, 199; reaction to, in America, 51; and Coercive Acts, 58-59; personally unpopular, 59; quarrel with Germain, 69; and defeats in America, 69; power behind throne, 72-73; reported to profit from war, 72-73; finances of, 73; on Montgomery, 93; as conciliator, 123-24; and Mauduit broadside, 124-25; and Gordon riots, 160; fall from office predicted, 187-88; resignation predicted, 196; resignation, 197, 198

North Ministry: blamed by press for war, 58; attacked by press, 63-66; reports of quarrels within, 69; corruption of Parliament by, 70-71; intransigence of, 74; good faith of, questioned, 74n1; reaction to Declaration of Independence, 76; and estimates of American strength, 80-81; and Trenton, 95; optimistic about war, 100; and Burgoyne's defeat, 106; false representation of Americans by, 107; blamed for defeats in America, 113; and parliamentary elections, 161-62; as block to peace, 192; end of, 197; corruption of, 197-98; vote for censure of, 198; credited with Rodney's victory, 204; fall of, and loyalists, 217; and press, 220

Northern confederacy: discussed by press, 177-78

Nova Scotia: to be lost, with Colonies, 187; description of, 214-15

O'Bryen (or O'Brien), Dennis: propagandist for Fox, 14; editor of *General Advertiser*, 14; mentioned, 199, 244

Official accounts: distortion of, 20

Official documents: withheld from press, 20

Official Government Publications, 224

"Olive Branch Petition," 53

Oliver, Andrew, 41, 42

Opposition party: and press in parliament, 7n23; control of press by, 12-13

Opposition press: task of, ix; unified in mutual defense, 33; hostility to Goverment, 34; blame of Ministry for war, 58, 106; joined by heretofore impartial papers, 60-61; reaction to Declaration of Independence, 76; and resemblance of American's demands to those of Englishmen, 77; on values of war, 77; certainty of American victory, 77, 79; effect of attitudes toward war, 81, 84; criticism of Howe, 89; criticism of Gage, 91; on use of mercenaries, 95; predictions of defeat, 106-7; on Saratoga, 109; and Fox, 109; opposed to war with Colonies, 113, 115; defense of Burgoyne, 113; pessimistic about reconciliation, 126; on European conflict, 133; pessimistic about American war, 156-57; on removal of Ministry, 188; seen as correct in judgments, 191; as loyal press, 200; on reform of Parliament, 216-17; power of, 219-20; public attitude toward, 221

Oswald, Richard: proposal by, 178-79; mentioned, 205

Otis, James, 39-40, 40n17

Packet: opposed to Bate, 27; and *Morning Chronicle*, 62; American cause related to English Whiggism by, 77; on Fort Washington, 100; prediction of long war by, 102; on Washington, 103; on silence of commanders, 106; on Burgoyne, 109; on Clinton, 119; reports of peace negotiations, 127; reports America lost, 128; on war with France, 136, 137, 139, 141; on economic conditions, 148; on Dutch neutrality, 172; on Russia, 176; on public apathy, 198, 206-7; on terms of European peace, 207; on trade with America, 216; mentioned, 224

Paine, Thomas, 46-48

Palliser, Admiral Hugh, 141

Paris agreements, 207